DEEP IN THE HEART

The Lives and Legends of Texas Jews

A Photographic History

Ruthe Winegarten and Cathy Schechter

Rabbi Jimmy Kessler, Consulting Editor

Eakin Press
Austin, Texas

The Texas Jewish Historical Society
Sponsor

Front Cover:

Clockwise, from top left: Sol Aron,
Pauline Mack, Mayer Brothers Store
(Sonora), Captain David Kokernot, Alex
and Alma Halff and Dave and Ida Straus,
Jacob de Cordova, Family of Temma
Tobolowsky, Alice Oppenheimer Steifel,
Philip Eldridge and grandchildren, Bern-
hardt and Max Goodman, Della Doppel-
mayer, and Rabbi Heinrich Schwarz.
Center: ark of Temple Moses Montefiore,
Marshall.

Title Page:

Eternal light of Temple Moses
Montefiore, Marshall
— *Photo by Louis de Luca*

Cover and Book Design: Peggy Parkhurst

Library of Congress Cataloging-in-Publication Data

Winegarten, Ruthe.
    Deep in the heart : the lives and legends of Texas Jews / Ruthe Winegarten and
Cathy Schechter : Jimmy Kessler, consulting editor.
        p.   cm.
    "The Texas Jewish Historical Society, sponsor."
    Includes bibliographical references.
    ISBN 0-89015-759-6 : $29.95
    1. Jews — Texas — History. 2. Texas — Ethnic relations. I. Schechter, Cathy.
II. Kessler, Jimmy. III. Texas Jewish Historical Society. IV. Title.
F395.J5W55 1990
976.4'005924--dc20   89-29770
                                                                                CIP

This book is dedicated to the grandparents of Ruthe Winegarten.

Lena (Newman) Lewin and Ludwig Lewin from Berlin and Jastrow, Germany

Max and Jennie (Czernie Radunska) Cohen from Grodno, Russia

And in honor of Lucile Brilling Gruner, who lovingly shared her mother's scrapbook.

Contents

Foreword

The Talmud records the folktale of Honi the circle drawer, who learned an important lesson from watching an elderly man plant a carob tree. "You'll not benefit from your efforts, old man, it will be long after your death when the tree gives its fruit."

"Of course, but I do this work for my children and my students and their posterity, not for myself."

So it is with this book. It is written not just for our generation, but for many generations to come who deserve to know of their Texas Jewish heritage. Writing a history is one of those acts that adds to the Jewish collective memory.

A decade ago, the Texas Jewish Historical Society began its activities dedicated to the preservation and dissemination of the history of the Texas Jewish experience. In ten years, TeJHaS has sponsored and encouraged research as well as provided a forum for scholars and students of Jewish Texana. In addition to this book, the Society continues to encourage and support, where possible, numerous similar activities. Membership in TeJHaS has grown substantially as has interest in Texas Jewry.

This is not a "Who's Who" of Texas Jewry. That would require an encyclopedia. Clearly, it is impossible to include all who deserve mention in this work. It can only be considered a beginning. We have not sought to rank the accomplishments of one individual or institution over that of another, but to provide the reader with an overview and a representative sampling of the kinds of leaders and workers our community has nourished. Our objective was to allow the life experiences of those included to reflect their significant contributions to Jewry and to Texas. The choice of material included was based in part on a response to a survey carried out by TeJHaS. From that data obtained, as well as other acknowledged sources, those materials deemed complete were included. Those which were incomplete, will, with permission, be used for future research and publications. All original materials given to TeJHaS will be made a part of the Society's collection at the Barker Texas History Center, the University of Texas at Austin.

We attempted not to become entangled in the issue of who is (or was) a Jew. For most, the label was easily determined. For those who had been ruled out as being Jewish by reputable research, or chose to exclude themselves, we opted to abide by that research and that choice. We have tried to let the facts speak for themselves and allow each reader to reach individual conclusions. Where Jewish roots were identifiable, they were so indicated. All decisions were those of the authors and editor, and were made with the most sensitive of intentions.

Ruthe Winegarten and I decided over coffee and a croissant that this book had to be written. Ruthe, and her co-author Cathy Schechter, brought this to fruition, a clear tribute to their commitment, their research and abilities. Editorial activity was minimal due to their competent endeavors. Texana is better for this literary contribution.

This work is not only a tribute to that which was and is Texas Jewry, but also to TeJHaS and to the sponsors of this book. Their foresight and commitment in supporting this work reflect the highest level of devotion. Honoring a TeJHaS requirement for a reputable, independent publisher insured the highest quality for their support.

This book had to be written because the history of Jews in Texas is important. We know of our Jewish heritage only because our religious ancestors thought enough of their posterity to record their life experiences. We can do no less. In reality we must do more, for we are a part of an unequaled Jewish enterprise. Thousands have given of themselves, and continue to do so today, that Jewish life in Texas might be of a caliber equal to any. Their efforts cannot go unrecorded. Their lives are the fabric of Texas. They could have entirely disappeared into the growing populace, but they did not. Because of their tenacity, we are beneficiaries of a rich heritage. As the carob tree was planted, so too is this work for the generations of Texas Jews to come.

RABBI JIMMY KESSLER, DHL
Founding President, Texas Jewish Historical Society

For over 5,000 years, the Jewish people have adapted to life in many lands, creating a collective history that is vibrant and diverse, yet in constant evolution. History is as fundamental to Judaism as food is to the sustenance of life. One of the most widely observed Jewish holidays — Passover — is dedicated to remembrance and celebration of national liberation and freedom from bondage. Citizens of the Lone Star State, likewise, share a passion for Texas history; Texas has its own independence day, encyclopedia, and a historiography of 10,000 books.

Now these two colorful histories are merged into one with the unique story of Jewish participation in the birth and development of Texas. Because both Texas and Jewish history have traditionally focused on the activities of men, we have also enriched them both with a feminist perspective. The result is *Deep in the Heart: The Lives and Legends of Texas Jews,* a gift to the people of Texas and the Jewish community from the Texas Jewish Historical Society as it proudly celebrates its tenth anniversary in 1990.

The importance of ethnic histories was stressed by Professor Walter Buenger of Texas A&M University in a speech before the Texas State Historical Association [Lubbock, March 1989]. The value of "inclusionary history," he said, is to promote a cultural understanding of ourselves, identify useful ideas from other cultures, discourage anti-Semitism and racism, and promote tolerance, cross-cultural interaction, cooperation, and civic peace. Ethnic history contradicts Texas provincialism and its racist/sexist interpretation of the Texas myth as a land of cultural and ethnic homogeneity in which rugged Anglo-American males vanquished the frontier. It helps all Texans feel part of the body politic.

In that spirit, the Texas State Historical Association is revising the state's encyclopedia, *The Handbook of Texas,* to broaden its ethnic perspective. And that is where the story of this book begins. The Texas Jewish Historical Society implemented a modest project to provide articles about Jews for the new *Handbook* by sending out questionnaires to some 1,500 individuals, libraries, archives, county historical societies, and institutions to solicit information. The response was so exciting and overwhelming, so interesting and unexpected, that we decided to move beyond our original goal and write our own book.

For three years, we swept the state from the Red River to the Rio Grande with telephone calls, oral interviews, letters, and field visits, following up on leads and filling in the gaps. The raw material for this book came not only from Texas, but from descendants of Texas pioneers in California, Colorado, Louisiana, Florida, New York — and from the American Jewish Archives and other national sources.

What did we find? Jews came to Texas with the Spanish *conquistadores,* more than sixty years before the first Jews landed in New Amsterdam. Although numerically small, they have been part of the fabric of the state's history from the beginning as politicians, land developers, proprietors, and philanthropists. The first permanent Jewish settlers helped finance and fight the battles for Texas independence; they lived on the frontier, traded with the Indians, and participated on both sides of the Civil War. Jewish immigrants from all over the world were often literate, multilingual, and were endowed with organizational skills, contacts in other cities, and a global view. Jews promoted and developed land for settlement and set down roots in rural areas, small towns, and urban centers. They established businesses necessary for commerce and growth and used their insights, enthusiasm, and resources to help create the infrastructure of dozens of communities, whether by bringing in utilities or establishing institutions like schools, libraries, and symphony orchestras.

The evidence is overwhelming in every community we studied. Although Texas Jews have always constituted less than one percent of the population, they have functioned successfully in a predominantly Christian society, have assumed a visible and active role in the state's history, and have built an outstanding record of philanthropic and civic enterprises. They were valued citizens who were often elected to public office and participated in all aspects of community life. They translated their basic Jewish values of *tsedakah,* justice, respect for learning, and love of family beyond the Jewish community into the development of many of the state's educational, artistic, cultural, and social welfare institutions through their contributions of time, effort, and generous sums of money.

Texas Jews are not a homogenous group easy to categorize. They came from dozens of countries and different parts of the United States with a variety of cultural and linguistic backgrounds, representing all social and economic classes and a range of religious rituals and practices from the most Orthodox to the secular. While living side by side and sharing the commonality of belonging to the same ethnic minority, Jews have experienced intragroup disagreements and divisions. Painful and protracted arguments over Zionism raged for years, and debate over assimilation versus ethnic Jewish identity has persisted, along with differences over rituals and the roles of women. Without revision or gloss, we have tried to cover the diversity, warts and all.

The Jewish community is inclusive in many ways: you don't have to be religious to be Jewish and you don't have to believe in a certain doctrine. The Texas Jewish community began with a few modest benevolent and burial societies, and has evolved to include hundreds of temples and synagogues, social circles, and organizations running the gamut from men's lodges to women's leagues, day-care centers to homes for the aged, family services to singles' clubs. Through their organizations, Texas Jews absorbed and resettled thousands of immigrants; Jewish immigrants from the Soviet Union, South Africa, Israel, and Latin America are still coming to Texas. As elsewhere, Texas Jews have faced discrimination and anti-Semitism by fighting to establish and protect fundamental rights for themselves and others.

We believe contemporary public policy issues can be examined through a study of the Jewish experience. As the general community is faced with the challenge of absorbing and resettling thousands from Latin America and Asia, who speak many languages and need education and employment, much can be learned from the successful strategies used by Jewish institutions and organizations. What methods used by Jewish immigrant resettlement services have broader applications? In the fight against discrimination, what lessons have Jewish organizations learned and what techniques have been used to combat racist ideology and promote intergroup understanding in a pluralistic society?

The heartbeat of every community lies within its people, and our research uncovered a cast of thousands: a few heroes, a few villains, and hundreds of colorful personalities including peddlers and the grandest merchant princes; scientific inventors and mythical rainmakers; seamstresses, saleswomen, midwives, and dowager empresses who founded orphanages and charitable foundations. Texas Jews were slave owners and abolitionists, soldiers and spies, blacksmiths and doctors, mayors and lodge members, teachers and typists, nurses and Noble Laureates. They were judges and scoundrels, politicians and prostitutes, the rich, the famous, and the bankrupt and broken.

Julius Roth, in his book *Time Clock*, said that every concrete life is a typical life from which one can generalize. We have tried, as much as possible, to let the subjects tell their stories in their own words. Our hope is that their voices will speak for their peers and the times in which they lived, as well as for themselves. We also present, for the first time ever, a broad history of most Texas Jewish communities — from those that are now almost gone, like Jefferson and Marshall, to those that have grown exponentially, like Houston and Dallas. From the earliest Hebrew Benevolent Societies and ladies' groups to the myriad organizations that exist today, the history of Jewish institutions unfolds. From the circuit-riding rabbis and keepers of the early cemeteries to the schools, temples, and community centers, the vitality of Judaism is best reflected in its institutions.

The overwhelming amount of in-

formation available made it a difficult task to choose who and what should be included. With over 500 photographs, most never before published, we have made selections which we felt were a representative sampling of Jewish life, institutional development, community history, and social concern. For individuals, we looked at representativeness, uniqueness, significance, and parity for men and women. We also incorporated anecdotes and human interest stories. We were flexible in deciding, "Who is a Texas Jew?" Some were born elsewhere and made their marks in Texas; others, Texas-born, made their marks elsewhere. As to their Judaism, some were converts and some had vague Jewish origins; we opted for inclusion rather than exclusion.

We have our favorites: some because of their unusual nicknames ("Coonskin" Cohen and the "Jewish Adonis"), some because of their tenacity and will to survive (centenarians Freida Weiner and Bertha Bender), some because of their adventure stories (Morris Lasker and Jane Hart Levy), and some with big hearts (Sam Perl, who served his congregation for fifty years without pay). We admire those who took unpopular political positions as matters of principle: the Schlingers of Brownsville, who opposed slavery and left Texas until the end of the Civil War; Rabbi Maurice Faber of Tyler, who defied Governor Jim Ferguson; Rabbi Isadore Garsek, who spoke out for civil rights in the face of racist threats; and Hermine Tobolowsky, the Mother of the Texas Equal Legal Rights Amendment. Most Jews, though, were ordinary people who worked hard without achieving fame or recognition. As many as we could fit in are as many as you'll find, and we hope that most will serve as role models and an inspiration for young readers.

Invariably, as with any book of this size and scope, there are omissions. As recently as July 1989, Selma Levy of Houston told us she had been a radio station disc jockey and founder of a string of beauty salons. We wanted to stop the presses for Mrs. Levy, but it was too late. For every one of the approximately 100,000 Jews who live in Texas today, there is a worthy story; for every special person included, there are hundreds

more who, for lack of space, have been omitted. However, we believe that a representative sample of Jewish life and activity, from yesterday and today, is reflected in this work, and we hope that our readers will forgive our limitations.

This book is written in a popular style for a general audience, but has been carefully researched and documented for use by teachers, scholars, and historians. In-depth analyses of events, movements, and attitudes are precluded in this format, leaving a broad perspective. We have included an extensive bibliography which can serve as a stimulus for further work and research; the possibility for many more publications abounds.

As native Texas Jews, it has been our privilege and delight to have spent the past three years uncovering and writing a new chapter in the panoramic history of Jewish life in Texas. For us, it has been an intensely personal experience as our own family scrapbooks have found a place in the larger history of the Texas Jewish community. From Ludwig Lewin, a Dallas butcher on Deep Ellum who never set foot in a temple but anonymously donated meat to the nuns in an Oak Cliff convent for ten years, to Helen Schechter, whose Fort Bend County Hadassah Chapter anteed their poker stakes for charity every week, their Jewishness was manifested in many ways. Like Morris Schechter of Safed, Palestine, and the Cohens of Grodno, Russia, they came from many places to find a home free of persecution. They left a precious legacy to us which we have tried to honor on the pages of this book.

Our greatest hope is that *Deep in the Heart: The Lives and Legends of Texas Jews* will stimulate every Jewish family, organization, institution, and community to save, document, and write its own history and add it to our archival collection at the Barker Texas History Center at the University of Texas at Austin.

We are particularly grateful for the groundbreaking work of the Texas Jewish Historical Society, which sponsored this book and gave us complete editorial freedom. The decisions, interpretations, and errors are ours alone.

RUTHE WINEGARTEN
CATHY SCHECHTER

This book has been made possible through the generosity of the following contributors. We also would like to express our gratitude to several donors who wish to remain anonymous.

The Endowment Fund of the Jewish Community of Houston

The Foundation of the Jewish Federation of Greater Dallas

The Texas Jewish Historical Society

The Elizabeth Gugenheim Trust, Tyler, in memory of Elizabeth Gugenheim

Kempner Foundation, Galveston

Helen and Milton Smith through the Moshana Foundation, Austin

Milton Brenner, San Antonio

Eleanor Freed, Houston

Jacobs Iron & Metal Company and the Jacobs and Linksman families, Dallas

Mr. and Mrs. Harris L. Kempner, Jr., Galveston

Dr. Philip J. and Patti Edelman Leonard, Austin

Audrey and Louis Kariel, Jr., Marshall

Rosalie and Dave Lack, Victoria

Mrs. Alvin J. (Ann) Marks, El Paso

Marvin A. and Shirley M. Rich, Houston

Fannie Pravorne Wienir, Los Angeles

Dr. and Mrs. William C. Levin, Galveston

The book represents the joint efforts and contributions of hundreds of people and institutions. People from all around Texas and the country sent family photographs and dug through attics and trunks to share yellowed documents and scrapbooks; archivists and librarians responded to numerous requests with diligence and care. Our heartfelt thanks and appreciation to all of you. This is your book, too. In particular, we wish to acknowledge the following:

Advisory editors and members of the Readers Committee: Frances Kallison, Dr. Don Carleton, Ima Joy Gandler, Doris Glasser, Ginger Jacobs, Audrey D. Kariel, Dr. Kenneth Roseman, and Lonnie Schooler. For editorial assistance: Frieda Werden, Dr. Stanley Schneider, and Marc Sanders. A special thanks to Tom Shelton, Institute of Texan Cultures, San Antonio, and Kevin Proffitt, American Jewish Archives, Cincinnati, Ohio. For invaluable assistance: Rose Biderman, Dallas Jewish Historical Society Archives; Gerry Cristol, Temple Emanu-El Archives, Dallas; Ellen Brown, Texas Collection, Baylor University, Waco; Casey Green, Rosenberg Library, Galveston; Cindy Smolovik and Jean Hudon, Dallas Public Library; Allison Beck, Barker Texas History Center, UT Austin; Hannah R. Sinauer, B'nai B'rith International; Ellen Cohen, American Jewish Committee, Houston; Doris Glasser, Houston Public Library; Lynn Inselberg, Texas Tech University, Lubbock; Dr. Charles Schultz, Texas A&M University Archives, College Station; and Barbara Rubin and Ellen Mack, Fort Worth Jewish Community Sesquicentennial Archives. For processing the 500-plus photographs: Austin Prints for Publication, Andy Reisberg, Dallas, and Steve Nussenblatt, Galveston. Other thanks to Helene Levy, Alex Corman, Phyllis Harris, Harriet Rochlin, Rabbi Marc and Margo Sack, and Abe Reichstein. Numerous family members and friends offered moral support: Mr. and Mrs. A. J. Schechter, Arthur and Joyce Schechter, Robert and Mary Ethel Schechter, Cheryl and David Schechter, Mr. and Mrs. William Winston, and Rose Greenberg. Dr. Jaron Winston watched his daughters many long hours while his wife was hard at work. And Martha Winegarten Wilson kept her mom laughing.

DEEP IN THE HEART

The Lives
and Legends
of Texas Jews

THE MARTYRDOM OF DOÑA MARIANA NUÑEZ DE CARVAJAL

This illustration depicts the martyrdom of a Jewish woman, Doña Mariana Nuñez de Carvajal, who was burned at the stake in Mexico City on March 25, 1601. Although she seems to have sincerely converted to Catholicism in 1596, the inquisitors were unmoved by her pleas of conversion and the corroborating testimony of numerous witnesses. They tried her on the charge of having relapsed into Judaism and sentenced her to death. She was garroted before her body was set on fire.

Mariana's mother, brother, and three sisters were convicted of "Judaizing heresy" in 1596 and burned at the stake. Her uncle, Luis de Carvajal, who was governor of the state of Nuevo León (which encompassed part of South Texas including San Antonio), was arrested for harboring Jews and jailed.

— *Illustration by P. Miranda, from Vicente Riva Palacio,* El Libro Rojo *(Mexico, 1870), copy from Martin Cohen,* The Martyr

1

In the Shadows of the New World
THE SPANISH INQUISITION

The earliest history of the Jews in Texas is hidden in the shadows of the conquest of Mexico, when *conquistadores* and other Spaniards came to the New World in search of glory, God, and gold. The cruelties of the infamous Spanish Inquisition followed. Although the Jewish presence is a certainty, that presence has receded into the mists of history, hidden because its very discovery meant repression, and often death, by the Inquisition's New World deputies.

In 1492, the Spanish rulers Isabella and Ferdinand issued an edict ordering that Jews either be expelled from Spain or convert to Catholicism. Within three months, thousands of Jews fled, while thousands of others converted, some sincerely. Some of the converts conscientiously adopted Catholicism, while others continued to practice Judaism in secret. The converts have been referred to as New Christians, *conversos*, *marranos*, and crypto-Jews.

There was significant economic motivation for the Inquisition to turn against its new converts. Confiscations of their possessions filled empty church and crown coffers. Because of their high profiles and their vulnerability to the charge of "Judaizing," or secretly practicing Jewish rituals, they were an excellent target in those times of turbulence and financial trouble both in Spain and Nueva España.

Many *conversos* sought sanctuary in the New World, believing that scrutiny of their religious practices would be less diligent. They came with the *conquistadores* as soldiers, merchants, peddlers, or importers, and by 1545,

there were almost 1,400 Jews in Mexico City. Because of financial acuity and entrepreneurial abilities acquired in Spain as a result of limited occupational options, they were indispensable to the government and the church.[1]

The Holy Office of the Inquisition began in Mexico in 1571, but did not concentrate on attacking crypto-Jews until the 1580s. The Inquisition records of 1622 include evidence given of a synagogue in Mexico City and testimony by a man named Francisco that if inquisitors would guarantee his life, he would reveal the names of more than 500 Jews. Over 900 *conversos* were charged with "Judaizing heresy" in Mexico. About 100 Jews were burned at the stake. Others died or committed suicide in jail while another 100 were imprisoned for up to ten years. Over 300 were tried and did penance, and a few were judged innocent and released.

The most prominent of those victimized in the New World were Luis de Carvajal and his family. In 1579, King Philip II of Spain gave de Carvajal patents to explore, colonize, and govern the Kingdom of León, which today includes South Texas (including San Antonio) and northern Mexico. Many of de Carvajal's colonists were of Jewish origin, including members of his own family. De Carvajal was himself a new Christian, but this did not save him. In 1590, he was convicted of harboring Judaizers. Other de Carvajal family members only pretended to convert, but continued the secret practice of Judaism. They were arrested and burned at the stake.

Historian Carlos Larralde believes that in the 1700s a number of *conversos* settled in Texas. They included colonists from the Canary Islands, who established Texas' first European settlement in San Antonio in 1731. The Canary Islanders are reported to have resented the Spanish priests and were not interested in Catholicism. In 1755, Tomás Sanchez established Laredo with anticlerical settlers. Over 100 years later, another possible *converso*, Juan Cortina, tried to establish a separate state along the Rio Grande River. He never ate ham or bacon, cooperated with the Yankees during the Civil War, and hated slavery. Larralde reports that Cortina's descendants inherited a five-candle candelabrum which was sometimes lit just before sunset on Fridays.[2]

San Antonio historian Richard G. Santos has concluded that hundreds, if not thousands, of the Sephardic descendants of these early *conversos* now live along the Texas-Mexico border and in South Texas. Many still practice rituals reminiscent of Jewish customs, although the practitioners are unaware of their origins. These customs include lighting candles on Friday nights, a prohibition against eating pork, ritual slaughter of fowl, use of a dreidel, and eating *pan de semita* (Semitic bread) made with vegetable oil during Lent.[3]

The Inquisition continued to operate in the New World until 1802, when the last edict prohibiting the entry of Jews into New Spain was issued by the Spanish colonial Holy Office.

Luis de Carvajal y de la Cueva

The first governor of the New Kingdom of León, which included part of what is now South Texas including San Antonio and northern Mexico, was a Portuguese-born new Christian with Jewish roots, Don Luis de Carvajal. By age twenty-eight, he was already a successful merchant and sea captain living in Spain. He formed a partnership with a new Christian and married the partner's daughter. Soon after the wedding, de Carvajal was shocked to learn his new wife was devoted to the Jewish faith.

In 1567, de Carvajal left his wife behind as he headed for New Spain. In 1579, he was appointed by King Philip II as the governor of the Kingdom of León with the right to bring colonists at his own expense. Between 100 and 200 families came with him. De Carvajal's charter exempted the colonists from having to present legal proof of four generations of Catholic ancestry, in the form of *limpieza de sangre* certificates. Included among his colonists were members of his family who were practicing Jews, including his sister, Doña Francisca, her husband, and eight of their nine children, including Luis de Carvajal the Younger.

Luis de Carvajal's niece Isabel was arrested in 1589 and, under torture, denounced him, along with her mother, her two sisters, and her brothers. In 1590, de Carvajal was convicted of harboring "Judaizers" and was sentenced to one year in prison and six years in exile. But he thwarted his accusers by dying in prison. Over 100 others of his colonists were also denounced, and most confessed.[4]

The 1590–91 expedition and route of Gaspar Castaño de Sosa to establish a Spanish colony in New Mexico is commemorated by a historical marker. Castaño de Sosa may have been the first person of Jewish ancestry to set foot in what is now Texas, as he crossed the territory en route to New Mexico.
— *Photo by Alfred M. Gordon*

Gaspar Castaño de Sosa

Around 1583, Governor Luis de Carvajal appointed Gaspar Castaño de Sosa, then living in Saltillo just south of the Rio Grande River, as the lieutenant governor of Nuevo León. Castaño was of Portuguese descent and may have had parents who were *conversos* in Mexico City.[6] In 1590, Castaño succeeded to the governorship when Carvajal was removed from office by the Inquisition.

In July 1590, Castaño led an unauthorized expedition across the southwestern corner of Texas en route to establish a colony in New Mexico.[7] Therefore, he is arguably the first person of Jewish ancestry to set foot on Texas soil.

After conquering thirty-three pueblos, Castaño was arrested in 1591 and charged with organizing an illegal expedition and rebellion against the Crown. However, some historians claim he was a victim of the Spanish Inquisition. Castaño was convicted and expelled from Mexico before his appeal to the Council in Spain could be heard. He died in 1593 while fighting in a shipboard uprising en route to his exile in the Far East.[8] The Council later established his innocence, revoked his sentence, and ordered his reinstatement as governor. He was, however, already dead.

A drawing of the Spanish conquistador Hernán Cortés (1485–1547), who conquered Mexico in 1521. Cortés awarded a large land grant to the shipbuilder and *converso* Hernando Alonso for his role in the conquest of Mexico City. In 1528, Alonso was charged with practicing Judaism in secret and burned in an *auto-da-fé*.[5]
— *Drawing by Thom Ricks, copy from UT Institute of Texan Cultures*

— **Luis de Carvajal the Younger**

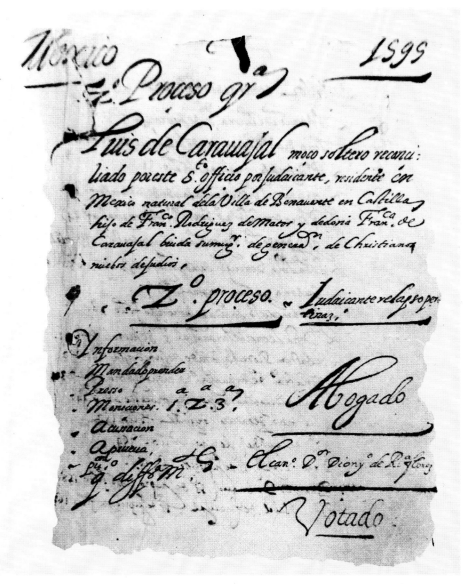

A page from the Inquisition proceedings against Luis de Caravajal [Carvajal] el Mozo, 1595, also known as Luis de Carvajal the Younger. Luis the Younger (1565?–1596), the nephew of Governor Luis de Carvajal, was burned at the stake in 1596.
— *Copy from Seymour Liebman,* The Enlightened

Luis de Carvajal the Younger was the nephew of Governor Luis de Carvajal. Luis the Younger went to New Spain, along with other family members, as part of his uncle's colonizing efforts. He was being groomed to succeed his uncle as governor, but turned his back on political ambition and took up the practice of the "Law of Moses." In 1590, at the age of thirty, he was indicted, based on testimony of his sister Isabel. His mother was subjected to the rack and cords, and her screams forced him to confess and name as crypto-Jews 116 fellow colonists. Luis had a reprieve of four years, during which time he worked in a hospital and a school, where he had access to a library. He secretly renamed himself Joseph Lumbroso

and wrote *Autobiography of Luis de Carvajal, the Younger,* as well as letters and a spiritual will in which he defended his desire to live and die in the Jewish faith. Luis the Younger's will gave arguments supporting his beliefs in the omnipotence of God, the practice of circumcision, and the coming of the Messiah. (Around 1595, Luis read the biblical account of Abraham's circumcision, grabbed a pair of shears, and ran to the bank of the Panuco River, where he painfully and clumsily circumcised himself.) He condemned the Spanish and Portuguese kings for spreading the Inquisition and held them responsible for the death of "the faithful and the true Jews who have died out of allegiance to this Law."

"The princes have persecuted them without cause," he wrote, "calling them Judaizing heretics, unjustly, for the practice of Judaism is not heresy; it is the fulfillment of the will of God our Lord." [10]

On December 7, 1596, Luis the Younger, his mother, and his three sisters were executed, along with forty-five other "Judaizers." Others who were punished that day included "fornicators, witches, bigamists," and some Negro slaves who, "when starved and inhumanely lashed, expressed the wish that they were not alive and said it was better to be a monkey than a Christian." [11]

TEXAS
FOREVER!!

The usurper of the South has failed in his efforts to enslave the freemen of Texas.

The wives and daughters of Texas will be saved from the brutality of Mexican soldiers.

Now is the time to emigrate to the Garden of America.

A free passage, and all found, is offered at New Orleans to all applicants. Every settler receives a location of

EIGHT HUNDRED ACRES OF LAND.

On the 23d of February, a force of 1000 Mexicans came in sight of San Antonio, and on the 25th Gen. St. Anna arrived at that place with 2500 more men, and demanded a surrender of the fort held by 150 Texians, and on the refusal, he attempted to storm the fort, twice, with his whole force, but was repelled with the loss of 500 men, and the Americans lost none. Many of his troops, the liberals of Zacatecas, are brought on to Texas in irons and are urged forward with the promise of the women and plunder of Texas.

The Texian forces were marching to relieve St. Antonio, March the 2d. The Government of Texas is supplied with plenty of arms, ammunition, provisions, &c. &c.

AN 1836 ADVERTISEMENT

An 1836 advertisement for land in Texas.
— *Broadsides, Barker Texas History Center, UT Austin, copy from UT Institute of Texan Cultures*

Milking the cows and gathering the honey
ADVENTURERS AND TRAILBLAZERS

"Thousands of acres of land can be bought, within settled portions of the state, for the small sum of from 25 cents to $1 per acre," wrote pioneer Houston Jew Lewis A. Levy. In an enthusiastic letter which appeared in the *Asmonean,* a New York Jewish newspaper, in 1850, he urged perse-cuted Jews to join him in Texas, "where a man can make his living to his liking, and [be] more independent than the Autocrat of Russia, or the Emperor of Austria." Inducements in the press from men like Lewis Levy fed Texas fever, and the Lone Star State became the destination of Jew-ish adventurers, opportunists, and pioneers.

In the first half of the nineteenth century, many Jews fled oppression, political upheaval, and forced mili-tary conscription in their native Euro-pean countries; others moved to es-cape family pressures and Orthodox practices. The mood of expansion and the spirit of independence found in the United States, along with the prospect of free land for a people tra-ditionally denied access to property ownership, drove Jewish immigrants westward to stake their claims on the new frontier.

About 200 Jews had come to Texas prior to 1836 and were among some of the more colorful characters of the times. The first Jew to settle perma-nently in Texas was probably Jao de la Porta of Portugal, who arrived in Galveston around 1814 and sold land to the infamous privateer, Jean Laf-itte.[1] Lafitte and his brothers used Galveston as their base from 1816 to 1821 as they plundered Spanish gal-leons.

Lafitte's hatred of the Spanish

stemmed from stories told to him by his grandmother, Zora Nadrimal, about the family's flight from Spain to Hispaniola (Haiti) to escape the Spanish Inquisition. The Nadrimals had converted to Catholicism but se-cretly remained loyal to Judaism. In spite of conversion, Lafitte's grand-father had been killed by inquisitors, and Jean's first wife, a Dutch Jew named Christina Levine, was killed on the high seas during a battle with the Spanish. Lafitte sought revenge against Spain in acts of piracy until he was driven out of Galveston by the U.S. Navy.[2]

Until 1821, Mexico, including Texas, was still a Spanish colony, and only "true members of the Catholic faith" could legally enter, reside, and own property. A few *conversos,* includ-ing descendants of the Carvajal fam-ily, settled along the Texas-Mexico border and in San Antonio. Samuel Isaacks and his family had come to Texas from Tennessee and settled on the Brazos River by December 1821 when Stephen F. Austin arrived with his first colonists (known as the Old Three Hundred). Austin drafted the Isaacks family as part of his colony. Isaacks, who was awarded land near present-day Rosenberg and later in Polk County, is widely considered to be Texas' first Jewish settler, though it has not been possible to document his Jewish ancestry from primary sources. There is a 300-year-old fam-ily tradition that the Isaacks family were Welsh Jews who originally spelled their name *Isaacs.*[3]

By the time the battles for Texas independence were fought in 1835–1836, there were Jews living in Ve-lasco, Bolivar, Nacogdoches, Goliad,

and San Antonio. Jewish participants in those battles included Maj. Leon Dyer, Dr. Moses A. Levy, and Capt. David L. Kokernot. Edward I. John-son of Cincinnati, Ohio, marched to Goliad with Fannin and was shot in the infamous Goliad Massacre. Eu-gene Joseph Chimene from France fought in the Battle of San Jacinto.

With independence won, the Re-public of Texas was eager to attract Anglos by giving development con-tracts to land agents, who advertised in the U.S. and abroad. Texas was described in German newspapers as a land of milk and honey, full of biblical promise. *"Geh mit uns Texas"* ("Go with us to Texas") was the slogan, and German steamship companies advertised passage to Galveston as early as 1848. That year, Isaac Leeser, editor of the *Occident,* sug-gested establishing a colony in Texas for Russian Jews who could farm or raise stock.[4]

Drawn by Texas' promise and fer-tility, thousands of immigrants, in-cluding Jews, arrived to build towns, cities, farms, and ranches from the vast expanse of prairies, forests, and coastal plains. Jews came from Ger-many, Prussian-controlled Poland, England, Holland, and Alsace; they also arrived from Philadelphia, Charleston, Baltimore, and New Or-leans. They came on foot, by ship, and overland by wagon or horseback. Some stayed to establish families and businesses and help build new com-munities. Others continued the west-ward trek. Some recorded their impressions; most moved silently and anonymously.

The majority of the early Jews in Texas were peddlers and merchants;

successful mercantile businesses often led to importing, exporting, and cotton brokering. Others contributed to the state's early development as publishers, politicians, and philanthropists. Some amassed large amounts of land as empresarios, farmers, ranchers, and realtors. There were Jewish slave owners and abolitionists, spies, soldiers, sailors, seamstresses, and boardinghouse operators. Jews were also teachers, lawyers, surveyors, doctors, and government clerks.

Until the 1850s, Jews coming to Texas found no communal life in place, although a scattering of Jewish families lived along riverboat and steamship routes. Larger populations lived in Galveston, Houston, and San Antonio. As they settled in Texas, many continued to practice Judaism, but institutions taken for granted in the Old World or in the Eastern or Southern U.S. had to be created anew. The first communal need was usually a burial ground, and Jews in Galveston, Houston, and San Antonio founded cemeteries in the 1850s.

Jews in Houston also established the state's first Jewish organization, the Hebrew Benevolent Society, in 1855, and the state's first chartered synagogue, Hebrew Congregation Beth Israel, in 1859. In 1855, a woman visiting from Philadelphia contributed $100 for a San Antonio Jewish burial ground, and the Jefferson Mount Sinai Cemetery was founded in 1862. In many towns, consecrated sections of city cemeteries were set aside for Jewish burials. The development of Jewish communal institutions was disrupted by the Civil War, with the exception of the establishment by Houston women of a religious school in 1864.

Many pioneer Jews came from Germany, as did a large number of other immigrants to Texas. For the most part, German Jews were regarded simply as other Europeans, and anti-Semitism was not a major concern. Exceptions included Jews who were perceived to be abolitionists, anti-secession, or business competitors, like the Sanger brothers in Weatherford. On the political issues of slavery and secession from the Union, Jews were divided. Some owned slaves; most did not. Some spoke out or voted against secession and had to flee; others fought in Confederate or Union armies or supported the war effort on the home front.

Jewish men were active in Masonic orders and the International Order of Odd Fellows (IOOF), thus becoming part of the community power structures. A few were prominent in the world of politics. Galveston elected a Jewish mayor, Michael Seeligson, in 1853, and others served in the state legislature and held local offices. For the most part, Jews were literate. Many were able to build successful businesses because they had access to credit or capital; contacts in New York, New Orleans, Chicago, and Europe enabled them to import desirable consumer goods.

As Jacob de Cordova, a Jewish real estate developer, wrote in his book *Texas, Her Land, Her People* (1858), "Although Texas is the finest state in the union, and may be literally regarded as a 'land flowing with milk and honey,' it is necessary to FIRST MILK THE COWS AND GATHER THE HONEY, before they can enjoy either the one or the other, for neither of them can be obtained without the aid of labor." Indeed, to live in Texas in the early days was arduous, and Jews, like other immigrants who came to Texas, worked hard to survive. Their letters, documents, photographs, and their descendants attest to their Jewish faith. They persevered and prospered in an atmosphere of religious tolerance and became inextricably woven into the events that became the early history of Texas.

— Sam Houston, of Adolphus Sterne

Adolphus and Eva Rosine Sterne

Nicholas Adolphus Sterne, one of the most colorful characters in early Texas history, was born in Cologne, Germany. His father was an Orthodox Jew, his mother a Lutheran.[5] While clerking in the Cologne passport office, he learned he was to be conscripted into the army. He forged a passport for himself and left for the U.S. in 1817.

Sterne landed in New Orleans, where he studied law and joined the Masonic order, an affiliation which later saved his life. He traveled often to the interior as a peddler; in Tennessee he met Sam Houston, with whom he formed a lasting but tumultuous relationship. Houston called him "the rosy little Jew." [6]

In 1826, Sterne established a mercantile business in the frontier town of Nacogdoches, Texas. He became involved in the struggle against Mexican dominance by smuggling guns in coffee barrels for the early, thirty-man Fredonian Rebellion. For this, he was sentenced to death, but his Masonic Lodge brothers in New Orleans had his death sentence commuted in exchange for his pledge of loyalty.

In 1828, he met and married Eva Rosine Ruff, a Roman Catholic from Germany. They built a home in Nacogdoches and raised seven children. Eva converted both her husband and Sam Houston to Catholicism and was godmother at Houston's baptism in the Sterne parlor. (Mexico allowed only Catholics or converts to hold office or own land.) Sterne's beliefs remained basically deist — having faith in reason, science, and goodness — much like those of Thomas Jefferson, Ben Franklin, and Thomas Paine.

Sterne served as *alcalde* (mayor) of Nacogdoches and local treasurer, 1831–1833. At the start of the Texas Revolution, he went to New Orleans as an agent for the Texians and paid for the transport of a company of New Orleans Grays. In the Republic of Texas, Sterne held many civil service posts including those of judge and postmaster. The Sternes owned

slaves, and by 1840, owned or controlled 16,000 acres of land.

Sterne was witty, charming, and a versatile linguist who spoke German, Yiddish, English, Spanish, French, Portuguese, Latin, and several Indian dialects. He was elected to the second Texas legislature in 1847 and was reelected in 1849. During one particularly dull session, Sterne amused his fellow lawmakers by making a speech in Choctaw.[7] He served in the Texas Senate from November 1851 until his death in New Orleans in 1852.

Adolphus Sterne (1801–1852) was one of Texas' early Jewish settlers, merchants, and officeholders. His diary *Hurrah for Texas* is one of the most important chronicles of life in the Texas Republic. The Sterne home in Nacogdoches now houses the Hoya Library and Museum; it is the oldest surviving wooden structure in the state.
— *Barker Texas History Center, UT Austin*

Eva Rosine Sterne (1810–1897) converted both her husband Adolphus Sterne and Sam Houston to Catholicism.
— *Special Collections Dept., Ralph Steen Library, Stephen F. Austin State University*

"Tuesday, October the 6th [1840] . . . tonight is erev Yom Kippur."

Adolphus Sterne's greatest legacy to Texas history is his vivid diary, written in English and published as *Hurrah for Texas* (1986). Among the many details of frontier life, the diary reveals Sterne's relationship with other area Jews. (Spelling and punctuation have been reproduced as edited by Archie McDonald.)[8]

1840 [November 2] . . . received back a contract made between Saml. Maas* & myself for some San Leon Property . . .

1841 [February 2] bought a Piece of Land to day for my wife . . . [May 19th] Court adjourned to day. All the lawyers got drunk . . . [July 15] mail from East-- rd A Book from Mr. [Michael] Deyoung* of San Augustin containing the Service of *Yom Kippur* in the Portuguese ritual . . . [August 3] the People . . . held a meeting in the Court House for the purpose of organizing a Patrol, to keep in due check the negro Population . . . [September 30] Dined at the house of Mr. Deyoung*, [in San Augustine] he is a German Jew of the *old reverend class*, his wife and the eldest Daughter most amiable. Mrs. D. Y. very much accomplished and deserves a better looking husband. [October 25] general [Sam] Houston here yet . . . had the pleasure of Mrs. Houston's playing a *tune* on the Piano . . . [after December 13] the inauguration took place . . . the President and vice President Elect [of the Republic of Texas] wore Hunting Shirts . . . a splendid Ball in the Evening . . .

1843 [April 22] had a devil of a rompuss with the negro woman Susan, after giving her a sound beating which she well deserved — she absquatolated to furrin parts . . . [October 3] . . . Today is Yom Kippur. Mr. Flateau* is doing Penance, nonsense, to keep up a Religion only one day in the year. [December 22] Mr. Reed . . . brought me several prospectuses for a Paper to be called the San Augustine Literary Intelligencer, edited or *Fathered* by L. A. L. Laird and *T. M. Flateau*,* the Paper is to be a *Methodist* Paper — (oh! dear) — and to be under the management of a *Son of Abraham* . . .

1844 [January 5] Mr. Orton arrived from New Orleans brought me a Letter from Bernard Cohen* a Step Brother of mine . . .

1851 [June 2] this is the 23rd anniversary of my marriage, all Sun shine yet, few dark clouds have obscured our matrimonial Hemisphere, all our children are now here, God Knows how long we may be permitted to remain together in peace. [Sterne died March 7, 1852.]

* indicates individual is Jewish

Captain Samuel Noah (1779–1871): disillusioned adventurer

The nineteenth century was a violent one in Texas history. A handful of Jews, mostly young men drawn to adventure, fought in the various battles for Texas independence, first from Spain and later from Mexico.

In 1807, Capt. Samuel Noah was the second Jewish graduate of West Point. Bored by routine duties as a U.S. Army officer and discouraged about slow promotion, he resigned his commission and joined the Gutierrez-Magee expedition to liberate Texas from Spanish rule, 1812–1813. The rebels temporarily took San Antonio in 1813, but were unable to hold it. Noah left the expedition in disgust, repelled by the brutal decapitation of Spanish loyalists. He returned to the U.S. but was unsuccessful in regaining his commission.[10]

Maj. Leon Dyer (1807–1883)

Leon Dyer moved from Dessau, Germany, with his family to Baltimore, Maryland, around 1810. He was self-educated, helped in his father's business, and even became acting mayor of Baltimore, restoring order during the bread riots. Dyer was president of the Baltimore Hebrew Congregation and helped organize the United Hebrew Society.

An adventurer, Dyer was a U.S. Army major in the Seminole War in Florida and later a quartermaster general for Louisiana. He brought several hundred men to help in the Texas War for Independence, but arrived too late to engage in the decisive Battle of San Jacinto where Sam Houston's forces were victorious (1836). Dyer was commissioned a major in the Texas Army and served as an escort to the captive Mexican General Santa Anna, who was taken to Washington, D.C. to see President Andrew Jackson. Dyer was appointed by President Martin Van Buren as a special envoy to Germany and later a consul-general in London. He also

fought in the Mexican War as a colonel under the command of Gen. Winfield Scott.[11] In 1850, Dyer conducted Yom Kippur services for a temporary congregation in San Francisco.

Leon Dyer and his wife, Sarah Ann, lived in Galveston and had two sons, Alexander O. Dyer, a dentist, and Joseph O. Dyer, a physician. Leon's siblings, Isadore Dyer and Rosanna Dyer Osterman, were Galveston pioneers.

Dr. Moses Albert Levy, Sam Houston's surgeon general

Moses Albert Levy (1814–1848) was among the 300 men at the Siege of Bexar in December 1835, a battle preceding the famous Battle of the Alamo in 1836. Levy served in both the Texas volunteer army and navy.

Born in Amsterdam, he moved with his family to Richmond, Virginia, around 1818. He married a non-Jew, Maria Bishop, around 1830 and graduated from the University of Pennsylvania Medical School in 1832. The marriage caused an estrangement from his family. The couple had one child, Rachel Cornelia. After his wife's death, Levy left Rachel with his sister and joined his older brother, Lewis A. Levy, in New Orleans.

Hearing of the revolutionary struggle in Texas, Moses joined the New Orleans Grays, traveled to Texas, and participated in the Siege of Bexar. He tended the wounded and fought alongside the other soldiers. Ultimately, he was Sam Houston's surgeon general. In 1836, Levy enlisted in the Texas Navy. When his warship *Independence* was attacked, he was imprisoned but escaped by swimming across the Rio Grande. One account of Levy described him as ". . . a swashbuckler cut from the cloth of a silent film star."[12]

Dr. Levy settled in Matagorda County on one of three land bounties he received for participation in the Army of the Republic. On August 2, 1837, he advertised his professional

services in the *Matagorda Bulletin*. His fees included $5 for day visits, $10 for night visits, $2 for bleeding, $5 for cupping, and $30 for labor cases. He married Claudinia O. Gervais, an Episcopalian, in 1838, and the couple had five children. In 1840, he was appointed to the Board of Medical Censors for the Republic of Texas. He again fought Mexico when hostilities broke out in 1842. He committed suicide in 1848, possibly during a period of severe emotional depression because of rejection by his Virginia family.[13]

"A double man being both soldier and surgeon."

Moses Levy's letter to his sister provides a vivid description of the Siege of Bexar.[14]

"San Antonio de Bexar, Dec. 20th 1835 . . . I am engaged for the first time in my life in the real, stirring, and precarious struggle of man with man, & should I succeed, I shall at once be elevated to such a standing in society as must ensure me independance *[sic]*, aye even a fortune, & an immortalized name. Should we fail, my life falls a sacrifice to outraged liberty . . . after a regular storm of five days and nights duration, during the whole of which the enemy kept up incessant firing we forced them to surrender . . . Our men fought like devils (even I fought). I worked in the ditches, I dressed the sick and wounded, I cheered the men, I assisted the officers . . ., for five days and nights I did not sleep that many hours, running about . . . dirty and ragged, but thank God escaped uninjured . . . I was a double man, being both soldier and surgeon."

I ever saw . . ." — Capt. David Levi Kokernot

David L. Kokernot

David L. Kokernot, a native of Amsterdam, went to New Orleans with his father in 1817. He was a pilot on the Mississippi River, traveled to the West Indies and Europe as a merchant seaman, and was a revenue agent in New Orleans. While chasing smugglers in 1830, his ship was wrecked on the Texas coast. Two years later, he moved to Anahuac, Texas, with his wife and children and opened a store.

Captain Kokernot was soon caught up in the Texas struggle for independence. He fought in the Anahuac disturbances of 1832 and commanded a schooner in the first Texas Navy. During a lull, he traveled to Nacogdoches to obtain land titles. He met two Jewish realtors, Simon Schloss and Simon Mussina, and a physician, Dr. Joseph Hertz. While in Nacogdoches, Kokernot met the future president of the Republic, Sam Houston. Kokernot moved his family to Nacogdoches and participated in the Grass Fight of 1835.

When Texas became a republic, Kokernot again moved his family — to Gonzales County — and became a rancher. When the Civil War broke out, he enlisted and served with Terry's Texas Rangers. The town of Kokernot is named for him. In later years, Kokernot wrote his "Reminiscences,"[15] which included a description of that first meeting with Sam Houston on May 15, 1834:

Capt. David L. Kokernot (1805–1892), an officer in the first Texas navy, is shown in his Confederate uniform around 1861.
— *UT Institute of Texan Cultures*

"From that day on I loved Sam Houston"

My first acquaintance with Sam Houston was in the year 1834 . . . I arrived at the town [Nacogdoches], and as I walked up the street I noticed the finest looking man I ever saw . . . He was dressed in a complete Indian costume made of buckskin and ornamented with a profuse variety of beads, and his massive head was covered with a fine broad beaver hat . . . He asked me whence I had come. I told him from Galveston Bay, Middle Texas.

Then he invited me to sit down and have a chat with him in reference to land matters . . .

"Now, my friend," said the General, "tell me the news."

I replied the news was war; that it was rumored that Santa Anna was gathering troops to disarm the inhabitants. "But," said I, "we are determined not to surrender our arms."

"Well, my friend," said he, "how will you act in that case?"

I replied, "We will fight them to the last, or die in the attempt."

"Who will command the army?" he asked.

I replied, "My dear sir, you are the man; for you are the finest looking man I ever laid eyes on."

He immediately replied, "Well, my dear sir, if I get the appointment of commander I will give you a commission."

From that day I loved Sam Houston. He proved a friend indeed in times of need, as many letters in my possession will show.[16]

A TALL TEXAS TALE

Louis "Moses" Rose (1785–1850) and the Alamo: "I am not prepared to die."

The most popular and romantic tale of the Alamo is that of the swashbuckling William B. Travis drawing the symbolic line in the dust with his sword on March 3, 1836, and inviting all who were willing to die for liberty to step over. But how could that tale have survived if no one lived to tell it?

The legendary Louis "Moses" Rose, who may have been Jewish, was by 1836 a seasoned fifty-year-old French soldier and pragmatist. Nicknamed "Moses" by the other defenders because of his gray hair and age, he was the only defender who refused to cross Travis' line. He said, "No, I am not prepared to die, and shall not do so if I can avoid it." Rose vaulted a wall of the Alamo and finally reached the home of a friend in Grimes County, Abraham Zuber. Abraham's son, William Zuber, published the tale of Travis and the line in the dust, as told by Rose, in the *Texas Almanac* of 1873.

Rose had probably participated in more military actions than any of the others at the Alamo. He had won the French Legion of Honor as a lieutenant in Napoleon's army. Prior to the Battle of the Alamo, Rose had already fought in two other Texas battles, the Fredonian Rebellion (1826) and the Siege of Bexar (1835). Recognizing the futility of 182 men defending the Alamo against thousands of Mexican troops without hope of reinforcements, he fled. Rose later operated a butcher shop in Nacogdoches until 1842, when he moved to Louisiana.

Was Rose Jewish? The historian Steven Kellman gives as possible evidence Rose's origins in a part of France with a sizable Jewish population, and the fact that Rose entered the French Army at a time when, after their legal emancipation, Jews were being conscripted for the first time. Rose also lived in Nacogdoches, which was then the home of a number of Jews.[17]

"It is a country where the poor man can easily obtain land."[18]

—Jacob de Cordova

One of the first Jews to capitalize on the new land opportunities available after Texas became a republic was Jacob de Cordova.[19] Famous as a land developer and promoter, he was also a visionary and planner, historian, botanist, business analyst, surveyor, public speaker, and publisher. De Cordova was pro-slavery, but worked for the importation of white labor and industrialization of the Brazos River Valley. His fortunes swung from bankruptcy in 1841 to control of one million acres of land by 1855. He died land poor: he owned land in forty counties, but left his family little but debts and dreams.

Jacob de Cordova was born to a Jamaican couple, Raphael and Judith de Cordova. His father was Jewish; his mother was not. When Jacob was eight, the family moved to Philadelphia, and Raphael was elected president of Pennsylvania's first Sephardic synagogue, Mickveh Israel.[20] Years later, Jacob entertained fellow stagecoach passengers in Texas by chanting portions of the Sabbath and holiday services in the styles of the various readers he had heard during his youth.[21]

In 1826, Jacob married Rebecca Sterling, daughter of a prominent Baptist family. They moved briefly to Jamaica, where he began a newspaper, *The Gleaner,* then to New Orleans, Galveston, and finally Houston, where they lived for almost thirteen years (1839–1851). Soon after his arrival, he helped found the Chamber of Commerce, and in 1844 was elected an alderman. He founded the first Odd Fellows (IOOF) lodge outside the U.S. In 1847, he was elected Harris County representative to the Texas legislature, where he voted to give state land for public schools. He was defeated in his second race because of his support for the railroads.

In 1845, Jacob began de Cordova's Land Agency, which lasted until his half brother and partner, Phineas de Cordova, died in 1903. Waco was laid

Jacob de Cordova (1808–1868) was a land developer, publisher, orator, surveyor, legislator, and a founder of the City of Waco.
— *The Texas Collection, Baylor University, Waco, Texas*

out on the site of an abandoned Waco Indian village by Jacob and two other men in 1849. In 1852, de Cordova moved his headquarters to Austin and began hiring land agents.

During the 1850s, de Cordova published three significant books that stimulated emigration to Texas, and he promoted the state on lecture tours to New York, Brooklyn, Newark, Philadelphia, and London. His encyclopedia, *Texas: Her Resources and Her Public Men* (1858), was the most complete sourcebook about Texas in its day.

Jacob and Rebecca had five children. She ran the home and farm in Jacob's absence, and in 1851, she moved the family from Houston to Wanderer's Retreat near Seguin. Jacob wrote to her: "There is a small piece of ground . . . that I wish broken up . . . for an early garden. Put on Irish potatoes, beets, peas, turnips." Rebecca, who was known for her gar-

dening, also raised cattle and registered a brand.

By 1855, de Cordova owned or controlled a million acres, but he was deeply in debt. Judgments were brought against him, and creditors seized his land. In 1856, Jacob again moved his family, this time to Bosque County northwest of Waco. He liked to stay just ahead of the westward-moving tide of Anglo-Americans, bringing his lands to market quickly. Jacob surveyed the Texas Panhandle with a team of men led by Indian guides and discovered mineral wealth. When the Civil War broke out, he became a tax collector for the Confederacy. After the war, he planned to industrialize the Brazos River Valley with textile mills and other factories. The machinery was en route to him when he died. He and his wife are buried in the Texas State Cemetery in Austin.

Phineas de Cordova: land developer, publisher, and politician

Phineas de Cordova was the half brother of Jacob de Cordova. The de Cordova family had emigrated from Amsterdam to Curacao (Netherlands Antilles, West Indies) in 1749 when their grandfather, Joshua Hezekiah de Cordova, was called to serve Congregation Mikveh Israel as a teacher. In 1755, Joshua went to Jamaica as rabbi for congregations in Kingston and Spanish Town. Joshua's son, Raphael de Cordova, left Jamaica for Philadelphia in 1816 with his sons Jacob and Joshua, following the death of his wife in childbirth. There Raphael remarried, and Phineas was born.

Phineas received a good general and Jewish education. In 1835, he moved to Jamaica, and in 1848 he married Jeminina Delgado. The couple settled briefly in Galveston, then moved to Houston, where Phineas joined Jacob in the land agency and newspaper publishing business. *De Cordova's Herald and Immigrant Guide* was a monthly publication devoted primarily to promoting the de Cordova lands.

At the request of Governor P. H. Bell in 1850, the de Cordovas moved their printing office to Austin, the state capital. They jointly published a weekly, *The Southwestern American*, for two years.

The de Cordova Land Agency grew rapidly. Jacob hired agents in many counties and gave Phineas his power of attorney to transact business throughout Texas. Phineas became an expert on land laws. In 1872, he published a topographical map of Austin, and together the brothers wrote a broadside, *Instructions to Heirs Claiming Estates Under the Laws of the Republic of Texas.*

Phineas was interested in politics and was a member of the Texas Democratic Party Executive Committee. Governor Bell appointed Phineas a notary public for Travis County in 1851, and Phineas was reappointed by every succeeding governor over the

Phineas de Cordova (1819–1903) was a partner with his half brother, Jacob de Cordova, in their land agency and publishing business.
— *Barker Texas History Center, UT Austin*

next forty years. He worked for the election of Governor E. M. Pease in 1853. During the Civil War, Phineas was elected to the Texas Senate for three terms and served as its secretary. As a member of the Ways and Means Committee, he strongly supported legislation to finance railroad construction. Later, Phineas made unwise investments in the New York, Texas, and Mexico Railroad Company. Unfortunately, he and the other investors lost everything.

During the Civil War, Phineas was responsible for the protection of the civilian population as secretary of the Texas Military Board. After the war, Phineas was appointed U.S. commissioner for the Western District of Texas (1879–1885). His friend, Governor Pease, who had been a Unionist, served another term, from 1867 to 1869. Phineas served as manager of the Pease family business affairs for fifty years.

Phineas was elected Grand Master of the Austin lodge (Milam) of the Independent Order of Odd Fellows. He was also a founder of Austin's Congregation Beth Israel, and was elected its vice-president on September 24, 1876. He died in 1903, probably from rheumatoid arthritis, and is buried in the Temple Beth Israel Cemetery.[22]

"First milk the cows and gather the honey."[23]

The following excerpts are from Jacob de Cordova's sourcebook, *Texas: Her Resources and her Public Men* (1858).

"As Texas is . . . an agricultural country, the immigration of the children of Israel has been very limited, and as yet there are no synagogues . . . Although they are very few in number, yet, they have established two burial-grounds, and a benevolent institution . . . The oldest of these burial-grounds is . . . in Galveston, and was donated by Joseph Osterman, Esq., and was consecrated . . . by the Rev. Mr. M. N. Nathan, in 1852. At the site of Houston through the exertions of Lewis A. Levy, Esq. [the older brother of Dr. Moses A. Levy], a benevolent association has been formed . . . This association has also under its control a burial-ground . . ."[24]

"It is difficult in this state . . . to find female help . . . plan not to have too great a burden of housework for women to bear. Remember, this kind of work is ever doing, never done, and incapable of being put off . . ."[25]

". . . although Texas is the finest State in the Union, and may be literally regarded as a 'land flowing with milk and honey,' it is necessary to FIRST MILK THE COWS AND GATHER THE HONEY, before they can enjoy either one or the other . . . neither . . . can be obtained without the aid of labor . . ."[26]

"[Texas] is not a paradise, but it is a country where the poor man can easily obtain land . . . We have large quantities of land for sale in various parts of the State . . ."[27]

". . . to win a home from the wilderness . . . is attended with a great deal of hard labor and fatigue . . . no one suffers more than the female emigrant, especially if she has been tenderly brought up, for those who have been unaccustomed to labor in the home of their childhood will find it a hard matter to commence on their arrival . . ."[28]

— **Lewis A. Levy**

Henri Castro (1786–1865) was a land empresario and founder of Castroville. Castro County is named for him. Rabbi Henry Cohen wrote that "during his [Castro's] surveying tours he would leave his companions in order to retire to the forest for the purpose of binding his Phylacteries."[30]
— *UT Institute of Texan Cultures*

Henri Castro

Along with new trade opportunities, Texas independence also marked the end of colonial land grants and contracts with Mexico. In 1841, a law was passed empowering the president of Texas to enter into colonization contracts. Henri Castro was a well-connected French banker, born of rich parentage descended from an old Portuguese *converso* family. After the fall of Napoleon, Castro emigrated to the U.S. and became a naturalized citizen. In 1838, however, he returned to France as a partner in Lafitte & Co., a Parisian banking firm. He tried to secure a loan for the Republic of Texas, a move that led President Sam Houston in 1842 to offer him a five-year contract to settle immigrants in an area west of San Antonio.

In the 1840s, Castro chartered twenty-seven ships. He ultimately brought over 2,000 European colonists from Alsace Lorraine and bordering German provinces to settle

four Texas towns in what are now Uvalde, Bandera, and Bexar counties. The center of the settlement was Castroville, where Castro made his home. He was appointed Texas' consul-general to France and helped popularize Texas by publishing pamphlets and maps in French and German. He spent large sums of his own money — over $150,000 — to furnish his colonists with cows, farm implements, seeds, medicine, and other essentials for survival in a rough, uncultivated area vulnerable to attacks from Indians and Mexicans trying to regain their land.

When Castro's contract expired in 1847, he continued living in Castroville. He and his wife, a devout Catholic, built a home there. He had expected to receive half the land awarded to each colonist, but the State of Texas overruled his claim and granted all the acreage to the other colonists. Like Jacob de Cordova, Castro lost most of his money in his Texas ventures, but continued to direct town affairs until his death in 1865. He is buried in a Catholic cemetery in Monterrey, Mexico.[31]

Simon Mussina

Simon Mussina, a newspaperman from Philadelphia, received a liberal education and lived in Mobile and New Orleans, before moving to the new Republic of Texas in 1837. He speculated in land with his brother, Jacob Mussina, and founded the Matagorda *Bulletin*. Simon was an attorney but was more interested in journalism, land acquisition, and merchandising.

During the Mexican War (1846–1848), Simon went to Matamoros, Mexico, as Jacob's agent. After Fort Brown was captured by U.S. forces, Simon was one of the first to begin buying land formerly held by Mexican citizens. These land acquisitions became the subject of litigation and ultimately became the City of Brownsville. In 1848, Simon began publish-

Simon Mussina (1805–1889) was a publisher, attorney, and land speculator.
— *Rosenberg Library, Galveston, Texas*

ing the *American Flag* in Brownsville. His last years were spent as a practicing attorney in Galveston.[32]

Other Brownsville Jews affected by the Mexican War were the John Melvin Hirsch family, who moved across the border to Matamoros. They were good friends of American Generals Winfield Scott and Zachary Taylor, who used the Hirsch home as military headquarters. Since the practice of Judaism was still not acceptable in Mexico, the Hirsches held secret High Holiday services in their attic.[33]

"More independent than the Autocrat of Russia . . ."
On May 24, 1850, the *Asmonean*, a New York newspaper, published a letter from Lewis A. Levy, a Houston Jew, urging persecuted European Jews to move to Texas. Excerpts follow.

". . . thousands of acres of land can be bought, within the settled portions of the State, for the small sum of from 25 cents to $1 per acre . . . where a man can make his living to his liking, and more independent than the Autocrat of Russia, or the Emperor of Austria . . . I would not exchange my fifteen acre lot, with the house on it, and the garden around it, . . . near the city of Houston for all the thrones and hereditary dominions of both those noted persons . . ."

Earning a living on the frontier

Most of the pioneer Jewish Texans were peddlers and merchants. Success led to land acquisition as well as entrepreneurial enterprises like cotton brokering. In the 1830s, Jews began settling in East and South Texas and along the Gulf Coast. When Abraham Cohen Labatt, a Sephardic Jew from New Orleans, visited Velasco in 1831, he found two Jewish merchants already established — Jacob Lyons from South Carolina and Jacob Henry from England. Henry left a sizable fortune to build a public hospital in Velasco, but his will was contested and the hospital was never built. After living for years in San Francisco before the Civil War, where he founded that city's first synagogue, Shearith Israel, Labatt himself settled in Galveston after the war. Solomon Parr opened a store in Bolivar in 1832, and Eugene Chimene arrived in Houston around the time of its founding in 1836.

Even before Texas won its independence, Jewish peddlers traded with the Kiowa Indians in northeast Texas and Oklahoma. The Cherokee Indians called them "egg-eaters" because the Jews carried hardboiled eggs to observe dietary laws. One story recounts Sitting Bear's first wife purchasing rolls of red and blue cloth from Jewish peddlers in northeast Texas. The other wives followed her, examining the goods which also included guns, lead, powder, and sheets of silver.[35]

After Texas became a republic, Samuel Maas operated a successful ship chandler's business in Galveston. In nearby Houston, Michael Seeligson ran a store near the steamboat landing, the Westheimers opened a stable, and Henry Wiener was an auctioneer. Henry S. Fox was a claims adjuster, while S. Raphael sold "Cigars, fruits, fancy groceries, nuts, confectionery . . . next door to Saloon, lately occupied by Rosenfield's Auction."[36]

By 1845, San Antonio was the largest city in Texas, and many Jews considered the city a good place to settle.

Louis Zork advertised in the San Antonio *Ledger,* June 5, 1851: "[We carry] an extensive assortment of staple and fancy groceries and cutlery at prices 20% cheaper." Henry Mayer carried men's and boys' clothing in his New York Clothing Store. Rebecca (Mrs. Sigmund) Feinberg, a woman of independent means, purchased a lot for "manufacturing purposes" in 1853. Miss Mollie Bergman advertised herself as a maker of mantuas, a loose-fitting woman's gown, with offices above *The Zeitung,* a German-language newspaper. Mrs. Mayers of New York opened a millinery shop, and C. M. Coen & Co. were forwarding and commission merchants.[37]

Jacob Samuels opened a trading post in Fort Worth, where skirmishes with the Indians were still common. Myer Levy traded on the Brazos River and later became a privateer for the Confederate Army. Bernard Kowalski joined the California Gold Rush, Simon Rosenbaum established a school in East Texas near Marshall, and Jacob Sterne worked in the Cass County clerk's office.

There were Jewish merchants in the border towns of Brownsville and El Paso and across the Rio Grande in Juárez and Matamoros. Samuel Schutz from Westphalia, Germany, settled in El Paso in 1854, where he founded the city's first railway system, the Old Mule Line, which crossed the river into Mexico. After the Civil War, he and his brothers built the Southwest's first steam-operated flour mill. Benjamin Moses was the captain of the Rio Grande steamboat *Aid* in 1847, freighting goods to Camargo, Mexico. He was also a Brownsville justice of the peace, a customs inspector, and an auctioneer. Moses sold a fleet of surplus government steamboats to Capt. Richard King, founder of the famous King Ranch.

Adolph Krakauer moved to El Paso in 1870 to work as a bookkeeper in the Schutz Brothers store owned by fellow Jews. In 1889, Adolph was elected mayor of El Paso, but had to give up his office because he had not yet received his second citizenship papers. He was the second president of Temple Mount Sinai from 1899 to 1900.

— *UT Institute of Texan Cultures*

The Isaac Gronsky family were sheep raisers in the West Texas town of Colorado City. They are shown eating watermelon, c. 1898. Standing far right is Estelle Gronsky. Others in the photo are not identified.
— *Sherwin Goldman (New York), Ronald Goldman (Fort Worth), Gayle Goldman Johansen (Dallas), and Carol Goldman Minker (Fort Worth)*

The beginnings of Jewish communal life

Texas Jewish institutions we take for granted today — synagogues and temples, federations and fraternal orders, sisterhoods, religious schools, and cemeteries — had their origins before the Civil War.

When the first Jews arrived in Texas, there were no communal institutions like the ones they had left behind in Europe, Philadelphia, Baltimore, New Orleans, or Charleston. There were no *cheders, yeshivas,* or synagogues; no *mohels, chazans,* or *schochets;* and the nearest rabbis were in New Orleans. Many of the first Jews lived in towns where they were the only ones of their faith. In Galveston, Houston, San Antonio, and Jefferson, after a period of ten or fifteen years, there were enough Jews to have a *minyan,* the ten men needed to conduct a service, and to establish at least a cemetery. Religious services were held in private homes, stores, or rented rooms.

Most of Texas' first Jews were young, single men who came from small towns in Bavaria, Prussian-occupied Poland, or the Eastern or Southern parts of the U.S. Many intermarried; others returned to Europe or to other parts of the U.S. to marry Jewish women and bring them home to Texas. Some tried to observe at least the Sabbath and the High Holidays with varying degrees of success. Others abandoned their faith. The tensions between Orthodox and Reform Jews surfaced early and eventually led to the establishment of religious institutions reflecting both points of view. The publication in 1857 of *Minhag America* by Rabbi Isaac Mayer Wise, the founder of Reform Judaism, facilitated the introduction of Reform rituals after the Civil War. Most Texas communities, however, could afford only one temple at first, and there was often an uneasy peace between the various religious factions.

Cemeteries were the first communal need. Before there were consecrated burial grounds, Jews were buried in city cemeteries. Jewish cemeteries were established in Galveston in 1852, Houston in 1854 (or possibly as early as 1844), San Antonio in 1855, and Jefferson in 1862.

Texas' first Jewish organization was the Hebrew Benevolent Association of Houston, founded in 1855 to help the poor. San Antonio organized a Hebrew Benevolent Society in 1856. The state's first chartered congregation was also a Houston institution — Temple Beth Israel, founded in 1859, and chartered by the state legislature later that year. (Beth Israel dates its official founding as 1854.) Houston women organized a religious school during the Civil War.

Communications between communities were enhanced by the founding of a national Jewish newspaper, *The Occident* (in Philadelphia, 1843) by Isaac Leeser, and *The Israelite* (in Cincinnati, 1854) by Rabbi Isaac Mayer Wise. Both papers ran numerous items from Texas correspondents from which we get a flavor of Jewish life on the frontier. Texas Jews responded to appeals for funds, sending money to Palestine and to yellow fever victims in other states.

The Civil War slowed the development of Jewish institutions because Jews, like other Texans, were preoccupied with wartime conditions. Some Texas Jews fought for the Confederacy, some for the Union Army, and some served on the home front. The Israelite Ladies of Houston donated funds to their local hospital society to care for wounded soldiers, and Jefferson Jews served the Confederacy as quartermasters and suppliers of food and clothing.

The Sigmund Feinberg tombstone, Temple Beth-El Cemetery, San Antonio, December 10, 1857. "And innocent blood shall not be spilled in Israel" is carved on this tombstone. The carving, which portrays two men dressed in Victorian frock coats and high "stove pipe" hats with pistols pointed at each other, led to the legend that Feinberg was killed in a duel. The duel allegedly followed a quarrel between Feinberg and another Russian Jewish immigrant, Benedict Schwartz, over a dog. According to the memoirs of Feinberg's stepdaughter, Rebecca Mayer, Schwartz actually shot Feinberg from ambush. Schwartz was never charged or brought to trial. Feinberg's wife, Regina Feinberg, was so incensed that she erected a wall around the Feinberg burial plot to prevent Schwartz' ever being buried nearby. Ironically, Schwartz was stabbed to death in his pawnshop twenty-five years later.[39]
— *UT Institute of Texan Cultures*

San Antonio

San Antonio's first Jewish family was that of Louis Zork, a native of Prussia. In 1847, he was a founder of the Alamo Lodge #44 of Ancient Free and Accepted Masons, Bexar County, and was elected senior warden. Many early Texas Jews like Louis Zork were active in the Masonic order, usually composed of the most influential men in town. The Jewish involvement in those early power structures may have served as protection against anti-Semitism and facilitated the acceptance of Jews as part of the inner circle of business and political decision makers.

Zork was a businessman who contributed not only to the local German-English School, but was also treasurer of Bexar County (1856–1865). The *Occident,* December 1858, reported that Zork had raised $59 among the few Jewish inhabitants of San Antonio for the Jewish Widows and Orphans Home in New Orleans. He was later a founder of San Antonio's Temple Beth-El in 1874.

Jewish services in San Antonio and an informal religious school were held as early as 1854 in the home of Rebecca and Henry Mayer. (The May-ers left San Antonio during the Civil War because they opposed secession.) The first Jewish cemetery in San Antonio was established in 1855 by Eleanora Lorch of Philadelphia, who was visiting her daughter and son-in-law, Regina and Sigmund Feinberg. Distressed by the absence of a Jewish cemetery, Eleanora contributed $100 for the purchase of four acres. In 1873, the land of the Hebrew burial ground was conveyed to the Hebrew Benevolent Society for $1 by Regina Feinberg, Louis Zork, and A. Morris.[40]

Galveston

Galveston's first known Jews, Samuel Maas, Michael Seeligson, and Joseph and Rosanna Osterman, arrived in 1839. They owned mercantile establishments and soon prospered. By 1850, there were four Jewish families — twelve adults and fourteen children.

In 1852, the six-year-old son of Isadore and Amelia Ann Lewis Dyer died in Galveston. Although his mother was an Episcopalian, the parents decided to give him a Jewish burial. The Jews of Galveston petitioned the city government to set aside a portion of the municipal cemetery for Jewish interments, and according to Jacob de Cordova, Joseph Osterman donated the land. The Ostermans and the Dyers sent for the Rev. M. N. Nathan of the New Orleans Portuguese Hebrew Synagogue, who performed the ceremony. His sermon reflected Nathan's understanding of the historic nature of the occasion, and in true rabbinic style, he admonished his listeners to adhere more closely to their faith. Excerpts follow.[42]

"Brethren, this . . . is the first public assemblage . . . of persons . . . to lay the foundation-stone . . . of the edifice of Judaism . . .

"At some distant day, when . . . large congregations of our brethren will abound in this gigantic State of the Union, curiosity will naturally be excited to ascertain who first unfurled . . . the standard of Judaism in this section of the West. Let, then, the particulars of the occasion be duly . . . recorded . . . [as] a chronicle for coming generations. Do not smile at the importance I attach to the act of consecrating a few feet of ground for a Hebrew burial ground . . .

"Neither you nor I can foresee what the vessel may ultimately hold. 'All beginnings are difficult.' . . . may we anticipate here the spread and growth of our peculiar institutions from this apparently inefficient beginning . . .

"It may be long ere another Jewish minister may address you in the language of admonition and warning . . . Fling away your indifference, your supineness, your coldness; and be warm, energetic, zealous in the cause of God . . . You are confessedly too few to build a Synagogue . . . But you can pray at home, instead of inconsistently going with your families to church and chapel . . . Can you not, also stamp your offspring with the seal of the covenant of circumcision? And is there any preventive to your children forming suitable alliances with Hebrew blood, when respectable and populous congregations are in your immediate neighborhood? . . .

"Robe your soul in light, in purity, in righteousness; clothe it with the panoply of good works on earth, that it may receive the . . . blissful immortality from our Father in heaven."

On October 8, 1859, the Galveston *Weekly News* carried this story: "Day of Atonement — today being the 10th day of the Jewish 7th month 'Tishri,' our Jewish fellow citizens have closed their places of business to celebrate it as a day of fast and prayer."

Galveston Jews would not form a congregation until 1868, when they established the state's first Reform temple, B'nai Israel.

Mr. Cohen of Galveston Circumcises his Son

The *Occident*, 1852, reported from Galveston that "A Mr. E. Cohen, lately from England, having a son born, . . . concluded with a praiseworthy courage to perform the circumsion *himself*, as we have no *Mohel* nearer than New Orleans. People endeavored to persuade him to wait till the child could be taken thither, or a *mohel* be sent for. But he replied, that our Father Abraham performed this duty on the eighth day, why should he not do it also? He therefore did as he contemplated, in the presence of a surgeon, and the child is doing well."

The home of Amelia and Isadore Dyer at 24th and Avenue I in Galveston is thought to be the site of the first Jewish High Holiday services held in Galveston — *Yom Kippur, 1856.*[43]
— *Barker Texas History Center, UT Austin*

Michael Seeligson (1797–1867) was Galveston's first Jewish mayor, elected in 1853.
— *Rosenberg Library, Galveston, Texas*

Early office holders

The election of Jews to public office in the days of the Republic of Texas and early statehood attests to a spirit of tolerance toward them.

Adolphus Sterne and Jacob de Cordova held local offices in Nacogdoches and Houston: Sterne was county treasurer (1831–1833) and de Cordova was a city alderman (1844). They were both elected to the state legislature in 1847. John Williamson Moses, a breeder of donkeys and mules, was a justice of the peace at Banquete, west of Corpus Christi, in 1852, and Louis Zork was Bexar County treasurer (1856–1865).

David Spangler Kaufman, from Lancaster, Pennsylvania, was the first Texan to be seated in the U.S. House of Representatives after Texas became a state in 1845. He was of Hebrew descent but not a practicing Jew after he moved to Texas. Kaufman also served in the Third, Fourth, and Fifth Congresses of the Republic of Texas, and was Speaker for two sessions.[44]

"I accepted the office . . . to thwart the designs of a certain clique who were preaching . . . against our nation . . ."[45]

— Michael Seeligson

One of the greatest myths in American Jewish history is that northeastern Jews were the first to break ground in the world of politics. Galveston in particular was one Texas city where Jews attained high office and positions of respect in public life very early. Galveston elected Michael Seeligson as its mayor in 1853 — 120 years before New York City had a Jewish mayor, Abraham Beame.

Seeligson was born in Holland to Sephardic Jewish parents whose ancestors migrated to northern Europe from Spain during the Inquisition. His family moved to Philadelphia in 1797, and he later married Adelaide Gottschalk, aunt of the famous composer Louis Gottschalk. Seeligson lived in Houston briefly in 1839, where he had a store near the steamboat landing. His wife and two children then joined him in nearby Galveston. Seeligson was elected a Galveston alderman twice (1840 and 1848) and mayor in 1853.[46] He described his election in a letter to Isaac Leeser, editor of the *Occident*, on June 19, 1853, excerpts of which follow.

"I accepted the office not for the sake of lucre, but merely to thwart the designs of a certain clique who . . . were preaching publicly the crusades against our nation. This is certainly an evidence, if our people would only sustain their rights and privileges in this republican country, and demean themselves accordingly, they can be elevated to any office they aspire."

The identity of the clique who opposed Seeligson is not known.

"Settle 'persecuted Israelites' at $1 to $3 an acre."

Seeligson and his family did not remain in Galveston. He bought 4,400 acres, and by 1856 the family settled in Goliad. In an 1856 letter to the *Occident*, Seeligson invited Jews to come to Texas and become landowners and farmers. He suggested that Jewish charities buy some of his land to settle "persecuted Israelites" at $1 to $3 an acre. He wrote, "if five or six [Jews] go together, they can make arrangements at once to keep the ceremonials of our religion fully as well as in cities." Seeligson and his wife are buried in the first Galveston Hebrew Cemetery.

Seeligson's son, George, who spoke fluent Spanish, got a job with a company on the Rio Grande River. He led pack trains into northern Mexico, returning with silver and information for the U.S. government about conditions south of the border. George and his brother Henry both served with the Confederacy. Henry also fought in the Mexican War under the command of Gen. Zachary Taylor.[47] George and Henry married non-Jewish women and became Episcopalians.

The Ostermans of Galveston

Rosanna Dyer was born in Germany, moved with her parents to Baltimore, Maryland, in 1811, and in 1825 married Joseph Osterman — a silversmith, diamond cutter, and merchant from Amsterdam. After financial reverses, Joseph moved to Galveston in 1838 and Rosanna soon followed. They went at the suggestion of Rosanna's brother, Leon Dyer, a major in the Texas Army.

In Galveston, Joseph opened an import enterprise and was assisted by Rosanna. Known for her tact, talent, and energy, she soon became his valuable business partner. Joseph's mule pack trains went to all parts of Texas. He was not only one of the first exporters of cotton to Holland, but also one of the first to advance money to planters on future crops. He financed the island's first ferry and supported one of Galveston's first newspapers.

The Ostermans built the city's first two-story residence, now the YWCA headquarters, at Broadway and 24th. Rosanna brought the first piano and iron stove to Texas and built the state's first hothouse. Her garden was noted for its almond and olive trees, and tea and coffee plants. She prepared meat biscuits from a pemmican of dried powdered buffalo meat, beans, and cornmeal obtained from trading with the Comanches. Gail Borden, a frequent visitor in the Osterman home, got his inspiration for processed evaporated milk (patented in 1856) from Rosanna. Other visitors included Texas presidents Sam Houston, David G. Burnet, and Mirabeau B. Lamar.

Rosanna brought the first rabbi — M. N. Nathan — to Texas for the consecration of the state's first Jewish cemetery in 1852. The first religious services were held in her brother Isadore's home at her urging on Yom Kippur, 1856.[49] The Ostermans had no children but helped raise her niece, Isabella Dyer. Isabella married

A black marble plaque hangs in the lobby of Temple Beth Israel in Houston, commemorating a bequest of $2,500 by Rosanna Osterman, which funded Beth Israel's Franklin Avenue building, dedicated in 1870. Rosanna Dyer Osterman (1809–1866) and her husband, Joseph Osterman (1796–1861), were Galveston pioneers.

— *Photo by Ruthe Winegarten*

Moritz Kopperl, who later served as president of the Gulf, Colorado and Santa Fe Railway.

Rosanna Osterman's abilities as a nurse were well known. During the 1853 yellow fever epidemic, she set up a tent on the grounds of her home to nurse the sick and dying, and sent $20 to help victims in other cities.

In 1861, Joseph Osterman was killed by the accidental discharge of a pistol, widowing Rosanna. During the Civil War, she dispersed the family's eight slaves but remained on the island herself. When most residents fled the occupation by Federal troops, she turned her home into a hospital to nurse first the Union and then the Confederate wounded. Three Confederate soldiers later wrote to her, "Your kindness to us in sickness can never be forgotten." Her carpets were made into slippers, her sheets into lint and bandages.

Rosanna allegedly helped the Confederates retake Galveston, based on information obtained from a wounded Union soldier. When she learned that Confederate plans to retake the island on January 12, 1863, had been re-

vealed to Union forces by a runaway slave, she alerted Confederate General John McGruder, who moved his successful attack up to New Year's Day.

Rosanna Osterman died tragically in the explosion of a steamboat on the Mississippi River, February 1, 1866, and is buried in the Portuguese Cemetery in New Orleans. She left an estate valued at over $200,000.

Recognizing the economic insecurity of women, Rosanna bequeathed the income from the Osterman Building to her niece, Isabella Dyer, her sister, Hannah Dyer Symonds, and a friend, Mary Ann Brown. After the last of these legatees died in 1902, the revenues went to the Osterman Widows and Orphans Home Fund. Among many bequests, she willed $5,000 toward the building of a synagogue in Galveston, Temple B'nai Israel, dedicated in 1870; $2,500 toward a synagogue for Houston, Temple Beth Israel, dedicated in 1870; $1,000 each for a Galveston and a Houston Hebrew Benevolent Society; $1,000 for a Galveston Sailors' Home; $1,000 for the Jewish Ladies Benevolent Society of New Orleans; and funds for Jewish hospitals and Hebrew schools in New Orleans, New York City, Cincinnati, and Philadelphia.[50]

— The *Occident*, Philadelphia, 1859

Lewis A. and Mary A. Levy: Houston Pioneers

Rosanne and Daniel Leeson

Lewis A. Levy (1799–1861) and his wife, Mary A. Levy (1800–1888), moved to Houston in 1841. They were married in England in 1817, lived in Richmond, Virginia, from 1818 to 1828, and then in New Orleans and Philadelphia. Shortly after moving to Houston, they began investing in land. Lewis bought a lot from Sam Houston in 1843, and Mary bought land in her own name from Jacob de Cordova in 1844. Since she was illiterate, she signed her name with an "x." The couple had twenty children; Mary was pregnant from the age of seventeen until forty-eight.[51] In 1847, their daughter Hannah married Henry Wiener, an auctioneer; it may have been the first Jewish marriage in Texas.

Lewis had several letters published in the *Asmonean*, a New York Jewish paper, in 1850. One urged European Jews to settle in Texas where, he said, "No obstacles are in their way to acquire property." The other was entitled, "The Punishment and Blessings of Israel" and dealt with the history of anti-Semitism through the ages. After Lewis' death, Mary went to live with her daughter Julia Levy Simon in Brenham. In 1989, gravestone markers for Mary and Julia were erected by the Daughters of the Republic of Texas in the Jewish section of Brenham's Prairie Lea Cemetery.   — *Rosanne and Daniel Leeson*

Houston establishes a cemetery (1854) and a Hebrew Benevolent Association (1855)

Although the first Jew to move to Houston, Eugene Chimene, arrived as early as 1836, it was almost twenty years before a formal community structure would develop. In 1854, Lewis A. Levy, Houston's first unofficial Jewish community leader, collected $33 for yellow fever victims in New Orleans. He probably organized the city's Hebrew cemetery the same year because the first burial was on December 10. By the spring of 1855, the city had a Hebrew Benevolent Association, chaired by Levy. It was apparently a well-respected institution and participated in the city's July Fourth celebration in 1856.

Beth Israel: Texas' first Jewish chartered congregation, 1859

According to the 1860 Census, there were 108 Jews in Houston: forty-two men, twenty-six women, and forty children. Most of the adults were young; a majority had been born in Germany. The others came from South Carolina, Louisiana, Virginia, and Mississippi. Only one had been born in Texas.

In 1859, Hebrew Congregation Beth Israel was founded as an Orthodox congregation. It was legally chartered later that year, on December 28. (The founding year is often given as 1854.) With an initial membership of twenty-two, the new congregation was headed by M. A. Levy from Charleston, South Carolina. (In Charleston, he had been vice-president of Shearith Israel, a splinter congregation formed by unhappy Orthodox members of Beth Elohim when the latter began moving toward Reform Judaism.)

The *Occident* reported on March 15, 1860, that Houston Jews were prosperous and well educated and had erected a wooden building in the downtown area, "the front of which is used as a Synagogue, the back portion as a meeting room."

Beth Israel adopted the Polish *Min-*

hag or ritual. Early minutes provide fascinating details of the congregation's members and the problems they faced. Forty-eight seats were sold to men and forty-three to women. A fine was levied against those who entered the sanctuary smoking or with their heads uncovered. The board suspended several members for keeping their businesses open on the Sabbath (November 4, 1861). The minutes have references to "problem children," relief for the poor, Jewish and secular education, and ritual matters. Cemetery concerns included protecting the graves from roaming hogs and cows.

"Hebrew ladies," possibly wives of non-members, were given temporary use of the synagogue in 1864 for a Sunday school. But the Beth Israel board soon disapproved of the ladies' classes, and their "objectionable Catechism." The ladies refused to compromise or cooperate in a joint effort. A committee was formed independent of the ladies, and Rabbi Emmich returned to supervise the religious school.[52]

The Reverend Zachariah Emmich was Texas' first formally ordained rabbi, educated at Frankfurt-on-Main, Germany. Houston's Temple Beth Israel hired him at an annual salary of $1,000 after advertising in the *American Israelite*, November 18, 1859, for a *chazan* (cantor), *schochet* (ritual slaughterer), and *mohel* (ordained to circumcise). One of Emmich's first responsibilities was to circumcise an eight-year-old boy. After Emmich's one-year contract ended, he went into the crockery business but from time to time conducted services and taught religious school for the temple.   — *Joyce Dannenbaum Wolf*

Skull and crossbones on the door

Around 1858, Isaac Sanger, the first of the Sanger brothers to arrive in Texas, opened a frontier store in Weatherford, west of Fort Worth. He and his brother Lehman, in partnership with a Mr. Baum, opened the Baum & Sanger store. Lehman Sanger recalled that they "met with considerable opposition because of their religion, and were put to a good many obstacles trying to break them up, but they held the fort." A former partner, Morris Lasker, wrote that the Sangers' pricing policies "aroused against them the enmity of their competitors, and all kinds of attempts were made to drive them out of Weatherford." He continued, "[Baum's] bride . . . found the new life hard at best, but imagine her horror when she saw a notice on her door that unless her husband and his partner left town . . . they would be subjected to dire punishment . . . this notice was repeated and emphasized by skull and crossbones being painted on the door . . . they were charged before a secret tribunal with entertaining abolitionist sentiment . . ."[53]

In 1859, the Sangers tried to overcome negative public sentiment by contributing $50 to the First Methodist Church and to the Cumberland Presbyterian Church. During the Civil War, Isaac and Lehman served in the Confederate Army, as did another brother Philip, then living in Savannah, Georgia.

Lehman Sanger (1838–1912) was one of the Sanger brothers who founded a mercantile empire before the Civil War. In Weatherford, they faced anti-Semitism.
— *Courtesy, Josephine Sanger Corman, photograph by Powell Studio, San Antonio, copy from UT Institute of Texan Cultures*

"Brothers awake. Strike high and strong."

When Adah Menken heard of the forced abduction and baptism of an Italian Jewish child, Edgar Mortara, she issued a call to arms to Jews:[54]

"Brothers awake. Strike high and strong
For danger that may come.
Strike high for Israel's holy right
And strong for hearts and home."

Her poem "At Spes Non Facta" sounds like an early plea for the establishment of the state of Israel:[55]

"Will he never come? Will the Jew
In exile eternally pine? . . .
Will he never his vows to Jehovah renew
Beneath his own olive and vine?"

Menken's essay on the "Jew in Parliament" [*Israelite*, September 3, 1858] was a powerful plea for the right of Baron Lionel de Rothschild to be seated in the British Houses of Parliament as an elected member without reciting a Christian oath. Rothschild called her "the inspired Deborah of our People." Her poem "Hear, O Israel!" includes these lines:[56]

"Brothers mine, fling out your white banners over this Red Sea of Wrath! . . .
Against the enemy lift thy sword of fire, even thou, O Israel! whose prophet I am.
For I . . . still see the watchfire leaping up its blood-red flame from the ramparts of our Jerusalem!
. . . I shall lead thee, O my people! back to freedom! . . .
Israel! rouse ye from the slumber of ages, and . . . carve a road through these tyrants! . . .
Rise up, brave hearts! . . .
The Lord of Hosts is in the field,
The God of Jacob is our shield."

Adah Isaacs Menken (1835–1868) condemned anti-Semitism in her writings. She lived briefly in Liberty, Texas, where she wrote for a local paper and gave readings. In 1856, she met and married Alexander Isaacs Menken, a traveling musician, from Cincinnati, Ohio. The couple moved to Cincinnati, where Adah fell under the tutelage of Rabbi Isaac Mayer Wise, editor of the *Cincinnati Israelite*. She converted to Judaism, and Wise published many of her poems and essays. Adah later left Alexander, married several more times, and achieved fame as an actress. She shocked Victorian society by appearing in a nude-colored body stocking in 1860 in the play *Mazeppa* and became known as the "Naked Lady of Nacogdoches." Adah never performed on Jewish high holy days, and a rabbi was in attendance when she died. She is buried in the Jewish section of the Montparnasse Cemetery, Paris, France. A book of her poems, *Infelicia*, was published posthumously.[57]
— *Hoblitzelle Theatre Arts, Harry Ransom Humanities Research Center, UT Austin*

The Landas of New Braunfels

Most Texans, including Jews, did not own slaves; however, a few did. In the Census of 1850, Galveston slaveowners included Joseph and Rosanna Osterman, who owned two women and three children; I. Dyer, who owned a couple, age fifty, and two girls, one eight and one sixteen; and Samuel Maas, who owned an older couple and a teen-age girl. Joseph and Helena Landa of New Braunfels, a Central Texas couple, freed their slaves amd suffered severe consequences.

Joseph Landa of Kempen, Prussia, was proficient in English, German, Polish, Russian, and Hebrew. The son of a livestock dealer who furnished cavalry mounts for the Russian government, Joseph's job was to parade horses before the Russian officers for inspection. Joseph's parents wanted him to become a rabbi, but he ran away to England. He sailed in steerage to America and worked his way west as a peddler.

Joseph arrived in San Antonio in 1844 and opened a store. But he felt that San Antonio would always remain a Mexican village, so he moved to the nearby German settlement of New Braunfels, drawn to its natural beauty and his familiarity with its German culture. During an annual trip to New York in 1851, he met and married Helena Friedlander from Hull, England. Helena had received a fine education both in English and German. They were married by Dr. Isaac Mayer Wise, a young Albany

Helena Friedlander Landa (1835–1912) of New Braunfels ran the family businesses and preserved Jewish traditions during the Civil War while her husband, Joseph Landa (1811–1896), was a fugitive from Confederate vigilantes.
— *UT Institute of Texan Cultures*

rabbi who became a prominent leader of Reform Judaism. The Landas established a home in New Braunfels and, by 1862, had seven children.

The Landas were prosperous merchants and owners of a grist mill, a cotton gin, and a saw mill. New Braunfels was on the frontier, and when Indians came by asking for food, Helena prepared meals for them. When the Civil War broke out, Joseph volunteered for the Confederacy but was rejected because of a disability. When President Lincoln issued the Emancipation Proclamation in 1863, Joseph and Helena freed their slaves. A secret society, the "Golden Circle," which harassed and even murdered those thought to have opposing views, tried Joseph in a "kangaroo court" proceeding. He was convicted of being an abolitionist and told to leave the country at once or be hanged. Joseph fled to Mexico, leaving Helena to care for their small children and businesses. On one occasion, when an armed gang invaded her store demanding clothing and tobacco, she took out a six-shooter and, with her children clinging to her skirt, threatened to shoot the first man who touched anything. They left empty-handed.

After the Civil War, Joseph returned home and rejoined his family. The Landas were the only Jews in New Braunfels for many years, and they sometimes rode their carriage into San Antonio to attend Temple Beth-El. But they usually worshiped at home. Their son, Harry, recalled the family's religious observances in his reminiscences, *As I Remember*.[59]

"A Nineteenth Century Texas Seder"

"Particularly did I enjoy the Passover services, for which great preparation was made . . . My mother

would brew sweet raisin wine . . . and of which, hanging to her apron strings, I managed to get more than my share. For weeks the female members were engaged in baking the unleavened bread *(matzoth)*. The dough consisted simply of flour and water, and was rolled out on a table in long thin sheets. A large tinform was used to cut them into the proper size, and several old fashioned spiked spurs with large rowels were run over them to make the air holes. Then the *matzoth* were baked in a large oven. A supply was necessary for fifteen people, including the servants, besides . . . our friends. The quantity that was baked would fill one side of a room. Several barrels of flour (196 pounds each) were necessary to supply the requirements.

"On Passover Eve the ceremony was very impressive . . . services were conducted in English and Hebrew. The family would gather around the large dining table with my father at the head. He would conduct the services in a most solemn manner, breaking the *matzoth* under a napkin, distributing them, and then passing around the bitter herbs and all of the other symbols commemorating the flight of our ancestors from the Egyptian Bondage . . . being the youngest son, I would have to 'open the door and let in the Angel' — to signify the welcoming of Elijah, harbinger of the era of peace and good will."

Kate and Nellie feed a slave woman

"Auntie" Clara Anderson, an ex-slave, remembered that, "This was what happened in Austin, Texas. Half of the time I was almost starved to death, and there was some little Jewish chillun who lived nearby, and every day when they would come from school, they'd leave me some food. They'd hide this food in a tree-stump, where I'd go and git it. Those chillun would bring me buttered bread, cakes and other things. I never did git much chance to talk with 'em, but I know one's name was Kate, and the other Nellie."[60]

For and against secession

Just as the Civil War set brother against brother throughout the nation, so did Texas Jews take up both causes. Emanuel Kahn of Marshall fought for the Confederacy while his brother Lionel fought for the Union. Many German Jews opposed slavery, and some from the small San Antonio Jewish community, like the Henry Mayer family, left Texas altogether. Michael Konigheim of San Antonio left but returned after the war and found those who stayed relieved that slavery was abolished and the Union preserved. The Schutz brothers of El Paso voted against secession and had to leave.

Texas Jews served in the Confederacy

Moritz Lichtenstein joined Sibley's Confederate Brigade in Victoria. He was taken prisoner, exchanged and rejoined his post, serving in New Mexico and Louisiana. Theo Keller of Houston, a member of the Second Texas Infantry, was wounded at Vicksburg. Morris Lasker voted against secession and then joined the Confederacy to fight in Louisiana, Galveston, and the Sabine Pass. Isaac and Lehman Sanger of Weatherford and Henry Hirshfeld of Austin also served.

Bernard Kowalski of Brownsville was an artillery major, and Capt. Levi Charles Harby (1793–1870) of South Carolina was a Confederate port captain in Galveston. Harby and his men captured the *Harriet Lane* in a decisive battle, and he was made a commodore in the Southern Navy.[62] A father and son from San Antonio, Samuel and Edwin J. Sampson, both served. Edwin was killed in action in 1862 at the age of nineteen.[63]

On the home front

Not all Civil War participants were in the armed forces. Some provided goods for the soldiers. Myer Levy received a Confederate letter of marque and was a privateer and blockade runner, trading among the Southern ports, England, and the West Indies. His wife, Jane Hart Levy (1840–1877) of Georgia, was imprisoned by federal troops in New Orleans for "impertinence to a Yankee officer."[64] In Jefferson, Confederate suppliers included Jacob Sterne, a quartermaster, and J. Nussbaum, who made soap and candles.

On March 26, 1862, the Houston *Tri-Weekly Telegraph* published a letter from three Jewish women to the president of the Houston Hospital Society: "Madame — the Israelite ladies of Houston have the pleasure to forward to you the sum of $131 for the benefit of the sick soldiers ... in the course of the most savage war, made against us by a malignant foe ... a committee is hereby appointed ... to ... solicit subscriptions ... and at the close of the war, whatever funds remain in their hands be divided among the widows and orphans of the soldiers from Texas ..."[65]

Max London (1838–1925) from Gratz, Germany, joined the Confederacy as a hospital steward in Victoria. He was captured and exchanged as a prisoner of war. After the war, he married Bertha Simon, and the couple lived in Hallettsville and Bremond. They settled in Corsicana, where he was a worshipful master in the Masonic order.
— *Robertson County Historical Commission*

"The testimony of one gentile": Confederate General T. N. Waul

"... I organized Waul's Texas Legion upon the express terms that they were to ... join in the fray where the blows fell heaviest and thickest ... Two of the infantry companies had a larger number of Jews in their ranks, and the largest company in the command, 120 men, was officered by Jews, and three-fourths of the rank and file were of that faith. There was also a number of Jews scattered through the command ... they were brave, orderly and well disciplined ... I never saw nor heard of any Jew shirking or failing to answer to any call of duty or danger ... The testimony of one gentile to attest the courage, endurance and patriotism of the Jew as a soldier."[66]

— **August Bondi**

Leopold and Regine Schlinger

Leopold Schlinger (1815–1892) came to the U.S. from Austria in 1847. He married Regine Wolf Schlinger (1818–1884), and the couple moved to Brownsville before the Civil War. They moved again, to Matamoros, Mexico, when the Civil War broke out, probably because of their opposition to the Confederacy and their sympathy with the North. When the Union forces retook Brownsville during the early part of 1864, the Schlingers returned home. Leopold joined the Loyal National League on May 26, 1864. Regine took an oath of allegiance on June 9, 1864, that she would faithfully support, protect and defend the Constitution of the United States and the Union, ". . . and I will support the Acts of Congress passed during the existing rebellion with reference to slaves." The Confederates retook Brownsville, and the Schlingers again had to leave. Their son, Louis, is said to have heard the last shot fired in the Civil War. After the war, the Schlingers returned to Brownsville, and he was appointed Cameron County commissioner in 1868.[68]

— *Schlinger Family*

August Bondi

As a boy of fifteen, August Bondi participated in the 1848 revolution in Vienna. In his *Autobiography*, he recalled, "We youngsters from the barricades and struggles of the revolutionary movements of Germany, Austria, and Hungary . . . were eager to grasp the opportunity which would prove our important political influence in our new home."

Bondi worked as a teacher in St. Louis and then as a bartender on a riverboat which stopped at Houston and Galveston in 1851. His attitude toward slavery was shaped in part by the brutal treatment of slaves in Galveston. Bondi later fought with John Brown's Fifth Kansas Cavalry in 1856 in a pre-Civil War movement against pro-slavery forces. He recalled:

". . . the howlings of the slaves [in Galveston] receiving their morning ration of cowhiding waked me at 4 o'clock a.m. I found the yankees the most cruel masters . . . I disliked to marry a woman with slaves . . . I felt that my father's son was not to be a slave driver." [70]

Leopold Karpeles (1838–1909), who lived in Galveston from 1849 to 1861, was one of only six Jews who received the Congressional Medal of Honor for service in the Union Army. After leaving Texas, he joined the 46th Massachusetts Infantry as a sergeant. During a three-day battle in 1864 in Wilderness, Virginia, he held up the Union colors and inspired the forces who rallied around the flag to stop the Confederate charge. He was in many more battles, including Gettysburg, and was wounded several times.[69]

— *American Jewish Archives, Cincinnati Campus, Hebrew Union College, Jewish Institute of Religion*

Leopold Karpeles

The treatment of slaves in Galveston also turned Leopold Karpeles against the institution of slavery and prompted him to take up arms. Leopold Karpeles was born in Prague (then Bohemia), and in 1849 he went to Galveston to live with his older brother, Emil. He accompanied caravans of merchandise across the Mexican border and into the Western territories. Leopold's daughter, Theresa Taussing, wrote: "Father, who had seen and abhorred slavery, came north when the Civil War started, to Springfield, Massachusetts; [and] joined the 46th Massachusetts volunteers." After the war, he married Sara Mundheim, one of the Jewish nurses who cared for him in a Washington, D.C. army hospital. She died in childbirth, and Leopold married her sister. He was appointed a post office clerk in the office of the auditor, Treasury Department. On April 30, 1870, Karpeles was awarded the Congressional Medal of Honor for gallantry in the field of battle.

THE SCHWARZ FAMILY OF HEMPSTEAD.

Gabriel and Jeanette Koppel Schwarz, seated center, traveled to Texas in a Conestoga wagon in 1864. They are surrounded by their children and grandchildren, including the Lustigs, the Rypinskis, the Emdens, the Newmans, and other Schwarzes. Gabriel's brother was Rabbi Heinrich Schwarz, a noted scholar.

— *Cathy Schechter*

After visiting Hempstead in April 1879, Charles Wessolowsky, editor of the *Jewish South*, wrote:

"How well it would be for some of our Jewish brethren living in those barbarous countries of Russia and Rumania to immigrate here to Texas, form Jewish colonies, on this fertile soil . . . become shepherds like Moses and David. Here in these prairies . . . Stock business is very remunerative and prosperous, let them throw off their Russian shackles and Rumanian fetters and come here to this land of liberty . . . where millions of uncultivated acres cry out for immigration, civilization and progress. Let them come here, rid themselves of the yoke of oppression, enjoy the freedom of our country, establish schools, secure enlightenment and advancement, and thereby enrich themselves and this country."[1]

3

"A word or so from these wild parts."
PIONEER FAMILIES AND BUSINESSES

When Hyman Perlstein was a young immigrant from Lithuania, his uncle advised him to "begin with a small town and grow with it . . . America is a young and vibrant giant, and the little cities are her arms and legs just beginning to stretch." Perlstein ultimately settled in Beaumont and became one of the town's leading citizens.

Hyman Perlstein's story is paradigmatic of thousands of Jews swept up in the powerful forces of world history who sought their fortune in the vast and unsettled land of Texas. European life in the nineteenth century had been transformed by the ideas of *Haskalah* (the Enlightenment). Increased anti-Semitism, manifested by the infamous May Laws of Czarist Russia in 1882, and subsequent political unrest, compulsory military conscription, and limited economic opportunities, hastened Jewish immigration to the U.S.

The world they found in Texas was one of rapid change. The Civil War had wrought a drastic dislocation of the political and economic structures of the South. Thousands of slaves had been freed. Patterns of patronage changed as the plantation system came to an end. Many slaveowners had been killed during the war or returned wounded. A new agricultural system, sharecropping and share tenant farming, emerged; both poor whites and ex-slaves worked for a share of the crops or for farm wages. Cattle, which ran untended during the war, multiplied and formed the basis for new industries — ranching, shipping, and meat-processing. Other changes occurred in the Texas econ-

omy with the advent of railroads, banks, utility companies, and an increase in international trade. Urban centers like Galveston, Houston, and San Antonio grew and increased in importance as commercial centers.

After the Civil War, some Jews who had left Texas because of their opposition to secession returned. Jewish veterans from both the Confederate and Union armies returned to their homes in Texas or migrated to the state for the first time. Along with increased immigration from Europe, the post-war Jewish population increased fivefold in twenty-five years — from 3,300 in 1877 to 17,500 in 1900.

Ironically, while many of the new Jewish immigrants traveled to Texas to gain the right to own land denied them by their respective European governments, land rights were denied to other Texas ethnic groups by treaty, force, or fraud. Hispanics along the Texas-Mexico border continued to try to reclaim land and properties they felt were unjustly taken from them, and Native Americans were driven from their Texas lands and exiled to Oklahoma. The birth of the Ku Klux Klan brought a reign of violence and terror across the state, aimed primarily against blacks. While the Jewish population grew and prospered during Reconstruction, blacks left Texas in large numbers for better opportunities in places like Kansas.

When Charles Wessolovsky, a journalist and B'nai B'rith leader, visited Texas in 1878–1879, he found Jews living in twenty-seven communities, and there were many towns he did

not visit. Their economic activities included merchandising at all levels: peddling, trading posts, retail stores, and import/export businesses.

The peddler was the sophisticate who brought news and goods from the outside world to customers on isolated farms and ranches and in the small towns. Many peddlers progressed to selling goods by horse and buggy and ultimately became proprietors of retail and wholesale businesses.

Many Jews chose to live in Galveston and San Antonio, the state's two largest cities. Others moved to small agricultural communities and towns to form businesses along the major railroad routes like Tyler, Waco, Marshall, Hempstead, Luling, Corsicana, Palestine, and Bryan. Austin, El Paso, and Dallas also became more important. E. M. Kahn chose Dallas for his store because, he said, "People here walk fast and talk fast." In Houston, Jews helped organize the Ship Channel Company and the Board of Trade and Cotton Exchange.

New towns spawned by the railroads after the Civil War provided new opportunities, and some merchants, like the Sanger brothers, followed the railroad terminus and expanded to a highly successful merchandising chain. By the late 1800s, San Antonio was a major trade center connected by train with New Orleans, San Francisco, New York, and Mexico City; Joske Brothers promoted San Antonio's first International Trade Fair in 1888.

By 1900, many Main Street shops in Texas towns were owned by Jewish merchants who carved an important niche in the agricultural economy. Jewish stores were often the most stable in town; they provided needed household goods, clothing, and agricultural tools to farm families. They also sold luxury items such as confectioneries, liquor, china, and crystal, and raised levels of taste with wares from New Orleans, New York, Chicago, and Europe. Many Jewish businesses extended credit to both Anglo and black customers and were often the only ones to allow blacks to try on clothing.[2]

Jewish businesses served the farm economy in other ways. Eugene Rosenbaum of Hillsboro founded a wholesale farm implement business, the Southern Plow Company, in 1898. Others went into cattle ranching and the wool industry; I. D. "Coonskin" Cohen was a fur trader in Navasota. Washer Brothers of Fort Worth outfitted ranchers, cowboys, and even sold western wear to President Theodore Roosevelt.

Some of the leading import/export businesses in Texas were owned by Jews. Moritz Kopperl's coffee business was so successful that by the 1890s, Galveston was the fourth leading coffee market in the U.S. Leon Blum developed the largest business in Texas, importing dry goods and exporting cotton from Galveston. Emmanuel Morris was an importer/exporter with offices in New York and branches in Corpus Christi, Alice, Laredo, and Nuevo Laredo, Mexico.

He transported the first oleomargarine produced by a Victoria packery to Hamburg, Germany, where the cargo was dumped into the harbor when it was found to be a butter substitute.

With the advent of electric power, some Jews founded power companies. Berg Brothers were the contracting agents for the Gulf, Harrisburg, and San Antonio Railroad and founders of Berg Electric Power Company in San Antonio. Harry Landa of New Braunfels and Joseph Deutschmann of Texarkana were also founders of power and utility companies. In the twentieth century, Jews would be largely excluded from utility company employment.

The 1880s and 1890s saw the emergence of the new Jewish professional as educational opportunities increased. In 1893, Jacob Henry Sampson graduated in the first class of the University of Texas Medical Branch at Galveston. John Pfeiffer, a graduate of the New York College of Pharmacy, lived in the West Texas towns of Dimmitt, Carrizo Springs, and Encinal. Benjamin Dubinsky was a pioneer San Antonio inventor who patented a part used in adding machines and cash registers and wired several small Texas towns for electric lights. And some had unusual occupations: Jonas Weil of Corpus Christi was a member of a rain-making group which fired a cannon into the clouds.

Although most Jewish women were homemakers, many worked by their husbands' sides in Mom and Pop

stores. Others were midwives, boardinghouse operators, and seamstresses. As ready-to-wear emerged in merchandising businesses, the job of sales clerk in a store was one of the most respectable positions a woman could hold.

Jewish businesses were also found on the frontier. Mr. and Mrs. Jack Schwartz operated a hotel for cattlemen in Fort Griffin. Nathan Sommer made uniforms for the officers at Fort Brown in Brownsville. In 1890, the prominent Hidalgo merchant Max Stein was shot to death by the wife of a suspended county judge whom he had replaced.

With the rapid increase in the Jewish population, the necessity for cemeteries, benevolent and burial societies, temples and synagogues took on added urgency, and during the latter half of the nineteenth century, Texas Jews created a wide array of institutions for relief and religious purposes. In the larger community, they supported the social order and participated fully as Jews, businessmen and women, and as civic, political, and cultural leaders.[3] Not all Jews prospered. There were those who struggled, failed, went bankrupt, and even left Texas — but that is the subject for another book. The families covered in this chapter are those who left extensive records or whose achievements, through either civic contributions, economic advancement, or personal accomplishment, have earned them a place in Texas history.

— **Sidney Samuels**

Fort Worth pioneers are shown, c. 1905, seated left to right: Jacob Samuels and Sam Woody; standing: Joseph C. Terrell.
— *Amon Carter Museum*

Julius Kuttner (1846–1920), a Union Army veteran, received patronage jobs after the war in several Texas counties and later moved to Waco.
— *The Texas Collection, Baylor University, Waco, Texas*

Eva Gabert Kuttner (1850–1912) helped support her family in Waco by teaching embroidery skills to other women and selling her handwork.
— *The Texas Collection, Baylor University, Waco, Texas*

Jacob Samuels (1836–1906)

After the Civil War, veterans from both sides of the conflict returned to their homes in Texas or migrated to the state for the first time.

In 1857, Jacob Samuels and his father, Lemuel Samuels, moved to Fort Worth from Louisiana. Jacob joined the Confederacy to fight with Tom Green's First Brigade beside a man he idolized, Capt. J. C. Terrell. Jacob wrote to his father, describing regimental injuries and the death by cannon ball of General Green on the Red River. Samuels' "colored" body servant made sure he and his friend, Captain Terrell, were well fed and clothed. Terrell's granddaughter, Mrs. Ed Hudson, wrote, "grandfather [Joseph Terrell] said they always had a clean shirt and also he [the body servant] would go catch a chicken or rabbit . . . so they always had something good to eat."

After the war, Jacob Samuels returned to Fort Worth and built a trading post with his partner, B. Berliner, on the courthouse square. The store carried a wide range of items for a frontier town. Jacob married Bertha Wadel, and the couple had three sons. One son, Sidney, was in the first class of the University of Texas

at Austin and began practicing law in Fort Worth in 1895. Sidney recalled, "We sometimes wore patched garments, but we always had good books and loved classical music."[4]

Julius and Eva Kuttner

Julius Kuttner traveled to New Orleans from Prussia before the Civil War and studied law. He was a sergeant in the Louisiana Volunteer Infantry and later joined the Union Army, serving under the assumed name of George Harrison. After the war, he moved to Madisonville, Texas, where he received patronage jobs under Reconstruction. In 1869, he was appointed registrar of Madison County; in 1870, surveyor. In 1871, he married Eva Gabert in Navasota, was appointed clerk of the District Court, and in 1873, became postmaster of Marquez in Leon County. Later, the couple moved to Waco, where he was secretary of the Hebrew Benevolent Association, secretary of Agudath Jacob, and caretaker of Rodef Sholom. Eva, also from Prussia, was secretary of the Waco Ladies Hebrew Aid Society and was instrumental in getting a wall built around the Hebrew Rest Cemetery.[5]

The Carbs

Babette Rosenbaum Carb (1831–1910) was a Confederate widow who settled in Fort Worth around 1880. Born in the German Rhineland, she witnessed the burning of Paris in 1848. She married a Mississippi farmer in 1850 in New Orleans, and they had six children. Her husband joined the Confederacy and was wounded. After their slaves were freed and their Mississippi home burned by Union troops, Babette found her maimed husband in New Orleans and supported the family by running a confectionery. She received letters praising Texas from her oldest son, Isadore, who had moved to Fort Worth. Enthralled with the West, he wrote her, "I'm gonna stay right here . . . Oh, you oughter see the cowboys lopin' up Main Street." After her husband's death, Babette moved to Fort Worth to be with her grown children. Her life was dramatized in a novel, *Sunrise in the West*, written by her grandson, David Carb.[6]

Henry Hirshfeld (1834–1911) was a Confederate veteran who became an Austin business and religious leader.
— *Hirshfeld Papers (AR/H.24), Austin History Center, Austin Public Library*

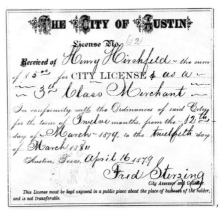

Henry Hirshfeld's Third Class Merchant License No. 62, issued by the City of Austin in 1879.
— *Hirshfeld Papers (AR/H.24), Austin History Center, Austin Public Library*

The Hirshfelds of Austin

Having served in the Confederacy, Henry Hirshfeld signed the following oath in Galveston on July 14, 1865:

"I, Henry Hirshfeld, do solemnly swear in the presence of Almighty God that I will hereafter faithfully defend the Constitution of the United States and the union of States thereunder; and that I will in this manner abide by and support all laws and proclamations which have been made during the existing rebellion with reference to the Emancipation of Slavery so help me God."

Born in Posen, Prussia, Henry Hirshfeld moved to Georgetown, about thirty miles north of Austin, in 1859. During the Civil War, he joined the Confederate Army, serving with Morgan's Battalion. He married Jennie Melasky in Austin in 1868 and opened a downtown store at the corner of Sixth and Congress. He was so successful, he retired in 1886 and began investing in real estate.

Henry was a founder and the first president of Temple Beth Israel when it was organized in 1876. He was a founding director of the Austin National Bank in 1890, a member of the Masonic Order, B'nai B'rith, and the Saengerrunde, a German cultural organization. His son Morris (1875–1949) became the first vice-president of the Austin National Bank, working there for forty-eight years (1891–1939). Another son, Jacob, was a mechanical engineering student at Texas A&M University from 1894 to 1896. The Hirshfeld family mansion at 814 Lavaca in Austin was donated to Texas A&M University, which uses it for a variety of purposes.[7]

Jennie Melasky Hirshfeld (1850–1920) married Henry Hirshfeld in Austin in 1868, and the couple had eight children. Jennie was treasurer of the Ladies Hebrew Aid Society in 1893.
— *Hirshfeld Papers (AR/H.24), Austin History Center, Austin Public Library*

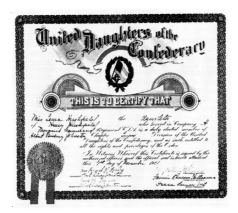

A 1921 certificate of the United Daughters of the Confederacy, belonging to Laura Hirshfeld, the daughter of Henry and Jennie Hirshfeld, who was one of the few Jewish members of the organization.
— *Hirshfeld Papers (AR/H.24), Austin History Center, Austin Public Library*

— Eva L. Sterne

The Sterne Fountain in Jefferson was donated to the city in 1913 by the children of Jacob and Ernestine Sterne (Eva, Leopold, Alfred, and Fred). The thirteen-foot-high bronze statue was cast by a New York foundry. Italian sculptor Guiseppe Moretti recreated Hebe, the mythological Greek goddess of youth, who serves rejuvenating nectar from her urn. The fountain is still used, as was originally intended, for people, horses, and dogs.[8]
— *Photo by Ruthe Winegarten*

Jefferson during Reconstruction

Jacob Sterne (1826–1872) was a McKinney merchant before marrying a Swiss Jewish girl, Ernestine, whom he met in 1853 while she was visiting her sister in Houston. They settled in Jefferson around 1855. He had a "Gentleman's Furnishing Goods" store in Jefferson and Marshall, worked in the county clerk's office, and was postmaster. They lived in a small house with their two slaves, although Jacob is said to have opposed slavery. Ernestine supplemented their income by taking in roomers and boarders, including six single Jewish men who lived there in 1860. In 1862, under Jacob's leadership, the Hebrew Benevolent Association founded the Mount Sinai Cemetery.

During the Civil War, Jacob was a Confederate quartermaster. After his death, Ernestine was appointed postmistress in his place.[9] After the war, the Jewish population of Jefferson grew rapidly: by 1873, twenty-six percent of the merchants on the tax rolls were Jewish. But in the late 1870s, when the U.S. government removed a natural dam of logs which made Jefferson a major steamboat port, the waterways were lowered and the railroads bypassed Jefferson. An economic panic hit. By 1880, most residents, including the Jews, had left.[10]

"He was an Israelite."

The history of the Sterne family is described in a novel by Eva L. Sterne, *The Little Immigrant: A True Story*.[11] Excerpts from the book give insights into Jacob's character, his feelings about slavery, and the period of Reconstruction. In the book, Jacob Sterne is given the fictional name of Jaffrey, and Ernestine is called Renestine. When Jaffrey buys his wife a slave, he says,

"I've bought a nurse girl for you, Renestine . . . I felt like a mean creature when I paid the money for that girl, but I knew that we needed a nurse . . . so what was to be done. This slavery system is frightful, and mark my words, Renestine, the day will come when the darkies will be free. Where I was born, on the Rhine, no one would believe for a moment that I would buy a human being. They would hate me, as I hate myself, for bartering in human flesh."[12]

The novel describes an anecdote occurring in 1870 during the Federal Army's occupation of Jefferson, following the murder one night of a "carpet bagger":

"It was necessary for Washington to send troops to Jefferson to restore order. A stockade was built . . . near the new home of Jaffray . . . and into this stockade some of Jefferson's prominent citizens were thrown and kept until they could prove their innocence of the charges brought against them, namely that they had knowledge of the murder of the carpetbagger. Those were trying days . . . Things were going badly in the town, military law was established and all men found implicated in the disturbance were drastically punished. The war had reduced the prosperous store holder to penury . . . and Jefferson was demoralized in its business, civic and social life.

"General Buell, commanding the military occupation, asked as a favor to be put up at Jaffray's house, as it was one of the largest in the town and near the camp. Jaffray consented . . . This was a courageous thing for Jaffray to have done, for, with the spirit existing in the town at that critical time, not many residents would harbor the Yankees . . .

"In politics Jaffray was a Republican and he had the courage to live up to his convictions in a community that was enraged against Lincoln and his party. But the Republicans stood for free men, whatever color or creed, and Jaffray championed their doctrines. For him humanity, justice and liberty was the breath of his nostrils. This passion for men's rights he had inherited from a long line of ancestors reaching back into the mists of 'In the beginning.' He was an Israelite."[13]

Texas had its share of drugstore cowboys,
even in the nineteenth century. Bernhardt
Meyer Goodman (left) and his younger
brother Max (right), from Latvia, are pictured, c. 1880s, dressed in western finery,
although they were actually peddlers in
the Flatonia-Victoria area. They moved
to Waco in 1906 and ran saloons and taverns.
    — *The Texas Collection, Baylor University,
    Waco, Texas*

The Mayers: pioneer ranchers

Ferdinand and Jette Mayer were married in 1866. They lived in San Antonio until 1879, when they moved to Fort McKavett for a year. Ferdinand ran a trading post and later a cattle business. Although the couple returned to San Antonio, Ferdinand and his son Sol continued to expand a successful stock breeding business. F. Mayer & Sons formed in 1888, and their cattle brand, a T-half circle, was registered in 1889 in Menard County. Sol eventually bought out his father's interests.

Ferdinand and Jette Mayer had six children: three daughters (Fanny, Josephine, and Therese) and three sons (Max, Abe, and Sol). The daughters remained Jewish, and the sons married non-Jewish women and adopted the religions of their spouses.

Jette Mayer sewed beautifully and was a fine lace-maker. A lace-trimmed dress she made for her sons' circumcision ceremonies, which is on display at the Fort Concho Museum in San Angelo, is now known as a christening dress. It has been used by all the Mayers' grandchildren and great-grandchildren — for Jewish circumcisions and non-Jewish christenings. The museum also houses other Mayer family artifacts.

Sol Mayer (1869–1957), the son of Ferdinand and Jette, started as a cowboy at the age of fifteen and ended up as a successful rancher, banker, and founder of Schleicher County. He is featured in the Cowboy Hall of Fame in Oklahoma City. A descendant of Sol Mayer currently runs the family ranch near Sonora, and Sol's saddle is still in use.[14]

Jette Steiner (Mrs. Ferdinand) Mayer (1834–1913) was born in Bavaria and went to San Antonio in 1860 to live with her uncle, Abraham Steiner. When he left for Mexico City during the Civil War to avoid service in the Confederate Army, she ran his store.   — *Richard Mayer*

Ferdinand Mayer (1832–1913), born in Baden, Germany, was a successful rancher and founder of San Antonio's Temple Beth-El. His brother Samuel was its first president.   — *Richard Mayer*

Marcus Koenigheim founds San Angelo

Marcus Koenigheim, a prominent San Antonio businessman and a founder of Temple Beth-El in 1874, acquired the original townsite of San Angelo in 1878 in lieu of a $1,500 loan repayment. He tried to entice settlers by giving land for a school and for Methodist and Baptist churches. When San Angelo became the county seat, the town finally prospered, and Marcus persuaded the Oppenheimers of San Antonio to open a San Angelo branch of their store. Thus, a member of San Antonio's Jewish community developed a new city in West Texas.[15]

Other Jews soon followed Koenigheim to San Angelo. Gus Clements, author of *Concho Country*, wrote that in the 1880s, "The Jewish community was well represented along the Concho River. In addition to Koenigheim and his family, Sam and Jake Lapowski owned the largest dry goods store in the city." The Lapowskis, from Russia, owned a chain of stores in other West Texas cities. Some of the Lapowskis were not happy with their last name. With assimilation, some changed their name to "Lapp," others to "LaPosea," and still others to "Dillon." Sam Lapowski's grandson, C. Douglas Dillon, was U.S. ambassador to France and President Kennedy's secretary of the treasury.

Mayer Brothers and Company Ranch Supply Store in Sonora was owned in 1892 by Ferdinand Mayer and run by his sons, Sol and Max Mayer.
          — *Richard Mayer*

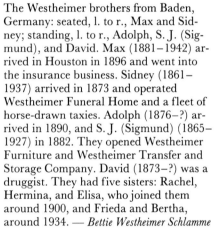

The Westheimer brothers from Baden, Germany: seated, l. to r., Max and Sidney; standing, l. to r., Adolph, S. J. (Sigmund), and David. Max (1881–1942) arrived in Houston in 1896 and went into the insurance business. Sidney (1861–1937) arrived in 1873 and operated Westheimer Funeral Home and a fleet of horse-drawn taxies. Adolph (1876–?) arrived in 1890, and S. J. (Sigmund) (1865–1927) in 1882. They opened Westheimer Furniture and Westheimer Transfer and Storage Company. David (1873–?) was a druggist. They had five sisters: Rachel, Hermina, and Elisa, who joined them around 1900, and Frieda and Bertha, around 1934. — *Bettie Westheimer Schlamme*

The Westheimer brothers of Houston

Mitchell (M. L.) Westheimer moved to Houston from Baden, Germany, about 1856. He bought a large cotton plantation southwest of town, where Lamar High School now stands at 3325 Westheimer. In the 1870s, he built a crude five-mile trail running east and west from his front door to downtown. In 1895, he deeded part of the trail to the city for a right-of-way, and Westheimer Road became a major thoroughfare. Fluent in seven languages, M. L. frequently served as an interpreter at the bank and post office. He built the city's first streetcar rails, which were made of wood.

Since there were no public schools in Houston in the 1860s, M. L. built one on his farm. He hired a teacher, and all the community children attended free. He and his wife raised sixteen children: eight of their own,

three orphans, and five relatives.

M. L. established the Houston Livery Stable on Market Square around 1869.[16] He sent for two of his nephews, Adolph and S. J., who later established a moving service, now Westheimer Transfer and Storage Company, and a funeral home. Eventually, ten of his twelve nieces and nephews moved to Houston. His daughter, Mrs. Hettie Westheimer Ray, was born on the Westheimer farm in 1869. She recalled her parents warning the children not to run when chased by cows. Mrs. Hettie, as she was known by her friends, made her living at the age of eighty-two by altering clothes.[17]

Sid, the first nephew who arrived, worked first for a flour mill, then as a grocery clerk. In 1880, he shipped seven cars of cattle and cotton on the first train arriving in Houston from Nacogdoches. In 1883, he turned over his transfer and storage business to his brother S. J. In 1894, Sid organized the Westheimer Undertaking and Embalming Company and held one of the first embalming licenses issued, No. 12. He was active in the State Funeral Directors and Embalmers Association. He married Lola Spiers in 1902.

Sigmund J. and Hannah Fox Westheimer

Hannah Fox Westheimer was the daughter of a pioneer Houston couple, Samuel and Bertha Fox from Mississippi. In 1859, Samuel was a charter member of Congregation Beth

Seated, Hannah Fox Westheimer (c. 1870–1963) and her husband, Sigmund (S. J.) Westheimer (1865–1927). Standing, their children, Bertha (Furman), I. B. (Senior), and Leona (Liedeker). The photo was taken c. 1914. Bertha was a vocal teacher, and Leona was an actress. In 1906, Bertha directed a vaudeville show as a fundraiser for the Jewish Literary Society at the Prince Theatre in Houston.   — *Bettie Westheimer Schlamme*

Israel. Hannah was one of the first students to attend Houston public schools in 1876. The story is told that she was so tiny the trustees didn't want to register her, but she climbed into the lap of one and convinced him she was old enough.

S. J. and Hannah married in 1890 and had three children. S. J. was president of District #7 B'nai B'rith Lodge, the Jewish Literary Society, and the Young Men's Hebrew Association. The Westheimers were active in Congregation Adath Yeshurun. In 1921, S. J. donated to the City of Houston the Attwater Collection of Natural History, Relics and Curios Peculiar to Texas, to be exhibited in the new public library. The collection later went to the Museum of Natural Science.

In 1883, S. J. took over the Westheimer Transfer and Storage Company and was joined by his brother Adolph, who later operated the ABC Transfer and Storage Company. In 1904, S. J. hired Ben Hurwitz as bookkeeper, dispatcher, and collector. By 1909, Hurwitz became a partner in the firm. S. J. operated the business until his retirement in 1923.[18]

— San Francisco *Jewish Progress,* June 10, 1878

"Uncle Joe" and "Uncle Ben"

Joseph Levy arrived in New York City from Alsace in 1865 and lived there for a year before moving to Galveston. He was a great storyteller who claimed he walked to Texas from New York. He had worked with his father dealing in horses and mules back in Alsace, so it was natural that he would found a related business in Texas. In 1868, he and his brother Ben established J. Levy & Bros., a livery and undertaking business, which lasted over 100 years. They were known affectionately as "Uncle Joe" and "Uncle Ben."

In the days before the automobile, the Levy stables provided carriages for their fashionable clientele and huge carryalls for the popular oyster roasts on the beach. Their funeral processions were noted for their handsome steeds, followed by beautifully marked Dalmatian dogs. The Levy Bros. funeral home served not only Jews but the whole community.

The same year Joe and Ben founded their business, in 1868, they also helped found Congregation B'nai Israel. Joe was president of the Hebrew Benevolent Society and a director of the City National Bank. The brothers invested in real estate and owned the Harmony Hall, which housed an early Jewish social club.

Joe was a Galveston alderman in charge of the fire, police, and public works departments. Following the 1900 flood, he served on the committee which undertook to rebuild the city. One famous "flood" story has the brothers meeting the morning after the flood to assess the damage. Ben said to Joe, "Everything all right?" Joe answered, "Yes, everything's fine, except I lost my cistern. What did you lose, Ben?" Ben: "I lost my cow." Joe: "Well, we can get another cow and another cistern. If you need water, I've got water." Later, Ben's cow was found in Joe's backyard, and Joe's cistern was found in Ben's backyard.

After the brothers' deaths, the firm was run by Sam, Joe's son, and Jack,

Joseph (Joe) Levy (1844–1922), left, and his brother, Bernard (Ben) Levy (1849–1908), right, were prominent Galveston businessmen and partners in the livery and undertaking business.
— *Helene Levy, print by Steve Nussenblatt*

Ben's son. In 1915, they modernized, making the transition from horses to motorized ambulances. After Jack withdrew from the partnership in 1920, Sam ran the business for ten years. In 1926, he built the first structure in Texas designed specifically as a funeral home. The home and their ambulances were air-conditioned. Sam founded the Galveston Memorial Park Cemetery, the first perpetual-care cemetery in the county. Sam was killed by a competitor's ambulance at the scene of an accident, when he ran out to caution the driver to be careful of the crowd.

Sam's son, Joseph Levy, assumed management of the business after his father's death in 1930, and continued until it was sold in 1969. Joseph was a charter member of the Junior Chamber of Commerce and served on the board of the YMCA, chairing its capital fund drives. He was active in the United Fund, American Red Cross, the Hebrew Benevolent Society, and Temple B'nai Israel. He was also chairman of the committee for resto-

ration of the opera. His wife, Helene Samuels Levy, was from a pioneer Galveston family. She was active in Temple B'nai Israel, the Red Cross, and the Galveston Nursing Service, and was an accomplished piano accompanist.[19]

J. Levy & Bro. [sic], founded in 1868, was the first Jewish funeral home in Texas. This ad appeared in the *Galveston City Directory* in 1903–04. The business was run by the Levy family for over 100 years.
— *Rosenberg Library, Galveston, Texas*

Morris Lasker (1841–1916) of Galveston made fortunes in milling, banking, and real estate, and was a Texas state senator.
— *Temple B'nai Israel, Galveston, copy from UT Institute of Texan Cultures*

Nettie Davis Lasker (1856–1930) was vice-president of the Galveston Women's Health Protective Association from 1908 to 1910.
— *Courtesy Mrs. Albert Lasker; copy from John Gunther,* Taken at the Flood; *print from Barker Texas History Center, UT-Austin*

The Lasker home in Galveston at the corner of Broadway and 18th was the first in South Texas with an indoor toilet. The mansion looked like a castle out of *Grimm's Fairy Tales*. The library was lined with books; the dining room held forty guests.
— *Courtesy Mrs. Albert Lasker; copy from John Gunther,* Taken at the Flood; *print from Barker Texas History Center, UT-Austin*

The Laskers of Galveston

Morris and Nettie Lasker were pioneer Texas Jews who not only made an impact on the Galveston community, but whose children, Albert, Etta, Flora, and Loula, went on to distinguished careers in business and social service.

Morris was born in the East Prussian village of Lask. Like many Jews, he fled the unrest and anti-Semitism after the revolutions of 1848 and at age fifteen, landed penniless in Virginia. For three years, Morris traveled westward as a peddler, reading Aristophanes aloud as his amusement. He was sheltered by slaves in Georgia and tutored the young mistress of a plantation who had failed a course in Greek.

In Weatherford, Texas, Morris worked for Sanger Brothers. Nearly lynched for voting against secession, he joined the Confederate Army, serving under "Rip" Ford on the Rio Grande and with Dick Dowling's Fighting Irish at Sabine Pass. After the war, goods were scarce. Morris peddled with a horse and wagon and made $1,500 in gold within a few months.

In 1872, Morris settled in Galveston. Within a few years, he was president of two banks and a real estate company and had founded the Texas Star Flour and Corn Mill, the second mill in the U.S. with the eight-hour day. "I don't deserve to make a decent living if the people who work for me don't make a decent living," he said.

A venture capitalist, Morris Lasker made and lost money in many enterprises. Having invested too heavily in real estate, he was wiped out in the Panic of 1893. By 1895, he had made a comeback and was elected to the Texas Senate. He introduced important bills, including one relating to drainage and another to the regulation of the fishing and oyster industries.

Nettie Davis Lasker was born in Albany, New York. Her father, Schmul Schmulian, changed his name to Abraham Davis (after the janitor at his rooming house) to be more American. Nettie married Morris in 1876. She became a prominent civic leader and philanthropist, was vice-president of the Women's Health Protective Association from 1908 to 1910, and was on the board of the Lady Managers of the Galveston Orphans Home.

Four of the Lasker children became prominent. The three daughters, Etta, Florina, and Loula, moved to New York. Etta became national president of Hadassah; the others had social service careers. Their brother Albert became a multimillionaire Chicago tycoon known as the Father of Modern Advertising. Another brother, Edward, named for his uncle, a liberal German statesman, served on the Galveston School Board.[21]

Mrs. Harris (Elizabeth Seinsheimer)
Kempner (1852–1947) was a Galveston
civic and religious leader for sixty years.
— *Rosenberg Library, Galveston, Texas*

Harris Kempner (1837–1894) was a Galveston wholesaler, cotton broker, railroad
promoter, and director of ten banks.
— *UT Institute of Texan Cultures*

Harris and Elizabeth Kempner of Galveston

Harris Kempner left Poland in 1857 to avoid service in the Russian army. He settled first in Coldspring, Texas, where he opened a small business as a door-to-door peddler, selling everything from brandy to corset stays. Like Morris Lasker, he was personally opposed to slavery but joined the Confederate Army.

After the Civil War, Harris returned to Coldspring, then in 1870 moved to Galveston and opened a wholesale grocery business. He became one of the largest cotton middlemen in the Southwest by advancing credit against the future cotton crop. After the crop was picked, Kempner shipped it overseas and to cotton mills in the Northeast. His major investments in South Texas farm land provided a strong financial basis for later business expansions. He orga-

nized and promoted the Gulf, Colorado, and Santa Fe Railroad and was partially responsible for its consolidation with the Atchison, Topeka and Santa Fe. After his death, his eldest son, I. H. Kempner, took over the family enterprises. [23]

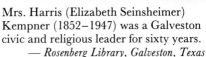

"The purposes of this Society are to assist women of the Jewish faith, to perform such duty to dead Jewesses as ought to be done by women only, and generally to act in harmony with the Hebrew Benevolent Society of this city."
— Constitution of the Galveston Ladies Hebrew Benevolent Society, 1903

Elizabeth Seinsheimer Kempner was born in Cincinnati, Ohio, and came to Galveston in 1872 when she married Harris Kempner. The Kempners had eleven children, three

of whom died in infancy.

Elizabeth was a charter member of the Galveston Orphans Home (founded in 1880 with a bequest from Rosanna Osterman) and served for fifty years. In 1900, Elizabeth donated a home to Temple B'nai Israel for the use of Rabbi Henry Cohen and his family, and in 1916 donated the Community House and the Memorial Hall for the Temple's Sunday School. She was the president of the Ladies' Hebrew Benevolent Society and also president of the Board of Lady Managers of the Letitia Rosenberg Home for Women from 1917 to 1934. She lived to be ninety-six and described her hobby as "bossing my children and working in my garden." After Elizabeth's death, her children established the Harris and Eliza Kempner Fund to support charitable, educational, religious, and medical research projects. [24]

Meyer Halff (1836–1905) was a pioneer rancher and businessman. His brother, Solomon Halff (1838–1905), and he worked together.
— *Halff Family, copy from UT Institute of Texan Cultures*

"Texas-size" cattle ranchers

The Halff brothers, natives of the French province of Alsace, controlled six million acres of Texas ranchland. Meyer arrived in Texas first, opening a business in Liberty, northeast of Houston, in 1850. He was followed by Solomon in 1857. They became involved indirectly in the cattle industry. Before the prevalence of banks and ready currency, the barter system was widely used in Texas commerce. As the Halffs began to receive cattle in payment for their merchandise, they acquired land for grazing and were soon in the ranching business.

After the Civil War, they moved to San Antonio and founded Halff & Levy, later M. Halff & Brother, one of the largest wholesale dry goods companies in the Southwest. But Meyer preferred cattle to calico and soon switched to ranching, traveling thousands of miles in a buckboard wagon to oversee his cattle empire. In the 1870s, the Halffs acquired the 50,000-acre Circle Dot Ranch in

Brewster County. By 1882, when the Southern Pacific Railroad was completed to Marathon, Meyer became a pioneer in shipping cattle to northern markets by railroad from West Texas and the Big Bend area.

The Halffs owned countless Longhorns and owned and leased over one million acres in Texas and Wyoming, where their Texas steers were fattened. In 1904, Meyer was instrumental in the development of the great artesian water belt in arid Frio County. Solomon not only ran their San Antonio store; he was a director of the San Antonio Gas Company. Both were founders of the Alamo National Bank.[25] They also were active in Temple Beth-El. Solomon was a founder in 1874, and Meyer was a member of the Building Committee, whose job was to solicit funds from Jews in New York, Boston, and Philadelphia. They were successful.

The Halff brothers were among the first Texans to import Hereford cattle. Their 200,000-acre *Quien Sabe* ranch near Midland held the largest herd of Hereford in the Southwest at one time.
— *Photo by Martha Winegarten Wilson*

Abraham Rosenthal (1850?–1945) stands in front of the Fort Worth stockyards. The only Jewish buyer for the Fort Worth Packing Company, he bought cattle, hogs, and sheep. He learned the meat-packing business in St. Paul, Minnesota. He took a job as a ritual slaughter and prayer leader at Congregation Shearith Israel in Dallas around 1900 and brought his wife Rachel and family to live there. In 1908, the family moved to Fort Worth, where Abraham established a meat-packing business. His son Harry was fined in 1912 for driving too many cattle up Lamar Street in downtown Dallas.[26] All of Abraham's sons went into the meat industry.
— *Mrs. Leon Brachman*

The interior of the D. & A. Oppenheimer Bank, San Antonio, c. 1900.
— *Dan Oppenheimer, copy from UT Institute of Texan Cultures*

Alice Oppenheimer (Mrs. Max) Steifel was the daughter of Mr. and Mrs. Dan Oppenheimer and the sister of Mrs. Alex Halff. She is shown here in 1902.
— *Mrs. Harry Halff, copy from UT Institute of Texan Cultures*

San Antonio after the Civil War

By 1870, San Antonio was the largest city in Texas, with a population more German in origin than Mexican. With its face turned southward, the city was the gateway to Mexico. Merchants transported their wares by huge wagon trains to Mexico. San Antonio was also a supply depot for military forts in West Texas and the Indian Territory. These factors, coupled with the arrival of the Galveston, Harrisburg and San Antonio Railroad in 1877, brought prosperity and growth.

Many Jews began settling in the city. Julius Joske, assisted by his two sons Albert and Alexander, established a general store, Joskes. Simon Suhler, a Union veteran, came in 1878 and was the deputy county tax assessor. He was one of only two Jewish Medal of Honor awardees for service in the Indian Wars.[27]

Henry Berg served as the enrolling clerk for the Texas Senate in 1873. His wife, when interviewed by the San Antonio *Express* on July 22, 1894, spoke out in favor of women's suffrage for female heads of household who earned the livelihood, paid taxes, and had no man to represent them.[28]

Daniel and Anton Oppenheimer

The Oppenheimer brothers were born in Burgkundstadt, Bavaria. Dan came to Texas first, working as a peddler in Palestine and Rusk. Anton followed, and in 1858 they established D. and A. Oppenheimer in Rusk. Both served in the Confederate army; after the war, they moved to San Antonio and prospered with a wholesale and retail store on the Main Plaza.

In the 1870s, banks were prohibited by Texas law, so the Oppenheimers conducted a type of banking operation as an adjunct to their mercantile business. They advanced merchandise or money to customers until crops were harvested and livestock sold at market. Since the brothers were men of integrity, farmers and ranchers left their gold or silver for safekeeping. They also accepted cattle for payment, bought land, and became cattle ranchers and livestock financiers.

By the 1890s, the brothers incorporated the wholesale business into the American Hat and Shoe Company, and by 1902 dispensed with the retail store. In 1908, they sold their ranch and cattle for $1 million and invested it in the bank.

Dan Oppenheimer was also treasurer of the Prospect Hill Street Railway Company. He was a founder and served two terms as president of Temple Beth-El.[29]

"Private San Antonio bank to close doors . . ."[30]

The Oppenheimer Bank was always unincorporated — it never had a charter, and its deposits were not covered by the Federal Deposit Insurance Corporation. All officers and partners were direct male descendants of Dan Oppenheimer. During the Depression, the bank was secure and none of its customers' funds were lost. The owners always felt that character was more important than collateral, and third- and fourth-generation customers were common. When the Oppenheimers decided to close in 1988, the bank was one of only two of its kind in Texas. Jesse Oppenheimer recalled, "It's sort of a dinosaur." The decision to liquidate had nothing to do with financial problems; there was simply no young male family member to take over. Oppenheimer said in an interview with the San Antonio *Express News*, August 30, 1988: "We were almost completely liquid — all money and bonds."[31]

Abraham Levi (1822–1902) (center with beard) on the occasion of the marriage of his youngest daughter, Melanie Levi, to Julius Hexter, December 1, 1886. Every member of the Levi family was present. Abraham founded one of Texas' first banks in 1875. His wife, Mina Halfin Levy (1827–1867), died at the age of forty. She bore eight children, two of whom died in infancy.

— *Henry J. Hauschild, Victoria, Texas*

The A. Levi & Co. Bank building in Victoria was built in 1890 and housed the institution for fifty years. After the Civil War, Abraham Levi and a cousin formed a grocery business. By 1875, the business' banking functions became so profitable that the partners decided to conduct a private banking business as well. Thus, the A. Levi & Company Bank was a natural outgrowth of the mercantile firm. By the time the new building was constructed in 1890, the firm consisted of Abraham Levi, his two sons, Godcheaux, president, and Charles, vice-president, and his son-in-law, Jules K. Hexter, cashier. Eventually, the A. Levi & Co. Bank became the Victoria Bank & Trust Company, the largest state-chartered bank in Texas.

— *Victoria College/University of Houston-Victoria Library Photographic Collection*

Godcheaux Augustus Levi (1852–1911), the oldest son of Abraham and Mina Levi, was treasurer of the "Macaroni" Railroad (New York, Texas, and Mexico Railroad) from 1881 to 1885; secretary-treasurer of the Texas Continental Meat Co.; president of the A. Levi & Co. Bank; and president of the Texas Bankers Association. He endowed the first scholarship and chair at the University of Texas. He was president of Victoria's Temple B'nai Israel, 1901–06, when he moved to Dallas. In 1911, he became the president of the Dallas United Jewish Charities.

— *Henry J. Hauschild, Victoria, Texas*

Abraham and Mina Halfin Levi

Abraham Levi, a native of Hutte, Alsace, France, arrived in Victoria in 1849 with goods purchased in Mississippi and opened a dry goods store with Henry Halfin. They advertised in the Victoria *Texian Advocate* of October 17, 1850, offering to sell for "low rates for CASH or PECANS. Please call at the CHEAP CASH STORE." The Levi firm kept its customers' money for safekeeping and gradually began lending money, discounting notes, and performing other banking functions. In 1851, Abraham married Henry's sister, Mina Halfin. By 1860, the tax rolls valued the partners' property at $70,000.

Although Abraham supported the Confederacy, he would not own a slave because he thought it was not right for one human being to own another.

In 1858, a Jewish section of the city's Evergreen Cemetery was consecrated. The Victoria Ladies Hebrew Benevolent Society was founded in 1871. The Society supported needy families and sent funds to the New Orleans Widows and Orphans Home. Victoria's Temple Beth Israel was founded in 1872, and Abraham Levi was the second president of the Temple.

With no rabbi, Victoria Jews depended upon Rabbi Henry Cohen of Galveston for guidance. In 1895, Mrs. M. L. Potash, a milliner, wrote to Rabbi Cohen for advice, explaining that she was trying to start a Bible class. She praised one of Cohen's books, *Talmudic Sayings:* "[It] is a gem . . . of incalculable value to all who like myself have never had an opportunity to sip at the Talmudic Fountain." Godcheaux A. Levi also wrote to Rabbi Cohen the same year: "At our Congregation meeting yesterday the purchase of a cheap second hand Sephar Torah was discussed by some of the old Orthodox school . . . What information can you give us." [33]

Gabriel Matthew Raphael (1845–1898) was a partner in the firm Bloomberg and Raphael, Brownsville wholesale dealers in dry goods, staples, boots, shoes, and groceries. He was also a banker with mining and ranching interests in South Texas and Mexico.
— *Alice Raphael Collection, Barker Texas History Center, UT-Austin*

Eugenie R. (Salamon) Raphael (1855–1926) was born in Scotland and married Gabriel Raphael in Edinburgh in 1885. She was descended from French Jews.
— *Alice Raphael Collection, Barker Texas History Center, UT-Austin*

Bloomberg and Raphael: Border Merchants

All kinds of hats, caps,
skirts, drawers,
notions and family groceries
A full assortment of European goods
kept in our Matamoros house.
Mail orders promptly attended to
Brownsville, Texas
Matamoros, Mexico

In 1865, A. J. Bloomberg of New York City opened commercial houses in Brownsville, Texas, and Matamoros, Mexico. He was the New York buyer, while his partner, Gabriel Raphael, also of New York, moved to Texas in 1866 and kept the firm's books. The Matamoros store sold only European goods. In 1868, the firm was changed to Alexander and Co., composed of J. Alexander (who was Jewish), Bloomberg, and Raphael.[35]

Gabriel Raphael did business on both sides of the border. He had mining interests in Tamaulipas, Mexico; he was the first president of the first national bank on the Texas-Mexico border; and he owned a 60,000-acre ranch in South Texas, *Las Mestagnas*, which was managed by Mexican *vaqueros*. Mexican President Porfirio

Díaz addressed him as a *"muy estimada amigo"* [very dear friend]. The men in Gabriel's *minyan* came from both Brownsville and Matamoros, and High Holiday services were held in the Brownsville Masonic lodge.

Gabriel married Eugenie Salamon in Edinburgh, Scotland, in 1885. She was Scots-born to a French family. Her French-Hebrew Haggadah was inscribed, "The book unites in a bond of living friendship two limbs of Judeo-European Culture." Eugenie was musical and subscribed to many magazines which arrived by stagecoach — Brownsville was 160 miles from a railroad. She gave thread to local Hispanic women and promoted their handwork to First Lady Mrs. Grover Cleveland.

The Raphael daughters were raised by a nanny and studied piano at an early age, but they attended public school. Alice recalled she was the only "American" girl in her class. She also remembered that a Mexican was dragged from jail and lynched. On Gabriel's death in 1899, Eugenie moved the family to New York. Claire became a music historian; Alice was a famous translator whose version of Goethe's *Faust* was staged at Yale, in California, and in New York.[36]

L. to r., Claire Raphael (Reis), Angus Raphael, and Alice Raphael (Mrs. Henry Eckstein), children of Gabriel and Eugenie Raphael. Claire was a music historian who wrote *Composers in America*,[37] *American Composers*, and *Composers, Conductors, and Critics*. Alice studied in France and Germany and at Barnard College in New York City, and became a well-known translator of Goethe's *Faust*.[38] Her translations were published in several editions, and in 1931 Max Reinhardt produced her translation of the play in Los Angeles and San Francisco. It was later produced by the Yale Drama School (1949) and at the New York City Center by the Deutsches Theatre (1961).
— *Alice Raphael Collection, Barker Texas History Center, UT-Austin*

Letters of Ernst Kohlberg (1875–1877)

Ernst Kohlberg wrote dozens of letters to his family back in Germany.[39] He wrote that El Paso was "nearly the end of the world and the last creation. If I had known what I know now I would not have come here."[40]

"At first chile . . . was a hellish . . . food for me, but . . . now I almost can swallow it like a Mexican . . . The revolution in Chihuahua continues unabated" (September 8, 1876). His letter of April 27, 1877, urged his parents to take out an emigration-pass for his brother Moritz. "One at least has one's freedom here if nothing else . . . He will always at least have beans . . . Do not forget to get the pass *at once.*"

Ernst Kohlberg (1857–1910) went to El Paso [then Franklin] from Westphalia, Germany, in 1875 to avoid the draft. He founded the International Cigar Factory in El Paso in 1886, the first in the Southwest. His deluxe brand was "La International." Ernst was a city council member and a founder of the city's Electric Light Company. He operated the St. Regis Hotel, where President Howard Taft met Mexican President Porfirio Díaz in 1909. Kohlberg became a deputy U.S. consul in Juárez, Mexico. He married Olga Kohlberg from Germany, who became one of El Paso's noted civic leaders. The Kohlbergs belonged to the Progress Club for German Jews and were active in Temple Mount Sinai. Murdered by a drunken tenant in 1910, Ernst was the prototype for the character of Ludwig Sterner in Tom Lea's novel, *Wonderful Country.*[41]

— *Southwest Collection, El Paso Public Library*

"Charley [Lesinsky] is a classy fellow for a Jew."
— *Montezuma Weekly Times,* El Paso, December 14, 1868

The Kohlberg Cigar Factory, c. 1915. The cigar makers were mainly Mexican workers who hired a reader to read the daily news and books in the Spanish language for three hours each day as they labored.

— *Southwest Collection, El Paso Public Library*

A circumcision in Corpus Christi: 1875

Letter from a Corpus Christi correspondent to the *American Israelite,* June 27, 1875:

"A word or so from these wild parts . . . within this body of Christ there lives [sic] no less than forty-five Jews and Jewesses . . . Most . . . have come here, some with their families, within the last five years . . . now we number eleven families . . . the object of this communication is to put on record this day . . . a joyous re-union of all the males professing Judaism, at the house of our worthy fellow-townsman and co-religionist, Mr. Julius Henry, to assist in the initiation of his infant son into the creed of his fathers, or, in other words, a *brit melah* [original phrase in Hebrew]."

The rite was performed by Dr. Aaron Ansell [presumably from out of town] with prayers from the Portuguese *Minhag.* Refreshments were served and "right merrie was the day." After the happy celebration, those gathered remembered "the distressed and oppressed, the widow and the orphan, the poor and the friendless," and decided to form a Hebrew Benevolent Society. "This being the stepping-stone to the erection of a temple . . . The response from fifteen souls was as one voice, all vociferated 'YEA!' "

Julius Henry (1839–1912) of Posen, Prussia, moved to Corpus Christi in 1858, the first Jew in town. He was an Indian fighter, a farmhand, and a baker. During the Civil War, he sold salt and also ran a bakery for the Union Army. Later, he became a grocer, an alderman, and the postmaster. His cousin, Bertha Nathan, came from Europe to marry him, and they had seven children.[42]

— *Copy from* Temple Beth El History of the Jewish Community 1957 — 5717, Corpus Christi, *print by Applied Photographers, Inc.*

— H. O. Gordon

Hyman and Mamie Gordon Perlstein

Hundreds of Jews settled in small Texas towns like Beaumont. They built families, founded businesses, and contributed to the civic lives of their communities. In the absence of Jewish institutions, many struggled to observe religious traditions and obtain a Jewish education for their children. They attended Jewish services in nearby towns or were fortunate to have occasional visits from circuit-riding rabbis. Some married non-Jews but retained their Judaism. Others adopted the religion of their spouses.

The New Orleans *Democrat* observed on September 8, 1881, that "Seven new stores have been built in Beaumont in the past forty days, and a number of Israelite merchants have settled here, a sure precursor of the prosperity which is to follow." The Beaumont *Enterprise* reported that same month that "Today and tomorrow are Rosh Hashanah, or the Jewish New Year. All the stores and places of business kept by the Israelites will be closed."

"Begin in a small town and grow with it," was H. O. Gordon's advice to his immigrant nephew from Lithuania, Hyman Perlstein: ". . . you must learn a trade. I don't want you to peddle . . . America is a young and

Hyman Asher Perlstein (1869–1948) and Mamie Gordon Perlstein (1872–1952) on their wedding day, March 19, 1893. The Perlsteins later became a prominent Beaumont family.
— *Eleanor Weinbaum*

vibrant giant, and the little cities are her arms and legs just beginning to stretch."[43]

In 1889, Hyman Perlstein decided to follow his Uncle H. O. Gordon's advice and settle in a small town. Hyman remembered, "I was on my way from Houston to Orange, but got off the train here [Beaumont] thinking it was Orange. By 9 o'clock that morning I had bought a blacksmith shop and have been here ever since. It was one of the most fortunate mistakes of my life." Hyman branched out from the blacksmith shop into the buggy, harness, and implement business and gradually started buying property. He had an interest in the Spindletop Oil Field which struck near Beaumont in 1901. In the wake of the oil boom, he developed a successful real estate business.

"Hyman Perlstein . . . was an institution."

Around 1907, Hyman Perlstein built the city's first skyscraper, the six-story Perlstein building, where the art museum now stands. He was a charter member of Temple Emanuel in 1895, serving as president, secretary, and treasurer. The first temple was built in 1901 with funds raised in a series of annual balls by the Hebrew Women's Benevolent Association. A Masonic leader, Perlstein summoned members to a meeting by leaning out a window and blowing a large horn, loud enough to be heard all over town.

In 1947, he received the Exchange Club's Golden Deeds Award. Mamie Perlstein was an active supporter of the Sabine Oaks Home for the Aged. Hyman and Mamie were generous philanthropists who gave an ambulance to the Red Cross, paid off the note on the Children's Day Nursery, and deeded land for a park. When

Hyman died, Rabbi Samuel Rosinger said, "Hyman Perlstein was not an individual, he was an institution." The Perlstein story is told by the couple's daughter, Eleanor Perlstein Weinbaum, in her book *Shalom America*. A memorial statue dedicated to Hyman Perlstein by the Beaumont Art League stands on the grounds of the Southeast Texas Art Museum.[44]

L. Roos' advertisement in the *Liberty Gazette*, April 10, 1867. Louis Roos (1844–1882) came from Belfort, France, to Liberty in 1866; there he opened a department store. He later moved to Houston and was shot by an irate customer in his downtown store, The Bazaar.
— *W. L. Melasky*

Alice Echo, September 14, 1899
LOCAL TOPICS
"You might mention that N. Cohn observed the Jewish New Year 5660 Monday. This will let the new people who are settling here know that Alice has a Jew store and that's a good thing for the town for it is a drawing card."

44   *"Quite a colony of Syracusans have settled in Texas and are*

meeting with splendid success." — Syracuse [New York] *Journal,* November 11, 1879.

The Joe Weisman & Co. Department Store, Marshall, 1895. Far left, Morris Kariel.
— *Audrey D. Kariel, Marshall, Texas*

From Syracuse to Marshall

One of the first Jews to settle in Marshall was Isaac Wolf of Syracuse, New York, who moved there in the late 1850s because of his health. He entered the cotton brokerage business, and members of his family soon followed, including his brothers-in-law, Daniel and M. L. Doppelmayer.

The Doppelmayers had been brought to the U.S. by their sister, Mary Doppelmayer Weisman (1822–1912). Mary went to New York City from Germany in the 1840s, using money she won in a lottery. She married Meyer Weisman, and the couple moved to Syracuse. Louis Weisman Kariel, Sr., who still lives in Marshall, recalled in 1988 at the age of ninety-one, "Little did my grandmother, Mary Weisman, know that when she won the lottery ticket in Germany she would be using the proceeds to start a colony in the U.S., including one in Texas."[45]

Mary and Meyer Weisman had seven children, six of whom eventually settled in Marshall. During and after the Civil War, many other members of the Weisman and Wolf families joined them.

J. Weisman & Co.: "Open with a rush, crush, and a jam."
— Marshall *News Messenger,* September 18, 1878

Joe Weisman (1848–1918), the son of Meyer and Mary Weisman, went to Marshall in 1866 to assist his uncle, Daniel Doppelmayer, in establishing one of the first department stores in East Texas. In 1878, the partnership merged into J. Weisman and Company. The June 28 issue of the local paper published the following notice:

"Mr. Joe Weisman . . . ᵗ on a train for New York . . . to buy a large, fresh stock of dry goods, notions and etc . . . He will open his own house . . . with honest and fair dealings, promptness and polite attention."

In 1879, Joe sent for his brother Jacob, whose departure was noted by the *Syracuse Journal* of November 11, 1879: "The many friends of Mr. Jacob Weisman will hereafter miss him at the post he has so long occupied . . . in the office of the W.U. [Western Union] Company . . . He leaves for Marshall, Texas, tonight . . . Quite a colony of Syracusans have settled in Texas and all are meeting with splendid success."

In 1880, another brother, M. L. Weisman, arrived from Syracuse just in time to avert a municipal energy crisis caused by a price increase of the local coal oil company. M. L. bought up a large quantity of oil to break up the local company's monopoly.

Joe Weisman was a prominent businessman and a charter member of Temple Moses Montefiore. His wife, Lena Young Weisman, was a homeopathic healer. Their two-and-a-half-story luxurious home (now known as the Weisman-Hirsch-Beil home) bears a Texas Historical Commission medallion and is on the National Register of Historic Places.

In 1898, Joe Nathan Hirsch joined Weisman & Co. and later married the Weismans' daughter, Valrie. When Joe Weisman died in 1918, Hirsch became general manager, a position he held for almost fifty years. After Hirsch's death, his two sons, Martin and Joe Weisman Hirsch, continued to manage the store. In 1972, the firm was sold to Joe Weinberg of Kilgore. The sale ended ninety-four years of a single-family ownership recorded to have been the oldest in Texas at the time. As of 1989, the store was still in business.[46]

The Doppelmayer Brothers

Meyer and Daniel Doppelmayer were the only Jews listed in the Marshall, Harrison County, Census of 1850. They ran a confectionery, the first Jewish business in town. Daniel baked gingerbread in a shed and cooked candy in open kettles. During the Civil War, he served in the Confederate Army while Meyer ran the business.

In 1866, Daniel sent for his nephew, Joe Weisman, and they formed a dry goods partnership, Weisman and Company. Daniel was president of Congregation Moses Montefiore when it was formed in the 1880s. When the temple building was dedicated in 1900, Daniel, the oldest member of the congregation, was given the honor of opening the ark for the Torah to be placed inside. One of his daughters, Della, married Rabbi Max Handman, who moved to Marshall in 1910.

At the height of Jefferson's prosperity in the 1870s, M. L. operated the Alhambra Hotel. In 1904, he began importing bananas, then considered an exotic fruit, including a rare red one, for his candy store customers. He acquired the name of "Banana King" and made headlines with an after-school banana festival such as "was never seen in any country. Mr. Doppelmayer had two or three doctors present . . . who assured him that no harm could come of overeating bananas, so he did not limit the children, and some few ate as many as 18 or 20."[47]

The family of Meyer L. Doppelmayer (1823–1910) and his wife, Rosalee Doppelmayer (?–1910). Front row, l. to r., Meyer, Amelia, and Rosalee; back row, Mose, Bett, Eva, and Jim. They lived in Marshall, Jefferson, and Sherman.
— *Audrey D. Kariel, Marshall, Texas*

A fan advertising the M. L. Doppelmayer Ice Cream Parlor.
— *Audrey D. Kariel, Marshall, Texas*

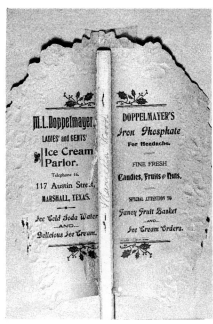

Mendel Bromberg (1845–1919) and his wife, Etta Bromberg (1849–1933) of Crockett.
— *Eliza Bishop, author-editor,* Houston County History, Crockett, Texas

The Brombergs of Crockett

Mendel Bromberg came from the same Polish village as his lifelong friend, Harris Kempner, of Galveston. In 1861, Mendel landed in New York, where he studied English, worked as a day laborer, and saved his money. He headed for Texas and opened a store in Crockett. He and his wife Etta built a home behind their store, one of the first in town with electricity and a telephone. In 1911, they built a new store with bricks from their own kiln.

Mendel was one of the first East Texans to be interested in soil conservation. He kept a bountiful garden, which he tilled, and built roads at his own expense, one of which is captioned in historic maps as the "Bromberg Road." With no Jewish congregation in town, the Brombergs traveled thirty-five miles to Palestine for services and also belonged to Galveston's B'nai Israel, 175 miles to the south. The Brombergs gave generously of land and money for the building of Protestant churches.

The Brombergs had six children. Etta put her son, Perry, through Vanderbilt Medical School by sewing and selling bonnets; he became a surgeon. Lena taught mathematics and literature to three generations of Crockett children and founded study, social, and historic groups that still meet today. Moses ran the family store and farm and was a president of the East Texas Chamber of Commerce. Sara Bromberg (Harrison) and Pauline Bromberg (Weis) moved away but returned to care for their mother. Sol was a Galveston attorney and executive of the Moody Cotton Company. His two children have made valuable donations to Crockett's public library.[48]

This "I. Jacobs Dealer in Pure Liquors, Tyler, Texas" amber strap-sided liquor flask was excavated near Starrville. Many Texas Jews have run saloons and been in the liquor business. Isaac Jacobs (1849?–1925) was a Tyler merchant for fifty years. His saloon was on the south side of the square in the Odd Fellows building. Jacobs advertised in the 1887 *City Directory* as a dealer in pure liquors, including California wines, and as the agent for the Klansman Brewery Company. By 1904, he was out of the liquor business and clerking in B. Sandolowsky's store. Jacobs was a founder of Tyler's Temple Beth El in 1895, and he and his wife, Annie, are buried in the Temple cemetery.
— *Smith County Historical Society Archives*

The dry goods and men's clothing firm of Lipschitz & Weyl (owners, Sam Lipschitz and Emil M. Weyl) opened in 1895 in Hearne.
— *Robertson County Historical Commission, copy from W. Baker,* A History of Robertson County, *286.*

Jesse James, $4, and a barrel of apples

Luling was a prosperous nineteenth-century community about fifty miles east of San Antonio. Silver trains from Mexico, ox carts, cotton, and cattle were all part of the economy. Although Luling had many Jewish residents, there were never enough to hire a rabbi or build a temple.[49] The closest congregation was in San Antonio. The cemetery, with about 100 gravestones, is maintained today in perpetual care by the Luling Cemetery Incorporated.

Today, there is only one Jewish-owned store in Luling, the Salt Flat Pipe and Supply Company, serving the oil industry, but descendants of the original pioneers tell colorful tales about Luling's early Jews.[50]

William M. Finklestein (1843–1879), the first Jew to be buried in the Luling Jewish cemetery, was killed in a dispute over a sale at his store. His widow, Reva Leah Finklestein (1843–1890), borrowed $4 from her in-laws for a barrel of apples and supported her four children by making pies and jellies. The story is told that Jesse James and his men stayed with her twice and paid a total of $500 for room and board. Reva was able to send her sons to college and give her daughters generous dowries.

Sarah Edloff (1856–1925) of Utica, New York, married Reuben Jacobs (1851–1936), and the couple settled in Luling around 1876. Reuben wanted Sarah to keep kosher, but kosher meat from San Antonio often arrived spoiled. Sarah belonged to the Blue Stockings Literary Club, and one daughter was Queen of the Fire Department. Reuben, a cattle buyer for Harris Kempner, had a hot temper. Once a man pulled a knife on him; Reuben hit the man so hard that he later died. The eldest Jacobs daughter, Mamie, was murdered by her first cousin because she refused to marry him. One story says the murderer hopped a freight train; another says he was taken by a highly incensed mob.

The original name of Luling was Joseyville, named after Joseph Josey. Joseph Josey (1821-1889) of Bavaria, shown here, opened a general store in Caldwell County after the Civil War. When the railroad considered coming to Luling, it was understood that a town would be built at Josey's Store. He offered the railroad twenty-five acres to locate the center of town in front of his store, but the store ended up outside the city limits.[51]
— *Mrs. Monte Harris, photo by D. B. Barr, Photographer, copy from UT Institute of Texan Cultures*

Noah Josey, son of Joseph and Fannie Goldsticker Josey, was a cadet at Texas A&M University from 1885 to 1888. He was given the name "Noah" because he was born during a flood in Luling.[52] His mother was put on a raft of cotton bales and towed to safer high ground to give birth. Noah was later a merchant, a bookkeeper, and manager of the San Luis Potosí Electrical Company in Mexico and San Antonio.[53]
— *Mrs. Monte Harris, photo by McNair, Bryan, copy from UT Institute of Texan Cultures*

Louis Goodman (1844–1920) went to Luling in the 1880s and was given the honorary title "Rabbi." He is known as "the Rabbi with the five wives" and is buried alongside three of them in the Luling Jewish Cemetery. His first wife died at the age of forty; his second died in childbirth, also at forty.[54] One daughter, Fannie Goodman Freed, became a prominent Houston civic leader.[55]
— *Richard Mayer*

Sanger Bros. Monthly Magazine, November 1890.
— *Dallas Public Library*

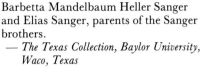

Barbetta Mandelbaum Heller Sanger and Elias Sanger, parents of the Sanger brothers.
— *The Texas Collection, Baylor University, Waco, Texas*

The Sanger brothers' story began in Obernbreit, Bavaria, where their parents, Barbetta and Elias Sanger, had a small farm and orchard. The Sangers had seven sons and three daughters. The second son, Lehman Sanger, recalled in his 1908 unpublished "Autobiography" that his father, Elias, was a wine trader, and worked looms making flannel and skirting. Jews, at that time, were an important part of European fairs; women and children often managed the stalls while the men moved about buying or peddling. Lehman remembered: "And he and mother [Barbetta] attended the various fairs . . . on Sundays. Mother always accompanying father as his main clerk, riding on top of one of the goods cases on the wagon carrying the goods to the fair. Mother was a valuable assistant." [56]

Sam Sanger (1843–1918) studied at the University of Berlin and at Berlin's leading rabbinical seminary. He came to the U.S. as a teacher of Jewish religious studies in Cincinnati, where he married Hannah Heller, the daughter of a rabbi. After three years as rabbi of a Reform congregation in Philadelphia, he joined his brothers in Texas in 1872. He opened the Waco Sanger Bros. store in 1873, one month after the arrival of the railroad. In a 1915 speech, he articulated the Sanger Bros. basic marketing policies as a desire to please the public and a belief in "truth in advertising." Sanger was president of Congregation Rodef Sholom and a patriarchal civic figure, whose "acuity, education, enlightened employee policies, forward looking business relationships and rapidly established reputation for high ethical standards quickly brought him weighty responsibilities . . ." [57] He died on December 18, 1918, the day after the firm received its charter of incorporation. His wife, Hannah Heller Sanger, donated the first parsonage to Rodef Sholom in 1919. [58]
— *The Texas Collection, Baylor University, Waco, Texas*

L. & P. Sanger store in Bryan, c. 1867. When the Sanger brothers decided to open a store in Bryan, no space was available, so they bought a wooden building in nearby Millican and had it shipped in on a railroad flatcar.[61] The greatest demand was for shotguns, revolvers, and accordions. Notice the names of other Jewish merchants on the block, N. Grossmayer and R. Oscar.
— *The Texas Collection, Baylor University, Waco, Texas*

Texas' first chain store

Sanger Bros. was founded in 1857 by the oldest of the Sangers' seven sons, Isaac, who opened a general store in McKinney, a town thirty miles north of Dallas. The rest of the Sanger sons followed. Lehman arrived in 1859 and opened stores in Weatherford and Decatur. In Weatherford, the Sangers experienced anti-Semitism and harassment, possibly because of their pricing policies or because they were believed to harbor abolitionist sentiments. During the Civil War, the stores closed while Isaac and Lehman fought in the Confederate Army.

After the war, the other brothers came to Texas: Philip, Alex, Sam, Jacob, and David. (Jacob and David died in an 1867 yellow fever epidemic.) The brothers began opening stores along the northward expanding route of the Houston and Texas Central Railroad. They built one of the country's first department chain stores with stores in thirteen cities at various times. In addition to the three founded before the Civil War, they opened stores in Millican, Bryan, Hearne, Calvert, Bremond, Kosse, Groesbeck, Corsicana, Dallas, and Waco.[59] Dallas and Waco were finally selected as permanent locations, founded in 1872 and 1873 respectively. Philip and Alex headed the Dallas store; Sam and Lehman ran the Waco store. Isaac lived in New York City, where he served as purchasing agent. All the brothers and their wives were active in civic and religious affairs.

The Sangers were leaders in innovative merchandising. They were the first to adopt fixed pricing. In 1880, they opened a mail-order department; in 1884, they published their first catalog, and by the mid-1890s, Sanger Brothers had annual sales of $1 million. They were the first in Dallas to offer credit, to have a telephone shopping service, a mail-order department, home delivery, and fashion sketches in their advertisements. They were also the first to install elevators, escalators, gas, and electric lights. Their pioneering employee benefits included a night school and a savings and loan service. By 1900, Sanger Brothers was the largest dry-goods company west of the Mississippi River. It had two major retail department stores (Dallas and Waco) and a wholesale business second only to Chicago's Marshall Fields.[60]

Isabella Wenk Sanger (Mrs. Lehman Sanger) (1849–1923) with her grandchildren, l. to r., Adrian Sanger, Evelyn Belle Sanger (Badt), and Dorothy Ettelson, c. 1912. Lehman Sanger recalled a revealing anecdote about his wife. In 1873, his sister, Sophie Sanger, came from nearby Calvert to visit. After her arrival, word came that yellow fever had broken out in Calvert. "The Bryan Board of Health attempted to compel us to leave town. My wife was pleased to hold the fort, and when they threatened to make us move, she told them she would shoot the first man that crossed her threshold, and they concluded to let her alone."[62]
— *The Texas Collection, Baylor University, Waco, Texas*

A WOMAN'S DREAM.

SHE SAT ALONE

In the moonlight, her beautiful cheek resting upon her hand, so soft and white and dimpled. You could tell as you looked at her, that her thoughts were far away, and that she was thinking of something beautiful. Her eyes were wistful, the dimples in her cheeks had died out, and only the dimple in her chin remained, that little rosy cleft, the impress of Love's finger. She was less glowing than at times, but none the less lovely. I thought to myself, as I looked at her, that she was nearer heaven than we coarser mortals, and I longed to know whither her pure heart turned itself. I approached her; she did not hear me. I spoke; she did not answer. I touched her softly on the arm, she looked up and smiled, a far-away smile, such as an angel might have given. "You are thinking very intently," I said. She answered, "yes, I am thinking of SANGER BRO'S, who, owing to the Removal of their Goods, and the want of room to exhibit their great quantity of Goods, are determined to reduce their stock at great sacrifice."

All goods reduced from former prices. Special bargains in Dress Goods and Silks. WHITE GOODS at greatly reduced figures. Notions, Ribbons, Embroideries, Corsets, Laces, Hosiery, &c., for less than can be had elsewhere.

CLOTHING, GENTS FURNISHING GOODS,

From 10 to 25 per cent less than ever.

GREAT BARGAINS IN HATS.

Great Inducements

TO WHOLESALE TRADE.

We are determined to sell goods at astonishing low rates. Call and examine our stock and prices, with the assurance that it will be to your advantage in making your purchases at the Store of

SANGER BRO'S,

DALLAS, TEXAS.

The earliest existing Sanger Bros. advertisement is this handbill entitled "A Woman's Dream," 1873. The ad claims that the woman sat alone in the moonlight thinking of Sangers' forthcoming sale and all the beautiful goods being offered at greatly reduced prices.
— *Texas State Historical Association, copy from Leon Rosenberg,* Sangers, Pioneer Texas Merchants

---

"I am thinking of Sanger Bros. . . ."

The earliest existing Sanger Bros. ad, which ran in 1873, could have been written by a contemporary Madison Avenue publicist.

"A Woman's Dream. She sat alone in the moonlight, her beautiful cheek resting upon her hand, so soft and white and dimpled. You could tell as you looked at her, that her thoughts were far away, and that she was thinking of something beautiful. Her eyes were wistful . . . she was nearer heaven than we coarser mortals . . . I approached her; she did not hear me . . . I touched her softly on the arm, she looked up and smiled, a far-away smile, such as an angel might have given. 'You are thinking very intently,' I said. She answered, 'Yes, I am thinking of SANGER BRO'S, who owing to the Removal of their Stock, and the want of room to exhibit their great quantity of Goods, are determined to reduce their stock at great sacrifice.' "[63]

A new sphere for women

The department store was a new sphere for women — both customers and female employees — in the late 1800s. Female clerks forged bonds of solidarity with each other, and many were elevated from "shopgirl" to "saleswoman." They exercised initiative, autonomy, and creativity. The department store, with its bargain basement as well as its "snob" appeal, provided something for women of all social classes. By allowing customers free access to goods without any obligation to buy and by providing free services in a congenial, home-like, and luxurious atmosphere, the store aimed at developing customer loyalty.[64]

Attracting the female customer

One Lancaster woman, Mrs. C. A. Bryant, Sr., recalled her first trip in 1872 to the Sangers store in Dallas. "We felt as though we had been in a city when we came to Sangers and met the gracious gentlemen at the door. The small store alone was a bright spot, full of beautiful things."[65] The creation of a new social class — the middle-class consumer — was on the horizon.

Female clerks in the ladies ready-to-wear department of the Dallas Sanger Brothers store, 1888. Sangers was one of the first stores to hire women to sell women's ready-to-wear and to use separate departments for different kinds of merchandise. Sales work in department stores was considered to be the "Cinderella of occupations." It provided a new, respectable, and desirable occupation for nineteenth-century women, including Jewish women. Although the pay was low and the hours were long, opportunities for upward mobility included advancement to the position of buyer or supervisor of personnel. A few clerks even married their bosses or their customers.
— *Texas State Historical Association, copy from Leon Rosenberg,* Sangers, Pioneer Texas Merchants

— Mrs. Herbert Marcus, matriarch of the Neiman-Marcus family

Fannie Fechenbach Sanger (1857–1898), the wife of Alexander Sanger, was an early Dallas philanthropist and civic leader.
— *Dorothy M. and Henry S. Jacobus Temple Emanu-El Archives, print by Andy Reisberg*

Alexander Sanger (1847–1925) was a Dallas business leader, alderman, the first Jewish regent of the University of Texas, and a founder and president of Temple Emanu-El. He was also president of the Texas State Fair and the Texas Manufacturing Association.
— *Dorothy M. and Henry S. Jacobus Temple Emanu-El Archives, print by Andy Reisberg*

Fannie Fechenbach Sanger

Fannie Sanger, a native of Wurtemburg, Germany, went to Cincinnati, Ohio, with her parents in 1866. The family moved to Dallas in 1876, and in 1879 she married Alexander Sanger. She was a patron of the arts whose elegant home was filled with European art treasures. She was a founder of the Dallas Woman's Home and a leading member of the Ladies' Hebrew Benevolent Association. A lover of literature, she was a member of many social and literary clubs.

Her last notable achievement was the presidency of the *Jahrmacht*, a German-style fair, which took place April 13–20, 1898. The successful benefit raised $11,000 to build the second Temple Emanu-El structure at Ervay and St. Louis streets. Her funeral was attended by hundreds of Dallasites of all denominations, rich and poor, black and white.[67]

Alexander Sanger

Alexander Sanger, one of the seven Sanger brothers, arrived in the U.S. in l865. He worked as a bookkeeper in Cincinnati, Ohio, before joining the Sanger Brothers firm in Corsicana, Texas. In July 1872, he moved to Dallas, where he and his brother Philip opened what would become the premier Sanger store. Alex ran the wholesale operations, supervised the employees, and was involved in community affairs, while Philip ran the retail operations. As Dallas boomed with the crossing of two railroads in 1873, the Texas and Pacific and the Houston and Texas Central, so did Sanger Brothers. Alex even signed a $100,000 bond issue for the T&P Railroad as chairman of its finance committee.

Alex Sanger's civic and cultural activities were far-ranging. Within six months of his arrival in Dallas, he helped found Temple Emanu-El and was elected to the city's Board of Aldermen. He received seventy-two votes of a possible seventy-three. The one dissenting vote was his; he voted for his opponent. In 1888, he was a member of the exclusive "male only" Dallas Club. In 1894, he served as president of the Texas State Fair. In 1911, he became the first Jew to serve on the University of Texas Board of Regents, holding that office until 1917, when Governor Jim Ferguson asked him to resign over a dispute. During World War I, Alex was a representative to the U. S. Food Administration. He was a director of the Dallas Public Library and president of the Dallas Fire Department. A Dallas branch library, an elementary school, and a town in Denton County are named for him.[68]

From the 1870s, Sanger Brothers was the outstanding department store in Texas. The Dallas store was so successful that the two brothers built mansions in Dallas' first prestigious residential section, the Cedars. Edna Ferber recalled that it was worth a trip to Texas just to see Philip's home. The brothers and their wives entertained lavishly. Their guests included President Howard Taft, actors, writers, and musicians like Paderewski and Heifetz, and the birth-control crusader, Margaret Sanger (no relation).[69] Both brothers were presidents of Temple Emanu-El.

In 1926, a year after Alex died, the mercantile business was sold. It had been sixty-nine years since the firm's beginning in 1857. The firm's real estate holdings, including what would become significant petroleum leases, were retained by family members. In 1951, Sangers' ownership changed again, after purchase by Federated Department Stores of Cincinnati. And in 1961, the Sanger Division of Federated merged with another old Dallas firm, A. Harris, to become Sanger-Harris. In 1988, it was sold to Foley's.

JOSEY FAMILY, LULING, 1889

The Josey family in Luling, Texas, is pictured on October 21, 1889, apparently the day of Joseph Josey's funeral. His hat is on the floor, and his wife holds his photograph. Front row, l. to r., Hermann Josey, Fannie Goldsticker Josey. Back row, l. to r., Rachel Josey, Noah Josey, Clara Josey Kahn, and Abe Josey.

— Mrs. Monte Harris, copy from
UT Institute of Texan Cultures

"The Israelites are fast increasing in numbers."
NEW JEWISH INSTITUTIONS

When Houston's Temple Beth Israel was chartered in 1859, the congregation was Orthodox and used the Polish *Minhag*. Within fifteen years, the congregation joined the Union of American Hebrew Congregations and adopted the *Minhag America*, with prayers in English. When the *shamas* was instructed to ask worshipers to remove their hats before entering the temple in 1879, the transformation to Reform was complete.

The period immediately following the Civil War was one of radical religious ferment among American Jews. Reform rabbis fresh from Europe promoted the Americanization of Jewish ritual with greater use of English over the traditional Hebrew liturgy. As at Temple Beth Israel, Texans joined the dispute within their communities. With the exception of Beth Israel, all the congregations established in Texas before 1880 were Reform, due in large measure to the predominance of Jews from Prussia.

The Reform movement was well suited to Jewish life in the primarily non-Jewish Texas communities. Dietary laws were largely abandoned; kosher meats could not be easily obtained or arrived spoiled when brought from other towns. Sunday schools, choirs, sermons, and organs were adopted in the manner of Christian churches, and Reform rabbis often called themselves "Rev." or "Dr." Head coverings were no longer required, or even permitted, in the temples, and women worshiped alongside men in family pews.

By the 1870s, congregations were established in the growing urban centers of Galveston, San Antonio, Houston, Austin, and Dallas, but many smaller towns with fewer than ten families could not support a rabbi. Often, laypersons conducted the services, and Torahs had to be borrowed from as far away as New Orleans. City rabbis began visiting the small towns to establish Sunday schools and conduct services. By 1880, the rabbis of Galveston, Houston, San Antonio, and Dallas met in Houston to draw up an official "circuit preaching" plan.

The Texas group was among the first in the U.S. to think of this innovation. The Union of American Hebrew Congregations — the organization of Reform congregations founded in 1873 — discussed circuit preaching as a revolutionary new idea in the 1880s, but did not develop its own plan successfully until 1895. The Hebrew Union College (HUC) for the training of Reform rabbis was founded in Cincinnati in 1875 and graduated its first class in 1881. The Jewish community of Galveston donated $3,500 toward its founding, perhaps in the hope that more Reform rabbis could be drawn to Texas.

In addition to the founding of congregations, Jewish organizations began to proliferate as the Jewish community faced the need for cemeteries, self-help, and relief work. The purchase and improvement of land for a cemetery usually led to incorporation of a Hebrew Benevolent Association, which offered charity to the bereaved and the needy. These associations also made contributions to the community at large and to Christian charities. The Jewish ladies of Houston donated funds for a hospital to treat Civil War wounded, and in San Antonio, the Sisters of Charity of the Incarnate Word thanked the ladies of Temple Beth-El for their "constant liberality toward our poor." Temple Emanu-El ran a non-sectarian school in Dallas for years before the city's public schools were established.

In 1879, Charles Wessolowsky, a correspondent for the *Jewish South*, toured twenty-seven Jewish communities in Texas and created a valuable, though opinionated, record of what the state's Jews were doing at that time. Wessolowsky was convinced of the value of Ladies Aid Societies and exhorted the women in every town that didn't have one to form one at once. Victoria, one community he did not visit, had established a Ladies Hebrew Benevolent Society by 1871. In 1877, they voted to organize a Sabbath school and sent money to yellow fever victims in Mississippi and Tennessee. In 1879, they donated $15 to the Jewish Widows and Orphans Home in New Orleans, raising funds from a masked ball. They later donated funds for an iron fence for the cemetery. As they developed, Ladies Hebrew Benevolent Societies expanded their role beyond care for the bodies of female deceased and charity; they were often the force that raised money to build the temples.

By 1873, the International Order of B'nai B'rith began to establish fraternal lodges in the South. By 1900, almost twenty Texas cities had a B'nai B'rith lodge. The lodge was a familiar model for organization because Texas Jews were already active in the Odd

Fellows and the Masonic Order. David Abrams of San Antonio, for example, a linguist and manager of a circus which traveled throughout Central and South America, was affiliated with a Masonic Order in Madrid, Spain. His certificate #139, dated May 15, 1894, was issued by the *Antiguo y Primitivo Rito Oriental de Memphis Y Mizraim.*

Communication between Texas Jews and the rest of the American Jewish community was facilitated by the national Jewish newspaper, the *American Israelite.* Births, deaths, social events, business news, and formations of congregations were often announced, and numerous letters from Texas correspondents included "Tall Texas Tales."

In the 1880s, intensified legal and political persecution in Eastern Europe hastened the departure of Jews from Russia, Rumania, and Hungary. Orthodox Jews began arriving in Texas in sufficient numbers to establish their own synagogues and institutions in many towns. Among the Eastern European Jews there were also secularists, Socialists, and early-day Zionists. But Zionism was so far from the minds of most Texas Jews that the Jews of Palestine, Texas, omitted the "next year in Jerusalem" prayer from the Passover *Haggadah.* They apparently preferred their own fertile Palestine with its freedoms to the arid Palestine of old.

Records from the period between the end of the Civil War and the turn of the century show a great variety among Texas Jewish communities and render lively details of Jewish life. As Jewish institutions and organizations developed, Jews took their place in the larger community as civic, political, and cultural leaders. Between 1865 and 1900, Texas Jews built a solid foundation to support their social and religious lives. As the twentieth century dawned, new opportunities were over the horizon, along with thousands more immigrants on their way to Texas to take advantage of them.

David Hirsch had to carry his dead wife's body in a wagon to Gonzales

In the words of historian Frank Wagner, "The practice of Judaism was a risky business in South Texas during the latter part of the nineteenth century. Most of the people in Corpus Christi were antagonistic toward Jews, and made no bones about it. Sabbath and Holy Day observances were regarded as examples of the Jews going out of their way to annoy the community."[1]

When Jeanette Weil Hirsch died of puerperal fever in 1873, a son-in-law of Capt. Richard King, founder of the King Ranch, blocked her burial. Her husband, David Hirsch, had to carry her body 140 miles by covered wagon to reach the nearest Jewish cemetery in Gonzales. In 1875, Captain King compensated for the action of his son-in-law by deeding a plot of ground to the Jewish community to be used for the Hebrew Rest Cemetery. King expressed "the hope that such wicked prejudice would not again occur in Corpus Christi."

David Hirsch, who was born in Darmstadt, Hesse, arrived in Indianola, Texas, in 1854, peddling goods on foot. He bought a horse in Gonzales, and in 1858 opened a general store in Belton. He married Jeanette Weil of Lockhart in 1860, and they had two children. When business declined during the Civil War, the family moved to Matamoros, Mexico. He ran a small store there until the end of the war, when the family settled in Corpus Christi.

After Jeanette's death, Hirsch married Olivia Benedict. In 1870, he switched from retailing to money lending and wool speculation. In 1875, he was a member of the planning committee for the construction of the Corpus Christi, San Diego, and Rio Grande Railroad and was chief of the Corpus Christi Fire Department. In 1891, he founded the Corpus Christi National Bank. He was the first president of the Corpus Christi Independent School District and ad-

vocated free public education, regardless of national origin or skin color. A school is named for him.[2]

Although Jews in Corpus would not found a synagogue until 1928 (Temple Beth El), Miss Grace Rice wrote to Rabbi Henry Cohen in 1896, requesting advice: "I intend to organize a Sabbath School in this town."[3]

Pioneer Corpus Christi families[4]

Other early Jewish settlers included the Weils, the Lichtensteins, and the Morrises. Charles Weil married Sarah Hymans in 1874, and they had eleven children. All Charles' sons except Jonas worked in the Frank-Weil General Store (which he owned in partnership with Emanuel Frank). Jonas Weil was the area's first Jewish farmer, expert cattleman, and rancher, who always wore cowboy boots.

Morris Lichtenstein, a Confederate veteran, was in business in Goliad and Indianola before moving to Corpus in 1874. He and his wife, Selina, had three sons, one of whom, Emil, became a commodore in the U.S. Navy. Lichtenstein's store had a delivery service in which their salesmen rode specially built hacks through the brush and hill country until the roads ended, when they switched to horses

David Hirsch (1834–1902) was a Corpus Christi businessman, civic leader, and a trustee of the first Jewish cemetery in Corpus Christi.
— *Copy from* Temple Beth El, 1957, Corpus Christi, History of the Jewish Community

and foot. They were often the only outsiders seen by isolated ranch families for weeks on end.

Emanuel Morris, an importer/exporter with a New York office, owned stores in many small Texas towns. His wife was voted the most beautiful woman in Corpus, and their son later became editor of the Victoria *Texas Advocate*.

Brownsville and Matamoros

South of Corpus, on the Texas-Mexico border, the Hebrew Benevolent Society of Brownsville and Matamoros received a deed of land for its cemetery in 1868 from Charles Stillman, the non-Jewish founder of Brownsville. Among the earliest proofs of a Jewish presence in the Brownsville area are tombstones in the Hebrew Cemetery. Some of the inscriptions read, "Joseph, son of Benjamin and Maria Moses, died October 13, 1858"; "Adolph Asheim, died 1869"; "Joseph Alexander, born in Tarnow, Galicia, died August 11, 1872"; and "S. M. Price, born in Memel, Russia, died June 22, 1879."[5]

Columbus and Wharton

In 1879, Columbus, Texas, had twelve Jewish families, some single men, and a B'nai B'rith lodge.[6] Wharton's first Jewish settlers were Aaron Casper Finkelstein and Ben Peine, who came in the 1880s. Within ten years, there were enough Jewish families in town to begin worshiping together.[7]

— **Charles Wessolowsky**

Congregation Beth Israel of Houston dedicated a new building on Franklin Avenue with funds donated by Rosanna Osterman. The dedication was June 16, 1870.
— *Congregation Beth Israel Archives, Houston*

Beth Israel

Congregation Beth Israel was organized in Houston before the Civil War as Orthodox, but began moving toward Reform after the war. In 1868, the Reform-minded members succeeded in getting the *Minhag America* prayerbooks adopted, but soon after the books arrived, they were mysteriously "stolen." By 1874, Beth Israel had joined the Union of American Hebrew Congregations.

The spiritual leader, Rev. Jacob Voorsanger, who had arrived in 1878, was "doing all in his power to build up and elevate Judaism, and with his eloquence and learning, he succeeds to have a full attendance of Jew and Gentile to the Friday evening service . . . one of the few fine English Jewish pulpit orators."[9] In 1886, he became the spiritual leader of San Francisco's Temple Emanu-El.

The Beth Israel "Minutes" of May 11, 1879, specify that "the *Shamas* be instructed to have all non-members visiting the Temple for services take off the hat before entering." The Sunday school had about 100 pupils, and Mrs. Larenden was the principal.[10]

The congregation tried to regulate behavior by passing some "Rules of Order": "Every one entering . . . must repair to his seat in a noiseless and becoming manner. All conversation is strictly prohibited . . . Parents are . . . responsible for the behavior of their children. It is strictly forbidden to gather together in the vestibule . . . prior to, during or after divine service." And finally, "The foregoing rules apply equally as well to the ladies as to the gentlemen." ["Minutes," September 26, 1886][11]

The congregation hired Rabbi Wolf Willner in 1891, but the board objected to his wearing a head covering and talith. He left in 1893. In 1899, Beth Israel advertised for a new rabbi, emphasizing that it was Reform and used the *Hebrew Union Prayerbook*.

By 1879, Houston had a B'nai B'rith Lodge (Lone Star) and a Young Men's Hebrew Association. The Ladies Hebrew Benevolent Association (organized in 1874) gave a "Calico Ball" and a cake raffle to raise funds in Turner Hall. The Hebrew Ladies also sold ham, which upset some of the more pious gentlemen.[12]

Adolph Harris (1842–1912), a native of Prussia, was a member of Beth Israel's first finance committee. In response to an invitation from Rabbi Isaac Mayer Wise in 1873, Harris joined delegates from thirty-three other Western and Southern synagogues to form the Union of American Hebrew Congregations in Cincinnati. He moved to Dallas in 1886 and opened A. Harris Department Store.
— *Leon A. Harris, Jr.*

Adath Yeshurun

In 1891, a traditional group of men from Russia and Poland split off from Beth Israel to form Adath Yeshurun, an Orthodox congregation. Their first synagogue was a frame building at Preston and Hamilton. Rabbi Willner returned to Houston to serve as their rabbi from 1907 to 1924.

". . . Rev. Rosenstein does not speak to any of my family."
The following letter suggests that Jewish communal squabbles have been going on for a long time in Texas.[13]

"Houston, Texas   10-3-1895
Rev. Dr. [Henry] Cohen
Galveston
My Dear Sir
  . . . I wish to ask you if you will come to Houston Sunday November 3rd to unite in wedlock Miss Jeannette Emmich and myself. I am *not* a member of the [Beth Israel] Congregation here [Houston] neither is my Intended, . . . am joined in this wish by Mr. and Mrs. Emmich [the former Rabbi Zachariah Emmich and his wife] and my dear Mother, none of whom are members of the congregation . . .
Most Respectfully
Jonas Dannenbaum, % Brown Bros.

I might add that the Rev. Rosenstein does not speak to any of my family and to only a few of the Emmich family."

— **Rabbi Julius M. Magil**

Temple Beth-El, Corsicana

The first Jews arrived in Corsicana in 1871 along with the Houston and Texas Central Railroad. By 1879, there was a B'nai B'rith Lodge and by 1887, a Hebrew Cemetery Association. In 1890, Jews began holding services in a store, in City Hall, and by 1898, upstairs over Freedman's Dry Goods Company.

In 1897, Mrs. S. S. Freedman became the first president of the Ladies' Hebrew Society and was instrumental in organizing Temple Beth-El, chartered in 1898. Within two years, the temple was dedicated. The local paper described the dedication ceremonies for the new temple, and reported a speech given by Mrs. Freedman, perhaps the first time a woman had spoken from a *bima* in Texas: [15]

"The synagogue is a credit to the city, especially to the indefatigable energy and zeal of the Ladies' Hebrew Society who were largely instrumental in bringing about its building, especially Mrs. S. S. Freedman, the president . . . Mrs. S. S. Freedman . . . then read a splendid and touching address, presenting to President Costa the pulpit, the Ark, furniture and interior decorations . . .

"President Costa gave a history of the Temple dating from the first meeting called by Mrs. Freedman for the purpose of inaugurating the Temple movement. In conclusion, Rabbi Julius M. Magil called Mrs. Freedman to the front of the pulpit, and said, 'It was you who built the temple . . . you never faltered in your work, never cooled in your devout enthusiasm, but . . . kept at your noble work until you see the temple built as a result of your efforts. You are entitled to the credit for this beautiful synagogue . . . Had it not been for your untiring efforts there would have been no Jewish place of worship here now . . .' The orchestra played a selection while Mrs. Freedman was given an ovation, being kissed by a host of ladies and her hand shaken by troops of gentlemen, and everybody went home in good humor."

By 1900, Corsicana's Jewish population was about 500. The Orthodox members began meeting in the International Order of Odd Fellows building, and in 1915, chartered Agudas Achim (A Union of Brothers). [16]

In 1900, a group of Reform Jews in Corsicana built Temple Beth-El, a stunning Moroccan-style building with two octagonal towers and onion-shaped domes, the only structure of its kind in the South. In 1987, the building was rededicated as a community center with funds raised by the "Save the Temple" Committee.

— Sketched by Jeremy Pereira

"Rope Walker, Rope Walker, What was Your Name? Did you defy death in search of fame?" [17]

A most unusual grave marker in the Corsicana Hebrew Cemetery with the inscription "Rope Walker" is a poignant reminder of a man who is still a mystery. In 1884, a circus came through town. One of the performers was an acrobat who strapped a cast-iron stove to his back and attempted to cross a tightly pulled rope stretched between two buildings. The rope failed, and the man plunged to the ground. A Methodist preacher came to comfort him, but the man cried, "Please get me a rabbi. I am a Jew." Since Corsicana had no rabbi, a Jewish merchant came, and the two men prayed in Hebrew just before the Rope Walker died. [18] His identity was never discovered, but the legend is remembered in the ballad, "Rope Walker, Rope Walker, What was Your Name?", written in 1976 by Patty George and Nancy Roberts.

Rabbi Henry Cohen (1862–1952) was the spiritual leader of Temple B'nai Israel in Galveston from 1888 to 1952. He is shown here with his wife, Mollie Levy Cohen,

and their children, Ruth Cohen (Frisch) and Harry Cohen.
— *Temple B'nai Israel Archives, Galveston, print from UT Institute of Texan Cultures*

The Temple B'nai Israel Sunday School faculty in 1895.
— *Helene Samuels Levy Archives, Congregation B'nai Israel, Galveston, print by Steve Nussenblatt*

Henry Cohen served for sixty-two years

Until the time of his death in 1952 at the age of ninety, Henry Cohen had served as the rabbi or rabbi emeritus of the same congregation longer than any other rabbi. Brought to Galveston's Temple B'nai Israel during the presidency of Leo N. Levi, Henry Cohen became "the rabbi of Texas."

Born in London in 1862, Henry Cohen's early training included serving the needy of London, studying at Jews Hospital, and a stay of several months in Capetown Colony, Africa, learning native dialects. Trained as a *mohel,* a *shochet,* and a reader, Cohen served Kingston, Jamaica, and Woodville, Mississippi, before moving to Galveston Island.

After one year on the island, Rabbi Cohen followed in the steps of his predecessor, Joseph Silverman, by marrying a Galveston woman, Mollie Levy. For most of their lives, the Cohens lived in the "rabbinage," one of the first parsonages to be so named. This home and subsequent housing owned by the congregation were substantially provided by the Kempner

family. Henry Cohen was a beloved leader in his own time. In Galveston, the man in the frock coat with removable sleeves, upon which he listed his daily activities, was everywhere. In the aftermath of the 1900 hurricane, Dr. Cohen worked closely with Clara Barton, who came to supervise the Red Cross work, and busied himself rendering aid to anyone in need.

In his own congregation, B'nai Israel, Rabbi Cohen was a source of wisdom and leadership. Though raised with a more ritually observant approach to Judaism, he found a new home in the budding Reform Jewish movement. He adopted their prayerbook, removed his head covering, and joined the Central Conference of American Rabbis.

Henry Cohen's good deeds included helping new immigrants, prison reform, circuit-riding rabbinic responsibilities, and serving as an intermediary for disputes. He taught and published many articles, as well as a book, *Talmudic Sayings.* Thanks to Cohen's efforts, the early history of Texas Jewry has been preserved in his *One Hundred Years of Jewry in Texas.* A linguist fluent in thirteen languages, Dr. Cohen was often called on as an

interpreter. His private library of 12,000 volumes, as well as his voluminous personal papers, were donated to the University of Texas at Austin.

Rabbi Cohen founded the Galveston Open Forum, but he aroused opposition by inviting such speakers as Socialist Party leader Norman Thomas. Dr. Cohen's answer was, "If any religion, which has been taught to a person for a lifetime can be shaken in an hour's talk over the platform by a man whose belief is different, then that religion is not worth anything." He said repeatedly that all religious groups had something to contribute to the world.[19]

When World War I started, Rabbi Cohen was upset that there was no provision for Jewish chaplains in the U.S. Navy. Upon Cohen's insistence, U.S. Senator Morris Shepherd, from Texas, saw to it that Congress amended the law. President Woodrow Wilson called Rabbi Cohen the "first citizen of Texas," and sent him the pen with which the act was signed into law.

— *Galveston News*, 1866

Galveston

Galveston's Hebrew Benevolent Society was founded in 1865 to bury the dead and aid those in need. It was formally incorporated the following year upon receiving a $1,000 bequest from Rosanna Osterman. A yellow fever epidemic in 1867 killed forty Jews, and the Society's donations to communities near and far exhausted their funds.

In 1868, Galveston Jews obtained a second Jewish cemetery and formally organized B'nai Israel — the oldest Texas congregation established from the beginning as Reform. B'nai Israel's first secretary was Samuel K. Labatt, who had been the first president of Los Angeles' Hebrew Benevolent Society in 1854. Mrs. Leonora De Lyon Harby (1824–1888) was hired to teach Sunday school at B'nai Israel for $25 a month. She was the widow of Capt. Levi Harby, a Confederate hero, and later married Dr. Edward Randall, a prominent physician. Prior to Mrs. Harby, the religious school was run by the Temple's first officiant, Alexander Rosenspitz.[20]

Galveston was a wealthy nineteenth-century city with Jewish bankers, notaries, lawyers, and merchants. In the 1870s, most of the 200 Jewish families were so prosperous that the Hebrew Benevolent Society and the Ladies Hebrew Benevolent Society dispensed much of their charities outside the city. The community gave $3,500 for the support of the Hebrew Union College — an institution founded in Cincinnati in 1875 to train Reform rabbis.

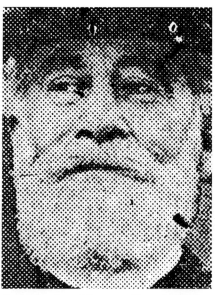

Rev. Abraham Blum was Temple B'nai Israel's first spiritual leader from 1871 to 1885. He received a degree from the Medical College of Galveston in 1872, was president of the Galveston School Board, and active in the Masons, Odd Fellows, and B'nai B'rith. In 1875, he delivered the opening prayer before the Texas House of Representatives. He also traveled in the countryside establishing Sunday schools and in 1880, met with other rabbis in Houston to organize circuit preaching. His wife, Mrs. Abraham Blum, a Sephardic Jew from New Orleans, was in charge of the higher branches of learning in two female academies.[22]

— *Helene Samuels Levy Archives,
Congregation B'nai Israel, Galveston*

"Russian Israelites"

In 1888, a group of "Russian Israelites" borrowed a Torah from B'nai Israel to hold their own services, and a second group of new immigrants from the Austro-Hungarian Empire formed another Orthodox group. These two Orthodox congregations, the Hebrew Orthodox Benevolent Association and the Young Men's Hebrew Association, finally merged in 1930 to form a new Galveston congregation, Beth Jacob.[23]

"Texas Brags"

On June 10, 1878, the San Francisco *Jewish Progress* published an article about Galveston, probably written by the Blums, that was an early-day example of "Texas Brags." Excerpts follow.

"I suppose a good many people in your city think that Texas is an entirely wild country, for they hear of so many rough things happening along the Mexican border. But let me tell you that here in this Island City, on the beautiful Gulf of Mexico, everything looks as pleasant as in any other city twice or thrice its size. The Israelites . . . number only about 200 families, but . . . were they to leave, Galveston would soon become provincial . . .

". . . we have a B'nai B'rith Lodge of 85 and a fine Sunday School which numbers 120 pupils. The synagogue has been in charge of Rev. A. Blum since its consecration, and the Hebrew and Sunday schools are flourishing . . . Last Sunday the closing exercises took place. The children [were] questioned on the whole 24 Books of the Bible, then in Jewish history down to the period of Moses Mendelssohn . . ."

The cornerstone of Congregation B'nai Israel's first building in Galveston, shown here, was laid on June 9, 1870, with Masonic rites, funded with a $5,000 bequest from Rosanna Osterman. The building's Gothic style is combined with Moorish revival features. The building was sold in 1953 and has now been converted into a Masonic Temple.[21] It is the oldest structure ever used for a Jewish house of worship still standing in Texas.

— *Rosenberg Library, Galveston, Texas*

— **A French visitor to Dallas, 1864**

Temple Emanu-El's first building was dedicated on the eve of *Shavuoth*, 1876. The small red brick structure, on the corner of Field and Commerce, cost $25,000. In 1899, the congregation moved to a larger building at St. Louis and Ervay.
— *Dorothy M. and Henry S. Jacobus Temple Emanu-El Archives, print by Andy Reisberg*

Reverend Aaron Suhler (1845–1916) was Temple Emanu-El's first rabbi (1875–1879). He later accepted a pulpit in Jefferson, thinking the city would prosper. When Jefferson's economy declined, Suhler moved to Waco to serve Temple Rodef Sholom (1883–1885). Suhler was a graduate of the Jewish Seminary in Würzburg, Germany; he came to the U.S. in 1872, serving congregations in Akron, Ohio, and Vicksburg, Mississippi, prior to arriving in Texas.
— *Dorothy M. and Henry S. Jacobus Temple Emanu-El Archives, print by Andy Reisberg*

Mrs. Louis (Ottlie) Arons (1848–1940) from Poland was Dallas' first Jewish bride. She came by train in 1872 from New Orleans over the new roadbed of the first railroad ever to reach Dallas. She married Louis Arons (1824–1889), a grocer, in 1873.   — *Dallas Public Library*

Temple Emanu-El, Dallas

The first Jew in Dallas was probably Alexander Simon, who arrived in 1858. He married Julia Levy, the daughter of pioneer Houston Jews, Lewis A. and Mary Levy. Around 1866, the Simons heard the railroad was coming through Brenham in Central Texas. They sold their downtown Dallas property and moved there.

By 1865, Dallas had four Jewish merchants, and on April 1, the *Archives Israelites*, a French newspaper, published the following note, about the previous year's (1864) holidays: "In Dallas, all along Main St., the shops are closed for Rosh Hashonah."[24]

In 1872, eleven Jews from Alsace and Northern Germany organized the Hebrew Benevolent Association, conducted the city's first Jewish services using a Torah borrowed from New Orleans, and bought a cemetery plot. By 1875, Temple Emanu-El (Reform from the beginning) was founded and received a charter — the first temple in North Central Texas.

In 1875, *The American Israelite* described the process by which Mr. Aaron Suhler was selected rabbi.[25] The two candidates, Suhler and the

Rev. Mr. Rosenspitz, delivered Friday night sermons in the B'nai B'rith Hall. Suhler wore plain clothes and delivered a sermon in German, which was "short, earnest, and impressive, carrying his audience with him from the very start and virtually electing himself." Rosenspitz, wearing full robes with cap and *talith*, spoke in English for forty-five minutes. Mr. Suhler was elected almost unanimously.

In 1876, Temple Emanu-El adopted the *Minhag America* prayerbook and dedicated its first building. (Dallas had about 500 Jews.) One-half of the temple was used as a synagogue and the other half as a nondenominational public school. Suhler founded a Sunday school which, by 1879, had fifty students and two female assistants. The *American Israelite* of March 28, 1879, noted that "The parents of the children seem to be . . . remiss, for . . . none of them ever think of visiting the school." In 1896, the temple adopted the *Hebrew Union Prayerbook* and advertised in 1897 for an "English scholar, Rabbi and Lec-

turer, with a yearly stipend of $2,000." In 1906, the temple joined the Union of American Hebrew Congregations.

Temple Emanu-El's early roster included the city's "merchant princes" and their wives: Sanger, Kahn, and Linz, mainly German Jews, who contributed to the general community as city councilmen, volunteer firemen, school board members, and later as leaders in cultural institutions like the symphony orchestra and the Grand Opera Association.

Jewish social and philanthropic organizations also sprang up. The B'nai B'rith lodge, organized in 1873, soon had sixty-one members. The Ladies' Hebrew Benevolent Society was active. The Southwest's first YMHA Hall was in downtown Dallas, and in 1879 Dallas delegates attended the national convention of the American Hebrew Association.[26]

Small surrounding towns without burial grounds often took bodies to nearby cities. When the Jews of Corsicana sent the body of a fellow Jew to be buried in Dallas, Temple Emanu-El complied and even paid the $10.25 funeral expenses. However, they wrote to Corsicana stating they would appreciate *not* receiving any more bodies without the accompanying funds.

Samuel Iralson, "a scholarly gentleman," was the first president of Congregation Shearith Israel (1884–1892). The congregation was originally known as Shaareth [sic] Israel, "A remnant of Israel."
— *From the Archives of Congregation Shearith Israel*

Charles Goldstein, Shearith Israel's second president (1892–1896), joined the Klondike, Alaska, Gold Rush in 1896 and made a fortune. He donated funds for a down payment on a lot in downtown Dallas as the site for the congregation's first building. He died in 1904, leaving a bequest which was sufficient to clear the building's mortgage.
— *From the Archives of Congregation Shearith Israel*

Congregation Shearith Israel

Jewish immigrants coming to Dallas after 1880 from Eastern Europe and Russia were not comfortable with the Reform movement. In 1884, J. Emin, L. Levy, and M. Wasserman organized an Orthodox congregation, Shearith Israel. Mr. Wasserman secured a *Sefer Torah,* and with his own hands sewed and decorated its white satin cover with gold braid and embroidery. By 1886, the congregation had twenty families and a state charter. Shearith Israel dedicated its first building in 1892, and the next year hired its first rabbi, Nehemiah Mosessohn of Philadelphia, a noted scholar who stayed for five years. Mosessohn worked closely with the rabbi of Temple Emanu-El, Dr. George A. Kohut.[27]

Goosevalley: "Everyone tried to help the greenhorns."

Dallas' early Eastern European Jews lived in an area nicknamed "Little Jerusalem" and "Goosevalley" because the residents owned geese. It was located on the northern edge of present-day downtown Dallas (Alamo, Caroline, and Wichita streets). Most residents were poor Jews who had fled the Russian Czar and the pogroms of Eastern Europe. Early residents recall their strong sense of community and sharing. Reminiscences included the following: "Few . . . had money . . . Many in a family would work — money was pooled together" . . . "[They] shared everybody's joys and everybody's sorrow."

People came to weddings whether they were invited or not. Cooking, baking, and sewing were communal activities. Women could not enter bars but little girls could. Annie Donosky Margules (b. 1892) recalled earning a few pennies by buying a bucket of "suds" for adult women.[28]

Congregation Tiferet Israel

Goosevalley residents received a charter for the Orthodox congregation, Tiferet Israel, on March 15, 1890. Frank Byers was president from 1893 to 1927. The first services were held at the home of Jake Donosky on Alamo Street. His was one of the few homes which were so *frum* (ritually clean) that Orthodox rabbis ate there. In 1893, Byers and Donosky advanced $1,050 to buy a house on

Wives of the founders of Shearith Israel, l. to r.: Mrs. M. Wasserman, Mrs. Charles Goldstein, and Mrs. S. L. Myer.
— *From the Archives of Congregation Shearith Israel*

Highland Street (now Akard) to use as a synagogue. Men and women entered the sanctuary through different doors and sat in separate sections, the women in an area behind the Torahs, separated by a curtain with a small opening at the top. Services were held there until 1902, when a building was erected.[29]

Prayer in the Dallas public schools was a problem as early as 1884, when Miss Leila Cowart, the principal of Columbian Elementary School, led students and teachers in a daily rendition of a Christian hymn, "Come, Thou Almighty King." Although three-fourths of the students were Jewish, their parents were too afraid to protest.[30]

Shearith Israel's first building, an imposing red brick structure on Jackson Street in downtown Dallas, was dedicated in 1892.   — *From the Archives of Congregation Shearith Israel*

Temple Beth-El

In 1870, the San Antonio Ladies Hebrew Benevolent Society was organized in the home of Mrs. Louis Zork "to relieve families of Jewish faith in distress and to do such duties to dead females of the Jewish faith as are necessary." In 1872, a handful of Jews held religious services in the Ruellman Hall opposite Joskes, near the Alamo. By 1874, a B'nai B'rith lodge was founded, and a group of men met to organize Temple Beth-El.

Temple Beth-El's first building was dedicated on September 10, 1875. A resolution was passed asking local Israelites to close their businesses during the Friday evening dedication services. The board voted to join the Union of American Hebrew Congregations and by a 16–5 majority, to adopt the *Minhag America* prayerbook. The trustees authorized the building to be lit by gas. The first rabbi was hired in 1879–1880, at which time there were about thirty-five Jewish families in town, totaling 250 individuals.

In 1882, the Temple Ladies held a fund-raising fair. One of the items donated was from the Sisters of Charity of the Incarnate Word — a beautifully worked Old Irish Point handkerchief in appreciation for the Jewish women's "constant liberality towards our poor." In 1891, the temple orga-

Samuel Mayer (1837–1920), a native of Heidelberg, Germany, was the first president of San Antonio's Temple Beth-El, serving two terms, 1874–1880. Samuel, who had been a Confederate officer, married Carolyn Jacobs Mayer (1840–1938), and the couple established a millinery business. After the war, the couple and their infant son drove with an ox team to Bagdad, Mexico, where they embarked in an open boat for New York. The boat was seized off Key West by a U.S. cutter looking for contraband. None was found and the boat was released. During the voyage food was so scarce that a porpoise was caught and eaten.[31]
— *UT Institute of Texan Cultures*

nized a Ladies' Hebrew Cemetery Association. Rabbi J. Hyman Elkins served from 1892–1897 for $175 a month. His Saturday morning lectures were found distasteful and he was told to dispense with them. Rabbi Samuel Marks came to the temple in 1897 and remained until 1934.

The dedication plaque for Agudas Achim Synagogue, 1898.
— *UT Institute of Texan Cultures*

"Do you want to go to America and become a *shaygetz* (Gentile)?"

Orthodoxy, too, made its way to San Antonio. When Jacob Schmidt wanted to emigrate to the New World, his father objected, asking, "Do you want to go to America and become a *shaygetz* (Gentile)?" Jacob *did* emigrate — to Texas — and was a founding member of Congregation Agudas Achim. His father would have been proud.

In 1883, Gemilath Hasodim (The Practice of Kindness) was organized to care for the sick, bury the dead, comfort the bereaved, and assist the needy. The group dedicated a cemetery and organized a Ladies Auxiliary in 1885. In 1889, they reorganized as Congregation Agudas Achim and in 1890, hired Rabbi Moses Sadovsky of Savannah, Georgia. He founded a Talmud Torah (religious school), which lasted until 1954. (By then, the city had three local congregations who decided to operate their own schools.) At first, Agudas Achim was Orthodox, with women sitting in the balcony, apart from the men. It is now Conservative.

Social activities have always been important in San Antonio. A YMHA was organized in 1879. Jewish social clubs in 1881 and 1882 included the Casino Club, the Turners' Association Masked Ball, and the French Social Club.[32]

Temple Beth-El's first building was dedicated in 1875 at the corner of Jefferson and Travis streets in San Antonio. It cost $25,000.
— *Wanda Graham Ford Collection,
San Antonio Conservation Society,
copy from UT Institute of Texan Cultures*

— Charles Wessolowsky

The Temple Beth Israel Sunday school class, c. 1880. Henry Hirshfeld was the temple's first president in 1876, and his daughter, Laura, was a student in the Sunday school.
— *Hirshfeld Papers (AR/H.24), Austin History Center, Austin Public Library*

Temple Beth Israel, Austin

Austin's first Jewish resident was probably Phineas de Cordova, who moved to the capital city in 1850 at the request of Governor P. H. Bell to publish a newspaper, the *Southwestern American*. Phineas' son, Samuel (1861–1909), may have been one of the first Jewish babies born in Austin. Phineas was a founder and the first vice-president of Temple Beth Israel in 1876, and a Grand Master of the Odd Fellows lodge.

By 1866, there were a sufficient number of Jews in Austin to set aside a section of Oakwood Cemetery for "Israelites." Temple Beth Israel, a Reform congregation, was organized in 1876 and bought a downtown site at 11th and San Jacinto in 1877. By 1879, there were about thirty-five Jewish families, and the temple applied for a charter.

When Charles Wessolowsky visited Austin in 1879, Phineas de Cordova gave him a tour of the city. Wessolowsky reported that the Jews "are carrying on a vast and extensive business, and some of them are old citizens of Austin, having resided there for the past 26 years; and those in particular are enjoying the respect and goodwill of all." The Sunday school had been recently established "under the call of the *Jewish South,*" Wessolowsky's newspaper. Mr. S. Philipson was superintendent, "full of zeal," and Mrs. D. Friedman (formerly principal of a Sunday school in Chattanooga) was "principal in the female department." Bro. A. Goldbaum was president of the B'nai B'rith lodge. Wessolowsky lamented the absence of a Hebrew Ladies Aid Society: "Our Jewish ladies in Austin, no doubt, fully understand their duties and all they would need, perhaps, is a 'reminder.' "[33]

In 1880, the women of Beth Israel organized a masked ball to raise money for the construction of a new synagogue, and by 1883 had organized a Ladies Aid Society.[34] By 1884, the temple, which had been meeting in the Odd Fellows Hall, held their first services in the new sanctuary at 11th and San Jacinto and hired their first rabbi, Tobias Schanfarber.[35]

Malevin was known as the "Walking Talmud."

While in the Austin area, Wessolowsky visited Jews in nearby communities.[36] In Rockdale, there were 100 Jews and a B'nai B'rith lodge whose members planned to inaugurate a Sunday school. However, there was disagreement over rituals. Wessolowsky reported that "some of them still cling and hold fast to the doctrines and dead forms of the so-called *chasid* (pietist), while others require and ask for 'progress' . . . Marlin, with half as many Jews, boasted of a Mr. Malevin, who was known as the 'walking Talmud.' "

In Calvert, with over 100 Jews and twenty Jewish families, Wessolowsky met Leon Strauss, who taught English and Hebrew to twenty young pupils. A certain "F" had written to the *Jewish South* that Strauss was an old fogey and a "northern importation," but Wessolowsky thought Strauss was doing a good job. The next year, Rabbi Jacob Voorsanger of Houston went to Calvert and encouraged the Jews to build a synagogue. Though money was raised and land procured, no structure was ever built.

Miss Emma Beer was organist and Sunday school superintendent for Waco's Temple Rodef Sholom from 1893 to 1897 at a monthly salary of $20. At one point, she clashed with Rabbi E. M. Myers over the selection of hymns. The dispute was brought before the board, who sided with the rabbi, "that hymns of Jewish character shall be sung." The board instructed her henceforth to submit a list in advance to the rabbi.
  — The Texas Collection, Baylor University, Waco, Texas

Temple Rodef Sholom (Pursuing Peace), Waco, was dedicated in 1881 with a spectacular affair. The building cost $8,000 which was raised from non-Jews as well as Jews. The Waco *Telephone* [September 17, 1881] reported that "The edifice recalls . . . the oriental era in Jewish history . . . Byzantine . . . The spires and minarets are the perfection of symmetrical beauty . . ."
  — Ima Joy Chodorow (Mrs. J. E.) Gandler

"Alas!, only one family is orthodox, the rest reform."
— American Israelite, 1876

In the early 1860s, the Reform movement newspaper, the *American Israelite,* had several subscribers in Waco, and by 1869, it published frequent reports from local correspondents. Most of Waco's pioneer Jews were Reform but kept *kashrut.* In 1869, they organized a Hebrew Benevolent Association, bought land for the Hebrew Rest Cemetery, and in October, according to the Waco *Weekly Register,* closed their businesses for the Jewish holidays. The Waco B'nai B'rith lodge was formed in 1873 — the same year B'nai B'rith was founded in the South.

By 1876, there were 150 Jews in Waco, and religious services were held in rented rooms, in stores, or in homes. Peddlers and small merchants came to worship from fifty miles around, arriving by foot or on horseback.

Rodef Sholom

In 1879, the Hebrew Benevolent Association's Torah passed into the hands of the newly organized Rodef Sholom, whose first president was Sam Sanger. The temple soon had regular worship services and a flourishing religious school. A Ladies Hebrew Aid Society was organized and sponsored a dance which raised $500 for the new temple building, dedicated in 1881. Women played an important part in the religious and cultural life of Waco. They not only raised funds for the temple's first building but raised funds for the YMHA and the cemetery, and taught Sunday school.

In 1887, the city's Jewish youth founded Our Unique Club. One of its first projects was a musical to raise funds for a resident rabbi. The program included Jennie Friedman singing, "The Convention at Sanger's Front Gate," which brought down the house. Apparently, the group was successful because Rodef Sholom soon hired its first rabbi — Rev.

Abraham Levy. He left after one year for a pulpit in Chicago, where he was arrested on charges of embezzlement.

In 1888, the Ladies Society gave its annual Calico Hop: "The young ladies looked sweeter than ever in their calico costumes . . . chewing gum was supreme." The temple hired a rabbi from Brooklyn, Dr. J. Rosenburgh, whose activities, such as his appeal for a public hospital, received frequent coverage in the daily papers. He invited the entire community to a lecture in German on the absolute necessity of the Hebrew language for Judaism.

The temple's early rabbis didn't stay long. Dr. Rosenburgh left in 1890, and the temple advertised for a rabbi who could officiate in *Minhag Jastrow* and deliver sermons in English. By 1898, the temple's rabbi, H. Weiss, was circuit preaching to nearby towns, along with Rabbi A. Suhler.

Agudath Jacob

By 1886, an Orthodox segment in Waco was holding services in a room over a grocery store. Samuel Levy came from Minsk, Russia, via Troy, New York. Many Reform families used him as their *schochet* and probably also as *mohel.* In 1888, the Orthodox group chartered Congregation Agudath Jacob, and in 1894 they bought a lot and built a frame synagogue.[37]

Sam Sanger

In 1882, Sam Sanger organized the Russian Refugee Society after the passage of the Czar's infamous May Laws.[38] By 1888, the Waco B'nai B'rith lodge had seventy-five members, and Sanger was on the board of the B'nai B'rith Orphan Asylum in Cleveland. In 1900, he raised an emergency fund of $50 for twenty Romanian Jews, who had been apportioned to Waco.

In 1892, Brenham Jews built their first synagogue, B'nai Abraham, but it soon burned. It was immediately rebuilt in 1893 and is still used on occasion for High Holiday services. Said to be the oldest Orthodox synagogue in continuous use in Texas, its architectural style is similar to that of many rural Baptist churches.[39]
— *Texas Historical Commission*

Rabbi Heinrich Schwarz (1824–1900) and his wife Julia Nathan Schwarz came to Hempstead around 1875 at the urging of his large family, who had settled there. He was ordained in Germany and is said to have had a Ph.D. from the University of Berlin. He was rabbi of the Hempstead congregation, consisting largely of members of his extended family. The couple both wrote poetry and were educated in German, English, French, Hebrew, and Latin. Rabbi Schwarz also wrote Talmudic interpretations in German and Aramaic.[40]
— *The Texas Collection, Baylor University, Waco, Texas*

Rabbi Jacob Voorsanger visits Brenham

B. Levinson, the first Jewish immigrant in Washington County (Brenham) arrived in 1861 and was followed in 1866 by Alex and Julia Simon from Dallas.[41] By 1880, there were about fourteen Jewish families, all in retail businesses. The only Jewish organization was a B'nai B'rith lodge. When Charles Wessolowsky visited the community in 1879, he "found no unity nor sociability among them. Every one seems to live within himself and for himself, always believing and thinking how mean and low his neighbor." Wessolowsky found Jewish children regularly attending "Christian" Sunday school. One "noble widow lady" offered her services to the other parents as a religious teacher, "but met with no success."[42]

Another visitor in 1879 was the Rev. Jacob Voorsanger from Houston, who had responded to an invitation from the city's Hebrew Benevolent Society (HBS). The Society may have been disturbed by the remarks of Mr. Wessolowsky. The *Brenham Banner* (November 18, 1879) reported that Voorsanger delivered an interesting lecture at the Opera House to an appreciative audience of Hebrews and Christians. The paper reported that Voorsanger was "a man of great learning, deep research, a fine theologian and an orator of the 'first water.'" The HBS organized a Sunday school and a Bible class.

By 1885, there were apparently enough Jews to organize a congregation, and B'nai Abraham was founded. Louis Fink was the president in 1892. Hortense Yarno Kamin recalled how her family settled in Brenham: "They had started west when they arrived from Lithuania, speaking no English; only Yiddish and German. They boarded a train, and a conductor who spoke German told them Brenham was the place to go because so many people spoke German and they would feel right at home . . . The synagogue still stands just as it was built . . . everything except the *mikva*, which I'm told my grandfather did away with . . . The men sat downstairs on benches that pinched; the women sat upstairs. Someone was always calling upstairs for the females to be quiet . . ."[43] Kamin recalled that their rabbi killed chickens in the morning and taught Hebrew in the afternoon.

Why did Jews come to Hempstead?

Edis Schwarz, the wife of a Schwarz descendant, speculates that Jews settled in Hempstead because, "That was where the horse died."[44] One of the first Jews in Hempstead was Sam Schwarz (1840–1918) from Kempen, Prussia, who came in 1866.[45] His brother Gabriel, a traveling optometrist, had settled there two years before. Sam was a Civil War veteran and a member of the Hempstead School Board for twenty years. In 1928, the Sam Schwarz Training School for (Negro) Teachers was dedicated in his honor. His daughter, Gussie Schwarz Galewsky, a musician and a member of the local literary society, spoke at the ceremony and presented the deed to the property. She said, "A good name is rather to be chosen than riches."[46] The building was funded by the Rosenwald Foundation, established by Julius Rosenwald, Sears Roebuck chairman, to help Southern Negro schools.

Giddings and Navasota

In 1879, the nearby towns of Giddings and Navasota had about fifty Jews each. In Navasota, Wessolowsky met a thirteen-year-old correspondent for the children's department of the *Jewish South,* "very tall and advanced in her studies," who used the pseudonym "Gussie." The Navasota Jewish cemetery in Navasota was started in 1900.[47]

In the days before photojournalism, the only known likenesses of Diamond Bessie Moore and Abe Rothschild were taken from newspaper sketches based on photographs of the couple sold in Jefferson during the murder trials. Diamond Bessie was also known as Annie Stone Moore (Rothschild).
— *Jefferson Carnegie Library, copy from Fred Tarpley,* Jefferson: Riverport to the Southwest

The Diamond Bessie Murder Trials

On January 17, 1877, a couple arrived in Marshall, Texas, and registered in the Capitol Hotel as "A. Rothschild and wife, Cin'ti, O. [Cincinnati, Ohio]." On Friday, January 19, they traveled to nearby Jefferson, at that time the greatest inland shipping port in the Southwest. They checked into the Brooks House Hotel as "A. Monroe and wife" with a trunk marked "Annie Moore, New Orleans." The gentleman was handsome; the lady was beautiful and bedecked with diamonds. Soon after their arrival, they were overheard arguing in their room. The next Sunday, a mild, drizzly, foggy day, the couple left the hotel for a picnic in the woods. The man returned later in the day without his wife but wearing her two diamond rings. When questioned as to her whereabouts, he said she was visiting friends. On Tuesday, he left town with the trunk.

For the next two weeks, Jefferson had cold weather, sleet and snow. On February 5, Diamond Bessie's body was found in the woods, a bullet hole through her forehead and without her diamonds. The Dallas *Weekly Herald* of March 10, 1877, reported, "At Jefferson . . . the sentiment is almost unanimous — that hanging is almost too good for the woman murderer, and that a slow fire should be started under him . . . it is pretty certain that

if Abe Rothschild is brought back to Jefferson from Cincinnati, he will not escape a felon's death."

Before Rothschild could be extradited, he attempted suicide by firing a pistol at his head, blinding his right eye. His family fought extradition, but the Ohio court denied their request. The Marion County sheriff brought Rothschild back to Jefferson in April 1877. Although his family had disowned him before the murder because he had a reputation as a gambler, they hired the best available attorneys for his defense.

Rothschild's attorneys successfully obtained a change of venue to nearby Marshall on the grounds of extreme prejudice in Marion County. His first trial was not held until December 1878. He was found guilty of murder in the first degree and sentenced "to be hanged by the neck until he is dead and that he pay the cost of this prosecution." Tradition has it that the foreman drew a picture of a noose on the wall, signed his name, and said, "That's my verdict."

The verdict was overturned by an appellate court, and the second trial took place two years later, on December 14, 1880. The verdict of not guilty was rendered two weeks later. The next day, the *Jefferson Democrat* reported that Rothschild "left the same night" on the train with his parents for their home in Cincinnati.

Soon after the trial was over, the myths and legends began. It was al-

leged that the jurors had been bribed with thousand-dollar bills stuffed down through the jury room ceiling. Although much of the circumstantial evidence pointed to Rothschild, the well-preserved condition of the body indicated that perhaps it could not have lain in the woods for two weeks, and therefore, someone else must have killed Diamond Bessie. Other tales abounded: that she was a prostitute, Rothschild's common law wife or his legal wife, that she was pregnant, that he murdered her to steal her diamonds to pay off his gambling debts, or that he was related to the European Rothschilds. Today, the most frequently visited grave in Jefferson's Oakwood Cemetery is Diamond Bessie's.[48]

Diamond Bessie

The Diamond Bessie murder trial was the most sensational event of its day in Texas. High-powered attorneys wanted to be involved, and David B. Culberson, the district's U.S. congressman and defense lawyer for Rothschild, staked his political career on the case. Today, the mystery of Diamond Bessie's murder continues to fascinate historians and folklorists alike.

Since the late 1950s, fact and fiction have been inextricably mingled in a popular folk drama, "The Diamond Bessie Murder Trial."[49] In a kind of supreme irony, the play is reenacted annually in the Jefferson Playhouse, which was once the Hebrew Sinai Synagogue. The murder has never been solved, and the mystery continues to intrigue the public as well as historians. Dr. James W. Byrd, a professor at East Texas State University, says that Rothschild did not kill Bessie, while Dr. Fred Tarpley, also at ETSU, disagrees: "There's no question about it. Abe murdered Bessie."[50]

— Brenham *Weekly Banner,* August 29, 1879

Rear view of the Hebrew Sinai Synagogue in Jefferson which once housed a convent owned by the Sisters of Charity of St. Vincent de Paul. After the Hebrew Sinai congregation was incorporated in 1873, they bought the building from the Sisters of Charity. The facility consists of the original convent and school building, as well as an addition built in 1876 by the Congregation.[51] In the 1950s, the property was transferred to the Jessie Allen Wise Garden Club in exchange for their perpetual care of the Jewish cemetery.[52] It is now known as the Jefferson Playhouse.
— *From the papers of Judge Sam C. Eldridge, copy from UT Institute of Texan Cultures*

Eva Eberstadt (1880–1974) (top) was a Jefferson music teacher who is shown here with her friend, Daisy Benefield Bower, c. 1910. Eva studied music at the Kidd-Key Female Academy in Sherman, as well as in New York and Europe. Her father, who was from Darmstadt, Germany, played an important role in the founding of the Hebrew Sinai Synagogue.[53] Eva's inlaid mother-of-pearl lap desk, black walnut music cabinet, and book of prayers in German for Jewish women are on display in the Jefferson Historical Museum.
— *Bower Family Album, print by Frankie McConnell*

Philip Eldridge (1833–1924), who came to Jefferson around 1867, is shown with his grandchildren, l. to r., Zellner Eldridge, and Zellner's first cousins, Margaret Eldridge and Elizabeth Eldridge (Bettelheim), c. 1911. The Eldridges lived next door to the Hebrew Sinai Synagogue, and after it closed, they became custodians of the synagogue records and ritual objects. They transferred the eternal lamp to the Jefferson Museum, where it is now on display. When Philip died at age ninety-two, he was thought to be the oldest living member of B'nai B'rith. (He had originally been a member of the lodge in Sherman.)[54] Two of Philip's sons became prominent attorneys: Samuel was a county judge and secretary of San Antonio's Temple Beth El for forty-six years; David was a Dallas County judge and secretary of Temple Emanu-El. Another son, Henry Eldridge, was one of the founders of Jefferson's Carnegie Library.[55]
— *Margaret Eldridge, copy from UT Institute of Texan Cultures*

The Hebrew Sinai Congregation

After the Civil War, Jefferson was a thriving commercial riverport which reached its peak of prosperity in the mid-1870s. On June 2, 1873, Jewish leaders organized the Hebrew Sinai Congregation, and in 1875 purchased a convent and school from the Sisters of Charity of St. Vincent de Paul. The congregation built an addition in 1876. In June 1879, local Jews presented an opera, "Esther, the Beautiful Queen," which deals with the oppression of Jews in ancient times. Queen Esther was portrayed by Eva Sterne, the daughter of postmistress Ernestine Sterne. The pianist was Eva Eberstadt. In August 1879, Rabbi Aaron Suhler of Dallas' Temple Emanu-El, was hired as Jefferson's spiritual leader.

The same year Jefferson Jews incorporated the Hebrew Sinai Congregation [1873], the U.S. government removed the natural dam of logs which had made steamboat travel to Jefferson possible. Jefferson began an economic decline, and most Jews left. In 1989, only one Jew remained.

Burial Rights

In the absence of a resident rabbi, Jefferson Jews, like those in other small towns, were frequently faced with trying to interpret Jewish law. In 1873, E. Eberstadt read a letter from Isaac M. Wise to the Jefferson Hebrew Benevolent Association,[56] apparently in response to a previous inquiry from the Association about an uncircumcised child who had been buried in the city's Jewish Cemetery.

Cincinnati, Novr 28, 1872
Mr. E. Eberstadt
Dear Sir:
    According to the Talmud and the Orthodox rule, the child of a Jewish mother is a Jew to all intents and purposes, hence may be buried, or rather ought to be buried according to Jewish rites and on Jewish burial grounds. I must tell you that the above rule is not mine, but in regard to burial the Talmud says, "Also the dead of heathens may be buried with the dead of Israel, to serve the cause of peace," hence in this case there can certainly be no objection.
        Yours,
            Isaac M. Wise

Temple Moses Montefiore, Marshall

In 1868, a Hebrew Benevolent Society was organized in Marshall, and by 1869, it had twenty-five members. In 1873, Rabbi M. Greenblatt of Shreveport, fleeing from a yellow fever epidemic, wrote to the *American Israelite* that he celebrated *Rosh Hoshanah* in Marshall with ten Jewish families in Bernstein's Hall. "The audience was large and appreciative," he reported.

In 1877, a Sabbath school was organized with twenty children. Weekly meetings were held in the home of Mrs. E. Baerwald under the direction of Mrs. Goldstein, "a very able teacher, in both English and Hebrew." In 1879, Joe Weisman was president of the B'nai B'rith lodge. By 1887, Jews in Marshall founded a new congregation, Temple Moses Montefiore Adath Israel. The first president was Daniel Doppelmayer. Rabbi Hyman Saft came from Mt. Vernon, Indiana, to serve as their rabbi. He and his family remembered using mosquito netting over their beds to keep away lizards, bats, and snakes.

In 1892, the Hebrew Ladies Aid Society organized. Membership was limited to twenty married women and carried considerable social prestige. This kind of limitation was the rule in many non-sectarian Texas women's clubs of the day. In 1899, the Society organized a Moses Montefiore Fair Association with the help of several prominent Christian women. They raised $1,500 to help build the temple, which was dedicated the following year. In 1909, a masquerade ball was held to raise money for a new organ for the temple. One woman came as an organ grinder and carried a live monkey. They raised the money.[57]

The ark of the covenant, housing the Torah scrolls of Temple Moses Montefiore, was donated by the late Morris Kariel. The temple, named for the British Jewish philanthropist Sir Moses Montefiore, was dedicated in 1900.
— *Photo by Frankie McConnell,* Marshall News Messenger

The tombstone of Lion Kahn is one of the largest in the Marshall Hebrew Cemetery. Lion fought for the Union. His brother Emanuel fought for the Confederacy. Their business, the Great Railway Supply Store, became the major supplier for Jay Gould's Texas and Pacific Railroad. Lion Kahn left $5,000 in his will to establish a hospital, which was named for him — the Kahn Memorial Hospital.
— *Louis DeLuca*

Ike Hochwald

Ike Hochwald came to Marshall in 1877 from the New Orleans Jewish Widows and Orphans Home to begin a new life as the ward of a bachelor merchant, Lion Kahn. After the death of Lion and Emanuel Kahn, Hochwald inherited their business, the Great Railway Supply Store, and prospered. The store's primary customers were sharecroppers and employees of the Texas and Pacific Railroad.

Hochwald and his wife, Amelia Raphael Hochwald, built a large and ornate two-story clapboard Queen Ann mansion. He owned the city's first car, which ran on electricity. To compensate for the absence of a reverse gear, he installed a revolving iron turntable in a driveway next to their home so that the car would always be aimed forward. Hochwald was a trustee of the school board, introduced Rotary and scouting to Marshall, and was president of the East Texas Baseball League.[58]

Isaac (Ike) Hochwald (1865–1956) was the president of Temple Moses Montefiore when it was built in 1900.
— *Audrey D. Kariel, Marshall, Texas*

— Fort Worth *Gazette,* March 10, 1886

"This is somewhat of a frontier place . . ."[59]

— Charles Wessolowsky

By 1874, Fort Worth had a B'nai B'rith lodge and a Hebrew Educational and Charitable Society. Rev. Abraham Blum of Temple B'nai Israel in Galveston established a Sunday school with Joseph Meyer as principal, and Misses Julia and Rosa Weiner and Dora Fry as teachers.[60] In 1879, John Peter Smith, a non-Jewish community leader, donated an acre of land "to the Israelites of the city, . . . to be used as a burial ground." The Jews received a deed to the Emanuel Hebrew Rest Cemetery in 1882.[61]

In 1886, Jewish women gave a select ball to raise funds for the cemetery. The local paper reported that "There was a joyous scene . . . a long table spread with a super abundance of refreshments, while above the spacious hall was devoted to dancing, in which all participated 'till past the midnight hour. Among the ladies present were Rosa Kahn, in pale pink and blue silk; Miss Mary Friedman, white nun's veiling and pink plush; . . . Miss Rachel Gabert, brown silk." In 1896, Mrs. Babette Carb organized the Emanuel Hebrew Association to maintain the cemetery grounds.

In 1892, Ahavath Sholom, an Orthodox congregation, organized and received their charter. In 1894, they bought a lot, and the following year, built a small synagogue which cost $640. By 1906, the congregation had grown to the extent that a new building was constructed, and yet another in 1914. Congregational minutes were in Yiddish, and the synagogue served as the site for a Hebrew school, as well as dances, luncheons, dinners, and later, meetings of Hadassah and Young Judaea.

Unlike most of the other Texas cities, Fort Worth's Orthodox Jews organized before the Reform group. The Reform congregation, Beth El, was not organized until 1902.[62]

The Philip Greenwall family, c. 1891, Fort Worth. Seated is Philip Greenwall. Also pictured are his wife, Almira Greenwall, and their children, Mary "Mamie" and Mitchell. Philip Greenwall was a founding member in 1902 of Temple Beth El in Fort Worth.
— *Pan Greenwall Jones, copy from Tarrant County Historical Commission*

Moses Shanblum was a devout Jew from Russia who moved to Fort Worth in the 1880s. Concerned that local Jews were adapting to Christian ways, he founded Congregation Ahavath Sholom, chartered in 1892. He left his wife to tend their store, while he spent his time raising money for a synagogue. As a result of his efforts, by 1895 enough money (including all of his funds) was collected to erect a small frame building. Shanblum was also an ardent Zionist, chair of the building committee for the Hebrew Institute, c. 1914, and president of the Hebrew School in 1925.[63]

— *Congregation Ahavath Sholom*

The Fort Worth Opera House, the Finest in the State

The Greenwalls were theatrical impresarios whose influence was felt throughout the Southwest. In 1867, Henry Greenwall and his brother Morris were partners in managing the Old Galveston Theatre. In 1871, Henry leased opera houses in Houston and Galveston and soon expanded to Dallas. He even took over the Grand Opera House in New Orleans. Henry and a partner organized the American Theatrical Exchanges, with offices in New York City, and booked shows throughout the South.

In 1890, Henry Greenwall bought the Fort Worth Opera House. He changed its name to Greenwall's Opera House and hired his brother Philip as manager. It featured new and intricate lighting and sound systems and booked world-renowned acts like Sarah Bernhardt, Douglas Fairbanks, John Philip Sousa, and the Barrymores. With the growth of the film industry, the Opera House became the Palace Movie Theatre in 1936.

70   *"Palestine, Texas. Rosh Hashanah and Yom Kippur were duly*

celebrated here."   **American Israelite, October 2, 1885**

Tyler

Many towns in North and East Texas, like Tyler, Palestine, Wichita Falls, Sherman, Denison, Paris, and Gainesville, had dozens of Jewish merchants who served the predominantly agricultural communities.

By the 1880s, Tyler had about an equal number of Reform immigrants (many from Posen, East Prussia) and Orthodox Jews from Russia. Fifty-three families chartered Temple Beth El, a Reform congregation, in 1887. Their first building was consecrated on June 16, 1889, with the Reverend E. M. Chapman, rabbi of Dallas' Temple Emanu-El, officiating.[64]

In 1897, Orthodox Jews began meeting in the Woodman's Hall. The *Sefer Torah* was kept in the home of Mr. and Mrs. A. Golenternek. By 1903, Congregation Ahavath Achim received a charter, and in 1910, built a small wooden synagogue. The mayor sent greetings, and a small girl, Hattie Fleischner, carried the Torah into the *shul*.[65]

"In Washington, it's the White House — in Texarkana it's I. Schwarz Co. Department Store."

By the late 1800s, Texarkana had a thriving Jewish community. Marks Kosminsky and Joseph Deutschmann

Sam Roosth (1888–1949), a native of Korycin, Poland, arrived in Galveston in 1907. He sent for and married Celia (1883–1928), his childhood sweetheart. They lived briefly in Marshall, where Sam worked as a baker's helper. They moved to Tyler in 1910 and operated Roosth Bakery. In 1931, Sam and his friend, Aleck S. Genecov, founded the partnership Roosth and Genecov. Their business interests have included real estate, cattle, and oil, and the association is carried on by family members to this day. The Roosths and the Genecovs have been major benefactors of many Tyler institutions and generous supporters of Congregation Ahavath Achim.
— *Jewish National Fund*

were among the first Jews to settle there in 1875. When Charles Wessolowsky visited in 1879, he found about ten Jewish families. The Jews tried to worship on the important holidays, and "at times an apostate Jew [Charles Goldberg], now being a staunch Christian . . . is the selected preacher. He like others of his kind . . . are neither Jews nor Christians . . ."[66] Goldberg reverted to Judaism on his deathbed in 1886, sent for the rabbi, and asked to be buried in the Jewish cemetery.

In 1885, Jews held their first High Holy Day services, led by Rabbi Friedman of Camden, Arkansas. Nettie Marx married Larry Klein and their wedding gifts, listed in the paper, included a bronze lamp, a gold thimble, and a glove stretcher. In 1903, Nettie received a medical degree from the Dallas Medical College.

In 1890, Deutschmann, president of the Hebrew Benevolent Association, purchased the Episcopal Church and moved the building to Eighth and State Line, where it became the synagogue for the Mount Sinai Congregation. It burned in 1892, and a new building was dedicated in 1894. The first full-time rabbi, A. Shriber, was hired around 1900. Deutschmann was part owner of the first streetcar lines (mule-driven), and the water and gas company. Kosminsky was the town's leading merchant. The local paper reported on October 15, 1884, that Kosminsky set a worthy example, "by employing a young lady clerk

behind his counters to attend to lady customers. In the East, dry goods houses employ female clerks in preference to males."[67]

Nearby towns

By 1880, Sherman had a B'nai B'rith lodge, Denison had a Jewish editor of the local *Evening Herald,* and Paris (Texas) had ten Jewish families. In 1881, the United Hebrew Congregation of Gainesville was chartered, and a building was constructed and used until the 1920s. Jewish merchants catering to farmers in much smaller towns came to worship and socialize in these outposts.[68]

"Palestine, Texas.

Rosh Hashanah and Yom Kippur were duly celebrated here. The Jewish business houses were closed . . . Services were impressively delivered at Library Hall by Mr. M. Winner . . . The Home Social Dramatic Club, composed almost entirely of Israelites, . . . will commence rehearsing at once. All the Jewish merchants who have been East to purchase their stocks are home again. The social season will soon begin here, then there will be plenty of fun for everybody."
— *American Israelite,* October 2, 1885

When Charles Wessolowsky visited Palestine in 1879, he found 100 Jews, but no Sunday school, no Ladies' Society, "nothing that . . . could . . . make them feel that they are Israelites." They did not observe the Sabbath, and were no longer willing to repeat the prayer of the Haggadah, "next year in Jerusalem." He told them they were committing a sin, but "Alas, after due reflection we thought that they may be correct in their views after all and that this land of liberty and freedom, this State of fertile soil and rich prairies, with all of its facilities and advantages may perhaps be preferable and more sought for than the dry and barren country of the Palestine of our fathers."[69] The town acquired its name from Protestant settlers who thought the area reminded them of the Holy Land. The town once had a temple, Beth Israel, which met in private homes until the 1940s. Now all that remains is the Jewish cemetery and one Jewish resident.

— Olga Kohlberg

Olga Bernstein (Mrs. Ernst) Kohlberg
(1864–1935) was an El Paso civic and
club leader.
— *UT Institute of Texan Cultures*

In 1888, Sally Dysterbach (Cohn) was
confirmed at Temple Emanu-El in Dallas.
— *Dorothy M. and Henry S. Jacobus Temple
Emanu-El Archives, print by Andy Reisberg*

The report card of Sally Dysterbach
(Cohn) for the school year 1879–1880.
When Aaron Suhler arrived in Dallas in
1875 as rabbi of Temple Emanu-El, one of
his first actions was to establish a non-
sectarian school. The school employed
both Jewish and non-Jewish teachers, and
if a child's parents could not pay the tuition, instruction was free. The school with
sixty boys and seventy girls was one of
Dallas' first interfaith endeavors. It was
discontinued in 1884 after the establishment of the city's public schools.[71]
— *Dorothy M. and Henry S. Jacobus Temple
Emanu-El Archives, print by Andy Reisberg*

Olga Kohlberg founded Texas' first kindergarten

In 1883, Olga Bernstein married
Ernst Kohlberg in Germany and returned with him to El Paso, where he
had a cigar factory. She was well educated and soon mastered both English
and Spanish. Believing that "what
you learn in childhood will have a
lasting effect on your life," she
brought the idea of preschool training
to El Paso from her native land and
led the El Paso Woman's Club to establish the first private kindergarten
in Texas in 1892. Soon, women
around the state took up the kindergarten movement.

Olga was a founder of the El Paso
Public Library in 1895 and president
from 1903 to 1935. She was instrumental in establishing El Paso's first
public hospital and the Cloudcroft
Sanitarium for Underprivileged Children in New Mexico. In 1902, she
was a delegate to the General Federation of Women's Clubs Assembly in
Los Angeles and hosted 500 women
who came through town on their way
to this West Coast meeting. She and
her husband were founders of the
Mount Sinai Congregation in 1898.[70]

Certificate from Congregation Emanu El School, Dallas, Texas,

To Miss *Sally Dysterbach*

FOR THE TERM COMMENCING SEPTEMBER 1879, AND ENDING JUNE

ENGLISH.		GERMAN.		GENERAL REMARKS.
Reading	*Perfect*	Reading	*Good*	*A bright studious*
Spelling and Definition	*very good*	Writing		*little girl, a pleasure*
Grammar		Grammar		*to all her teachers.*
Composition		Russian		**MARKS DURING THE TERM.**
Geography				PERFECT IMPERFECT BAD
Arithmetic	*Good*	**HEBREW.**		
Penmanship		Reading	*Good*	

DEPORTMENT:

Perfect

DR. H. M. BIEN, Superintendent.
Mrs. GEORGIE F. FELTON, 1. Assistant.
Miss ROSIE ROSENTHAL, 2. Assistant.

G. SCHIFF, M. D   } School Committee.
DAVID GOSLIN

SAM. KLEIN,
President Congregation Emanu El

Della Doppelmayer (Handman), c. 1900. Della was the daughter of Daniel Doppelmayer, a Marshall pioneer. In 1914, she married Rabbi Max Handman. Her sister, Bella D. Doppelmayer (Pearce), was in the first graduating class at the University of Texas at Austin in 1886.
— *Mrs. Ruth Ruben, Shreveport, Louisiana*

Music was important in many Jewish homes

Amelia Barr, an Austin writer, recalled in her autobiography (1856) that she knew of only two pianos in town, "one was in the Governor's mansion, the other belonged to a rich Jewish family named [Ben] Henricks."[72] In 1884, Houston had a Jewish Ladies Literary and Musical Union,[73] and in 1893, Austin young ladies organized the Young Hebrew Literary Society.[74]

In 1907, *Beau Monde*, a Dallas society magazine, reported on the marriage of Felice Kahn to Alex Sanger of Waco: "The bride is . . . a young lady who has been carefully reared and beautifully schooled, being devoted to and gifted in music, with a fine discrimination of the classics." Felice, who had been a violinist with the Dallas Symphony Club in 1900, re-

called growing up in a home where the whole family participated in musicals and the reading of Dickens.

Annie Harelik (Novit) remembered that music was important in their home in Dublin, Texas. "We bought Lillie a violin from Butler Brothers for $12.75 . . . Velvel would sing Yiddish songs accompanied by Morris on the clarinet and Fannie on the piano."[75]

Isabella Offenbach Maas

In 1844, Isabella Offenbach (1817–1891), a celebrated German singer, married Samuel Maas (1810–1897), a Texas pioneer. Isabella, the daughter of a rabbi and sister of composer Jacques Offenbach *(Tales of Hoffman)*, had been a soloist in the Cathedral at Cologne and was much admired and courted by nobility.

Isabella and Samuel Maas had four children, including a daughter named for Rosanna Osterman. In 1887, Samuel built Isabella a Queen Anne mansion at 1727 Sealy in Galveston and put the property in her name. She lived there with her daughter Rosanna and son-in-law Nathan Redlich until her death.

After moving to Galveston, Isabella sang on occasion for members of her family, for friends, and for charity benefits. And in the tradition of Ger-

man Jewish women, she was active in the community. She belonged to both the Hebrew Ladies Association and the non-sectarian German Ladies' Benevolent Society, founded by the ladies of the Lutheran Church to help women and children. She was known for her heroic nursing work during smallpox and yellow fever epidemics. She died from exposure to inclement weather while providing food and gifts to needy families during the Christmas season of 1891.[76]

Isabella Offenbach (Mrs. Samuel) Maas (1817–1891), with her grandchildren in the living room of her Galveston home, c. 1887. She was a cultural leader and philanthropist who nursed the sick and cared for the needy. An eternal lamp, which she donated to Temple B'nai Israel in Galveston, now hangs in their small chapel.
— *From the papers and records of Sam J. Maas*

— Lee Cohen Harby, Houston, 1883

Jewish women get an education

Before 1900, a few Jewish females were attending private schools or colleges, a few Jewish women were writers, and a few were teachers. In the 1880s, the Waco Female College had a number of Jewish students, including local girls like Libbie Goldstein, as well as Pauline Kuttner (Gaber) of Navasota and Rosa Sanger (Ettleson) of Bryan. Jeanette Goldberg taught English literature there in 1893 and edited the *Critic,* a YMHA journal. The three daughters of H. A. Jacobs of Grimes County went to colleges in Hamilton, Kentucky, and Nashville, Tennessee. An early catalog of the North Texas College, Kidd-Key Conservatory, in Sherman noted that "All pupils except Jewesses must attend church on Sunday."[77] In 1894, Birdie Landman was valedictorian of her Waco high school class, and Miriam Myers, daughter of the Waco rabbi, E. M. Myers, had her play, *Under a Cloud,* produced by the YMHA. She also wrote articles for the *American Israelite,* the Chicago *Reform Advocate,* the *World,* and the *Sun.*[78]

"Cultivate self-reliance"

Lee Cohen Harby (1849–1918) was born in Charleston, South Carolina, a descendant of two well-known Southern Jewish families. Both her great-grandfathers fought in the American Revolution. She was educated by her father and great-aunt. Lee married her second cousin, J. D. Harby, whose mother, Mrs. Leonora Harby Randall, was one of the state's first Jewish Sunday school teachers in Galveston. When the elder Mrs. Harby was widowed in the 1870s, the young couple joined her, and in 1879, moved to Houston.

In 1880, Lee Harby read one of her poems at the opening of the Texas Press Association meeting. She published in prominent Eastern periodicals and was a regular contributor to the New Orleans *Times-Democrat.* In the 1890s, her work appeared in magazines such as the *Ladies Home Journal* nearly every month. In June 1893,

Lee Cohen Harby (1849–1918) was a nineteenth-century author who strenuously denied that women were inferior to men. — *Copy from Frances E. Willard,* American Women, *print from Texas Woman's University*

her first long story, "Judy Robinson, Milliner," was published in *Godey's* magazine, and *Harpers* published her essay on "Texas Types and Contrasts." Her essay about Texas Germans in New Braunfels, "The City of a Prince," appeared in the *Magazine of American History,* and she was elected a member of the American Historical Association. At their 1891 annual meeting, she read a paper on "The Earliest Texans."[79]

On November 1, 1894, the *Dallas Morning News* reported on a paper read by Harby at the Women's Congress, "The Literary Opportunities of Women." Harby's remarks closed the program: "A Jewish rabbi . . . said, 'It is greater to be a woman than a man. Man has a thousand aids . . . to help him up; woman has ten thousand clogs to impede her ascent. Woman's achievements are, nevertheless, the greatest of the age.' "

In 1895, while living in Velasco on the Texas coast, Harby corresponded with Rabbi Henry Cohen, another early Texas historian. Because she was living in a town without reference books, she asked Cohen "to be my encyclopedia."

When he inquired about African Jews in West Columbia, Texas, Harby replied: "I have taken the

trouble to type-write my notes and send them to you as a gift." Her "Notes on the Africans of Brazoria [Texas]" describe interviews with ex-slaves conducted by a friend of hers.

On October 8, 1882, a New York woman wrote the Jewish *Messenger* on the lack of eligible male suitors. Harby responded in an article, "Our Women and their Possibilities," writing that educated women had no trouble attracting male visitors. She advised Jewish women to spend less time on fashion and gossip and more time on reading and ideas. "I say educate, cultivate, read, listen, and discuss. Try and understand *yourself* physically, mentally, and morally . . . Take broad views, look on both sides of a question . . . Cultivate self-reliance. A woman with resources within herself stands independent of fortune and imparts that quality to her children."[80]

Moselle Littman of Austin was one of the first Jewish women to graduate from the University of Texas at Austin, c. 1900. Her parents moved to Austin because of the university's reputation and their desire that their nine daughters get a good education. — *Queenie Littman Collection*

Directors of the Waco Cotton Palace in 1894. Bottom row, far left, Sam Sanger, a civic and business leader, was vice-president. Young Jews from the neighboring towns of Dallas and Fort Worth often traveled to the Waco Cotton Palace festival.
— *The Texas Collection, Baylor University, Waco, Texas*

Social life in Waco

Social life for Waco Jews in the 1880s and 1890s was typical of other towns with sizable Jewish populations. There was an active YMHA, for whom Jewish women gave lawn parties as fundraisers. The *American Israelite* (1888) reported one interesting meeting which was called to discuss "whether poker shall go or not." In May 1889, "a bevy of young ladies and gentlemen met in the hall of the YMHA and boarded the electric car to the suburban residence of Mr. and Mrs. J. Lesinsky."

In 1893, Teshla Weslow, a local talent, sang at the Chicago World's Fair. The Waco papers carried frequent notices of engagements and weddings between local youth and mates from other Texas towns such as Corsicana, Dallas, Houston, and Buffalo, as well as Ardmore in Indian Territory; St. Louis, Missouri; and Peoria, Illinois.[81]

OPENING ENTERTAINMENT

—OF THE—

Young Mens Hebrew Assoc'n

Sunday, Sept. 19, 1886.

Programme:

PART I.

Overture, - - - - - - Prof. Will J. Frees.
Address, - - - - - - - D. A. Eldridge.
Piano Solo, - - - - - Miss Hattie Baum.
Song—"Joy of Song." - - Miss Annie Frees.
Recitation, - - - - - Miss Anna Goslin.

PART II.

Violin Solo, - - - - Miss Ida VanRonkle.
"When you Slept (a) - - - Halpen Kjemef.
Last Night," (b) by W. H. Boyer, of Cincinnati.
Recitation, - - - - - Miss Sophia Getz.
Flute Solo, - - - Miss Emma VanRonkle
Accompanist, - - - - - Ben R. Irelson

ENTERTAINMENT COMMITTEE:

Ben Irelson, Chairman.
A. S. Getz.   Will J. Freez.

A D ALDRIDGE & CO STEAM PRINT, DALLAS

Program of the Young Men's Hebrew Association, Dallas, 1886. According to the *Jewish Advocate*, November 1879, a Dallas YMHA was formed in 1879. It dedicated the first YMHA hall in the Southwest in downtown Dallas in 1887. By 1890, the name changed to the Phoenix Club, and later evolved into the exclusive Columbian Club. There were also YMHAs in San Antonio, Houston, Waco, and Austin.
— *Dorothy M. and Henry S. Jacobus Temple Emanu-El Archives, print by Andy Reisberg*

An invitation to a Grand Masquerade Purim Ball given by the Hebrew Ladies Aid Society in Waco, March 11, 1884. Waco's first Purim Ball was sponsored by twenty young men in 1873 to raise money for a cemetery fence. Purim Balls were popular fundraisers for Jewish organizations.
— *Ima Joy Chodorow (Mrs. J. E.) Gandler*

PURIM BALL

You are respectfully invited to attend a Grand Masquerade Ball, given by the Hebrew Ladies Aid Society, at M'Clelland Opera House, On the night of March 11, 1884.

Invitation Committee:

A. CANMANN,   J. S. SMITH,   DAN WEIL,
S. MARX,   I. S. LEVY,   DAVE WEIL.
(RED BOWS.)

Floor Managers:

DAVE WEIL,   GUS HEINEMAN,   I. S. LEVY,
SAM GAINSBURG,   LEOPOLD LYONS.
(WHITE BOWS.)

Reception Committee:

A. S. HABER,   L. MIGEL,   J. LEVINSKI,
NATHAN HYMAN.
(BLUE BOWS.)

Examining Committee:

A. ALEXANDER,   M. F. KILSHEIMER,
I. LOWINGER.
(YELLOW BOWS.)

— Maj. William Levy

In the 1880s and 1890s, El Paso had three Jewish mayors, Solomon Schutz, Adolph Solomon, and Adolph Krakauer. Shown here is Adolph Solomon (1853–1905), who was elected mayor of El Paso in 1894. Before moving to El Paso, he represented Cochise County in the Arizona Territorial Legislature.[82] Solomon Schutz was elected mayor in 1881.[83] Adolph Krakauer was elected mayor of El Paso in 1889, but had to give up his office when it was found he had not yet received his second citizenship papers.   — *Southwest Collection, El Paso Public Library*

Samuel Freudenthal moved to El Paso in 1884 from Arizona Territory, where he had been a clerk and bookkeeper for a mining company and the unofficial postmaster of Clifton, Arizona. He served on the El Paso city council, school board, and county commission.[84]
— *UT Institute of Texan Cultures*

Political and civic leaders

Many Texas Jews held public office and founded community institutions before 1900. They were mayors, volunteer firemen, city councilmen, aldermen, and state legislators. Even so, a Jew lost a race for the Texas legislature in Bell County in 1888. The Waco *Evening News* reported: "The regular Democratic nominee for the legislature in Bell County was defeated simply and solely because he was a Jew . . . hide bound fanatics refused to vote for a Democrat of Hebraic descent."[85]

William Levy dedicates college for "colored citizens" in Sherman (1890)

William Levy from Altona, Germany, had an advanced Jewish and secular education. After demobilization from the Confederate Army, Levy opened a men's clothing store in Sherman. There he was an alderman (1873–1881 and 1883–1889), the mayor (1881–1883), and a member of the school board. In 1890, Levy was the principal orator at the dedication of the College of Northwest Texas Colored Citizens. His speech was remarkably tolerant for its day. Although patronizing in tone, the speech included a plea for blacks to seek an education, using the Jewish love for learning as a model. Excerpts follow.[86]

"My Colored Fellow-Citizens:
". . . behold in me a man whose ancestors were also slaves . . . they were . . . persecuted, in times ancient, middle and modern . . . We believe in one fatherhood of God and one brotherhood of men, be they Jews or Christians, Mohammedans or pagans, whites or blacks; . . . we judge people not according to their nationality, creed or color, but according to their heart, deeds and actions . . . the time will come when it will be acknowledged that not creed, nationality or color of a man make him a gentleman, but intellectual education, moral conduct and nobility of the heart . . ."

Isidore Lovenberg (1844–1917) was a member of the Galveston School Board from 1887 to 1917 and was elected president in 1905. He was on the board of the Rosenberg Library and chairman of the Galveston Orphans Home. He helped organize Temple B'nai Israel and was president of B'nai B'rith District Grand Lodge #7. A junior high school is named for him. Born in Paris, France, he lived in Alabama and New Orleans before moving to Galveston in 1867. He was prominent in the insurance business and president of the Galveston Board of Underwriters.[87]
— *Rosenberg Library, Galveston, Texas*

Isaac A. Goldstein was known as the "Father of Waco's library." He founded Waco's first circulating library in his place of business, Goldstein-Migel department store, because he wanted those who could not afford books to have access to them. He was president of the Public Library Association of Waco (1900–1920) and donated the site on which the Carnegie Public Library was built. He was also the superintendent of the Rodef Sholom Sunday School.
— *Ima Joy Chodorow (Mrs. J. E.) Gandler*

STEERAGE DECK, 1893: THOUSANDS OF JEWS CAME FROM EUROPE ON SHIPS

Thousands of Jews came from Europe on ships like the S.S. *Pennland,* pictured here in 1893. Most immigrants traveled under miserably crowded conditions in steerage class, the least expensive fare.

— *Museum of the City of New York, photograph by Byron*

Getting to America required courage and stamina

Jennie Radunska Cohen of Grodno, Russia, smuggled herself and her infant daughter Celia out of the country in 1905. Traveling with their next-door neighbors, a doctor and his family, Jennie and Celia were listed on the doctor's passport as his sister and daughter. They joined Jennie's husband, Max Cohen, who had left the previous year for Boston. Jennie and Celia traveled in steerage on the *Vaderland (Fatherland)*. Although Celia was too young to remember the crossing, she recalled the story as her mother told it to her:

"The voyage was very rough. We came in steerage, the third or fourth layer down where you feel the pull of the ocean, and most of the immigrants came that way because they couldn't afford any other way and they didn't care. We came with all our belongings . . . I know Mama

brought two big featherbeds and you can imagine how it was, with all her possessions and a baby in diapers. She also brought with her some big copper pots which she later sold to a junkman for twenty-five cents.

"We settled first in Boston, but Papa got in a fight with his partner in the fish market. So around 1909 we moved to Wills Point, Texas, where Mama had a cousin. I'm not kidding, Texas was wild. Wills Point had one street and boards for a sidewalk. When Mama saw this, she didn't know what to do. She couldn't talk English, she didn't see a Jewish face, and no place to buy kosher meat. My parents were very Orthodox Jews. So Mama told Papa, 'You either take me where there's some Jewish faces, or else . . .' "

The family moved to Dallas, where there was a *schochet,* an Orthodox congregation, Agudas Achim, and a thriving Jewish community.[1]

1900 to 1920

"The bearer of this certificate is a political refugie."
THE DAWN OF A NEW CENTURY

By the turn of the century, most Jews who had been in Texas for a decade or more thrived. In towns and cities across the state, their mercantile establishments and businesses were some of the most stable and elegant to be found. Many lived charmed and privileged lives, and their prosperity increased with the oil boom that started with Spindletop in 1901. It was a sign of times to come, and the future looked bright.

As they prospered, Texas Jews built new temples and synagogues to accommodate the larger population, and the edifices were impressive brick structures that represented permanence. Jews were here to stay, and they took their place alongside Catholics and Protestants as community builders and leaders.

But all was not well for Jews in the rest of the world. The cries of suffering by co-religionists living in poverty and fear in Eastern European *shtetls* under repressive regimes reached the ears of Texas Jewry from across the Atlantic Ocean. Outrage at the pogroms led to action as Jews protested and opened their doors to the immigrants. Families sent for loved ones left behind, and new immigrants saved their money and sent for sweethearts, parents, siblings, and friends. And when the Galveston Movement brought Jews to the portal of Texas, the newcomers were provided with food, shelter, and jobs until they could plant their feet firmly on Texas soil or move on to other states.

Between 1900 and 1917, the Jewish population in Texas more than doubled, from 15,000 to over 31,000. Although Jews from Eastern Europe began coming to Texas in the 1880s, the large influx occurred after 1900. Older Reform temples like Austin's Temple Beth Israel and other established congregations expanded. Beth Israel added electric lights, heating, and a pipe organ. But most of the newcomers to Texas were Orthodox, and they added new dimensions to the theological landscape. New congregations formed, new organizations developed, and new ideas emerged. The differences in liturgy and ritual and the heated debate that ensued as Zionism gained in popularity during the early 1900s reflected the diversity among Texas Jews which continues even today.

During these years, the American Jewish Committee and the Anti-Defamation League of B'nai B'rith were organized nationally. In 1906, the Immigration Restriction League tried to get a federal bill requiring a literacy test for prospective immigrants passed in Congress to keep out the worst of the "racially unfit." Largely through the efforts of AJC, the bill was defeated. Unfortunately, a similar one passed in 1917.

The Jewish National Fund was established in 1902 to buy and develop land in Palestine. The concept of Zionism gathered momentum as the Balfour Declaration was issued in 1917, pledging British support for a Jewish national homeland in Palestine.

Aside from political and social problems, the many newcomers, who often came with few resources, posed a financial strain on family members and the Jewish community. To serve the needs of poor Jews and address broader concerns, the forerunners of today's federations formed, like the United Jewish Charities of Dallas in 1911.

The Great Storm of 1900, which devastated Galveston Island, was one of the chief causes of expansive growth in Houston. After a deepwater channel was dredged, the city exploded with opportunity, and many Jews flourished. The dynamic community had a number of Jewish organizations, and the Jewish Welfare Association was created in 1913 from the merger of the Ladies' Hebrew Benevolent Society, the Bikur Cholim Society, and the Beth Israel Immigrant Society. The expanded group raised funds for the Hebrew Immigrant Aid Society (HIAS) and the Joint Distribution Committee (JDC). By 1915, there were four congregations, three B'nai B'rith lodges, a Workmen's Circle, five fraternal lodges, three Zionist societies, and several women's and men's clubs. In 1908, Edgar Goldberg started the *Texas Jewish Herald* in Houston, the forerunner of today's *Jewish Herald Voice,* to report it all.

In the community at large, Jews were at the forefront in establishing symphonies, libraries, and hospitals. Though Texas Jews freely associated with non-Jews in the course of business, cultural and civic affairs, and in fraternal organizations like the Masons, lines were still drawn at night for social contact. Jewish literary societies and social clubs, which sprang up in the larger cities, sponsored Purim balls, citywide seders, musicales, plays, book reviews, and debates on issues like Zionism and suffrage for women. The societies created an active Jewish social milieu which facilitated marriages and enhanced Jewish life. Some Jewish social clubs, like the Concordia Club in Houston, were composed primarily of German Jews.

Along the Texas-Mexico border, Jews participated in the revolution to the south as soldiers, arbiters, and businessmen. Jewish life on the border took on a distinct flavor of its own as the warm climate and good business opportunities led to family enclaves that exist even today.

While some Jews struggled to maintain a minimum standard of living, many others bought land, built homes, and began sending their children to universities as they reached for the American dream. A Jewish presence in the professions, in white collar jobs, and in the military became noticeable. Emanuel Raphael served on the first board of trustees of Houston's Rice University in 1911. Gus Kowalski of Brownsville, a graduate of the University of Texas Law School, was elected Kleberg County attorney. Leonce Kosminsky of Texarkana got degrees in pharmacy and medicine and became a professor at the College of Physicians and Surgeons in Little Rock. In 1918, M. M. Harris became editor of the *San Antonio Express* and *San Antonio Evening News*.

When the U.S. entered World War I in 1917, Texas Jews answered the call of their homeland with patriotism and valor on the battlefront and the home front. In Europe, there were thousands of suffering Jewish victims. After the war, the American Jewish Relief Committee raised $14 million, calling for the rescue of 300,000 orphans.

The period of 1900–1920 was one of unbridled growth in the Texas Jewish community. It paved the way for its constituents, both native-born and immigrant, to enter political and professional life and to participate in the greater community, with a strong religious and cultural heritage as a backbone.

"The bearer of this certificate . . . is a political refugie [sic]."

"The bearer of this certificate, David Rappoport, is a political refugie [sic]. For the socialistic propaganda among the Russian peasantry he had been sentenced by the Russian High Court of Appeal to two years & eight months' hard labour, and as an additional punishment, to the perpetual exile in Nord [sic] Eastern Siberia. Having happily fled from there, he is now going to settle in the United States of America with his brother Raphael Rappoport (1474, Matamora str., San Antonio, Texas). 27-IX-1913. Signed by W. MaKnichine The Secretary of the Russian Social Revolutionary Party's group in Brussels, Belgium."[2]

After moving to San Antonio, David Rappoport joined the Socialist Party of America in 1914.

Nationally acclaimed poet Fania Feldman Kruger (1892–1977) (top row, far right and left) was only admitted to the gymnasium in Sevastopol, Crimea, Russia c. 1907, after her fourth try.
— *Personal Collection of Bert Kruger Smith*

Fania Feldman Kruger

In spite of three rejections from the local *gymnasium* in her home village of Sevastopol, Crimea, Czarist Russia, Fania Feldman (Kruger) fought for her education and ultimately became an award-winning poet. Though her poetry recounted the suffering and terrorism her family endured at the hands of Czarist thugs, the *Saturday Review of Literature* said, "There is no shrill wailing, no personal complaint, but rather a quiet nobility in her impassioned statement."

Born in 1892, Fania finally was accepted to the *gymnasium* (similar to a junior college) on her fourth try. Because she and her sister became involved in revolutionary politics, their parents feared for their well-being and sent them to live with relatives in Fort Worth in 1908. Fania continued her education in night school, while during the day she did manual labor carrying buckets of beer. Driven by her father's word — "Knowledge is the Messiah of Humanity" — she read and studied into her seventies as she took classes in English and poetry at UT Austin.

In 1912, Fania married Sam Kruger, another immigrant. They moved to Wichita Falls in 1914 and opened a jewelry store. She began writing poetry in 1937 and met with critical acclaim for her three books — *Cossack Laughter, The Tenth Jew,* and *Selected Poems* — as well as numerous essays published in such periodicals as *Redbook* and *Southwest Review.* She received numerous awards for her poetry, including the National Poetry Society of America Prize. She was a member of the Texas Institute of Letters and the International Mark Twain Society.[4]

"Cossack Laughter"

Our raftered hut was near a wood
Where, crowned with snow, the dark trees stood

With sheltering arms. When April stirred
The budding flower, the migrant bird,

Proclaiming spring, a cruel wind
Withered the leaf and rudely thinned

The boughs of bloom, while skies turned gray
As pools upon a foggy day.

Life, too, was torn with a gale of grief
Like that which seared the flower and leaf.

That dusk, I, but a girl of ten,
Witnessed the rage of Czarist men.

The Cossacks, who, like winds of hate,
Battered the fence, smashed down the gate,

Shattered the windows, broke the door,
Ripped up the boards of the worn pine floor.

"Death to all Jews!" Their drunken yell
Rang through the hut; our hearts as well.

Father, undaunted with death at his face,
Pled with the Cossacks to leave our place.

A saber's thrust . . . My father's words
Caught as he sank on blood-soaked boards.

My mother cried: "Is God a word,
A broken shield against the sword?"

Only a sudden burst of laughter
From the Cossacks shook the leaning rafter.

With bitter rage, bewildered, wild
I turned on them, a helpless child,

Trod on their boots that seemed as steel,
Prayed they be crushed beneath my heel.

With lead-tipped knoughts they scourged my legs
As they gulped again the vodka dregs.

Our hopes were broken like the chairs;
Blood was clotted on wall and stairs.

Grief-crazed beside the unhinged door
My mother scrubbed the spattered floor.

• • •

The hut is lost, the czar is gone,
But certain as the dark, the dawn,

Memory of blood upon a rafter
Brings back the ruthless Cossack laughter.

My mother, locked behind a door,
Still scrubs and scrubs a stainless floor.

Max Cohen (1879–1963) served in the Czar's army from 1897 to 1903. After six years of military service, he was discharged, but with the Russo-Japanese War on the horizon, he feared reconscription. He left his pregnant wife, Jennie Radunska Cohen, behind in Grodno, Russia, stole across the border, and made his way to Boston, where he had an aunt. His wife and baby daughter Celia followed in 1905. The family moved to Dallas in 1909. Life in the Russian army was especially difficult for Jews because of anti-Semitism and the absence of kosher food. Unable to eat the meat or poultry, Jewish soldiers subsisted on cabbage soup, black bread, vegetables, and tea. Many who were conscripted never returned. Others tried to avoid service by cutting off a finger or puncturing an eardrum.
— *Ruthe Winegarten, granddaughter*

Dora Solomon (Mrs. Ben) Levinson (1865–1940) came to America seeking a better life. She and her husband were the tenth Jewish family in Fort Worth.
— *Mrs. Leon Brachman*

Seeking a better life

Violent anti-Semitism, poverty, and lack of opportunity caused many Jews to flee Russia and Eastern Europe for the U.S., seeking a better life for themselves and their families.

Like many of her counterparts, Dora Solomon was encouraged by her parents to join relatives in the "new world" because of their hope for a better future. Like most of the other immigrants, she never again saw her parents. Dora washed and cooked in her brother's New York boarding-

house until illness caused her to move to a warmer climate. She joined another brother in Forney, Texas, where she met her future husband, Ben Levinson.

Dora and Ben Levinson became the tenth Jewish family to settle in Fort Worth in 1891. Together they built a family, a successful business, and became leaders in Fort Worth's fledgling Jewish community.

Freida Weiner

Freida Mirochnik Weiner (1890–   ) (far right standing) came from the Russian *shtetl* of Korostishev to Galveston in 1915 and has spent a lifetime organizing for the Workmen's Circle. This photo was taken in 1913, one week before Freida left for America. Also pictured are, l. to r., her sister Malka Mirochnik Fleishman, her brother Froika, mother Genendel, and her youngest sister Chana. All except Freida perished in the Holocaust.
— *Freida Weiner*

"The Revolutionaries" from
My Shtetl Korostishev
Freida Mirochnik Weiner

Chai Dvorah, Freida Weiner's grandmother, was a midwife and practical nurse in Korostishev, Russia, a town of 7,000 (90 percent Jewish). After Dvorah became too old to practice, she turned her trade over to her two daughters, one of whom was Freida's mother, Genendel. After becoming a widow, Genendel delivered babies and ran a grocery and a whiskey bar whose best customers were men dropping by after morning prayers at the synagogue.

During the 1905 revolution, Freida, a tailor's apprentice in nearby Kiev, hid in a basement with her fellow workers, while mobs rampaged, plundered, beat, and killed Jews. Freida's cousin, Tillie, was raped during a pogrom, so they married her off to an old man. Freida and her husband-to-be, Itzik Winokoor (Isaac Weiner), became members of a small group interested in socialism.

They later married in Detroit, Michigan, where Isaac worked for the Ford Motor Company. They both became active in the Arbeiter Ring (Workmen's Circle). After the family moved to Galveston around 1915, Freida continued organizing for the Arbeiter Ring for sixty years. She also organized a chapter of Pioneer Women and was president for thirty years. During the 1930s, she sup-ported the Joint Distribution Committee, the Jewish Labor Committee, and helped raise money for striking coal miners in Pennsylvania. She moved to Houston in 1979 and organized the Senior Yiddish Culture Club and the Yiddish *Vinkle* for children.[6]

"Annie, The Immigrant"

One typical family who came through Galveston around 1907 were the Hareliks. The story of Annie Harelik Novit and her husband, Wolf Novit, is recounted by their daughter, Minnie Siegel, in "Annie, The Immigrant."[7] Annie Harelik of Slavan, Russia, was a successful seamstress and designer who owned a Singer sewing machine and employed three young women. Groups began to form in her town to help the working class reduce the number of hours of labor from eleven or twelve a day. "This cause of the working class gave us something to . . . become involved in."

Annie and her fiance, Velvel (Wolf Novit), began meeting secretly with friends in the forest where they heard lectures on Zionism. Annie's brother Haskell did not want to be a scholar; he wanted to be a member of the working class. He got a job as an iron worker in a factory making anchors for ships. Wolf Novit came through Galveston in 1907 and became a banana peddler around Dublin, Texas. Later, he sent for his wife Annie and her brothers, Haskell and Morris Harelik. In turn, the family assisted others who came through Galveston. Sometimes their houses in Dublin were so crowded that the newcomers had to sleep in the bathtub.

Of them, the "respectable Jews" used to make fun and derided them [the revolutionaries] generally. The saying was: "So you common trash are going to depose the Tsar?" Later on, when the "respectables" own sons and daughters, and also the Rabbi's grandchildren, Mosheela, Rivkele and Chanah-Rochel joined this group, their attitude changed and they sang a different tune: "Who are we to complain, when the Rabbi's own grandchildren are consorting with the shoemakers?" The prestige of these nonentities further rose when they succeeded in exerting pressure on the various shop owners, forcing them to reduce the long work hours of their workers. When any shop owner failed to comply, he was simply waylaid and beaten up. One time, just before Passover, they forced a work stoppage in the Matzoh bakery [by extinguishing oven fires], because the women dough rollers and cutters were kept working very late into the night.

Threshka, the local constable, who made an attempt to restrain the fellows, had his front teeth knocked out. And Chaim-Moshe, who informed the constable of this group, was so badly beaten up that he remained a cripple for life.

Our Korostishev group of these Revolutionaries was very strong and had a very good reputation. They were feared and respected by all classes of people. Often, they were called on to arbitrate differences.

". . . for the guidance of all civilized men, none shall suffer in person, property, honor or life because of his religious belief."

— Leo N. Levi's Kishinev Petition to Czar Nicholas II, 1903

Leo Napoleon Levi (1856–1904) was a prominent Galveston attorney and civic activist who framed the famous Kishinev Petition in 1903.
— *Temple B'nai Israel Archives, Galveston, copy from UT Institute of Texan Cultures*

Leo N. Levi

Texas Jews were sympathetic to the plight of Eastern European Jewry. As the immigrants poured into the state, established Jews offered food, shelter, jobs, and English classes. For those who remained behind, however, the pogroms made life more unbearable and led to vigorous protests by co-religionists in the U.S.

After the particularly brutal Easter 1903 massacre of Jews in Kishinev, Russia, Leo N. Levi framed the famous Kishinev Petition. The petition deplored the riots and asked that Czar Nicholas II publicly oppose religious persecution. President Theodore Roosevelt cabled the petition with its 13,000 signatures to St. Petersburg, but the Czar refused to accept it.

Leo N. Levi was born in Victoria in 1856 to a pioneer Jewish couple, Abraham and Mina Halfin Levi. Leo graduated from the University of Virginia Law School and began his legal practice in G lveston in 1876. He was active in ci .c affairs, often representing Galveston as an unofficial lobbyist before the Texas legislature. In 1887, he was elected president of Congregation B'nai Israel and was instrumental in hiring Rabbi Henry Cohen, who would remain for the next sixty-two years.

Leo Levi was president of B'nai B'rith District Grand Lodge #7. After moving to New York in 1899, he was elected national president.[8]

Leo N. Levi left his fortune to establish the Leo N. Levi Memorial Hospital in Hot Springs, Arkansas. The hospital was a free non-sectarian institution founded in 1914 by B'nai B'rith for the treatment and research of arthritic diseases.
— *B'nai B'rith International Archives*

— **Jacob de Haas**

"I established . . . the first Zionist organization in Texas . . ."

Dr. Sigmund Burg recalled the early days of the Texas Zionist movement:[9] "Dr. (Theodore) Herzl started the convocation of the first Zionist Congress. German Jewry, in the greater majority imbued with the idea of assimilation . . . prevented the holding of the first International Zionist Congress in Germany. It was held . . . in Basel, Switzerland, in 1897. In that very year . . . I had already established in . . . San Antonio, Texas, the first Zionist organization in Texas and possibly the first in the United States."

As a political idea, Zionism arose out of the spread of the French Revolution, the seeds of emancipation of West European Jewry, and the ideas of Haskalah (the Enlightenment). The bloody pogroms of Eastern Europe further nourished hope for a Jewish homeland. But it was Theodore Herzl, a young Viennese journalist, who first advocated the establishment of a Jewish state with his book *Judenstaat* (1896).

Herzl had covered the infamous Dreyfus Case in Paris, in which a French Jewish military officer was wrongly accused and convicted of being a traitor. After years of imprisonment on Devil's Island, Alfred Dreyfus was finally acquitted. But the case had a lasting effect on Herzl. In 1905, the Texas Zionist Association (TZA) was organized in Houston at Adath Yeshurun Synagogue; it supported not only a Jewish homeland in Palestine, but Hebrew schools and Young Judaea chapters. A monthly magazine, *The Jewish Hope,* was edited by a University of Texas professor, Dr. C. Pessels. The passage of the Balfour Declaration in 1917 was a great encouragement to the Zionist movement. In 1920, District Grand Lodge #7 of B'nai B'rith contributed $500 to the Palestine Restoration Fund. By 1939, chapters of the Texas Zionist Association existed in many Texas cities.[10]

"A petition was made to send $10 to the Kishinev Relief Fund."
— Esrath Zion, Waco, Minutes, May 10, 1903

In the meantime, Waco Jews organized Esrath Zion in 1898 and within ten years had seventy members and a women's auxiliary, Daughters of Zion.[11] In 1909, the group began selling $5 shares for a Texas colony in Palestine. In 1910, the men and women merged into one organization. Disagreements were so serious that a resolution was passed outlining punishments for those "disturb[ing] order and harmony . . . either by abusive, disorderly or profane language, or [those who] shall refuse obedience to the chair . . . shall be excluded from the meeting room . . . A member shall not speak more than once on the same subject . . . until all who wish to speak shall have had the opportunity to do so." Many Texas Jews were opposed to Zionism because it ran contrary to their belief that Judaism was a religion rather than a nationality.

Dr. Sigmund Burg of Vienna founded the first local Zionist organization in Texas, and possibly in the U.S., in 1897 in San Antonio. He later became the first president of the Texas Zionist Organization, founded in 1905. A graduate of the Imperial University of Vienna, he was president of Kadima, the world's first organization of Jewish university students. In Texas, Burg was a member of San Antonio's Agudas Achim Building Committee, the city's health officer for ten years, and secretary of the Western Texas Medical Association. In 1925, he gave up his practice for a year and moved to Palestine.

— Jewish National Fund

The Travels of Jacob de Haas
Following are excerpts from the diary of Jacob de Haas, editor of *the Maccabaean,* who traveled through the South promoting Zionism in 1904.[12]

"Galveston, Dec. 22, 1904 . . . the most unique community in the country, for a species of purely English Judaism prevails . . . all the Jews may be said truly to be Zionists in spirit though the minority only believe in our actual Zionism. A great deal of this seems due to Rabbi [Henry] Cohen, who is sanely orthodox, and has the unqualified confidence of the orthodox. The Zionists are today a handful . . ."

"Waco, Tx., Dec. 25, 1904. I snugged away into a little Texas town, but though I did not come into contact with any of our people, I found their names written over stores . . . And so I begun *[sic]* a cautious inquiry into the Jewish settlements in this portion of Texas . . . almost every town on the route between Houston and Waco had its little collection of Jews, from a single family to 20 or 25, whose spiritual affairs are being . . . ministered to by the . . . circuit Rabbis initiated by the Central Conference of Reform Rabbis . . . the orthodox Jew is allowed to shift for himself, there is no organization to strengthen his consciousness, . . . orthodox in the South is more a matter of opinion than a matter of practice." [There was an active Orthodox congregation in Waco, Agudath Jacob.]

". . . [in a local] newspaper . . . I read that a Rabbi had made a brilliant, and witty speech at a 'possum and 'tater supper. It seemed so unique, so bizarre, from what we consider ordinarily to be Jewish life, and yet I felt that it was all so natural here . . . this morning [I was] introduced to that same Rabbi as Dr. [B.] Wolhberg, the Rabbi of Waco, and a Zionist."

The first group of Jewish immigrants pictured here in 1907 arrived as part of what would become known as the Galveston Movement (Galveston Plan). From 1907 to 1914, 10,000 Jews came through the Texas port city, and each boat was met by Rabbi Henry Cohen, second from left.[13]
— *Helene Samuels Levy Archives, Congregation B'nai Israel, Galveston*

In July 1907, a small group of Russian Jewish immigrants stood on the docks of Galveston Island after eighteen days on a transatlantic steamer. After a hearty welcoming address from Galveston's mayor, translated into Yiddish by Rabbi Henry Cohen, the mayor shook each immigrant's hand. One man stepped forward, rolled up his sleeve, and showed thin red lines along his arms. In broken English, he said that this scene could not have happened where he came from.

"The *knout* (whip) was our greeting. You have clasped hands. A time may come when your country will need us; we will not hesitate to serve with our blood."[14]

Rabbi Cohen reported that during World War I, he related this story to a group of army soldiers. A soldier stepped forward and said, "I am that man."

The Galveston Movement

The outrage of American Jews did not stop the pogroms in Eastern Europe, and the idealistic dreams of Zionists would not become a reality until 1948. Russian Jews poured into the East Coast cities of the United States where, even though free, many remained in ghettos. Thousands crowded into substandard tenement housing, where frequent illnesses, piece work at home, sweat shops, and child labor prevailed. The New York City Triangle Shirt Waist fire of 1911, in which almost 200 immigrant girls died, became a major scandal. Anti-Semitism began growing, along with the cry for restrictive immigration laws.

Jacob Schiff, a New York financier, took action by establishing the Jewish Immigrant Information Bureau (JIIB) with $500,000 of his own money. He enlisted the aid of Israel Zangwill, the director of the Jewish Territorial Organization in Europe. Schiff wanted to settle immigrants in the southwestern and midwestern parts of the U.S. Zangwill wanted an autonomous state for the world's Jews. They compromised and began working together. Zangwill would supply the immigrants from Europe, and Schiff would assist their resettlement in the U.S. To that end, Morris Waldman of New York was hired to establish local JIIB offices and, ultimately, locate a port to reroute Jewish immigration westward.

San Francisco and New Orleans were considered but dismissed for fear that the populous areas would spawn new ghettos. Galveston was chosen for several reasons. It had existing rail connections to major cities in southwestern and midwestern states. A German steamship line was already making regular stops at the port. And Galveston, it was felt, would not be attractive enough to induce the newcomers to remain. But most important was the presence of Rabbi Henry Cohen, who had served his community for eighteen years and was one of the country's foremost Jewish leaders.

Rabbi Cohen met every ship that arrived and worked tirelessly to arrange for food, shelter, and jobs for the newcomers. He also arranged for travel to points west of the Mississippi — New Orleans, St. Louis, Chicago, San Antonio. Tanners, cabinetmakers, butchers, and other tradesmen were often sent to Omaha or Kansas City or Fort Worth. Unskilled workers went where jobs could be found. Most of the newcomers stayed in Galveston less than twenty-four hours. Some, like Haskell Harelik, peddled their way to small towns like Hamilton, Texas, and started a new life. Others, like Clara Reinhardt, remained in Galveston. Clara arranged for her "brother," Fred Nussenblatt, to come to Galveston; he was actually her fiance. They married, and their descendants still live in Galveston: a granddaughter, Shelley Nussenblatt Kessler, and two great-grandchildren, Andy and Jenny Kessler.

Many Galveston Jews helped Rabbi Cohen care for the newcomers. Abram Geller of Houston recalled going to the dock and awaiting the landing of the immigrants. "If they wanted kosher food, my father, Rabbi Jacob Geller, would take them in our buggy to our home."[15]

The Galveston Plan did not live up to Schiff's expectations. A tightening of immigration policies, changes in Russian governmental policies, American economic insecurity, the duration and difficulty of the voyage, the outbreak of World War I, and the enactment of restrictive federal immigration laws in the 1920s all contributed to the demise of the plan. Still, modest success was attained by resettling some 10,000 immigrants, many of whose descendants still live in Texas.

Any person who went to Galveston in need of a hot meal, a bed, medical care, or a job found a friend in Rabbi Henry Cohen. The rabbi of Temple B'nai Israel for sixty-two years, he was a nationally known humanitarian and a legend in his own time. His good deeds were as varied as the Central Relief Committee after the 1900 Galveston storm to directing aid in 1914 for American citizens stranded during the Mexican Revolution. As a catalyst for Jacob Schiff's Galveston Plan, Rabbi Cohen helped welcome every Jewish immigrant who landed. Cohen, a leader in prison reform, was appointed, along with Rabbis Ephraim Frisch and Dr. Max Handman, to the Texas Committee on Prisons and Prison Labor in 1928. Most of Rabbi Cohen's recommendations for prison reform were eventually adopted.
— *Rosenberg Library, Galveston, Texas*

Rabbi Cohen's wide-ranging concerns are reflected in samples of letters from his collection at the Barker Texas History Center, UT Austin.[16]

His Excellency, James E. Ferguson,
Governor of Texas,
Austin, Texas.

Dear Governor:
I am interested in the case of Louis Himelfarb who four months ago was sent up for five years, for felony.

I cannot presume to pass upon the legal merits of the case. I think, however, that the punishment was excessive and am asking you to extend your clemency in the man's behalf.

Himelfarb has a wife and four children, only one of whom is working, earning four dollars a week. The boy next in age sells newspapers and earns little or nothing. The family being in the meanwhile supported by the Hebrew Benevolent Society, and some charitable people of the City.

The amount involved is some Twelve or Fifteen Hundred Dollars . . . I am of the opinion that after Himelfarb has served a given time in the Penitentiary, he should be paroled, with the understanding that he make good the sum in question . . .
With regards, I am,
Yours faithfully,
/s/ Henry Cohen
Galveston, Texas. June 23, 1915

San Antonio, Texas
Oct 11th 1903
Reverend H. Cohn [sic]—

Dear Sir
You will pardon the liberty I take being unknown to you, but wishing to come to your city and being alone, I thought you would kindly give me the advice I so much need . . . I would like a position in a coat and Suit "Dept," . . . I have always worked in our own store, but now circumstances have made it necessary for me to support myself . . . if you could kindly send me the names of some such store in need of my services I would indeed be very grateful . . . will you please send me the address of some Jewish boarding house or rooming house, where I could stay for a reasonable price . . .
/s/ Miss R. Picurd #812 Austin St., San Antonio, Texas

4/12 1905
Bisbee Ariz
Dr. Cohen, Galveston Tex.

Dear Sir:
I heard from Mr. L. Dreeben that you have inquired of him about me. What I intended doing about my family. I am willing to send my wife every week 4.00 to live on and take care of my boy. The reason why I didn't send money so far was because since I came to Bisbee nearly 4 months, it has rained mostly, and I barely made my own living, and my expense is about 3-1/2 dollars a day.

. . . everything is very high here, and still it rains, and makes it hard for me . . . but still I will send my wife from the 25th of this month 4.00 every week . . . Hoping my wife and boy are well . . .
Max Schwartz

The Jewish Farmer was published monthly in Yiddish by the Jewish Agricultural and Industrial Aid Society, which provided loans to farmers in the Midwest and South.
— *Copy from Kenneth Libo and Irving Howe, We Lived There Too*

"Who says that Jews cannot be farmers?"[18]

Because Jews were traditionally deprived of land ownership in Europe, some Jewish families dreamed of farming. Not all plans for a return to the land involved Palestine. The Jewish National Farmers Alliance Movement and other farm programs sponsored by the Hebrew Immigrant Aid Society (HIAS) were associated with the efforts of Baron Maurice de Hirsch, who funded agricultural experiments to place Jews on the land. As a result, Jewish farm communities were established at various places in the U.S.

In 1881, a group of prospective colonists were sent to work on Texas farms for three months. They reported back that the land was too arid.[19] In 1888, the Waco B'nai B'rith lodge had as one of its philanthropic concerns the Dakota Colony, one of several Jewish agricultural cooperatives established around the country by the Am Olam movement.[20] Some Texas Jewish farmers were successful. W. Bluestein of Beaumont shipped 100 barrels as part of the first boxcar of rice ever shipped from Orange County in 1892, and Sam Lederer operated a rice farm south of town in 1900.

In the early 1900s in St. Louis, Missouri, a *chevra* (group of friends) associated with the Jewish National Farmers Alliance met every Thursday night with each family contributing twenty-five cents to the *pushke* (collec-

tion box). By 1912, there was enough to buy land near Conroe (Montgomery County), about forty miles north of Houston. Finally, the small colony of men, women, and children moved to Montgomery County onto land which they named the Ida Strauss Plat after the fiance of Isidore Fry (one of the colonists), who had perished on the *Titanic*. Their plan to raise peanuts and do subsistence farming failed either because the land was unsuitable or for lack of know-how. Some of the children became ill with pellagra and died. The families eventually returned to St. Louis but kept ownership of the land, which ultimately became valuable for real estate development and oil and mineral exploration.[21]

Five cents a boll weevil

In 1892, the boll weevil came to Texas from Mexico, and by 1904, had infested much of the state's cotton crops. However, crops were not all that was under attack. One cause of anti-Semitism in Corpus Christi was the rational approach taken by a local Jew to the problem. While fundamentalist Christians blamed the boll weevil on the will of God, a Mr. Goldman paid five cents for each boll weevil brought to him. Even though he was called an agent of the devil, his approach did reduce the boll weevil population.[22]

The Werlin farm near Pearland, Texas, c. 1910. L. to r., Joe (a worker); the Werlin children: Jacob, Reuben, Eugene, and Sam; and their father, Jacob A. Werlin. Jacob Werlin grew pears, strawberries, and pecans. He wrote *The Progressive Farmer*, a book recommending that farmers use scientific methods to record their yields. Werlin lost everything to a drought and returned to Houston to live.[17]
— *Rosella Werlin, copy from UT Institute of Texan Cultures*

— **Morris S. Schechter (1898–1970)**

Rosen Heights: Fort Worth

It didn't take long for some families to establish successful mercantile businesses in the early Texas boom-times. Land in Texas was plentiful, and success brought the opportunity to buy land — land for homes, land to rent, land to farm or ranch, land to develop, land for land's sake. As Rosenberg merchant Morris Schechter, along with many other Jewish parents, advised his children: "Everybody should own a little piece of Texas." For a people who had been deprived of land rights for centuries by laws or by poverty, land ownership was a dream-come-true and a good investment.

Sam Rosen was one Jewish immigrant with a *Yiddishe kupp* (loosely translated — a smart thinker). He came from Russia at age twelve, began his career as a peddler, and soon amassed enough capital to open a dry goods store in Fort Worth. When the Swift and Armour meat-packing companies moved to town in 1902, Rosen bought 1,500 acres of land west of the stockyards for subdivision into housing lots.

Land development also meant providing transportation since there were no automobiles, and horses and buggies were few. So Rosen built a streetcar line. He also created White City, an amusement park with a baseball diamond and a grandstand, a theater, a carnival with a Ferris wheel, an artificial lake, and a dance pavilion. Unfortunately, the amusement park showplace burned down.

But Sam Rosen had other plans for enticing people to Rosen Heights. He gave away lots if he knew a fine home would be built, provided land for a church, paid water and electric bills during hard times, and never foreclosed on a house.[23]

Louis and Bessie Novich Lazarus with their son at home in Waco, c. 1902. Even in towns like Waco, some Jewish families kept chickens and garden plots.
— *The Texas Collection, Baylor University, Waco, Texas*

Sam Rosen predicted that employees of the Fort Worth stockyards and packing companies would want homes close to work. In 1902, he bought 1,500 acres of land, subdivided them into residential lots, and took elaborate measures to make sure his land was purchased. The area became known as Rosen Heights.
— *Fort Worth Public Library*

Once the immigrants arrived, they set about looking for work. Some were able to use skills they had in the old country such as tanning, blacksmithing, baking, or sewing. Others took work where they could find it. Many acquired a horse or a wagon and set out to peddle. Wagons quickly gave way to stores as Jews settled in to make a living.

It was common to have a photo made into a postcard to send home to one's family in Europe. Charles Hoffman had this picture made in Fort Worth, c. 1915. He is pictured here looking at a blown-up photo of his girl friend in Russia to let her know he was thinking of her. However, he met another young girl in the U.S. and married her instead.

— *David Hoffman,* A Family Portrait, *privately published, Austin, Texas, print by Andy Reisberg*

Max Rachofsky of Dallas became a blacksmith, c. 1900.

— *Mrs. Max Blend*

Harry Ladabaum, left, and Alex Dochen,
right, peddled their wares between Austin
and Taylor around 1910.
— *Blanche Ladabaum Sheiness*

This photo c. 1910 shows a Tyler general
store owned by the Friedlands. Posing
with townfolk are Minnie Friedland, age
seventeen, who is standing between the
two men in suspenders, and Sam and
Henry Friedland, the two young boys, left
to right, in the foreground. The caption
on the back of the photo says, "I don't
think the horse was a Friedland." Rev.
Julius Friedland and his daughter Czernia
came from Minsk, Russia, through Galveston around 1904. He settled briefly in
Meridian, Mississippi, as an itinerant
rabbi, *mohel*, and *schochet* before accepting
a better position in Tyler, Texas, where
Czernia could work as a seamstress. In
1907, his wife, Esther, and their five
younger children arrived in Tyler via Galveston.

Several years later, the family moved to
New York, where they felt they would be
more comfortable among their *landsmen*.[24]
— *From the Collections of the
Dallas Jewish Historical Society*

Joe Rudnitzky, far left, came to Texas through Galveston c. 1907, and worked his way to Dallas as a chicken plucker. Notice the size of the bird Joe and his fellow worker are holding.
— *From the Collections of the Dallas Jewish Historical Society*

Brickman's Bakery, 111 Elm Street in Waco. Ida Brickman is the first woman on the left.
— *The Texas Collection, Baylor University, Waco, Texas*

Allfand & Chazen of Galveston bought and sold second-hand clothing and shoes.
— *From "West of Hester Street," produced by Cynthia and Allen Mondell, print by Andy Reisberg*

The Max Bettin Grocery was one of Victoria's leading and most prosperous stores around 1903. It advertised itself as having "the freshest goods and . . . all the articles to be found in an up-to-date grocery (horse collars, too)." Pictured are l. to r., Max, Regina, Izzy, and Frank Bettin. The local chapter of B'nai B'rith was named for Mr. Bettin.

— *Maxine Yonet*

Issie Wyll is shown in 1915 selling butternut bread for the Schepps Bakery in Dallas.

— *From the Collections of the Dallas Jewish Historical Society*

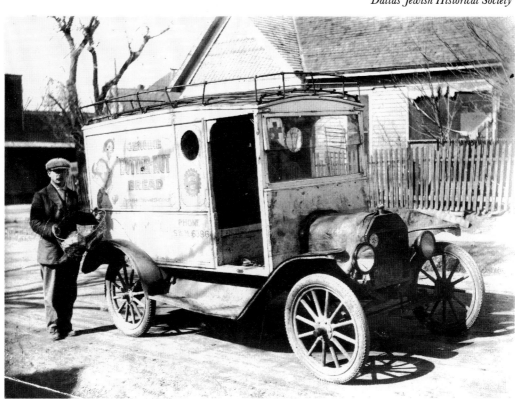

Waco tailors used the name "New York" as a draw to their business. "New York" suggested high fashion.
— *The Texas Collection, Baylor University, Waco, Texas*

Rag men and junk dealers were the first recyclers in Texas, and often turned junk into gold. Lipshitz took everything from copper, brass, and iron to bottles and rags.
— *The Texas Collection, Baylor University, Waco, Texas*

Sol Aron (above) started his business career in Texas as a peddler on a horse, but by 1917 was well established in his Crosby store, where he is pictured below with his wife, Sadie.
— *Rabbi James L. Kessler*

Charles Brachfield (1871–1947) of Henderson practiced law for fifty-seven years. He was the first Jew to seek statewide office in Texas when he ran for attorney general in 1926. He did not win, probably because of his strong prohibition stance, but came within 3,600 votes of a runoff—a remarkable showing in a decade dominated by Klan activity. Born in Vicksburg, Mississippi, Brachfield moved to East Texas at age two. He was admitted to the Texas Bar in 1890, was elected Rusk County judge in 1897, and to the State Senate in 1903, serving until 1911. In 1918, he was appointed a district judge by Governor W. P. Hobby, serving until 1928. He was active in the Masons and Odd Fellows and was a director of Henderson's First National Bank.[25]
— *Dr. E. Wolfe and Dr. A. S. Wolfe*

Victor H. Hexter, Sr., was a prominent Dallas attorney who was president of many groups, including the Dallas School Board in 1907, the Dallas United Jewish Charities in 1917–1919, and the B'nai B'rith District Grand Lodge #7, 1920–1921. Hexter was also a member of the city council, 1931–1935, and mayor pro-tem, 1932–1935. He was known as "Mr. Victor" by the new Jewish immigrants from Eastern Europe whom he assisted.
— *Dorothy M. and Henry S. Jacobus Temple Emanu-El Archives, print by Andy Reisberg*

Dr. Perry Bromberg, left, of Crockett, became a renowned surgeon and professor at Vanderbilt University in Nashville. His brother, Sol, right, was an attorney and an executive of the Galveston Dry Goods Company. He later became an executive officer of the Moody Cotton Company.[26]
— *Eliza Bishop, author-editor,* Houston County History, Crockett, Texas

"I do not care to bandy words . . ."
— Governor Ferguson

As Jews entered the professions, became prominent in business, and assumed leadership in their communities, some received government appointments. Rabbi Maurice Faber of Tyler was appointed to the University of Texas Board of Regents in March 1915, but was soon embroiled in a controversy with the man who appointed him, Governor Jim "Pa" Ferguson.

Governor Ferguson was not formally educated and was suspicious of University of Texas professors for what he viewed as misappropriation of state funds for salaries and other "extravagances." The governor demanded the firing of certain professors and a line-item veto over the university's budget. Because he viewed appointment to the Board of Regents as a political payoff, he expected "full cooperation" from his appointees. When he failed to receive it, he demanded their resignation.[27] One of these regents was Rabbi Maurice Faber.[28] Another, Dallas civic leader Alex Sanger, who had been appointed a regent in 1911 by Governor O. B. Colquitt, also resigned.

Correspondence between Rabbi Faber and Governor Ferguson over differences in policy reached a fever pitch in September 1916.[29] Excerpts follow.

From Rabbi Faber, September 20, 1916:

". . . I cannot give you the assurance of my 'full and complete cooperation' with your avowed plans concerning the internal affairs of the University of Texas without a thorough investigation into the merits of each individual case. I cannot pledge myself to follow the arbitrary will of any person, no matter how high and exalted, without being convinced of the justice of his demands. In my humble opinion such course will disorganize and disrupt the University, the just pride of the people of Texas. It will produce untold harm to the cause of Higher Education and prac-

tically destroy the labors of a generation to bring up the University of Texas to the high rank it now occupies among the universities of the land. With all due respect to you, my dear Governor, I do not concede to you the right or the authority to interfere in the internal management of the University of Texas. That is the sole business of the Board of Regents and for that purpose they are created. I would by far rather return to my honorable obscurity than stand in the lime light of public glamour purchased at the cost of manhood and conscience . . ."

Governor Ferguson responded on September 25, 1916:

". . . I do not care to bandy words with you further but simply put you on notice of these facts, and if you continue to allign [sic] yourself with the crowd who wants to perpetuate this policy, I shall not hesitate to repair the wrong which I have done in appointing you, so far as I am able to do under the powers given me under the Constitution of removal of appointees. If you want to force me to remove you, you can rest assured that I shall not shirk from the task . . .

Rabbi Maurice Faber (1854–1934) served Temple Beth El in Tyler from 1900 to 1934. He was appointed to the University of Texas Board of Regents in 1915, but resigned after refusing to accede to Governor James Ferguson's demands.
— *Eugene Lipstate*

". . . Your bold statement that the Governor of the State has no right or authority to interfere or inquire into the management of the University proves conclusively the arrogance which has attained to a marked degree in the institution, and shows how far the idea has gained credence that the people are to have nothing to do with this institution except shoulder and pay high appropriations to be turned over to a set of men to continue their unholy spree of establishing an educational hierarchy."
Yours truly,
Jas E. Ferguson.
Governor of Texas.

Needless to say, Faber resigned. He also testified against Governor Ferguson during his impeachment hearings in 1917. Ferguson was impeached and made ineligible to hold any office of trust or profit under the state. He ran again for governor in 1918, but was defeated by W. P. Hobby.

Simon Sakowitz (1883–1967), left, and Tobias Sakowitz, (1882–1970), right, from Kiev, Russia, opened a store in Houston around 1910. They recalled that their first customer, a longshoreman, came from the Galveston wharves and "bought some jeans, a work shirt, and a pair of Otis underwear." Following the 1915 hurricane, they moved their business permanently from Galveston to Houston, where Sakowitz became a local tradition. The Sakowitz brothers were not only successful retailers but also generous philanthropists and leaders of Temple Beth Israel.

— *Photo by Gittings*

Merchant princes

The turn of the century saw a few pioneer Jewish merchant families, like the Joskes and the Sangers, and new immigrant families, like the Sakowitzes, catapulted to immense success. The advent of ready-to-wear and general department stores brought a new kind of merchandising to what were previously specialty stores. In every major Texas city, Jewish merchants built department store dynasties that strengthened the economic health of their communities. The stories all have a similar ring: treat the customers kindly, give generous credit terms, and be considerate of your personnel. All led to legends of "merchant princes."

These families not only built fabulous businesses; most set examples with their generous personal involvement in civic enterprises like schools,

symphonies, and hospitals.

In addition to those businesses pictured, many others flourished and left their marks on their respective cities, such as Battelsteins and Foley's in Houston, Frost Bros. in San Antonio, E. M. Kahn in Dallas, and Goldstein-Migel in Waco.

Sakowitz: A Houston Tradition

Since its move after the Galveston storm of 1915, Sakowitz has been a name synonymous with taste in Houston retailing. From "Mr. Simon" and "Mr. Tobe" (as the two founders were fondly called by employees and patrons alike), the business has passed to two succeeding generations, with each shaping the Sakowitz stores to meet the needs of Houston buyers in times both expansive and austere.

In 1929, Simon and Tobias moved their business from the Kiam building to a new downtown skyscraper built by Jesse Jones at Main and Rusk. Opening day brought 40,000 people to shop and gawk at the unprecedented elegance of the store, which had now added women's apparel. The new store also marked the ascendancy of Tobias' son, Bernard (1907–1981), a graduate of the Wharton Business School. Solicitude of the customers and liberal credit policies turned Sakowitz into a Houston institution.

In 1951, Sakowitz again moved to a new downtown location, this one 100 times larger than the original Galveston store. Over the next twenty years, several new locations opened, including a men's shop in Glen McCarthy's lavish Shamrock Hotel. As Houston stretched to the suburbs, so did Sakowitz.

One legend has Tobias and Bernard sitting on the undeveloped corner of Westheimer and Post Oak boulevards, counting cars on their way to nearby elegant neighborhoods like Memorial and River Oaks. They counted a lot of cars and made their decision accordingly. The flagship Post Oak Sakowitz store opened in

1959. It stands across the way from Houston's famous shopping area, the Galleria, which opened ten years later.

In 1973, Bernard and his son Robert expanded Sakowitz beyond Houston, to Scottsdale, Arizona, Tulsa, Oklahoma, and Midland, Texas. But the 1985 downturn in the Texas economy led to reorganization under Chapter 11 of the Federal Bankruptcy Code. All downtown stores closed, and eighty percent of the business was sold to an Australian investor. Today, Sakowitz is still partially owned and operated by Robert T. Sakowitz. Few stores of this size in Texas or the U.S. are currently run by descendants of the founders.[30]

Joske's: "The pioneer one cent store"

In 1873, Julius Joske returned to San Antonio from a trip to Berlin, Germany, and opened a store in an adobe structure on Austin Street. By 1900, Joske's was one of the state's largest department stores, having added items such as fans, parasols, lace hosiery, and corsets to their standard military and outdoor equipment.

Joske's was responsible for a number of Texas "firsts." In 1886, the nickel was the lowest standard of value since pennies were scarce. Julius Joske considered it an insult to small quantity customers that penny items sold for a nickel, so he began to mark goods at the closest price to the penny. The *San Antonio Light* praised Joske for his fairmindedness in an article, "The Pioneer One Cent Store."

Under the leadership of Alexander, Julius' youngest son, Joske's grew to be one of the largest department stores south of St. Louis. Alexander was known for his literary and philosophical interests and regularly bought space in the newspaper next to his ads to communicate his opinions to the public. In one article he wrote that "prejudice is the greatest evil to humanity." After Alexander's death in 1925, his son-in-law, Dr. Frederic Oppenheimer, succeeded him as president.[31] Joske's was later bought out by Dillard's.

Galveston after the flood

As the wind roared at speeds well over 120 miles per hour in Galveston on September 8, 1900, the family of I. H. (Ike) Kempner huddled on the upper floor of their home at 1528 I Street. Half a dozen neighbors and servants from less sturdy residences found refuge there, as well. Before the storm was over, Ike Kempner tied a long rope around himself, secured the other end to his back porch, and swam from house to house to assist friends and neighbors. All about his neighborhood and city, he discovered snakes, open sewage, sparking electric cables, debris, and the corpses of humans and animals. Galveston Island, whose downtown Strand Street was known as the "Wall Street of the Southwest," was in ruins.[32]

In the weeks and months that followed, Isaac Herbert Kempner, son of Harris and Elizabeth Kempner, and one of Galveston's most powerful men, was more than a "search and rescue" hero. He became, according to history professor Harold Hyman of Rice University, "a pivotal force in post-storm rehabilitation and reform in the governance of the city." The 1900 storm proved to islanders that the city government was unprepared for disaster relief. It had no mechanism to recoup the loss of tax revenue

I. H. "Ike" Kempner (1872–1967) was in the Law School at Washington and Lee University in Virginia when his father, Harris Kempner of Galveston, became fatally ill. Ike returned home and assumed control of the family's cotton, banking, and ranching interests. Around 1890, he was elected a director of Galveston's Cotton Exchange and served as its president from 1905 to 1919. In 1907, he and Col. W. T. Eldridge bought the Cunningham Sugar Refinery in Sugar Land and reorganized it as the Imperial Sugar Company. He was also a director of various financial and industrial enterprises, including the U.S. National Bank and the Gulf, Colorado and Santa Fe Railroad. He was commissioner for finance for Galveston from 1901 to 1916 and mayor, 1917–1918. He was married to Henrietta Blum Kempner, also a prominent Galveston civic leader.

— UT Institute of Texan Cultures

due to flight from the island, and it had a less than amiable relationship with the state legislature. Galveston was on the brink of hopelessness after the massive devastation.

On the day after the storm, Kempner and fifteen other prominent Galvestonians, including Rabbi Henry Cohen, Morris Lasker, and Bernard Levy, formed an *ad hoc* relief committee which sought to reestablish order and allocate money and supplies pouring in from all over the nation and the world. After basic needs were met, Kempner and his colleagues addressed more far-reaching problems. The erosion of the city tax base and the damage to the deepwater port and other parts of the infrastructure that sustained Galveston, such as

wharves, piers, breakwaters, and warehouses, were all matters of grave concern. Kempner and his fellow committee members cataloged the losses and began exploring ways to improve the city as it was rebuilt.

Self-help was the order of the day, and within a week, Galveston businesses were functioning again and streets were clear. Kempner himself provided indefinite interest-free loans to Temple B'nai Israel, Catholic and Protestant churches, the orphans' home, and the library. Rabbi Cohen was "busier than ever, serving as a conduit for Kempner funds" (Hyman). Mrs. I. H. Kempner and other Galveston women started beautification programs by planting palms and oleanders along Broadway.

As city treasurer, Ike Kempner sought out new revenue sources by taxing peddlers, licensing taverns, and charging hookup fees for sewer connections. As a leading proponent for government reform, he promoted changes in the city charter as he spoke widely to fraternal and religious organizations, legislators, and journalists. In addition to his vast holdings as a businessman, Ike Kempner served the city as the first commissioner of finance and revenue from 1901 to 1916 and as mayor from 1917 to 1918. He was also the state treasurer of the National Jewish Relief Committee for World War I sufferers.

This photograph was one of hundreds taken showing the devastation caused by the 1900 storm in Galveston.

— Rosenberg Library, Galveston, Texas

The 1915 all-star basketball team of the
Jewish Literary Society, which sponsored
many activities for Jewish youth.
— *Copy from* History of the Jewish
Literary Society of Houston, *print by
Barker Texas History Center, UT Austin*

Members of the Jewish Literary Society of
Houston pose in 1908 in front of Congre-
gation Adath Yeshurun at Walker and
Jackson streets.
— *Copy from the* Golden Book,
Congregation Adath Yeshurun

"Common meeting ground of young and old."

By 1900, Houston's Jewish community flourished with two houses of
worship, Temple Beth Israel and
Congregation Adath Yeshurun. On
June 27, 1906, Max Flaxman, H.
Grossman, and Boris Litovich called
a meeting of young people in the vestry of Adath Yeshurun to organize a
Zionist youth society. Thirty-four
young men and fifteen young women
came, and after much discussion, decided that a Zionist focus was too
narrow. Instead, the group decided to
"support literary and scientific un-
dertakings, maintain a library, contribute to the enjoyment of its members, and promote music, literature,
science, and other arts." Thus was
the Jewish Literary Society of Houston born.

During the next ten years, the Jewish Literary Society grew from fifty to
400 members. It sponsored cultural
and social events that brought together members of all congregations

and promoted a number of marriages.
The Society had boat outings, mock
debates, including subjects such as
women's suffrage, Purim balls, and
communitywide *seders*. Baseball and
basketball teams for both men and
women played in city leagues. Members monitored theater in Houston for
anti-Semitic references, and in 1909
passed a resolution to boycott any
theater "that would present a Jewish
character in any way that would give
offense to our people, or cast reflection on them."[33] Musicales, lectures,
book reviews, and classes in Bible and
Jewish history were all popular.

In 1909, the vacant lot next to
Adath Yeshurun was purchased and
in 1911, a building, which housed a
library, was erected. In 1916, the
Jewish Literary Society of Houston
published its ten-year history, which
also included a list of the local Jewish
organizations. Tremendous growth
had taken place in the Jewish community, which now had four congregations, three B'nai B'rith lodges, an
Arbeiter Ring (Workmen's Circle),

five fraternal lodges, three Zionist societies, a chapter of the National
Council of Jewish Women, two male
social clubs, a Menorah Society at
Rice University, a Yiddish library,
two alumni associations, two wom-
en's auxiliaries, and a United Jewish
Charity Federation.

As Judge H. J. Dannenbaum observed on the Society's tenth anniversary, "It [the Jewish Literary Society]
has become the common meeting
ground of young and old. Differences
of creed, of social standing and of education disappear in the democracy of
its affairs . . . The Jewish Literary Society has become the center of Jewish
cultural activity and it is our public
representative in this respect."[34]

After 1916, activities of the Jewish
Literary Society dwindled, possibly
because of the intensity of the World
War I effort. The library, the land,
and the social functions were ultimately absorbed into the life of Congregation Adath Yeshurun.

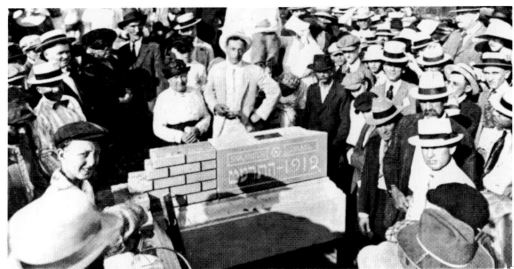

On March 9, 1919, Congregation Shearith Israel of Dallas laid the cornerstone for its new building on Park and Eakin streets. The honor, determined by competitive bidding, fell to Mrs. Rebecca Hurwitz and her son, Ben, with their bid of $1,000.   — *From the Archives of Congregation Shearith Israel*

Rabbi Wolf Willner (1863–1930) served in Houston eighteen years, first at Temple Beth Israel (1890–1892) and then at Congregation Adath Yeshurun (1907–1923). He led a group that split briefly from Adath Yeshurun to form Congregation Beth Sholom, which was primarily Zionist. They later rejoined Adath Yeshurun. Willner occasionally preached in German, but given the prejudice against Germans during World War I, he began calling the sermons "Yiddish."
     — *Copy from* Golden Book, Adath Yeshurun, 1891–1941

Rabbi Samuel Rosinger (1877–1965) served Temple Emanuel in Beaumont from 1910 to 1957.
     — *Jewish National Fund*

New temples and synagogues

Between 1900 and 1920, the Texas Jewish population grew from 15,000 to more than 30,000. Old congregations built larger structures, and new congregations formed to accommodate a variety of ritual preferences.

Jacob de Haas, editor of *The Maccabaean*, remarked in his 1904 Texas diary that "our people are far too ready to land themselves communally into debt in order to build synagogues and temples." But to Texas Jews, the buildings represented civic stability, and provided them with important social, and religious, outlets.

In the early twentieth century, new temples and synagogues sprang up throughout Texas. Beginning with Temple Moses Montefiore in Marshall, built in 1900, and extending to towns as far-flung as Wharton, which organized Shearith Israel in 1913, the growing population required new houses of worship. Existing congregations like Adath Yeshurun in Houston, Ahavath Sholom in Fort Worth, and Temple Emanu-El in Dallas, outgrew existing structures and moved to new ones. The Reform movement came to Fort Worth in 1903 with the construction of Temple Beth El at 5th and Taylor. And in Tyler, a small group of Orthodox Jews, who had founded Ahavath Achim in 1899, were able to build a simple wooden structure by 1910.

One of the first institutional synagogues west of the Mississippi and one of the first such buildings to be fully equipped was El Paso's new Temple Mount Sinai building in 1916. It had a gym, a stage, showers, a billiard room, a library, a moving picture booth, a large kitchen, and a social hall.

From the Carpathian Mountains to the Gulf Plains

Rabbi Samuel Rosinger (1877–1965) traveled far from his birthplace in Hungary to Beaumont, where he spent fifty years. Classically trained in Hungarian and Swiss *yeshivas*, he started at Temple Emanuel in Beaumont in 1910. (The congregation had erected its first building in 1901.) Rosinger served until his retirement in 1957, at the age of eighty.

Rabbi Rosinger was active in civic affairs, wrote editorials for the *Texas Jewish Herald*, and presented an annual paper to the Kallah of Texas Rabbis. He was once asked by a noted Jewish lecturer who visited Beaumont what "heinous sin have you committed that in expiation you have buried yourself in this hole?" Rosinger wrote: "The mystic magnetism that Texas exerts upon one by the vast reaches of its prairies, the matchless beauty of its skies, the luxurious growth of its tropical vegetation, and the warm heart of its people explains the secret of the long tenure of service of the Texas rabbis, and accounts, very largely, for my lifetime incumbency with my congregation." [36]

Eastern Europeans form new congregations

By 1900, German Jewry, with its emphasis on liberal Judaism, was entrenched in Texas. But the influx of immigrants coming from Eastern Europe, with their differences in ritual and liturgy, gave rise to new congregations.

Waco's Agudath Jacob had its first ordained Orthodox rabbi, Nachman Heller of Russia, by 1902. He served until 1921. Rabbi Heller was a frequent contributor to the American Jewish press and wrote a novel in Hebrew.

In Galveston, the Orthodox community was divided along cultural lines into two congregations. One had its origins in Russia, the Young Men's Hebrew Association (the Litvaks), and the other in Austria-Hungary, the Hebrew Orthodox Benevolent Association or Bikur Cholim (the Galitzianers). The two groups finally consolidated in 1931, with the founding of Congregation Beth Jacob.[37] Dallas had three Orthodox congregations around 1900: Tiferet Israel, Anshe Sephard (a Rumanian-Austrian *shul*) and Agudas Achim.

In some towns, dissatisfaction with existing congregations led to new groups. Agudas Achim, the Orthodox congregation of Corsicana, built its *shul* in 1915. During the same year, Agudas Achim members in Austin began meeting in homes, but the congregation was not chartered until 1924.

In San Antonio, controversy from within caused a new congregation to form. An active Agudas Achim member, Selig Deutchman, insisted on burying his Catholic wife in the synagogue's cemetery. The more Orthodox members withdrew and formed Congregation Rodfei Sholom in 1911.[38]

Reverend Sam Levy served Waco's Congregation Agudath Jacob as the circumciser and cantor from 1886 to 1934. In addition to being in charge of music and prayer, he was also the ritual butcher, certified to slaughter cattle and fowl in accordance with Jewish law. His son, Gus, recalled that as a young boy he delivered kosher meat for his father on horseback and that about half of his customers were Reform Jews.
— *The Texas Collection, Baylor University, Waco, Texas*

A celebration at Agudath Jacob in Waco, c. 1903, probably *Simchat Torah*.
— *The Texas Collection, Baylor University, Waco, Texas*

A Galveston *cheder*, c. 1903. Mr. Hirshfeld, the first trustee of the Young Men's Hebrew School, is pictured far left, and Rabbi L. Novich is at far right.
— *Copy from Shmuel Geller,* Mazkers Ahavah

Cheders and confirmation classes

Following the religious affiliations of their parents, young people studied Judaism. The Orthodox adhered to the rote style of learning of the old country *cheder,* or school, and education was not considered important for girls. Emphasis was on the study of Torah, Talmud, and Hebrew.

Many rabbis who came to Texas, however, were more steeped in secular learning. The *cheder* style of education was abandoned in the Reform temples primarily because education was regarded as a means of invoking Jewish ethnic consciousness in young people growing up in a pluralistic society.

Because the Reform movement was concerned with retaining the allegiance of these "Americanized" young people, a new ceremony called "confirmation" was developed. Confirmation was for both girls and boys ages fifteen and sixteen and gave girls educational opportunities alongside boys in temples and synagogues for the first time. The new curriculum emphasized the study of ethics and history, as well as Bible studies.

The confirmation class of 1917, Temple Beth Israel, Houston.
— *Temple Beth Israel Archives, Houston*

Rachel Edelstein and Michael Riskind on their wedding day in Chicago. Soon after the wedding, the Riskinds moved to Eagle Pass, Texas, where they operated a store catering to prominent Mexicans. The synagogue in their home was always open to Jewish soldiers stationed nearby.
— *Morris Riskind*

The Riskinds of Eagle Pass

The Texas-Mexican border represented both economic opportunity and a warm climate, and many Jews prospered in the area. Rachel and Michael Riskind moved to Eagle Pass from Chicago following the Panic of 1907 for opportunity and to improve his health. Their Eagle Store was popular among prominent Mexican politicians and generals.

Rachel, an excellent Hebrew scholar, came from a learned Litvak *Mitnaged* family. The upper level of the Eagle Store and the living room, dining room, and kitchen of the Riskind home were used as a synagogue with a holy ark for the Torah. The store is still operated by members of the Riskind family, though Eagle Pass has barely enough Jews for a *minyan*, including women.[39]

The Schwartzes of El Paso

Adolf Schwartz and Simon Picard's store in Juárez, Mexico, was named *Tres B* — for *bueno, bonita, barata* (good, pretty, cheap). Prior to 1900, Juárez was a tariff-free zone which flourished with European merchandise, while its sister city, El Paso, had a meager population of less than 1,000.

Adolf Schwartz, from Stropko, Hungary, came to Juárez via New York, Ohio, and California, and established successful business and financial enterprises. He married Fanny Amstater, also from Hungary, who was visiting her family in Juárez. But the lack of a Jewish life drew the couple to El Paso, where Adolph opened The Fair store. By 1900, El Paso's Jewish Cemetery Society evolved into Congregation Mount Sinai, where A. Schwartz became a leader. B'nai Zion, an Orthodox congregation, was organized that same year.

In 1902, Schwartz fell ill and closed The Fair, but became a silent partner in the Popular Dry Goods Company, run by his nephew Maurice and other relatives he had helped bring from Hungary. Maurice and his brothers turned the Popular into a successful dry goods store, widely known for clever merchandising schemes such as double-stamp days, clearance sales, and "markdowns." The Popular was also a reliable employer, boasting of many employees who spent their lifetimes working there. Many were Hispanic, and the Popular was also the first store in El Paso to employ black clerks.

Sometimes Maurice and Adolf Schwartz did not see eye to eye on political issues. During the Mexican Revolution, Maurice extended credit to Pancho Villa, while Adolf sided with the *Maderistas*. On a single day, soldiers from both sides shopped at the Popular, each unbeknownst to the other.[40]

In 1989, the Popular was still being operated in El Paso by members of the Schwartz family.

The Schwartz family was prominent on both sides of the border. This photo was taken in Juárez, Mexico, on July 29, 1911. Mrs. Adolph Schwartz (in flowered hat) stands beside Adolph. Mrs. Sara Perez de Madero (in black dress) stands beside Mexican General (President) Francisco I. Madero. The woman in front, far left, is Madero's nurse. The woman in back, far right, is the Schwartz's maid.
— *Copy from Floyd Fierman*, The Schwartz Family of El Paso, *print by Barker Texas History Center, UT Austin*

The Popular Dry Goods Company, which opened in El Paso around 1902, is still operated by members of the Schwartz family.
— *Copy from Floyd Fierman*, The Schwartz Family of El Paso, *print by Barker Texas History Center, UT Austin*

Oscar Sommer (1889–1971) was a prominent citizen both in Brownsville, Texas, and Matamoros, Mexico. When politicians like Lyndon Johnson and Ralph Yarborough wanted votes in the Rio Grande Valley, they posed in newspaper photos with Oscar Sommer. Upon Sommer's death, the mayor of Matamoros wrote a eulogy about him entitled, "Un Hombre Extraordinario."[41]
— *Ray S. Leonard*

Sam Dreben (1878–1925), center, fought in almost every revolutionary army in Mexico between 1911 and 1916. He also fought with distinction for the U.S. Army during World War I. Gen. John J. Pershing said that the short, stocky Dreben "was the finest soldier and one of the bravest men I've ever known."[42]
— *Southwest Collection, El Paso Public Library*

The Mexican Revolution (1910–1920)

Between 1910 and 1920, Mexico was embroiled in a bloody revolution. Many Jews living along the Texas-Mexico border in El Paso, Brownsville, Laredo, Harlingen, and Eagle Pass became involved in the struggle, some as soldiers, some as businesspeople, some as medical helpers.

Sam Dreben: soldier of fortune

Sam Dreben followed wars wherever he found them, and if he couldn't find one, he'd start one. A Russian immigrant who had seen family members slain in the pogroms, the short and stocky Dreben led guerrilla armies in Honduras and Guatemala and fought in almost every revolutionary army in Mexico.

After serving in the U.S. Army during the Philippine Insurrection, 1899–1901, Dreben joined international forces in the Boxer Rebellion in China.

Between 1911 and 1916, Dreben fought in Mexico. He served in Pancho Villa's army but quit after Villa's infamous attack on Columbia, New Mexico.

Sam Dreben reenlisted in the U.S. Army in 1918 and served with distinction in France. He was decorated by the French, Belgian, Italian, and U.S. governments.

When the Unknown Soldier was buried at Arlington National Cemetery, Gen. John J. Pershing chose Dreben to be a member of the honor guard. When Dreben died, the Texas legislature adjourned for a day and the flag flew at half mast over the State Capitol.[43]

Oscar Sommer

Oscar Sommer of Brownsville took a more Solomon-like approach to problem-solving than the fierce Dreben. A native of Rumania, Sommer also fought in the Philippine Insurrection before moving to Brownsville, where he became widely known and well-trusted on both sides of the border. He reclaimed hostages for both sides during the Mexican Revolution and transported the wounded from areas of attack to Brownsville hospitals. Many Mexicans mistook Sommer for a northern Mexican himself because he rode horseback wrapped in a *serape*. Sommer's wife, Laura, founded the local Hadassah chapter in 1954.

One popular story about Oscar Sommer was that one night, when a drunken young man with an unusually old gun boasted of his intention to kill someone, Oscar convinced him to try out the pistol in target practice on the outskirts of town. Once there, Sommer set up the target and let the young man shoot until the pistol was empty. Knowing that the shells could not be replaced, he confidently told the young man, "Now go kill the son of a -----." Thus, a tragedy was averted.

Sgt. Byron Gernsbacher of Fort Worth served in France during World War I. The *Jewish Monitor* of Fort Worth [June 20, 1919] reported that "Sergt. Byron Gernsbacher . . . while walking in the area around La Mans, France, met Miss Bessie Fox, head of the Jewish Welfare Board work in that section." Miss Fox was a sister of Rabbi George Fox, leader of Fort Worth's Temple Beth-El.
— *Fort Worth Jewish Community Sesquicentennial Archives*

Support of the war effort

Many Jewish Texans joined the armed forces and served overseas, like Sgt. Byron Gernsbacher of Fort Worth. Dr. Leonce Kosminsky of Texarkana was a founder of the American Legion Post #1 in Paris, France. Others lost their lives.

On the home front, Jews helped as soldiers, seamstresses, and bandage rollers. Many sold Liberty Bonds. Leo Krouse, president of the Texarkana Casket Company, was active in the War Industries Board. Other Texarkana Jews organized a Zionist Association and collected $1,000 for Jewish War Relief. Rabbi George Fox insisted that black workers in Fort Worth's Liberty Bond drive be allowed to attend and eat lunch at a bond drive event. Galveston Jews contributed $600 monthly for the relief of their European co-religionists.

B'nai B'rith organized a war services program. In District #7, most of the 6,000 members were beyond draft age, but 435 served in the armed forces. Others were volunteers in hospitals. Temples and synagogues from San Antonio to El Paso, Houston to Dallas, opened their doors and their hearts to Jewish soldiers far from home.

Sigmund Archenhold of Waco.
— *The Texas Collection, Baylor University, Waco, Texas*

Max Westheimer (1881–1942) of Houston joined the navy.
— *Bettie Westheimer Schlamme*

Left to right, Myron B. Marks and Zelig Maurice Jacobs, cousins in Corsicana, play dress up.
— *Audrey D. Kariel, Marshall, Texas*

Like many women's organizations, the Ladies Auxiliary of Congregation Shearith Israel in Dallas worked untiringly for the Red Cross, serving food and providing hospitality. They helped with bond drives, made bandages, and sewed hospital garments. L. to r., Mrs. Rosenberg, Miss Gertie Green, Miss Pearly Fried, Mrs. Marie Wolens, and Mrs. Ethel Ablon.
— *From the Archives of Congregation Shearith Israel, Dallas*

War bonds, Liberty Loans, Red Cross Motor Corps

Jewish women, like other Texas women, worked diligently to help the war effort. Members of the National Council of Jewish Women worked with the Red Cross and created sewing circles to make garments to send overseas. The Dallas section sold $176,000 worth of war bonds, practiced food conservation, and worked on the Soldiers and Sailors Welfare Committee. In Waco, the women sent garments to Belgium and to Ellis Island. In Texarkana, women worked in Liberty Loan, the War Stamps drive, and for Jewish War Relief. The exclusive Wednesday Sewing Club of Fort Worth, founded by Mae Davidson, was made up of twelve Jewish women who sewed warm clothes, knitted, and made bandages. And in Galveston, Henrietta Blum (Mrs. I. H.) Kempner was chair of the Jewish Women's War Bonds Sales Committee, for which she received a medal, and also drove in the Red Cross Motor Corps.

Dallas girls rolled bandages for the war effort in the alterations room of the old Sanger Bros. building on Main and Lamar. L. to r., left front table: Caroline Schinks, Fannie Koenigsberg Kahn, and Elise Corder. Front right table: center, Inez Munzesheimer Roth, far right, Juanita Bromberg Kramer. Back table, seated with head down, Alice Roos Ehrenfeld. Standing, Fanchon (Mrs. I. K.) Kahn.
— *Dorothy M. and Henry S. Jacobus Temple Emanu-El Archives, Dallas, print by Andy Reisberg*

Joyce Dannenbaum (Wolf) learns to play baseball

Joyce Dannenbaum, age four, learns to play baseball from her nine-year-old brother, Cecil, c. 1916, in Houston. Texas girls could be as rough and tumble as their male counterparts: as early as 1904, Ester Levi was a member of the Red Imps baseball team at the J. D. Mitchell School in Victoria.
— *Joyce Dannenbaum Wolf*

When Florence Ramer (Rabe) of San Antonio spoke to the Houston Jewish Literary Society in January 1916, she was one of the first female Jewish lawyers in Texas. Her words echoed the trend of Jewish womanhood as they went out to meet the pressing issues of their time: "Stand up for your Judaism . . . One of the greatest enemies to the Hebrew race is the Jew who seeks to push himself into society by trying to have people overlook the fact that he is a Jew . . . success comes only to those who do their own thinking."[1]

Florence Rabe was part of a new generation of women around the turn of the century who were getting an education, entering the work force, and taking their place as professionals. Jewish women like Rabe continued working in benevolent societies and Sisterhoods, organized local chapters of new Jewish women's groups, and participated in the newly organized suffrage societies and federated women's clubs.

Her speech captured the tone of the feverish work of the National Council of Jewish Women and Hadassah during those years, as well as of the Jewish women in the larger community who worked for suffrage and social reform. There were schools, libraries, and symphonies to build, dairies to sanitize, children to feed, immigrants to assimilate, and laws to pass. And to succeed ultimately, women needed the vote. Jewish women were community builders who tackled these causes with intelligence and elbow grease and helped change the social and cultural life of the state in the process.

The earliest Jewish women's institutions were the Ladies Hebrew Benevolent Societies (LHBS). In many Texas towns, LHBS members were ladies bountiful personified, with sewing circles made meaningful by charitable work. The 1900 minutes of the LHBS in Victoria gave insight

"The new woman, like the automobile, is here to stay."[2]
THE CHANGING ROLE OF WOMEN

into the many causes they supported: rent for a poor family, sufferers of the Galveston flood, the Victoria Hebrew Cemetery, and a $2.50 donation to Jerusalem.

Congregational sisterhoods, like that of Dallas' Shearith Israel (organized in 1913), slowly replaced the old-fashioned Ladies Hebrew Benevolent Societies. Jewish institutions were full of women who gave their lives to the fulfillment of the educational, fund-raising, and religious functions of the congregation. They taught Sunday school, raised money, made *hamentashen,* sang in the choir, and ran gift shops. And they reached out to the non-Jewish community. Dallas' first interfaith activity was a Silver Tea, held around 1900, to collect money for a non-sectarian old ladies' home. Many Jewish women, like Mrs. Leon Goodman of San Antonio, worked within both the general and Jewish communities. Not only was she treasurer of the San Antonio Associated Charities and secretary of the local library board, she was also president of the Ladies Hebrew Benevolent Society.

Individual philanthropists with strong personalities and iron wills were as relentless as dowager empresses in the pursuit of their causes. Minnie Mittenthal Marcus rode in her horse and carriage to collect money for the Dallas Jewish Benevolent Society; Rebecca Sakowitz Nathan started the Houston Humane Society in her home. Bertha Krakauer (Mrs. Gus) Zork gave $3,000 to Temple Mount Sinai in El Paso, and Pauline Sterne Wolff bequeathed $100,000 to establish a Home for Jewish Orphans and Indigent Widows in Houston in 1921.

Jennie Nathanson (Mrs. Joe) Schepps opened a home for unwed mothers in Dallas in the 1920s. She and her husband lived in Goosevalley. Her autocratic manner led her three children to call her Godmother;

her grandchildren called her Czarina, and others called her Duchess. After breaking her hip, she summonsed people by stomping her cane on the floor. In the 1940s, Jennie purchased a new building for the Dallas Community Chest. Her son, George, remembers when she announced to her children that "they" had bought the building and proceeded to tell them how much to pay.[3]

From kindergarten through college, Texas Jewish women were concerned with ensuring that their own sons and daughters, as well as others less fortunate, received an education. Mrs. Rudolph Liebman was founding president of the Dallas Free Kindergarten Association, which served the children of mill workers and Russian Jewish immigrants. The first kindergarten in Texas was started in 1892 by Olga Kohlberg, who brought the concept of early childhood education to El Paso from her native Germany.

Increasingly, in the early 1900s, Jewish girls began attending high school and college. Delano Levi (Hirsch) was valedictorian of Dallas High School in 1904 with an average grade of 97.7. Some went to college to become teachers, nurses, pharmacists, and librarians. Florence Ramer (Rabe) and Ray Karchmer (Daily) were early law and medical school graduates who paved the way for women to come. Nettie Marx Klein of Texarkana graduated from the Dallas Medical College in 1903, and in 1921 became the first female member of the State Board of Health. Jewish girls attending the North Texas Female Academy (later the Kidd-Key College) in Sherman were assured in the 1911 catalog that "all pupils except Jewesses must attend church on Sunday." Rose Toubin of Brenham attended Rice for a year in 1916; an observant Jew, she paid a dollar to take a test on Monday instead of Saturday.

Jewish women, along with their

non-Jewish counterparts, began entering the work force in larger numbers around 1900. Gertrude Predicki was a deputy clerk for the U.S. Customs Office in Galveston, Jennie Goodman was postmistress in Laredo, and Bee Goldberg monogrammed linens at Sanger Brothers in Dallas. Many women worked alongside their husbands in Mom and Pop stores.

The prosperity of some Jewish businessmen created a leisure class of wives who cared primarily for their homes and children. No longer content with cemetery and charity work, women changed focus as new organizations like the National Council of Jewish Women, Hadassah, and the Texas Federation of Women's Clubs were born. A new kind of volunteer emerged — one who was not afraid to confront painful social issues like white slavery, poverty, and medical care for mothers and children.

In the early twentieth century, the rights of married women in Texas were bound by legal restrictions. They could not control their own funds or property; their husbands' permission was needed for all financial transactions. Jewish women in many Texas cities were at the forefront of the suffrage movement, making it no surprise that the "Mother of the Texas Equal Legal Rights Amendment" more than fifty years later was a Jew, Hermine Tobolowsky.

The legacy of those gritty pioneer women lives on today in school cafeterias, sanitary dairies, libraries, symphonies, and laws protecting the rights of women. And Jewish cultural and religious institutions stand stronger today because of "women's work."

In the late 1880s, Sarah and Jake Shapira turned their Madisonville home into a boardinghouse which soon became popular with traveling salesmen known as drummers. The house burned in 1903, Jake died, and Sarah rebuilt a larger Victorian-style facility on the same site, the Shapira Hotel. It opened in 1904 as a haven for travelers and a center for community events. Known far and wide for her good cooking and hospitality, Sarah served her delicious meals to as many as twenty-six guests at a time until she retired in 1922.[4]

— *Texas Historical Commission*

Boardinghouses

Hospitality by Texas Jewish women found many expressions: a home for guests and travelers or a home-like atmosphere in the fitting rooms of their businesses. Many women, single, married, and widowed, supplemented family income or supported themselves and their children.

From the frontier to the blossoming cities full of newcomers, women ran boardinghouses. After the Civil War, Jewish peddlers in Jefferson boarded among the more permanent Jewish families. Mrs. J. Calisher ran an El Paso boardinghouse; Mary Levy Cohen ran one in Navasota, while her husband, affectionately known as "Coonskin" Cohen, bought furs and hides. The Cohens later operated a boardinghouse in Dallas.

Carrie Marcus Neiman

The most successful Dallas businesswoman was Carrie Marcus Neiman. She, her brother Herbert Marcus, Sr., and her husband A. L. Neiman brought high fashion to Texas when in 1907 they opened what would become the most famous department store in the world.

Stanley Marcus later said that Neiman-Marcus was founded on bad business judgment. When his father, aunt, and uncle completed a successful sales promotion campaign in Atlanta, Georgia, in 1907, they were offered the Missouri franchise for a new soft drink, Coca-Cola, or $25,000 in cash. They took the cash and opened Neiman-Marcus. Dallas was then a rich but still somewhat raw town with 200 saloons, and Oklahoma was still Indian Territory.

Stanley described Dallas as a city where women could wear white gloves for a week, white stone buildings stayed white, and there was no smog or smoke. It was "a city with a Southern climate, Northern enterprise, Eastern sophistication, and Western self-confidence."[5]

Carrie Marcus Neiman is much less known than her internationally famous nephew Stanley. But it was her fashion judgment, taste, and intuitive sense of stylish trends that were key factors in the store's fantastic success. She bought the store's initial stock of silks, satins, woolens, and furs with $17,000 in cash from New York wholesalers; the elegant inventory sold out within a month. She was soon traveling to Paris for merchandise. In 1928, Carrie divorced her husband. The intense, graceful, and charming Carrie never had an office or an assistant. She became chairman of the board in 1950, but often interrupted board meetings to wait on favored customers. Most would not think of making a purchase without the approval of Miss Carrie, a woman of understated elegance, who usually wore a simple black dress, a strand of pearls, and two gold bracelets. For fifty years, she was the arbiter of taste and fashion.[6]

Carrie Marcus Neiman (1883–1963) uniquely defined high fashion in Dallas, and ultimately, the world beyond as one of the co-founders of Neiman-Marcus. Launched in 1907 by Carrie, her husband A. L. (Al) Neiman (whom she later divorced) and her brother Herbert Marcus, the store was widely known for the personal attention lavished on its customers and its carefully selected ready-to-wear merchandise. Carrie became chairman of the board in 1950.

— *Neiman-Marcus Archives*

Neiman-Marcus' first ad, which ran on September 8, 1907, set out the store's philosophy: ". . . to be at all times leaders in their lines and to give buyers in Texas something out of the commonplace . . . a radical departure from the usual ready-to-wear department . . . exclusive lines of high-class garments . . ."

— *Neiman-Marcus Archives*

Temma Valnianski Tobolowsky from Poland (far right) was a Dallas practical nurse and midwife in the early 1900s. She gave vaccinations, delivered babies, and pierced ears in Goosevalley, where many immigrants lived. Temma was also a founder of Tiferet Israel, an Orthodox congregation.[7] Left to right are Temma's daughter, Lena Tobolowsky Rosenthal, and grandchildren, Sam Rosenthal, Leah Leventhal, and Lynn and Rube Rosenthal.

— *Annette Golman Jayson*

Lena Young (Mrs. Joe) Weisman (1858–1930) was a homeopathic healer who recorded her patients' prescriptions on the bathroom wall of her elegant Marshall home. She nursed her family and neighbors with a supply of homeopathic remedies from Los Angeles, which came in a large parcel every autumn and were stored in her medicine chest. Her granddaughter, Mary Hirsch Stern, recalled that on Saturday mornings, "The colored folks came to town in wagons. She [Lena] would stand on the back porch . . . as they would state their ailments and she regally dispensed her sugar pellets."[8] Lena's grandson, Dr. Raymond Kay, now of Upland, California, was inspired by her work to become a physician. He was a pioneer in the formation of health maintenance organizations like Kaiser, the first of its kind.

— *Audrey D. Kariel, Marshall, Texas*

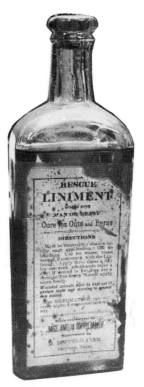

Amelia Dopplemayer's rescue liniment: good for man or beast.
— *Harrison County Historical Museum, Marshall, Texas, print by Frankie McConnell*

Amelia Dopplemayer's Rescue Liniment Good for Man or Beast.

Amelia Dopplemayer lived first in Marshall with her family, then in Jefferson and Sherman. Aside from producing her famed liniment, Amelia was a dollmaker who sent five homemade dolls to the Dionne quintuplets in 1934.

Amelia Dopplemayer's Rescue Liniment was a popular East Texas remedy for cuts, burns, and rheumatism. The bottle on display at the Harrison County Historical Museum has directions on the label:

Cure for Cuts and Burns.
Directions:
Must be thoroughly shaken before each application. Use no bandage. Clean wound, if necessary, with the Liniment. Apply three times a day for one week, afterwards, twice a day; if wound is too deep use a syringe. For Screw Worms apply more freely.

Wounded animals must be kept out of the pasture night and morning to prevent dew poisoning.

For rheumatism rub well every night; a most excellent remedy.

Made exclusively by Mrs. Amelia Dopplemayer.

Successor to M. Dopplemayer
Sherman, Texas

Carrie Pfeiffer Brown

Newfound prosperity for some Jewish families made it possible for their children, including the daughters, to go to college. Bella Dopplemayer of Marshall was in UT Austin's first graduating class in 1886. And during the 1880s, Myer Levy's daughters, of Navasota, attended girls' colleges in Kentucky. The daughters of Morris and Nettie Lasker went to New York for advanced degrees in social work and philanthropy. Most girls were not expected to obtain degrees in order to earn a living but were trained in the arts and letters to become "ladies." A few, however, went on to professional careers and positions of community leadership.

Carrie Pfeiffer Brown's passion for education led her not only to college but to work in her community to help those less fortunate. Born in Carrizo Springs, Texas, in 1886, to John and Sophie Pfeiffer, Carrie grew up in Encinal and San Antonio and was educated in the public schools. She entered the University of Texas at age fifteen, where she was a member of the student council, and graduated at nineteen.

After graduation, Carrie married Dr. Alexander Brown, a San Antonio physician. She was one of the first women in San Antonio to bob her

Carrie Pfeiffer (Mrs. A. A.) Brown (1886–1977) was a student at the University of Texas at Austin in 1905. She is the only Jewish woman to have served as Texas state president of the American Association of University Women (1941–1943).
— *Photo by Elliott, copy from UT Institute of Texan Cultures*

hair and drive a car. The Browns' home became a social center with an outstanding collection of fine books, art, china, and antique furniture.

In her ninety years, Carrie Pfeiffer Brown immersed herself in community affairs, both Jewish and non-sectarian. She worked with the San Antonio Kindergarten Association, the Immigrant Night School established by the National Council of Jewish Women, the City Federation of Women's Clubs, Crippled Children's Association, PTA, Bexar County Medical Auxiliary, the Texas Home-Finding Association, and taught Sunday school at Temple Beth-El.

Carrie Brown strongly supported the hiring of women on college faculties, the passage of child labor laws, and education for dependent children. Her activities prompted her friends, Rabbi David Jacobson and Archbishop Robert E. Lucey, to urge Governor Coke Stevenson to appoint her as a University of Texas regent in 1944–1945. However, a woman had never before been a regent, and the time was not yet ripe.[9]

"A CAPTIVE PRINCESS"[10]

One young woman who desired college but could not attend because of illness was Miriam Hirshfeld Frees, a granddaughter of Austin pioneers Henry and Jennie Hirshfeld. Miriam, who lived in Austin from 1912 to 1918, was stricken with a treacherous and fatal illness. She was unable to attend school but studied constantly at home. As an admirer wrote, Miriam "was as well informed as the average college graduate." She was intellectually gifted and was a delightful companion to teachers, students, and the learned.[11] Before her death at age nineteen, Miriam wrote *An Autobiography*, excerpts of which follow.

"When we girls used to talk over our plans, as to what we should do after high school, I always contended, in spite of their scorn, that college was my objective point. Father's teasing advice was: 'Look in the glass, if you're good looking you don't have to go.' I did not go to college — it was not a decision of mirrors, but rather thermometers. And so I became a 'Captive Princess.' . . . other prisoners keep me company . . . Little Women . . . Don Quixote and Uncle Remus . . .

"I can say, like the mouse in Alice in Wonderland, 'Mine is a long tale, and sad.' Please, let no doubting Alice make reply, 'I see it's long, but just where is it sad?' "

Miriam Hirshfeld Frees (1898–1918) was captive to a fatal illness but did not stop studying.
— *Hirshfeld Papers (AR/H.24), Austin History Center, Austin Public Library*

Dr. Ray Karchmer Daily (1891–1975) of Denison was one of the first women, and Jews, to graduate from a Texas medical school. She graduated from the University of Texas at Galveston Medical Branch in 1913, was a well-known ophthalmologist, and served on the Houston School Board from 1928 to 1952.
— *Moody Medical Library, University of Texas Medical Branch at Galveston*

Dr. Ray Karchmer Daily

Yale and Harvard would not accept Ray Karchmer to medical school because she was a woman, and the conventional wisdom in 1909 was that a woman would be embarrassed by the study of anatomy. But Ray Karchmer, born in Vilna, Russia, was undaunted by rejection on the East Coast. She became one of the first women — and Jews — to graduate from the University of Texas Medical Branch (UTMB) at Galveston in 1913.

Being accepted to medical school was the first of her challenges. With difficulty she found an internship in Pennsylvania, but her chosen specialty of ophthalmology had no residency for a woman in the U.S., so Ray went to Vienna, Austria, to complete her training. In 1915, she was the only female physician among the founders of the Houston Academy of Medicine.

After graduation, Dr. Karchmer married Dr. Louis Daily, an ear,

nose, and throat specialist who was her partner professionally and personally until his death in 1952. She later became partners with her son, Dr. Louis Daily, Jr.

Her experience with discrimination led her to become an active suffragist and supporter of equal rights for minorities. In 1928, Dr. Daily was elected to the Houston School Board opposing the influence of the Ku Klux Klan. She was president of the Texas School Board Association, and her support for federally funded free lunch programs for the needy led to her being labeled a "Communist." Her progressive stands were attacked by an opponent, who used McCarthyite tactics to defeat her in 1952.[12]

Throughout her career, Dr. Daily remained concerned about women in medical school. In 1943, after the women's dormitory at UTMB was badly damaged by a hurricane, she led a legal battle to provide housing for female students.[13]

"The doors were closed to women."

Fannie Pravorne Wienir of Dallas was one of the state's first women to pass the bar. She attended the Jefferson School of Law at night and passed the five-day Texas Bar Examination in 1928 with an average grade of 83-5/8.

"I was a rarity in those days," she recalled. "The doors were closed to women. Finally, I found an office where they allowed me to hang my hat, provided I would answer the telephone."[14] Fannie worked in Philadelphia as a legal secretary. After her marriage to Harry Wienir, they owned a wholesale pharmaceuticals business in St. Louis. "I was secretary-treasurer for twenty years and my legal knowledge stood me in good stead," she said.

In 1937, Fannie became a founder of Dallas' Business and Professional Chapter of Hadassah. Now a resident of Los Angeles, she is a Life Trustee of the American Society of the Technion in Israel.

Fannie Pravorne (Wienir) (1902–) of Dallas passed the Texas Bar Examination in 1928. — *Fannie Pravorne Wienir*

Tillie Harris Harmel (1900–) of Dallas was one of the first Jewish women to achieve certification as a pharmacist in 1919. — *Tillie Harris Harmel*

One of the first Jewish women to graduate from pharmacy school was Tillie Harris Harmel. She attended Baylor University Medical School in Dallas and finished school in St. Louis, where she received a Gold Medal.

She returned to Dallas in 1919 to take the examination for the Texas State Board. The law required that applicants be twenty-one; Tillie was only nineteen. A member of the board advised, "I won't tell — go take the exam." She did and earned pharmacy certificate #6606. Mrs. Harmel and her husband owned pharmacies in Dallas and Los Angeles.[15]

Few respectable jobs

In the early twentieth century, there were only a few jobs considered respectable for working women, such as clerking in a store or working as a secretary or telephone operator. For the educated "ladies," there was teaching, nursing, and library science. Some Jewish women became interested in schools, hospitals, and libraries through their clubs, and later made careers in those institutions.

Lena Bromberg Klein (1881–1966) taught mathematics and literature to three generations of Crockett public school students. "Miss Lena" graduated from Sam Houston Normal in Huntsville around 1900 and as a teacher, inspired students to read fine literature. Many gathered after school to listen to her read poetry and prose and to enjoy informal discussions. "Miss Lena" was founder of several Crockett study, social, and historic groups that still meet today.[16]
— *Eliza Bishop*

Miss Martha Schnitzer, a University of Texas graduate, is shown behind the loan desk in Houston's first public library building checking out books, c. 1904. In 1945, she was appointed acting head of Houston's Ideson Public Library. She also established a library for Temple Beth Israel's religious school.
— *Houston Metropolitan Research Center, Houston Public Library*

Jennie Hesselson Zesmer (1892–1944) taught at the Royal Street public school (now Leila P. Cowart school) in Dallas. She is pictured here with her class, c. 1912. Active in many civic and religious organizations, she was president of Shear-ith Israel's Sisterhood and the Texas-Louisiana Region of Hadassah, as well as vice-president of the National Council of Jewish Women, Dallas Section. Mrs. Zesmer also served as director of the Jewish Federation's Social Service Division.

— *From the Collections of the Dallas Jewish Historical Society*
— *From the Archives of Congregation Shearith Israel*

— Uniongram from Temple Beth Israel Sisterhood to Rose Brilling

Rose Brilling

As Texas congregations grew in strength and numbers, the Hebrew Ladies Aid Societies evolved into strong Sisterhood auxiliaries. In every congregation, there were Sisterhood women who devoted their lives to the nuts and bolts of congregational life. Most were volunteers, but some earned salaries. As bookkeepers they paid bills, as secretaries they typed sermons. They organized weddings, *bar mitzvot,* and funerals. They saw that there were fresh flowers for Friday night services and that the building was clean and well organized. They sometimes supervised the religious school and were usually in charge of *Oneg Shabbats* and holiday celebrations. Whether or not there was a rabbi or even a building, the women played leading roles.

Rose Brilling of Houston's Temple Beth Israel was at the center of all the congregation's activities. She was a consummate clubwoman when her young husband, Robert Brilling, died unexpectedly in 1925. It was the eve of laying the cornerstone of the new temple. Concerned that she was left practically destitute with three young daughters to raise, the Sisterhood gave her a job as staff secretary. She worked there for thirty-six years, until the day she died at her desk at age seventy-eight.

Every year at Beth Israel, Mrs. Brilling inscribed in calligraphic

handwriting the inside of the Bibles presented to confirmands. She coordinated Sisterhood activities and taught Sunday school. When another of her peers, Mrs. Baer, who also taught Sunday school for many years, quit, Mrs. Brilling's grandson, Joe Schechter, wrote to her, "Grandma, if *you* quit, too, the place will fall apart."

Much of the unofficial history of the congregation — the political intrigue and gossip — died with Mrs. Brilling. Day after day, her comfortably decorated office received a line of congregants who came to her for counsel and advice as they shared their joys and woes. One of her co-workers, Bea Joseph of Austin, remembers that "Rose was everybody's mother. She never pried and she never shared a confidence. She was a quiet, but strong presence in the Temple."[17]

Rose Emden Brilling (1882–1961) was one of many Sisterhood women who made a career out of temple life. Her name is inscribed in the Union of American Hebrew Congregations House of Living Judaism in New York.

— Cathy Schechter

"The women of our people were always a . . . vital force . . . as active in the cultural and religious survival of our people as the great heroes of Israel. Rabbi Akiba is great, but Rachael, his wife, stands right beside him . . . In over 5,000 years of our recorded history we can see the great personalities of Jewish women such as Judith and Shulamith; Emma Lazarus and Henrietta Szold . . ."
— Mrs. Abraham Herson, Congregation Ahavath Achim, Tyler

Temple Fredda in Bryan was built in 1912 and named in memory of Fredda Tapper, the grandmother of the congregation's founder, Max Tapper. Naming a congregation after a woman was unprecedented and very unusual, even today. Land for the temple was the gift of a non-Jewish banker, J. E. English, and money for its construction came from Jew and Gentile alike.
— National Register Program, Texas Historical Commission

"Of Judaism, she was the High Priestess."

Thousands of Jewish women have helped build and support community institutions at the local and national levels. Among the outstanding examples of women who used their talents and hard work to sustain temples and synagogues are Rose Brilling and Miriam Browning, both of whom worked for Temple Beth Israel in Houston for over thirty years. Brilling was the staff secretary, and Browning taught in the religious school.

On the national level, Jeanette Miriam Goldberg from Jefferson was secretary of the Jewish Chautauqua Society in 1923. A plaque on the wall of Jefferson's Hebrew Sinai Congregation describes her by saying, "Of Judaism, she was the high priestess."

It is possible that had these women been born in another time, they would have become rabbis. The idea of women rabbis surfaced early. In 1922, Rabbi Henry Cohen of Galveston chaired a committee of the Central Conference of American Rabbis, which passed a resolution by a 56–11 vote, recommending the ordination of women rabbis: ". . . [It] is a modern issue due to the evolution in her status in our day," the committee wrote. But it would be another fifty years before the first woman rabbi was ordained.

The National Council of Jewish Women

When the Parliament of Religions to be held at the Chicago World's Fair in 1893 was planned, women were left off of the program. That single act of omission led Hannah G. Solomon, Rebecca Kohut, and Sadie American to convene the first Congress of Jewish Women. The Congress voted to establish the National Council of Jewish Women (NCJW). By 1896, there were NCJW sections in fifty U.S. cities.

NCJW chapters were innovators in Sabbath schools and kindergartens, immigrant assistance, English classes, and job training programs. Early Council women supported women's suffrage and addressed difficult issues like white slavery and prostitution.

The first Texas NCJW section may have been the one in Beaumont, organized by a state vice-president, Miss Jeanette Goldberg of Jefferson, in 1901. The group established a library with 300 books in the vestry of Beaumont's Temple Emanuel and promised to promote a public library later. The San Antonio Section was organized in 1907 by a Mrs. Schwab of Chicago, who was visiting the city. She convened a meeting of thirty women, and Mrs. Anna Hertzberg was elected president. Theirs was the first Jewish women's organization in San Antonio to participate actively in civic and cultural projects.

In 1913, Miss Sadie American visited Texas, beginning her sweep across the state in Houston, where she enlisted seventy-five members to charter a section. She then traveled to Waco, Dallas, Galveston, and El Paso. The first president of the Galveston section was Mrs. Abe Blum, and the first president in El Paso was Mrs. Max Mayer (1917). The Sherman-Denison group, organized in 1917, was led by Mrs. Ray Exstein Tillman.

Texas sections of the NCJW worked from the beginning to feed needy children through penny lunch programs (which evolved into school

cafeterias), assisted in immigrant education through English classes in night school, and founded libraries, schools, and kindergartens.

Pauline (Mrs. Theodore) Mack (1873–1939) founded one of the first Texas sections of the National Council of Jewish Women in Fort Worth in 1902. The section not only organized the Fort Worth Baby Hospital, but members raised the funds, formed the hospital board, and operated it for many years. Under Pauline's leadership, the NCJW also raised sufficient money so that Temple Beth-El could hire a rabbi and erect a building.
— *Fort Worth Jewish Community Sesquicentennial Archives*

Sadie (Mrs. Henry J.) Dannenbaum (1872–1947) was the first president of the Houston Section of NCJW in 1913. Council dues were $2 a year, and the group met at Temple Beth Israel. By 1914, the NCJW had started the Working Girls Home for underpaid women, many of whom were immigrants. The sewing committee made clothes for the Autrey Tubercular Hospital and the Jewish Children's Home in New Orleans.[18]
— *Lasker M. Meyer, grandson*

In 1913, Carrie Sanger Godshaw (1884–1973) of Waco met with Sadie American, Rabbi Henry Cohen, and Rabbi I. Warsaw in a small hotel room in Waco to form the Waco section of NCJW. The Waco Council set up a soup kitchen at Bell's Hill School, which evolved into the Penny Lunches in 1919 and ultimately, school cafeterias. Carrie was a suffragist and a charter member of the League of Women Voters. She was the director of Planned Parenthood, and in 1916, established the city's first Montessori kindergarten.[19]
— *Elva Sanger Godshaw (Mrs. Robert E.) Levy*

Estelle Goodman (Mrs. Charles) Levy (1899–1963) was a leader and president of the El Paso section, NCJW, 1928–1939. She was also active in Temple Mount Sinai, the Cloudcroft Sanitarium for Underprivileged Children, World War II War Bond sales, and the Russian War Relief Committee.[20]
— *Levy Goodman Collection, Western Jewish History Center, Judah L. Magnes Museum, Berkeley, California*

Elizabeth Gaertner (Mrs. Alphonse) Levy (1849–1925) encouraged her daughter Estelle Meyer to abandon Galveston's more provincial Sisterhood in favor of aligning with the NCJW and to work for a Mother's Club. Elizabeth helped immigrants coming through Galveston to find jobs and housing and to learn English.[21]
— *Texas Division, American Association of University Women, copy from Evelyn Carrington, Women in Early Texas*

Minnie (Mrs. Victor) Hexter was president of the Dallas Section of NCJW from 1915 to 1919. Under her leadership, the Council began a free milk fund for needy children and families. Today, the Minnie W. Hexter Milk Fund is still the only consistent source of free milk in Dallas County. Minnie was also president of the Temple Emanu-El Sisterhood from 1933 to 1935.[22]
— *Dorothy M. and Henry S. Jacobus Temple Emanu-El Archives, print by Andy Reisberg*

A sewing class conducted by the Dallas Section of NCJW, c. 1917, at the Neighborhood House. In 1918, the Dallas Section also established a free clinic and free baths at the Cumberland School, attended by many immigrant children.
— *National Council of Jewish Women, Greater Dallas Section*

Ten Commandments[23]
Adopted by the Texas Federation of the Council of Jewish Women. By Mrs. Max Levy, President of the Galveston Section

1st. I am the Council, who brought the Jewish Woman before the eyes of the world — who opened the doors of Universal Service to Humanity.

2nd. Thou shalt have no other organizations before me — For I am a zealous body — desiring the cooperation of every individual member.

3rd. Thou shalt not hold lightly the obligation which thou hast assumed upon becoming a member of the Council of Jewish Women. For the Council will not hold thee guiltless shouldst thou fail her.

4th. Remember the Council Day to keep it surely — many days hast thou for Bridge, Mah Jong or Movies — but the 2nd Tuesday, is thy regular meeting day — and on it thou shalt have no other dates.

5th. Honor thy Council — that the Council may forever be a power for good in the community in which thou livest.

6th. Thou shalt not withhold thy dues or pledges from the Treasurer — but pay promptly, lest ye be dunned.

7th. Thou shalt not adulterate too much the business of the meetings, by side remarks to thy neighbor on extraneous matters.

8th. Thou shalt not be a kill-joy — nor a wet blanket — but enter heartily into any schemes for the filling of Council coffers.

9th. Thou shalt have no sidewalk Conferences — but thou shalt fight it out in open meeting.

10th. Thou shalt not covet — even the third Vice-Presidency — Chairman on Telephone, Rummage — or Home Economics. But serve in any capacity, however humble, for the good of thy Section.

Hadassah, the world's largest Jewish women's organization

During Purim in 1912, Henrietta Szold gathered thirty-seven women in the vestry of Temple Emmanuel in New York City to found Hadassah. Szold, who was an editor for the Jewish Publication Society and a student at the Jewish Theological Seminary, devoted her life to Jewish education through Young Judaea and Youth Aliyah and the establishment of health, education, and welfare agencies in Palestine.

Henrietta Szold undoubtedly traveled to Texas more than once, although records are sketchy. Prior to her first visit, there was a chapter of Daughters of Zion in Waco. The Texas Zionist Organization was active, and an Austinite, Lydia Littman, served as its secretary in 1912.

In 1914, Szold traveled to Wharton to organize a chapter of Hadassah. She recalled, "I remember the women's meeting . . . I remember the meeting with the children of the school — I remember the general meeting in the evening, when Zionists came from all around, from all the small settlements."[24] Ten women were required to form a circle, but in Wharton there were only seven adults. Three seven-year-old girls, Beatrice Zeidman, Esther Rosenfield, and Marjorie Wadler, were enlisted to round out the circle.

In 1919, Szold met with a sewing circle of seventeen women to form Houston's first chapter after an empassioned plea for money to send to the medical staff in Palestine. Other early chapters were organized in San Antonio in 1917 and in Dallas in 1918.

Today, Hadassah has 386,000 members nationwide. Its major project is still the provision of medical services in Israel, in particular, the Hadassah Hebrew University Medical Center, and it is the largest contributor to the Jewish National Fund. Hadassah supports a pro-choice stand on abortion.

Lydia Littman (1872–1965) of Austin joined the Texas Zionist Association in 1906. By 1912, she was the TZA secretary, and her name was inscribed in the *Golden Book* in Jerusalem. She began as a stenographer and built a forty-year career in real estate and insurance.[25]
— *Queenie Littman Collection*

Beatrice Zeidman, Esther Rosenfield, and Marjorie Wadler were present in 1914 when Henrietta Szold arrived in Wharton to organize a chapter of Hadassah. They are pictured here at the seventy-fifth anniversary celebration of Wharton's Congregation Shearith Israel in September 1988.
— *Photo by Ruthe Winegarten*

The Littman Sisters

"There are strippers *and* strippers," wrote Jeanette Littman Hammer of herself and eight sisters.[26] Leopold and Harriet Littman's daughters stripped tobacco leaves from the stems to help make cigars for their father's business — "when school work and other duties permitted."

Leopold Littman of Austin knew the meaning of "cheaper by the dozen" as he bought clothing and groceries for his nine daughters and their mother in wholesale lots. All the girls wore dresses made of the same fabric. Eggs were purchased by the crate, butter by the tub, and cucumbers by the barrel. Queenie, Clara, and Mayme later recalled wearing white stockings because they were less expensive, even though black was more fashionable. And the girls were expected to help in the cigar factory.

When Harriet Littman, the weary mother, was told she had given birth to her seventh daughter, she said, "Another girl? I don't want her." Leopold replied, "*I* want her, and I'll call her 'Myown.' " Her name was registered in the family Bible as "Myown Clara," and at home she was called Ownie.

For the nine Littman sisters, schoolwork was important as they went to their mother and asked, "Mama, please hear me" — which meant Harriet held the books while they recited. All nine attended high school with six graduating, and four of *those* graduated from college. Bella and Queenie quit school early to support the family. Rose became a stenographer, and Clara was a secretary in the legislature when Governor Jim Ferguson was impeached in 1917. Lydia, Mayme, Jeanette, and Moselle graduated from college with degrees in pedagogy and went on to teach school, although Lydia later entered the world of business.

Queenie and Lydia were both active in Hadassah, the National Council of Jewish Women, and the Business and Professional Women's Club. Though Lydia was not initially in favor of suffrage for women, she was one of the first women to cast a vote in Austin.

— Waco Women's Club motto

Anna (Mrs. Eli) Hertzberg (1862–1937) of San Antonio was one of the first Texas women and probably the first Jewish woman to hold elective office in Texas, eleven years before women won the right to vote. She was elected to the San Antonio School Board in 1909. From 1911 to 1913 she was president of the Texas Federation of Women's Clubs.
— UT Institute of Texan Cultures

Minnie Bertha Hirsh (1899–1972) was born in Lockhart and studied in San Antonio, where she won the Hertzberg Medal (named for Anna Hertzberg) for accomplished piano playing in 1915, 1918, and 1920. Minnie later studied at the Cincinnati Conservatory of Music, toured the Midwest, and taught at the Toledo Conservatory of Music.[27]
— Richard Mayer

Anna Hertzberg of San Antonio

The National Council of Jewish Women and Hadassah were part of a national trend in the late 1800s and early 1900s of women's groups turning from cultural self-enrichment to strong organizations designed to fight social ills and build community institutions. In the larger community, the Texas Federation of Women's Clubs (TFWC), founded in 1897, involved thousands of women in social reform. TFWC's first priority was to build libraries and improve schools. Many Jewish women, through both NCJW and other women's groups, joined the fight for public kindergartens, designating wife and child desertion a felony, the establishment of juvenile courts, regulation of child adoption, and marital blood tests.

Even before they achieved the vote, women worked to influence the men in their lives to vote for their causes. Anna Hertzberg was a great believer in this strategy. In 1902, she urged club women to persuade their male relatives and friends to vote for a proposed state constitutional amendment that would fund schools through a poll tax. "[It] is up to the Women of Texas," she said.[28]

Hertzberg was the quintessential club woman. A gifted musician, she

started the Tuesday Music Club to sponsor scholarships and concerts, and organized the first San Antonio symphony.[29] As the first president of the San Antonio NCJW in 1907, she started a night school which was taken over by the school board. By 1917, the NCJW had almost 200 members and was affiliated with the TFWC. NCJW started a free library and contributed toward the Texas building at the Panama-Pacific Exposition in San Francisco, of which Hertzberg was state chair.

Hertzberg was elected to the city's school board in 1909, one of the first Texas women elected to public office.[30] She was president of the Texas Kindergarten Association and a charter member of the History Club, Texas Landmarks Association, the Business and Professional Women's Club, and the American Association of University Women.[31] She was a Zionist and state secretary of the Palestine Welfare Society in 1915, which raised funds for the Medical Training School for Girls in Jerusalem.[32]

As president of the TFWC from 1911 to 1913, Anna Hertzberg was instrumental in the passage of laws protecting married women's property rights. Her son, State Senator Harry Hertzberg, was an outspoken advocate of suffrage during an anti-suffrage filibuster June 25–26, 1919.[33]

Though some garden and culture clubs excluded Jewish women, a number found a place in women's organizations outside the Jewish community. Annie Finger (top row, second from left) was a member of the Eastern Star in Shepherd. Eastern Star members are the female relatives of Masons.
— Mrs. Joe Kost

Henry J. Dannenbaum (1871–1940) of Houston was appointed by U.S. Attorney General George Wickersham as enforcement chief of the Mann Act, which made procurement of prostitutes across state lines a felony. He was president of District Grand Lodge #7 of B'nai B'rith, an active Zionist, and president of Temple Beth Israel. He was also president of the Houston School Board, chairman of the city's Civil Service Commission, and judge of the 61st Texas District Court (1915–1919).
— *Lasker M. Meyer, grandson*

The fight against prostitution

"They were in the sordid business because it was the only way they had of earning bread and butter," wrote Rabbi George Fox in his memoirs.[35] Fox, rabbi of Temple Beth El in Fort Worth from 1910 to 1922, was among Jewish leaders who became concerned with the issue of Jewish prostitution before World War I. Prostitution was an unfortunate circumstance for some Jewish immigrant girls who, arriving alone and vulnerable, were met by procurers who offered to pose as relatives, only to coerce them into "white slavery." Among the organizations working internationally to combat the problem were B'nai B'rith and the National Council of Jewish Women.[36]

Although Jewish prostitutes and pimps were largely concentrated on the East Coast, Texas had its share.

Galveston became a distribution point for Jewish prostitutes from Europe and South America. Fort Worth, San Antonio, and El Paso also became notorious for heavy concentrations of prostitutes, some Jewish. A U.S. inspector general, Stone, reported in 1909 that Jewish pimps were doing business at the "New York Restaurant" in Fort Worth and especially in San Antonio.[37] *The Blue Book,* 1911–1912, a guide to San Antonio's Red Light District, listed prostitutes, some of whom were Jewish. In El Paso, Rabbi Martin Zielonka reported Jewish prostitutes to the authorities, resulting in deportation back to Eastern Europe for some fourteen unfortunate women.

Rabbi Fox viewed Jewish prostitution as a disgrace and feared that its existence would tarnish the image of Jews in the community. He and several other Texas rabbis took steps to eliminate it. The unseemly phrase, "Jew whore," heard in Fort Worth, spurred Rabbi Fox into action. He sent notices to the whorehouses in "Hell's Half Acre" that they would be closed unless they sent the Jewish prostitutes to see him. A few surrendered to his office, but the rest were rounded up and arrested for disorderly conduct. He went to the jail with a Yiddish translator and heard some tragic tales. He recalled:

"Some were supporting their children in . . . foster homes. Some were supporting their parents, and one showed me a lavalier of her father . . . an old, bearded, co-religionist. We asked them to leave the city . . . told them of the disgrace they had brought upon the community . . . One asked me whether [any] Jews would take her into their homes and give her a job. Another asked me . . . how she could live, if she wanted to stop. A third challenged us, in Yiddish, to give her a job in some store. Of course we were stymied. Our women's committee wouldn't even speak to them. Two of them married men who were their pimps and went into legitimate businesses. They settled down to normal life and appeared to be happy.

The rest left town, and whether we were right or not we breathed a little more easily."[38]

Henry J. Dannenbaum and the Mann Act[39]

In the spring of 1910, the Rockefeller Grand Jury in New York City, empaneled to gather statistics on prostitution, received a visit from El Paso attorney Samuel London. London, whose good character was attested to by Rabbi Martin Zielonka, Rabbi Stephen Wise, and Adolph Kraus, president of International B'nai B'rith, had been a defense counsel for a number of procurers along the border. Overcome by a guilty conscience, London offered to make his expertise available to the grand jury.

London began working with Henry J. Dannenbaum, a Houston attorney who, at that time, was president of District Grand Lodge #7, B'nai B'rith. DGL #7 had shown active concern and had collected $5,000 to lobby for legislation to suppress the White Slave Traffic. Dannenbaum and London induced the federal government to organize a special section in the Justice Department.

In 1911, Dannenbaum was appointed by U.S. Attorney General George Wickersham to be enforcement chief of the Mann Act, which made procurement of prostitution across state lines a felony. London was put on the B'nai B'rith payroll from April 1911 to December 1912 and gathered intelligence for future prosecution by Dannenbaum, who moved temporarily to New York City. In 1913, London presented a voluminous report to a New York Aldermanic Committee. His testimony was featured on the front page of the *New York Times.*[40]

With the advent of immigration quotas, the number of Jewish immigrants, including prostitutes, decreased. The fate of London's report to the New York Aldermanic Committee remains a mystery, as does that of the Jewish prostitutes working in Texas.

— **Dr. Ray Karchmer Daily**

Votes for women

As Jewish women worked through their clubs to effect social reform, they were frustrated by being classified with "idiots, imbeciles, and the insane" as categories of Texans who could not vote. Not surprisingly, many of the same women who achieved higher education worked actively for women's suffrage. They were angry that illiterate men could vote, and they could not. As Dr. Ray Karchmer Daily said, "Women's suffrage . . . is just another step in the intellectual evolution of mankind, as powerful as the abolition of slavery or the explosion of the doctrine of the divine rights of kings."

Etta Lasker and her sisters, Florina and Loula, were heavily involved in the Galveston Equal Suffrage Association. Galveston men supported suffrage as well; Rabbi Henry Cohen and Edward Lasker (Etta's brother) were among seven male charter members of the Galveston Equal Suffrage Association.[42]

Others visibly active in Texas were Mrs. R. Tsarnoff, president of the Houston Equal Suffrage Association, and Carrie Sanger Godshaw of Waco. Anna Hertzberg was a board member of the Bexar County Equal Suffrage Society. Blanche Kahn Greenburg, the wife of Rabbi William Greenburg of Dallas' Temple Emanu-El, was vice-president of the Dallas Equal Suffrage Association from 1917 to 1919.

Mrs. Greenburg, like most suffragists, was concerned with other issues besides the vote. She was director of the Dallas Free Kindergarten and Day Nurseries, 1905–1919, and the Baby Camp and Child Placement Committee, 1913–1919. She was a founder of the Dallas Infant Welfare and Milk Association, the Dallas United Jewish Charities, and the Community Chest. After the Greenburgs moved to New York City in 1920, Mrs. Greenburg continued her work as a member of the New York City Commission for Public Adult Education and the American Com-

mission against Fascist Oppression in Germany.[43]

Texas women achieved the right to vote in Democratic Party primaries in 1918. In 1919, the Texas legislature ratified the Nineteenth (women's suffrage) Amendment to the U.S. Constitution; the federal amendment took effect on August 26, 1920.[44]

Mrs. Rob't *[sic]* I. (Agnes Lord) Cohen (1856–1934) was a leader of the Galveston Equal Suffrage Association in 1915. Her activism began in the Jewish Ladies Aid Society and evolved through the National Council of Jewish Women to conducting a survey of dairies for the Women's Health Protective Commission in 1915. The survey of eleven dairies led to the revision of the city's milk ordinance. Her husband was largely responsible for the institution of the Galveston United Charities (later the Community Chest). Agnes' sister, Miss Melanie Pimstein, a Galveston public school teacher for almost fifty years, was also a suffragist. On the occasion of Agnes' seventy-fifth birthday, her son and daughter-in-law, George S. and Esther Cohen of Houston, announced a $125,000 gift to Rice University for the Robert and Agnes Cohen House, to be used as a faculty club.[45]

— *Family Album*

EQUAL SUFFRAGE ASSOCIATION.

The members of the Equal Suffrage Assn. are cordially invited to meet Miss Anna Maxwell Jones, Wednesday, April ninth, from four to six o'clock, at the residence of Mrs. Thompson, 3224 Avenue J.

ETTA LASKER,

Corresponding Secretary

Etta Lasker (Rosensohn) (1885–1966) issued this notice in 1912 to Galvestonians interested in women's suffrage. She and her sisters, Florina and Loula, later attended the New York School of Philanthropy, and Etta received a degree in social work. She headed the Home Service Bureau on the Lower East Side and worked for the Bureau of Jewish Research. In 1914–1915, she became interested in the Leo Frank case and urged her brother, Albert, to organize mass meetings. In later years, Etta was national president of Hadassah from 1952 to 1953, the only Texan to hold that position. Florina was founder of the New York City Civil Liberties Committee. Loula was a specialist in urban housing and edited a liberal magazine, *The Survey Graphic*.[46]

— *Rosenberg Library, Galveston, Texas*

LARGE CANDLESTICK MADE BY A. LEVYTANSKY FOR TEMPLE BETH-EL

Floyd Goldenburg and his sister, Betty Goldenburg, stand beside the large candlestick made by A. Levytansky for Temple Beth-El's new building at Belknap and Ashby, dedicated in San Antonio in 1927.
— *The* San Antonio Light *Collection, October 10, 1927, copy from UT Institute of Texan Cultures*

7

"We lived by our Judaism in this beautiful town."
A FLOURISHING JEWISH COMMUNITY

The range of events covered in one edition of *The San Antonio Jewish Weekly* in November 1925 provides a bird's-eye view of the Texas Jewish community at that time: a Sisterhood Sabbath, a Young Judaea dance, a benefit for starving children in Russia by the Ladies Aid Society. A new kosher butcher had moved to town, and Rabbi Samuel Marks of Temple Beth-El prayed for peace at an interfaith Thanksgiving service. World Jewish news was reported on page one, while page five was full of local gossip. Young men and women traveled to Waco, Fort Worth, Houston, and Oklahoma City to be entertained in a thinly veiled search for suitable Jewish mates. Parents visited children, children were born, Mah-Jongg parties were held, college students came home from Austin and College Station for the holidays. Newcomers were ever welcome, and the poor were provided for discreetly.

Many Jews led comfortable lives, and those who had been in the state for decades had numerous friends and relatives in other Texas cities with whom they shared strong social bonds. But most Jews still struggled to earn a living, particularly the immigrants who had poured into the state since 1900. They worked hard to establish themselves, learn English, take out citizenship papers, and educate their children.

The influx of these Eastern European newcomers from traditional backgrounds resulted in the founding of new congregations and the expansion of older ones. Some of the Orthodox congregations joined the Conservative movement. In smaller towns, rituals and traditions were modified to find common ground for

members from diverse backgrounds. Older organizations like B'nai B'rith and the National Council of Jewish Women grew in influence as they grappled with issues like restrictive immigration laws and immigrant resettlement. The Jewish concepts of *tsedakah* and self-help were manifested in the creation of the Hebrew Free Loan Association, which gave interest-free loans to small businesses. Yiddish culture flourished in the larger cities with branches of the Workmen's Circle and Yiddish *schules* (or schools).

A population explosion in smaller towns because of the 1920s oil boom brought about the construction of new synagogues in places like Amarillo, San Angelo, Wichita Falls, and Lubbock. Interfaith relations became more important as Jews went out into the community through the Jewish Chautauqua Society and the Round Table of Christians and Jews (forerunner of the National Conference of Christians and Jews) to promote a better understanding of their religion. Rabbis became goodwill ambassadors both within their congregations and to the outside world.

As the nation fell into the Depression in the 1930s, many Jewish communities created or expanded welfare councils and began fundraising for Jewish survival both at home and worldwide. Austin Jews formed a Federation of Jewish Charities in 1924. Others followed, including Texarkana's Jewish Charity Chest in 1934, and the Houston and El Paso Jewish Community Councils in 1936 and 1937. The YMHA and YWHA were founded in Houston, and the Dallas United Jewish Charities (in existence since 1911) merged with the

Jewish Community Center.

Institutions serving youth and the aged sprang up. Through the impassioned teachings of men like Jacob Levin of Dallas and Rabbi Charles Blumenthal of Waco, Zionist youth movements, Habonim and Young Judaea, became a large influence in many young lives. In Houston and Dallas, Jewish homes for the aged were founded by visionary philanthropists.

The idea of a Jewish homeland in Palestine slowly gained in popularity, but not without a heated and painful debate which was often shockingly aired in the larger community. Many Reform Jews thought of themselves as Americans first and feared that the Gentile community would perceive Zionism as disloyal Jewish nationalism. Temple Beth Israel of Houston was torn asunder by its adoption of "Basic Principles," one of which repudiated Zionism. Antipathies among Reform, Conservative, and Orthodox factions were sharpened by differences of opinion over Zionism, assimilation, and ethnicity.

As news of the Holocaust reached Texas Jews, they redoubled their efforts to support the war effort and rescue European victims. Jews joined the armed forces, and many lost their lives.

At the end of World War II, the Texas Jewish community had almost doubled in size again, from 30,000 in 1918 to 50,000 in 1945. With the proliferation of new institutions during these years, Texas Jews stood organized and prepared to deal with the tragic consequences of the Holocaust and the fight for a Jewish homeland that came in its wake.

"For I give you a good doctrine: Forsake ye not my law."

— Words above the pulpit at Temple Beth Israel, Houston

Beth Israel's new temple at the corner of Austin and Holman was dedicated in November 1925. Designed by a Jewish architect, Joseph Finger, there were *Mogen Davids* on the ceiling and Jewish symbols on the exterior brickwork. After Beth Is-rael moved to Houston's suburbs in 1969, the old building became the Houston High School for the Performing Arts. It is now part of Houston Community College.
— *Houston Metropolitan Research Center, Houston Public Library*

Rabbi Henry Barnston (1868–1949) served Congregation Beth Israel from 1900 to 1943. Wrote M. N. Dannenbaum in *The Centenary History,* "His love for Beth Israel was matched only by our love for him."[1]
— *Temple Beth Israel Archives, Houston*

Growing pains in Houston

The period following World War I in Houston brought unprecedented expansion. Now a major port, Houston became headquarters to oil and gas industries; "King Cotton" made it a banking and commercial center, as well.

The Houston Jewish community continued to experience rapid growth. In 1925, Temple Beth Israel moved once again to a new facility; it would remain their home until 1969.

The battle over "basic principles"

Upon Rabbi Barnston's retirement in 1943, Congregation Beth Israel had 807 members. Some of its newest members came from Eastern Europe with more traditional backgrounds and were pro-Zionist. Within the temple, as throughout the nation, a debate raged over the establishment of a Jewish national homeland. With Assistant Rabbi Robert Kahn overseas, the congregation voted 346–91 to elect Hyman Judah Schachtel as rabbi. The minority opposed Schachtel's selection because he was an anti-Zionist. The temple was about to enter a tumultuous and painful chapter in its history.

A Policy Formulation Committee recommended the adoption of a set of "Basic Principles," which were accepted by a 632–168 vote at a special meeting of the congregation on November 23, 1943. The ensuing schism led to the resignation of Rabbi Kahn and some 140 members. A new Reform congregation, Temple Emanu El, was formed with Rabbi Kahn as its spiritual leader.

Voting rights in Beth Israel were granted only to those members who subscribed to the "Basic Principles." Principle No. 2 rejected the notion of Zionism, stating, "We are Jews by virtue of our acceptance of Judaism. We consider ourselves no longer a nation. We are a religious community, and neither pray for nor anticipate a return to Palestine . . . We stand . . . for the separation of Church and State. Our religion is Judaism. Our nation is the United States of America . . . With regard to the Jewish settlement in Palestine, we consider it our sacred privilege to promote the spiritual, cultural and social welfare of our co-religionists there."

The other "Principles" rejected the obligatory nature of dietary laws, priestly purity, and rabbinic and Mosaic laws observed by Conservative and Orthodox Jews. The use of Hebrew in religious services was to be downplayed, except where "sacred duty" needed to be fulfilled. Principle No. 5 stated, "We recognize the complete religious equality of woman with man."[2]

The "Basic Principles" created a national controversy which was widely reported, even reaching the pages of *Time* magazine (January 17, 1944). Criticism by the national Jewish community was intense.

The formation of the State of Israel in 1948 and the evolution of modern Reform Judaism rendered the "Basic Principles" obsolete within a few years. Rabbi Schachtel dropped his membership in the American Council for Judaism and became a supporter of Israel, as did most other Beth Israel members. The "Basic Principles" were formally dropped in the 1960s. But in Houston, the rift took many years to heal.

"They selected an improbable moment in history   **123**

to produce a 'Mitzvah.' " [3]   — Seymour "Slugger" Cohen

The religious school faculty of Houston's Congregation Adath Yeshurun, 1927–1928. Adath Yeshurun, like Beth Israel, continued to grow and eventually merged with Beth El in 1946 to become Beth Yeshurun. Beth El, founded in 1924 under the leadership of Phillip Battelstein, was the first congregation in Texas organized from the beginning as Conservative.[4] Feeling a need to attract the young, they kept the Orthodox ritual, but added English responsive prayers, allowed men and women to sit together, and had a mixed choir and an organ. Adath Yeshurun erected the Hebrew Institute in 1925; within ten years it had over 300 students, a program of adult education, the College of Jewish Studies, and Haskallah or self-enlightenment for the Sisterhood and the Ladies Auxiliary.

— *Copy from* The Golden Book of Adath Yeshurun, 1891–1941

Max Nathan (1887–1961) was the first president of Houston's Jewish Community Council in 1936. Operations were informal, and meetings were rarely held. Rabbi Robert I. Kahn recalled that, "Max Nathan would gather around with a few of the leading Jews in town and make public relations decisions when matters got hot." — *Doris Nathan Lascher*

Houston Jewish Community Council

In 1936, there was a full-blown Depression on the home front, and in Germany, Hitler's hatred for the Jews had exploded into violence. In 1938, *Kristallnacht,* the night of broken glass, rioting, burning, and looting, brought the plight of German Jewry to the forefront of Jewish consciousness at home.

"At a time when everyone was worried about self survival, they organized the Houston Jewish Community Council to concentrate on Jewish survival," wrote Seymour "Slugger" Cohen.[5] Thus was the Jewish Community Council of Houston born. Under the leadership of Max Nathan, the first United Jewish Appeal Campaign raised $47,437 in 1936 from 1,200 contributors. That year Mrs. Goldie Myerson (later known as Golda Meir) made her first fund-raising visit to Houston and spoke of her concerns for Palestine and German Jewry.

As the needs of European Jews became more acute, the Houston community responded with increased giving in each consecutive year for the Joint Distribution Committee and the National Palestine Fund. Under the leadership of Mose M. Feld, Joe Weingarten, and Simon Sakowitz, the campaign grew to 1,800 contributors and $105,600 by 1939. By 1940, the Community Council included thirty-five organizations and institutions, and a Refugee Service Office was opened.

Following the attack on Pearl Harbor December 7, 1941, the Community Council organized a boycott to prevent shipment of cotton from the Port of Houston to Nazi Germany. Refugees began to arrive and were helped by men like I. Weiner and Joe Weingarten, who provided jobs and affidavits of support for the newcomers. Ruth Fred, director of the Jewish Family Service, said her agency was busier with immigration work than family service.

Rebecca Sakowitz (Mrs. Max) Nathan (1887–1974) was a founder of the Jewish Community Council. She was president of the Houston Section, NCJW, and founded the Round Table of Christians and Jews. She co-chaired the Temple of Religion for the Texas Women's Advisory Committee during the 1939 World's Fair in New York, chaired the YWCA's World Fellowship Committee, and was a leader in the Houston Interfaith Workshops.[6]

— *Doris Nathan Lascher*

"Rev. I. Kulik has opened a Kosher market..."

— San Antonio Jewish Journal, **November 20, 1925**

Rev. Alexander L. Gurwitz (1855–1947) moved to San Antonio via Galveston and remained until his death at ninety-two. He was a religious scholar who translated the *Pentateuch* into Yiddish verse and taught many young San Antonio men in preparations for *bar mitzvah.* His book, *Memories of Two Generations,* published in Yiddish, was translated by Rabbi Amram Prero, formerly of San Antonio's Congregation Agudas Achim.
 — The San Antonio Light *Collection, UT Institute of Texan Cultures*

Rabbi Samuel Marks (1846–1934) was born in England. His first pulpit was in Montreal, Canada, where he established that country's first Reform congregation. He was the spiritual leader of San Antonio's Congregation Beth-El for twenty-three years (1897–1920). Soon after his arrival, he organized the Ladies' Hebrew Cemetery Association, and in 1902, his campaign for a newer and larger sanctuary bore fruit as a new facility was erected. Rabbi Henry Cohen said of him, "He had a deep compassion for the common man; he freely gave his time, talents, and substance to all who sought help . . . San Antonio was better for his far-sighted, tireless, selfless labors and for the 'law of kindness in his heart.' "
 — *Temple Beth-El, San Antonio, copy from UT Institute of Texan Cultures*

San Antonio

San Antonio had a lively Jewish community in the 1920s and 1930s with Reform, Conservative, and Orthodox congregations, a Yiddish *schule* for young people, a Workmen's Circle, a Zionist organization, a Mother's Club, a Hebrew Free Loan Association, and a number of active women's groups. There were two Jewish papers, the weekly *San Antonio Jewish Journal,* published by Leon Baer, and the *Jewish Record,* edited by Alfred Sack.

Temple Beth-El had already constructed two buildings at Travis and Jefferson streets (1874 and 1902). By 1924, the facilities had become inadequate, and a decision was made to move the temple, which now had a membership of 400 families. In a three-day ceremony (April 29–May 2, 1927), the new facilities were dedicated. The temple's spiritual leader was Rabbi Ephraim Frisch, son-in-law of Rabbi Henry Cohen.[7] Rabbi Frisch's wife, Ruth Cohen Frisch, was active in the Texas Federation of Temple Sisterhoods, and in 1924, addressed their statewide convention on the subject of "Peace." She urged her listeners to "live for our dearly beloved country, and work for it . . . but not one drop of our blood . . . shall be shed to settle economic, political, yea, even moral disputes between nations."

Temple Beth-El, San Antonio, laid the cornerstone for its new building in 1926. It is still housed in the same location at Belknap and Ashby.
 — *Ruth Caroline Friedman, copy from UT Institute of Texan Cultures*

Cantor Rubin I. Kaplan (1888–1951) from Minsk, Russia, studied with the renowned Russian cantors of his day. His forty-three-year Texas career began in Galveston, where he was chazan for the YMHA Congregation, 1908–1912. He then moved to nearby Houston, serving Adath Yeshurun from 1912 to 1932. He recorded cantorial music in 1921 for the Victor Talking Machine and Record Corporation, becoming the first Texas artist ever to make a record, and his recordings were widely sold throughout the U.S. and Canada. Kaplan's last post was as cantor and teacher at Congregation Shearith Israel in Dallas from 1932 to 1951.[9]
— *Photo by Gulf Photo, courtesy Mrs. Hyman Finger, copy from UT Institute of Texan Cultures*

Sylvia Mazur (Mrs. H. Raphael) Gold (1896–1937) of Dallas was a leader of the Literary Circle of the Women's Auxiliary at Congregation Shearith Israel. Her programs included book reviews and the study of philosophical movements from the Golden Era of Spain to the Chassidic movement. Her husband, Rabbi H. Raphael Gold, an active Zionist, served Shearith Israel from 1928 to 1941. He later became a psychiatrist.
— *From the Archives of Congregation Shearith Israel*

Dallas

As a center for apparel, banking, commerce, and oil-boom wealth in the Southwest, Dallas prospered. In spite of an active Ku Klux Klan in the 1920s, Dallas Jews were highly visible in the greater community as they built their institutions and worked for better interfaith relations.

After World War I, the Jewish population and its congregations, Orthodox, Conservative, and Reform, grew and shifted from downtown and near north Dallas to south Dallas. Temple Emanu-El relocated in 1917 to South Boulevard and Harwood; Shearith Israel dedicated a new building in 1919 and changed from Orthodox to Conservative. The Orthodox *shul*, Agudas Achim, built a new building on Forest and Colonial in 1920, and another Orthodox congregation, Tiferet Israel, moved to Grand Avenue in 1936. Dallas had an active Yiddish cultural life replete with Yiddish theater and kosher butchers and bakers.

By 1919, the YMHA, which had been moribund since the 1880s, was revived. It moved into a building on Pocahontas and Park streets near Shearith Israel, and by 1924 had merged with the United Jewish Charities. The "Y" sponsored sporting events, women's classes, a circus, and in 1924, a visit by Chaim Weitzman. By 1927, its name had changed to the Jewish Community Center, and it offered social work services. Unfortunately, one of its first workers, Mrs. Rose Goldstein Cahn, was assassinated at her desk by a disgruntled client in 1933.[10]

A Home for [Dallas] Jewish Aged was started in the late 1940s by Congregation Ohave Shalom in a family residence at 1825 South Boulevard. To insure a *minyan*, they hired older retired men to come for services, and soon were providing housing for some of the needier ones. Louis Kreditor became president and spokesman for the group which enlisted the support of the Jewish Welfare Federation in 1944. After a comprehensive study, the Dallas Home for Jewish Aged was chartered in 1949. On November 10, 1953, eight older men and women moved from south Dallas' Home for Aged Jews to the new Dallas Home for Jewish Aged (now Golden Acres).[11]

The *Chevra Kadisha* (burial society) of Shearith Israel in Dallas, 1936.
— *From the Archives of Congregation Shearith Israel*

Morris Levine founded the Levine Stores in Lubbock in 1929 and was president of Congregation Shaarith [sic] Israel in 1939. Jews from Slaton, Texas, and Clovis and Hobbs, New Mexico, also went to Lubbock to worship.[12]
— *Jewish National Fund*

Texas Jews from near and far went to the dedication of Temple Beth Israel in Breckenridge on April 21, 1929. Rabbi H. Raphael Gold, the leader of Dallas' Shearith Israel, is on the front row, fourth from left. The temple's largest booster and benefactor was Charles Bender.
— *Bertha Bender*

Small-town Judaism

From the heart of Texas to the vast reaches of East and West Texas, Jews settled in small towns. Drawn by economic opportunities, they arrived a few at a time in Amarillo, Abilene, Wichita Falls, Lubbock, San Angelo, Breckenridge, and Tyler. When there were enough to form a community, it was usually a blend of different cultural backgrounds. Often, divisions between traditionalists, non-traditionalists, Zionists, and anti-Zionists arose. Congregations became the central focus of Jewish life, and differences were laid aside to hold the community together.

Small-town Judaism required great determination to survive. Because their welfare was at stake, Jews had to nurture their relationships with Gentiles and were among the most active participants in the towns' organizations and institutions.

San Angelo had Jewish merchants as early as 1880. Newspaper advertisements announcing that they would be closed during the High Holy days attested to their faith, though they had no organized congregation at that time. Such was also the case in Amarillo, where there were

Jews as early as 1903. In the wake of an oil-boom economy in the 1920s, a series of small-town temples were constructed in West Texas: San Angelo's Beth Israel in 1928; Breckenridge's Temple Beth Israel and Amarillo's Temple B'nai Israel in 1929; and Lubbock's Shaarith Israel in 1931.[13]

The new temples hosted Jews from even smaller communities who drove miles for services. Abilene Jews went to Breckenridge. Jews from Menard and Colorado City went to San Angelo. Lubbock hosted people from Slaton, Texas, and Clovis and Hobbs, New Mexico; Pampa and Borger Jewish families traveled to Amarillo.

Most of the congregations used laymen to conduct weekly services and imported student rabbis or rabbis from larger communities for holidays and weddings. In Abilene, for example, Dallas' Aaron Klausner served Temple Mizpah as their lay rabbi from 1945 to 1990. The temple was originally built for the hundreds of Jewish servicemen stationed at Camp Barkeley. As the congregations grew, rabbis were hired. The small-town rabbi was often the Jewish community's best goodwill ambassador to the Gentile community and the arbiter of disagreements within the Jewish community.

Rabbi David Shnayerson served Beth Israel in San Angelo from 1951 to 1971. His congregation never affiliated with any American Jewish movement. In his later years, Rabbi Shnayerson went blind but continued to conduct services and give tours to Christian Sunday school classes. Barbara Rosenberg recalled that his sermons became more powerful because they came from the heart instead of a piece of paper.[14]

Amarillo hired Rabbi Arthur Bluhm, a refugee from Nazi Germany, in 1941. A popular speaker and civic activist, he remained there until his death in 1962.

Rabbi Wolfe Macht (1890–1952) served Temple Rodef Sholom in Waco from 1919 to 1952. He was born in England, ordained at the Hebrew Union College in 1918, and spent his entire ministry in Waco. He was the chaplain at the Veterans Hospital and Connally Air Force Base.

— *Ima Joy Chodorow (Mrs. J. E.) Gandler*

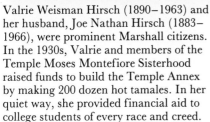

Valrie Weisman Hirsch (1890–1963) and her husband, Joe Nathan Hirsch (1883–1966), were prominent Marshall citizens. In the 1930s, Valrie and members of the Temple Moses Montefiore Sisterhood raised funds to build the Temple Annex by making 200 dozen hot tamales. In her quiet way, she provided financial aid to college students of every race and creed.

She delivered *matzahs* to Jews in nearby Longview and was active in the American Association of University Women's Book Circle. Joe Hirsch managed Weisman & Co. for forty-eight years, served on the Marshall school board, and was active in civic affairs.[15]

— *Joe W. and Phyllis Hirsch, Fort Worth*

Mrs. Ann Kusin and her husband David (1895–1938) were longtime leaders of Texarkana's Mount Sinai Congregation. David won $3,000 playing poker on his ship returning from overseas service during World War I. In 1919, he caught the train from Monroe, Louisiana, and stopped in Texarkana for a lunch break. He was so impressed with the bustling community that he decided to stay. He bought a harness shop, replaced the stock with second-hand furniture, and opened the Texas Furniture Co. He learned bookkeeping and taught himself English. After his death, the business was run by his wife and brother, and then his son Melvin until 1985.[16]

Texarkana's Jewish community grew during the 1930s. The temple was remodeled, and in 1934, the Ehrlich Education Building was added. At that time, Rabbi David B. Alpert, a prolific writer for both the Anglo-Jewish and the general press, served the congregation.[17]

— *Mount Sinai Congregation, Texarkana, Texas*

Frieda Lipman Pink (1877–1921) and her husband, Louis, moved to Wichita Falls in 1918 to open a drug store. They had come from Indianapolis, Indiana, where Frieda was active in the National Council of Jewish Women and had been an accomplished pianist. Within days of their arrival, the Burkburnett oil field was discovered, and the population of Wichita Falls exploded. In spite of a diagnosis of cancer, Frieda was determined to create a Jewish atmosphere. She helped raise money for Temple Israel, which was dedicated to her.

— *Pearl Pink*

Lay Rabbi Sam Perl (1898–1980) with
his wife Stella Cohn Perl, and children,
Frances Perl (Mrs. Stanley Goodman)
and Ito Perl.
— *Frances Perl Goodman*

Temple Beth-El, Brownsville, under construction in 1931.
— *Ruben Edelstein*

**"I had the reputation of being the
only rabbi who had to pay his
synagogue dues to get . . . his
pulpit."** [18]

— Sam Perl

Sam Perl loved to tell the story of
the time that his newlywed daughter
Frances wired him from her honeymoon in New Orleans that it was so
great she and her new husband
wanted to stay another week. Sam
wired back, "It's great everywhere.
Come home." For Sam, home was
Brownsville, and to a greater degree,
Brownsville's Temple Beth-El. As lay
rabbi in the Valley for fifty years,
Sam was the motivating force who
held the local Jewish community together.

Sam Perl, his brother Leon, and
their father moved from Austria to
Galveston in the early 1900s. There,
Sam helped Rabbi Henry Cohen
greet other immigrants coming
through the port city. In 1926, Sam
heard of opportunities in Brownsville,
so he and Leon moved there and
opened a men's clothing store. At that
time, the Jewish community was un-
organized and came from a variety of
religious backgrounds. Some even at-

tended Catholic or Episcopalian services for want of an alternative. Sam
organized Temple Beth-El, which
held services at the Masonic lodge.

In 1931, the Temple Beth-El Sisterhood, which was legally chartered,
purchased land in trust for the temple, raised money, and erected a
building. Sam led Sabbath and holiday services for the next fifty years
and officiated at *B'rit Melah, Bar
Mitzvot,* and weddings, though not a
rabbi. Originally, the services were
Reform, but as more Orthodox Jews
moved to Brownsville, Sam began to
wear a *yarmulke* and *tallis* to hold his
community together and give everyone a sense of belonging.

To conduct weddings, Sam originally had to be accompanied by a justice of the peace to make the ceremony legal. However, a JP once got
carried away and used the phrase,
"By the grace of Jesus." According to
Sam, "the county judge was appalled
and the next day called a meeting of
the county commissioner's court.
That day, he bestowed on me all the
rights and privileges of a rabbi of Israel."

Sam was also a founder of B'nai
B'rith of the Lower Rio Grande Val-

Sunday school students of Temple Beth-
El, Brownsville, 1941.
— *Temple Beth-El Archives*

ley, and the local Zionist Organization of America chapter was named in
his honor. He was active in the
Brownsville Chamber of Commerce
and the Kiwanis Club, and made
many goodwill trips to Mexico. He
was a local radio commentator, and
as chairman of the Housing Authority
he initiated housing for the elderly.

When Sam Perl retired from his
rabbinic duties, his congregation secretly raised funds to purchase a
Torah in his honor which had been
rescued from the Holocaust. When
they presented it to him, he responded as he always had during his
fifty years of service: he donated it to
the congregation. [19]

— Ida Orinovsky Zellen

"We . . . lived by our Jewishness in this beautiful town."

Judaism found its place in multicultural South Texas. In towns as far-flung as Laredo, Gonzales, Alice, and in the larger city of Corpus Christi, Jews held services, built religious schools, and organized chapters of Hadassah, B'nai B'rith, and ORT (Organization for Rehabilitation and Training).

In Laredo, services were initially held in a rented hall. In the 1930s, funds were raised for a two-story building: one story for the Reform Jews and another story for the Conservatives. The arrangement proved unsatisfactory, so the money was divided. The Reform became Temple B'nai Israel, and the Conservatives formed Agudas Achim. A similar arrangement existed in Port Arthur, with the Reform and Orthodox Jews sharing a building. When the Reform rabbi was on the Orthodox side, he wore a hat; he removed it when he walked to the other side.

Beaumont's Temple Emanuel, founded in 1895, completed its second structure in 1925. Jews in Richmond and Rosenberg, who found the forty-mile ride to Houston for services too tiring, used the hall owned by the Fort Bend B'nai B'rith lodge, located between the two towns. The hall was used for religious services and as a social center for poker games, barbeques, and parties where youth from nearby towns could meet.

For the most part, Jews in small South Texas towns were well assimilated into the larger community, and their Gentile neighbors often participated in their rites of passage. In Crystal City, the first *bris* was that of I. L. "Buddy" Freed in 1929. His father, Solomon, imported a *mohel* and got the whole town drunk, Jew and Gentile. For thirty years afterward, people told Buddy that they remembered his *bris*.

There were also a handful of Jews in Gonzales. Ida Orinovsky Zellen remembered the 1930s.[20]

Sadie (Mrs. Ed) Grossman (1892–   ) of Corpus Christi was active in the Jewish community for fifty years. In 1911, the Grossmans were the only family in town to subscribe to the Yiddish-language paper, *Tageblatt.* Sadie founded the city's Hadassah chapter and was the first president of Temple Beth El's Sisterhood.
— *Corpus Christi Jewish Community Council*

". . . my mother, Fanny . . . had the strongest sense of Jewish identity . . . Fanny set up the Sunday School in the back of our store . . . At the ripe age of 12, I was the teacher. With my two little brothers, two little cousins, and any other little kids whose parents could be cajoled, shamed, or persuaded . . . we had a class of children, ages five to eleven . . . We told Bible stories . . . celebrated all the Jewish holidays, and ended each class with . . . cookies or cake, or bread freshly baked by Mama . . . We studied, celebrated, and lived by our Jewishness in this beautiful town, and were respected for it by our Christian neighbors."[21]

Rabbi Martin Zielonka (1877–1938) served Temple Mount Sinai in El Paso and Jews along the border for thirty-eight years, from 1900 until his death.
— *El Paso Public Library*

A Figura Rara

The post-World War I period brought thousands of East European Jews to Mexico who found the doors of the United States closed to them. Many were poor, friendless, and vulnerable to unscrupulous people selling phony passports and entry permits. Rabbi Martin Zielonka of El Paso, with the help of B'nai B'rith, tackled the desperate situation with a vengeance.

Rabbi Zielonka, a native of Berlin, Germany, was ordained at Hebrew Union College in 1899. He served Temple Rodef Sholom in Waco briefly before going to El Paso's Temple Mount Sinai in 1900.

In 1921, Rabbi Zielonka took his concerns for Jewish immigrants in Mexico to B'nai B'rith. Zielonka and Archibald A. Marx, supreme lodge vice-president, spent a month in a number of Mexican towns arranging for Spanish-language courses, setting up job training and social programs, and advancing small business loans. Within a few years, Mexico had 10,000 Jewish immigrants, with problems beyond the scope of the local communities. Zielonka was elected president of B'nai B'rith's District Grand Lodge #7 in 1925, and under his leadership, B'nai B'rith organized a Mexico City bureau with a staff of ten. By the 1930s, Mexico had a viable Jewish community. Many of its members had been personally assisted by a *figura rara,* the Spanish-speaking rabbi from El Paso, Martin Zielonka.[22]

Rabbi Charles Blumenthal (1871–1957) served Congregation Agudath Jacob in Waco from 1926 to 1944 and was founder of one of Texas' first Young Judaea chapters in 1928.   — *Jewish National Fund*

Louis A. Freed was a prominent leader of the Texas Zionist Association from its inception in 1906. He was president of the TZA in 1926 and the Texas-Louisiana Zionist Association in 1933. He and his wife, Fannie Freed, were among those who resigned from Houston's Temple Beth Israel after the adoption of "Basic Principles."   — *Jewish National Fund*

Etta Lasker Rosensohn (1885–1966), a native of Galveston, was the only Texan to serve as national president of Hadassah. Elected in 1952, she was a dedicated Zionist whose life of community service began as a suffragist in Galveston in 1912. She was active in the National Council of Jewish Women and on the board of Hebrew University. As organizing chair of Hadassah's medical organization from 1947 to 1951, she played a leading role in shaping its health and social welfare programs.[24]   — *Hadassah, New York*

Zionism after *Kristallnacht*

Until the 1930s, Zionism was a small political movement among Texas Jews. Jewish institutions were concerned with the welfare of those at home, particularly the new immigrants, and the community was split between Zionists and non-Zionists.

But with the rise of Hitler, the Zionist movement gathered strength. With American doors closed to all but a few immigrants, Jews began to recognize the need for a Jewish homeland.

Jewish children in Houston and Dallas began standing on street corners with blue boxes called *pushkes,* collecting money for the Jewish National Fund to buy land for cultivation and settlement in Palestine. In 1938, Houston Zionists observed the twenty-first anniversary of the Balfour Declaration, including a radio address by Joe Weingarten. He was active in the Houston Jewish Community Council, which was raising funds for the National Palestine Fund.

By 1939, the Labor Zionist youth group, Habonim, had chapters in Dallas, Houston, and San Antonio, and was planning for summer camp. Young Judaea was also gathering momentum.

Zionism provoked some of the most heated debates the Jewish communities had yet withstood. The argument was manifested in events such as the time that H. J. Dannenbaum, while attending a Zionist meeting in Galveston, hoisted a Jewish flag alongside the American flag over the county courthouse. Rabbi Henry Cohen came and lowered it immediately.

In one of the most dramatic conflicts, Temple Beth Israel in Houston split over the adoption of "Basic Principles" in 1943. One of the principles repudiated Zionism as having no place in the temple because of Judaism's perceived status as a religion rather than a nationality. Many Reform rabbis, including Henry Cohen and Hyman Judah Schachtel, were members of the American Council for Judaism, an anti-Zionist organization.

One Reform Jew who did not share that view was Louis A. Freed of Houston. Freed grew up in San Antonio, where he fought with other boys who cast aspersions on his Jewishness. He and his wife, Fannie, moved to Houston in 1913, and he went into the insurance business.

Louis joined the Texas Zionist Association in 1906 and was elected secretary and chairman of propaganda.[25] He was president of TZA by 1926, the year it met in Houston with the Texas Federation of Hadassah. In a prophetic speech delivered to the 1933 convention in Beaumont he said, "While we are striving for the rebuilding of the Jewish Homeland, there comes the unhappy plight of German Jewry forcibly bringing the realization of Israel's uncertain position in the world. It becomes an historic irony that Palestine, through Zionist effort the last three decades, is now the only place of refuge in all the world for those who in earlier days had fought the movement with all their might."[26]

The tragic Holocaust of World War II catapulted Zionism into wider acceptance. By 1945, twenty-six of Houston's thirty-six member organizations of the Jewish Community Council considered themselves Zionist, and the Council censured the American Council for Judaism.[27] From then on, Texas federations moved to the national forefront in raising funds for the establishment of a Jewish homeland in Palestine.

— **Chaya Rochel Andres**

A scene from Clifford Odets' *Awake and Sing,* produced by the Dallas Jewish Art Theatre, c. 1935, is pictured here. The Yiddish Theatre flourished in the United States during the 1920s and 1930s, with traveling troupes from New York, as well as locally produced plays in larger cities.
— *Temple Emanu-El Archives, Dallas*

In 1934, the Dallas Jewish Art Theatre produced *The Dybbuk,* based on an old Jewish folk tale by S. An-ski. *The Dybbuk* tells the story of a migrant soul who enters the body of a living person and refuses to leave unless exorcised by a religious rite.
— *From the Collections of the Dallas Jewish Historical Society*

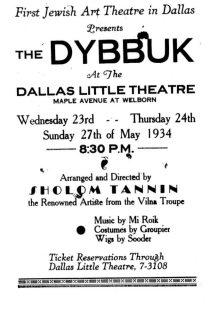

First Jewish Art Theatre in Dallas
Presents

THE **DYBBUK**

At The

DALLAS LITTLE THEATRE
MAPLE AVENUE AT WELBORN

Wednesday 23rd - - Thursday 24th
Sunday 27th of May 1934
———— **8:30 P.M.** ————

Arranged and Directed by
SHOLOM TANNIN
the Renowned Artiste from the Vilna Troupe

● Music by Mi Roik
Costumes by Groupier
Wigs by Sooder

*Ticket Reservations Through
Dallas Little Theatre, 7-3108*

Workmen's Circle, *schules* kept culture alive

From the turn of the century until World War II, most Jewish immigrants to Texas spoke Yiddish — at home, at *shul,* and with their friends and neighbors. Many subscribed to national Yiddish newspapers like the *Jewish Forward* and *The Day.* Others could speak Yiddish but could not read or write the language. Celia Cohen Lewin remembered writing letters in Yiddish for south Dallas neighbors to send home to Europe.

Another source of Yiddish culture and companionship was the Arbeiter Ring (Workmen's Circle). It was a "socialist inclined" nationwide fraternal organization, providing members with life insurance as well as financial and moral aid. Members supported the Hebrew Immigrant Aid Society (HIAS), ORT, and the Jewish Labor Committee. By 1912, chapters formed in Waco, Houston, Dallas, San Antonio, and Galveston. They provided Yiddish theater, music, and other forms of entertainment. Houston had a Yiddish Library and a Jewish Literary Society.

In Dallas and San Antonio, there were Yiddish *schules,* or schools, for children who gave musicals, plays, and readings in Yiddish. Rochel Andres was active in the Dallas chapter of Workmen's Circle (Branch 243), the largest in the region, with 100 members. The chapter opened a *schule* in 1926 with forty-three pupils. Mrs. Andres recalled in her book *Years Have Sped By:*[29]

". . . we wrote to New York, and were able to secure the best talent the Jewish stage had to offer, for our annual concerts. Very often we would also have a Yiddish poet, a lecturer or a speaker . . . The women . . . organized themselves into a Mother's Club [which] . . . transport[ed] the children to the *schule* five days a week. They would then wait in the building for an hour, till the class ended, and take the children home again.

"There was an awakening of Yiddish culture in the city of Dallas. Our concerts attracted large segments of the Jewish population, who previously knew nothing of the renaissance of Yiddish cultural activity in the United States."

Members of the Arbeiter Ring (Workmen's Circle) from Texas and Louisiana met annually. They are pictured on July 4, 1937, at the Sixteenth Conference of the Texas-Louisiana District, which was held in Galveston. It was also the 25th anniversary of Galveston Branch #307.
— *Freida Weiner*

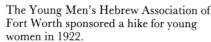

The Young Men's Hebrew Association of
Fort Worth sponsored a hike for young
women in 1922.
— *Congregation Ahavath Sholom*

"Who can forget those burning eyes peer-
ing into the depths of your soul?" This is
how David Zesmer recalled his charis-
matic teacher, Jacob Levin, forty years
later. Jacob Levin (1905–1983) was a
gifted scholar and leader who taught Hebrew as a living language at the Hebrew
School of Dallas, where he was principal
from 1929 to 1946. He is pictured with the
1939 graduation class. Levin organized a
chapter of the Labor Zionist youth group,
Habonim, founded Camp Bonim, and
Boy and Girl Scout troops. L. to r.,
seated, Meyer Rosen, Miriam Grabstald,
Ben Zion Kahn, Shulamit Sherrard,
Schmuel Mordecai Zimmerman-Glatzer.
Standing l. to r., Dov Lichtenstein, Zal-
mon Schneider, Rachel Kahn, Yaakov
(Jacob) Levin (principal), Zvi Rosen, and
Zvi Borofsky. All the students used their
Hebrew names in the school.
— *Zalmon Schneider*

Jewish youth organizations

Along with increased Americanization of first- and second-generation
children came parental concern that
assimilation would lead to intermarriage and/or a loss of Jewish heritage.
Organizations like the Young Men's
Hebrew Associations (YMHA), the
Jewish Literary Societies, and community centers sponsored card parties, lectures, gym classes, dances,
sports teams, and employment bu-
reaus. In 1922, the Parkview Club, a
Dallas social group of Shearith Israel
members, donated their building
across from the synagogue to the
YMHA. The board included representatives of several congregations,
the United Jewish Charities, and
B'nai B'rith. The "Y" became the
Jewish Community Center, and in
1942, hired its first full-time director.[31] San Antonio and Houston also
had YMHAs. In Houston, the
YMHA, the forerunner of the JCC,
was a Community Chest beneficiary,
sponsoring a debating club and
dances with big band music.

Other young people found Jewish
identity in Hebrew and religious

schools as well as in the growing Zionist youth movements. Jacob Levin,
principal of the Hebrew School of
Dallas, also promoted Labor Zionism
to his students.[32] Ginger Chesnick Jacobs recalled that "the blending of
Hebrew School and *Habonim* crystal-
ized my identity as a Jew."

Around 1915, the Galveston Harmony
Club staged a Purim Ball. Ben Cooper
Levy and Helene Rosa Samuels (Levy)
came as "Mr. and Mrs. Tom Thumb."
— *Helene Levy, print by Steve Nussenblatt*

— Annie Finger to her children

Sam Finger (1869–1958) and his wife Annie Finger (1874–1970) began their business in Shepherd, but moved to Houston in 1927. They were two of the founders of Houston's Jewish Home for the Aged, among their many philanthropic activities.

— *Mrs. Joe Kost*

Homes for the aged

In 1944, Ruth Fred of Jewish Family Service wondered if Houston needed a home for the aged. She later said, "As I look back, it was a good idea." Today, Seven Acres Jewish Home for the Aged is one of the premier geriatric facilities in Texas.

It took men and women of vision and philanthropic greatness to start institutions like a home for the aged. Two such Houston couples, Sam and Annie Finger and Ben and Rose Proler, were the movers and shakers behind the first Home for Aged Sons and Daughters in Israel, organized in 1942. The stories of these two immigrant families are the quintessential tales of "rags to riches." Their contributions to the community speak to the gratitude and generosity of many Jewish immigrants who made it in the *goldena medina* (golden land).

Ben and Rose Proler (standing, far right) were founders of Adath Emeth and the Jewish Home for the Aged in Houston. Bernard Rosmarin said of Ben Proler, "He stands on the proposition that *Pat's* welfare is as precious in the sight of God as *Abie's*. Tolerance and brotherhood are his personal creed."

— *Joyce Proler Schechter*

Sam and Annie Finger

Sam Finger was born in Latvia in 1869 and came to the U.S. in 1890 with one ruble in his pocket. He arrived in Houston in 1892 and later met Annie Gordon, who had come to the U.S. alone at the age of twelve to live with her sister. After their marriage in 1903, Sam and Annie moved to Shepherd and opened a store. In 1927, they "retired" to Houston, but ended up opening Finger Furniture with their oldest son Hyman. Annie was a founding member of City of Hope (a hospital and research facility in California), Hadassah, Mizrachi, and B'nai B'rith Women. Sam was president of Congregation Adath Emeth and a member of Beth Yeshurun and the Masonic lodges of Houston and Shepherd.[33]

Ben and Rose Proler

Ben Proler was widely known in Houston for being a blunt and outspoken personality with a heart of gold. Ben came to the U.S. as a Yeshiva boy from Lithuania. For a short time, he sang in the Yiddish Theater in New York with the comedienne Molly Picon (who entertained for him at a testimonial dinner in Houston fifty years later). For ten years, he lived in Pennsylvania, where he met and married Rose Stein. He sold bones for tallow, but gave up that grisly business to begin the junk business with a pushcart. Once in Houston, his business, City Junk, became Proler Steel, and ultimately, Proler International. Often giving anonymously to charity, Ben Proler was one of the founders of the Orthodox congregation Adath Emeth and the Jewish Home for the Aged. He was also president of the Independent Hebrew School of Houston.[34]

KU KLUX KLAN

Magazine cover, "The Ku Klux
Klan, The Strange Society of Blood
and Death Exposed," 1920s.

— Dorothy M. and Henry S. Jacobus Temple
Emanu-El Archives, print by Andy Reisberg

In 1924, Morris Zale saw the growing strength of the Ku Klux Klan in
Graham, Texas, as a personal danger,
and moved his store to Wichita Falls.
"I was the only Jew in town . . . I was
just a kid trying to make an honest
living . . . but when I saw that cross
burning, I was scared to death."[1]

Cross-burning was only one of the
many nightmares visited upon world
Jewry in the tumultuous era of 1920–
1945: from Graham, Texas, to the
grim revelation of the slaughter of six
million Jews during World War II,
organized anti-Semitism permeated
the collective consciousness of Jews.
Restrictive immigration quotas, quotas on campuses and in medical
schools, and "gentlemen's agreements" barring Jews from certain
clubs, corporations, and neighborhoods also provided significant stum-
bling blocks.

The tremendous upsurge of activity
by the Invisible Knights of the Ku
Klux Klan in the 1920s was aimed at
blacks, foreigners, and Jews. Blacks
were lynched; many victims were
beaten, tarred and feathered, run out
of town, or had their businesses boycotted. Frightened and angered, Jews
fought back and spoke out: Texas was
their home too. The National Federation of Temple Sisterhoods and the
National Council of Jewish Women
mobilized as members of the Association of Southern Women Against
Lynching.[2] Courageous newspaper
editors spoke out, and with the election of Miriam A. "Ma" Ferguson as
governor on an anti-Klan platform in
1924, the influence of the Klan in
Texas waned.

8

Despite the Klan, many Jews moved to the forefront of business, professional, and political life. They won political offices and were recipients of political appointments. Seizing new opportunities, Jews bought movie theaters, built department stores, imported citrus fruit from the Rio Grande Valley, went into apparel manufacturing, and struck oil. Increasing numbers of Jewish university students prompted the creation of Hillel Houses and Jewish fraternities and sororities. Jewish professors wrote textbooks and taught thousands of students. Jewish journalists, doctors, and lawyers became more numerous and visible as they contributed to their fields of endeavor.

The Roaring Twenties, the Jazz Age, and Prohibition produced Jewish bootleggers, gamblers, and flappers who bobbed their hair, danced the Charleston, and practiced birth control. Jakie Freedman bought a piece of the Hollywood Dinner Club and speakeasy on the outskirts of Galveston, sold out to the Maceos, and opened a gambling resort in Houston. In the 1930s, Mayor Adrian Levy of Galveston ordered slot machines removed from restaurants and other public places.

On the more serious side, the aftermath of the terrible destruction of World War I saw Jewish organizations working for world peace. In 1921, the sisterhood of Temple Emanu-El in Dallas established a Peace and World Relations Study Group, and Temple Mt. Sinai in El Paso held joint Armistice Day services with the Congregational Church. The Texas Council of Jewish Women

supported formal U.S. entry into the World Court in 1924. Church-state issues continued to plague Texas Jews, and in 1922, the Dallas Section, National Council of Jewish Women, opposed Bible readings in the public schools.

The Great Depression, which began with the stock market crash in October 1929, hit Texas hard, and many businesses and farms failed. Most Jews supported President Franklin Delano Roosevelt and his New Deal programs, such as Social Security, minimum wage and hour laws, and unemployment relief. Jewish owners of Mom and Pop stores in towns, large and small, suffered along with their customers. Jews raised money for relief and worked in soup kitchens; most simply struggled to survive those lean years.

As darkness descended over Europe with the emergence of Adolph Hitler, the security of Jewish life was in grave danger. One of the crucial events was *Kristallnacht,* November 9–12, 1938 — an organized pogrom in Germany in which Jews were killed, businesses and synagogues burned, and Jews shipped in cattle cars to concentration camps. At first, many Jewish leaders refused to believe that the Holocaust — the wholesale slaughter of Jews — was a reality. But as Hitler's intentions became increasingly clear, Jews throughout the world, including many Texans, frantically tried to rescue relatives.

After the Japanese attack on Pearl Harbor on December 7, 1941, the United States once again entered an international conflagration. Thousands of young Jewish men and

women from Texas served in the armed forces. Some were heroes, some liberated their co-religionists from death camps, and some never returned. Those who remained on the home front did their part to assist with the war effort by working in defense industries, selling bonds, recycling scrap metal, entertaining soldiers, and planting victory gardens.

Jews, like other Americans, were overjoyed when the war was over, but their joy was tempered with the revelation of Hitler's massacres. The aftermath impressed upon Texas Jewry the need for a Jewish homeland, as the remnants of European Jewry searched for a safe refuge to begin life again.

Once more, Jews began to immigrate to Texas in significant numbers, and there was new impetus and energy to build even stronger Jewish communities. With peace came a desire to return to normal life, but the world would never again be the same.

them now." [4] — **Sam Dreben, speaking out against the Klan**

Rabbi David Lefkowitz (1875–1955) was the spiritual leader of Temple Emanu-El in Dallas from 1920 to 1955. One of the city's most outspoken opponents of the Ku Klux Klan, he referred to its activities as "the mob spirit incarnate." Lefkowitz, a native of Austro-Hungary, was ordained in 1900 at Hebrew Union College. Before coming to Dallas, he served Temple B'nai Hesherum in Dayton, Ohio. His radio broadcasts in Dallas were legendary, and he was widely admired for his support of non-Jewish causes. He was a lecturer at the Perkins School of Theology, Southern Methodist University, president of the Central Conference of American Rabbis, vice-president of the World Union for Progressive Judaism, and a member of the executive board of the Union of American Hebrew Congregations.
— *Dorothy M. and Henry S. Jacobus Temple Emanu-El Archives, print by Andy Reisberg*

"The hooded night riders so terrorized the Jews in some parts of the state that . . . they gathered together and sat up all night fearing a pogrom."
— Ouida Nalle[5]

Since the Civil War, the Ku Klux Klan has experienced several peak periods of activity and influence: the 1880s following Reconstruction and the 1920s. From 1882 to 1930, 349 blacks were lynched in Texas.[6] During the 1920s, the Ku Klux Klan pervaded political and social life in both rural and urban areas. The Klan controlled the Democratic Party, and in 1922, Texas voters elected a Klansman, Earle B. Mayfield, to the U.S. Senate. Among those attracted to Klan membership were religious fundamentalists, members of the Masonic Order and the American Legion, and many prominent businessmen, lawyers, and doctors.

The Klan tried to enforce its brand of law, order, and morality against blacks, Jews, bootleggers, and aliens. Jewish businesses were boycotted, and in some cases Jews were beaten, tarred, and feathered.

The Klan was a powerful force among elected officials in the city governments of Dallas and Houston. In Dallas, the police chief, mayor, and district attorney were thought to be sympathizers. From 1920 to 1925, Dallas Klan membership was estimated at 13,000, the highest per capita in the U.S. On May 21, 1921, 800 Klansmen marched in Dallas carrying signs which read, "All Native

The Waco *Tribune Herald* reported that almost 16,000 people attended this Ku Klux Klan picnic and initiation service. The crowd sang "America the Beautiful" and "Nearer My God to Thee" and burned a huge cross.
— *The Texas Collection, Baylor University, Waco, Texas*

Born," "All Pure White," and "Our Little Girls Must Be Protected." A Jewish chemist for the Dallas Water Department lost his job, as Klan members took over many city and county departments. In March 1922, Philip Rothblum, a Dallas Jew, was kidnapped from his home, whipped, and told to leave town. Jewish stores were boycotted.[7]

When the Klan tried to march into Galveston over the causeway, Rabbi Henry Cohen and his friend Father Jim Kirwin, a Catholic priest, met them and said, "You are not going to pass us." They didn't. In Austin, a cross was burned in the yard of the Finklestein family. A Baptist minister stood on the family's porch and made the Klan leave. In Fort Worth, Jewish businesses suffered. Klansmen swooped down on horseback, burning crosses in front of Jewish homes and businesses like that of Seymour Drescher.

In April 1924, Mrs. Maurice L. Goldman, running for a second term on the Houston School Board, was endorsed by all the local papers. The Klan-controlled Central PTA ranked her fifth out of six candidates. Four of her fellow school board members supported her; two with alleged Klan affiliations refused. She won with the second highest number of votes.[8]

Out of ignorance, the Klan even invited some Jews to join, like the prominent Dallas merchant Edward Titche. When they learned he was a Jew, they said it was too bad — he would have made a good Kleagle. As a State Fair official, Dallasite Alex Sanger sat on the podium at the Fair's Klan Day in 1923. Hyman Perlstein of Beaumont was invited to join by an anonymous phone caller, but declined the offer, as did a Jewish Crosby merchant, who sold white muslin to the KKK to keep it from harassing local Jews.

As Klan violence increased, some Klansmen began to defect. Newspaper editors like the *Dallas News'* George Dealey and the *Houston Chronicle*'s M. E. Foster fought back with anti-Klan editorials. In 1924, Miriam A. "Ma" Ferguson ran for Texas governor on an anti-Klan ticket and defeated a Klan-backed candidate in the Democratic primary by 100,000 votes. One of her first acts was to get an anti-mask bill passed in the Texas legislature. From then on, the Klan was on its way out in Texas.[9]

Jews in public office

In spite of the penetration by Ku Klux Klan into state and local politics, Jews continued to run for public office and receive political appointments.

In 1926, Charles Brachfield of Henderson became the first Jew to run for statewide office in a race for attorney general. He missed the runoff by 3,600 votes, a remarkable showing at a peak period of Klan influence. In 1928, Governor Dan Moody appointed Rabbi Henry Cohen to serve on the State Board of Prisons, and Dr. Ray Karchmer Daily, who fought the Klan, was elected to the Houston School Board.

In the case of pioneer attorney Theodore Mack, the pervasive presence of Klan influence on Fort Worth juries changed the course of his career. He refused to try cases because of Klan-controlled juries and practiced appellate law instead. During his sixty-year career, he briefed and argued 1,500 cases in the state and federal courts. Before moving in the 1890s to Fort Worth, where he was the first Jewish lawyer in town, Mack had been the district attorney in Albany, Texas, in 1887. His son, Henry Mack, his grandson, Theodore Mack II, and his great-granddaughter, Elizabeth Mack, have all been attorneys.

Theodore Mack (1864–1952), a pioneer Fort Worth attorney, refused to try cases in Tarrant County between 1918 and 1924 because of Klan-controlled juries.
— *Fort Worth Jewish Community Sesquicentennial Archives*

Attorneys Hattie Henenberg (1896–1974), left, Hortense Ward, center, and Ruth Brazzil, right, were members of a special All Woman Supreme Court. They were appointed by Governor Pat M. Neff in 1925 to hear a case from which the three male sitting court justices had to disqualify themselves because of a potential conflict of interest. Henenberg graduated from the Dallas School of Law in 1916. She was a Dallas attorney from 1916 to 1966, director of the Dallas Bar Association, and an assistant district attorney in Dallas County, 1941–1947. A staunch Democrat, she was a delegate to the 1932 Democratic National Convention in Chicago, where Franklin Roosevelt won his first presidential nomination. She raised funds for social service agencies like the Free Legal Aid Bureau and a Loan Library for underprivileged West Dallas children. She was active in Temple Emanu-El and was listed in "Who's Who" in Jewry in 1928.[10]
— *Archives Division, Texas State Library*

Goldie (Thomas-Thomachevsky) Cohn (1890–1970) and her husband, Jacob Cohn (1886–1966), were garment manufacturers in New Braunfels, 1924–1931, and in Dallas from the 1930s to the 1950s. Goldie was the designer; Jacob was the cutter and production man. He was known as "Hattie Carnegie Cohn" because he was always a season ahead of everyone else. Their line of blouses was called Rosselee *[sic]*. In New Braunfels, they were concerned because their daughter had an anti-Semitic teacher, so they gave the teacher a dress every month so she would call on their daughter in class.
— *Rosalee Cohen*

Albert Lasker (1880–1952) moved from Galveston to Chicago in 1898 and became the "Father of Modern Advertising." Ads like this one were his creations.
— *Mrs. Albert Lasker, copy from UT Institute of Texan Cultures*

Businesses small and large

In the days before the mammoth chain stores, most Texas towns had a Mom and Pop department store. As one old Jewish Texan put it, "Whenever a town grew big enough for a post office, the next building on Main Street was the Jewish dry goods store." The Jewish Moms and Pops were Horatio Algers in the flesh; owning one's own business was a symbol of stability, respectability, independence, and self-pride.

Couples like Bertha and Archie Skibell established stores like Archie's Style Shop in Greenville and La-Mode's in Lubbock. Newspaper ads were only part of their public relations: they also concentrated on courtesy and personal attention to their customers. During the Depression, when cotton sold for five cents a pound, Archie bought a $25 bale of cotton and placed it in front of his Greenville store to show his support for the local farmers, who were undoubtedly his best customers.

The Father of Modern Advertising

The nature of merchandising changed with the ideas and genius of men like Albert Lasker, the "Father of Modern Advertising," who began life in Galveston. By the age of thirteen, he started his own newspaper. In 1896, he scooped all the other reporters in town by getting an interview with the Socialist Party leader, Eugene V. Debs. In 1898, Lasker moved from his hometown to Chicago and went to work for the Lord & Thomas Agency, where he started with a salary of $10 per week. When he retired, he was a multimillionaire, responsible for making Lord & Thomas the most prestigious advertising agency in the world.

Lasker promoted the merchandising of canned food and evaporated

milk and made citrus fruit something to drink as well as eat. Through his ads, he encouraged women to smoke and introduced them to Kotex. Radio commercials and soap operas were developed by Lasker, and many famous products and trademarks were his creation as well, including Pepsodent, Lucky Strikes, Kleenex, and Palmolive.

Lasker earned more money in advertising than anyone who came before him — $45 million, most of which he gave away. His most ardent cause was health; in 1928, he gave $1 million to the University of Chicago medical facility. In 1947, he testified before a U.S. Senate committee in support of public health programs. After his death, his widow founded the famed Lasker Awards for scientific achievement.

Albert Lasker was proud of his maternal grandfather, Schmul Schmulian (who changed his name to Abraham Davis). Whenever he met a stuffed shirt or a snob, it pleased him to announce that he was rightfully Albert Schmulian Lasker, grandson of Schmul. [12]

Bertha (1929–1981) and Archie Skibell (1905–1982) were prototypical Horatio Algers who owned clothing stores in Greenville and Lubbock.
— *Cynthia Winston*

"Haymon operated on the principle that the treasures of West Texas were limitless."[13]
— Rabbi Floyd Fierman of Haymon Krupp

By the time Haymon Krupp and his brother Harris arrived in El Paso in 1890, it was a booming frontier town. Haymon saw the opportunities and pursued them to enormous success — and on the way, brought great wealth to the University of Texas when he struck oil at the Santa Rita #1 in 1923.

Krupp began as a pawnbroker but quickly graduated to wholesale dry goods and apparel manufacturing. During peak times, Krupp's factory employed 500 workers who made shirts, dresses, pants, and *rebozos* (shawls). He hired his nephews as managers and sales representatives while he incorporated and sold stock in his companies.

With a keen eye for talent, Krupp picked Frank Pickrell as his partner in 1919 to form the Texon Oil & Land Company. They paid Rupert Ricker $2,500 for his oil leases on 430,000 acres of UT-owned land in the Permian Basin. Geological studies showed the land might have oil. Krupp went to New York to sell stock

to finance the drilling but investors were hesitant to buy non-producing wells, so Krupp purchased three producing wells at Burkburnett.

Two-and-a-half years of drilling began in 1921 at the Santa Rita #1, named after the Saint of the Impossible. Finally, in May 1923, the impossible happened, and Santa Rita struck. It was the first oil-producing well drilled on UT Permanent Fund Endowment Lands. The resulting millions of dollars in royalty income transformed the University of Texas and Texas A&M into major institutions. Part of the Santa Rita #1 is now enshrined on the UT Austin campus.[14]

In 1929, Texon's holdings were sold for $26 million. Krupp later organized new drilling companies, but never again struck it as rich. He was inducted posthumously into the Permian Basin Petroleum Hall of Fame in 1969.

Haymon Krupp was also a philanthropist who provided coal for poor people in winter and blankets for an infantry company stationed near El Paso in World War I. He was active in the Masons, the Elks, B'nai B'rith, and was a generous contributor to both El Paso congregations, Temple Mount Sinai and B'nai Zion.

"My father thought that American citizenship called for land ownership."
— Louis Wolens

Kalman and Ida Wolens bought 145 acres on the fringe of the Powell

oil field in Wortham, about twenty miles south of Corsicana, and struck oil. Mr. "K," as Kalman was called, took great pride in his success because it enabled him to give liberally to hundreds of worthy organizations, causes, and countless individuals.

In 1895, K. Wolens emigrated from Poland to Chicago with his family. Kalman and his brothers followed the Missouri Pacific Railroad to the end of the line in Palestine, Texas, and opened retail stores in Calvert, Palestine, and Corsicana.

With a $400 loan from Mrs. Abe Heyman, Kalman staged a sidewalk spectacle. In 1925, he expanded to Wortham, an oil boom town, and other stores followed in Palestine, Kaufman, Waxahachie, and Athens. Kalman's brothers, Nathan and Jack, and his sons, Joe, Max, and Louis, also helped.

Kalman and Ida Wolens maintained Orthodox traditions and were founders of the Orthodox congregation Agudas Achim in Corsicana. Their son, Louis, contributed $200,000 to Navarro College for the Wolens Health Building, $100,000 for scholarships at Navarro College, and funds for a day-care center.

The Wolens family of Corsicana. Top row: Joe, Louis, and Max Wolens. Bottom row: Daisy Wolens Silverberg, Kalman and Ida Wolens. Mr. "K" struck oil at Wortham and donated generously to numerous worthy causes.
— *Silverberg and Wolens families*

The Brachman family of Fort Worth. Top row: Rabbi Abraham Brachman, Solomon Brachman, and Elias Brachman. Bottom row: Lillian Brachman Raimey and Dora Brachman Ginsburg. The Brachmans owned Producers Supply & Tool Co., whose customers were oil producers. Solomon and his wife, Etta, were founders of the Jewish Federation of Fort Worth in 1936. — *Mrs. Leon Brachman*

"Brother can you spare a dime?"

— From a popular Depression tune

Mrs. Louis A. (Fannie) Freed (1880–1975) of Houston chaired the Women's Crusade in 1934, a group of Community Chest volunteers who raised money for needy families during the Depression. The overall chair was Oveta Culp Hobby. Born in Luling, Mrs. Freed was educated at a convent school in San Antonio. Active with her husband in Zionist causes, she was a pioneer member, along with Ima Hogg, of the Houston Symphony Society. She served on Houston's Recreational Board, the Interracial Commission, and for thirty-three years was on the Travelers' Aid board. She was twice president of the Houston Section of the National Council of Jewish Women, a founding member of the Houston Women's Building in the 1920s and Temple Emanu El in 1943. In 1966, she was honored by the YWCA for her contributions to Houston's human resources. Mrs. Freed still drove a car after she was ninety.
— *Eleanor Freed, copy from* Houston Post, *October 5, 1934*

Helping with relief efforts

The Great Depression hit Texas later than the rest of the country. While the oil boom and the growing petrochemical industry buffered the effect on Texas somewhat, Texans eventually suffered with the rest of the nation. Many fortunes were lost and in the small towns, the owners of Mom and Pop stores dependent on farmers struggled along with their neighbors to survive those dark years. Jews joined the ranks of the unemployed, and small businesses went bankrupt.

Many Jews were actively involved with the challenge of healing a broken nation. Their activism took many forms. Joe Weingarten, a Houston businessman, spoke before the President's Conference of Small Businesses on February 3, 1938, advocating the passage of a wage-hour bill "as the only democratic way to increase purchasing power." Other Jews worked in soup kitchens and raised money for indigent families. In the 1930s, Jewish federations organized or stepped up their activities, as much to assist local Jews in need as to begin rescue work in Europe.

Max Friedman's Home Industrial Tailors at 2200 Elm Street in Dallas made men's suits. Garment workers during the Depression suffered from the lack of minimum wage standards.
— *From the Collections of the Dallas Jewish Historical Society, print by Andy Reisberg*

— Louis W. Kariel, Sr.

Mayor Adrian Levy of Galveston (right) presided over a reception for President Franklin D. Roosevelt (far left) in 1937 when FDR came ashore from a Gulf fishing trip to take the train to Fort Worth. Also present were Governor Jimmy Allred (third from left) and a young, newly-elected congressman, Lyndon Baines Johnson (second from left).
— *Helene Levy, copy from UT Institute of Texan Cultures*

"We had soup lines in Marshall."

During the Depression years, the vast majority of Jews were supporters of President Franklin D. Roosevelt. Samuel Rosenman (1896–1973), born in San Antonio, coined the phrase "New Deal"; he was FDR's counsel in 1943, organized his brains trust, and during World War II helped create many national defense agencies.

Louis W. Kariel, Sr., was mayor of Marshall from 1935 to 1947 and recalled that, "Times were hard. We had soup lines in Marshall like every other place. FDR's fireside chats just got to you — he was such an able speaker. I thought he was great. He put things in motion that started us out of the Depression."

Louis W. Kariel, Sr. (1896–   ) was the New Deal mayor of Marshall from 1935 to 1947. A 1917 graduate of the University of Texas, Kariel worked as a chemist in sugar refineries before owning the Hub Shoe Store in Marshall. He has been active in many civic and fraternal organizations, and was lay leader at Temple Moses Montefiore when there was no rabbi. During the Texas Centennial celebration in Dallas in 1936, Kariel and other elected officials sat on the platform with President Franklin D. Roosevelt.
— *Audrey D. Kariel, Marshall, Texas*

Sara Borschow (Bormaster) of San Antonio was active in state Democratic politics during the 1930s. She fought for equal representation of women in the Texas Democratic Party. She was the first woman ever elected as sergeant-at-arms at a state Democratic convention and was the state secretary of Woman Democrats of Texas. In 1939, she was a member of the Advisory Committee on Women's Participation in the New York World's Fair. She was also a deputy sheriff and deputy district clerk in Bexar County. Writing under the pen name Rita Barr, Bormaster is an award-winning poet. Now a resident of Joplin, Missouri, she is the author of a collection, *Pinions of Wisdom*, and in 1988, won a Golden Poet Award in the New American Poetry Contest.

Sara Borschow (Bormaster) talks with St. Louis, Missouri, Mayor Bernard S. Dickman during a Young Democrats convention, c. 1945. She was active in Texas and Bexar County Democratic Party politics for a number of years. In addition to her political activity, she is a prolific and award-winning poet whose pen name is Rita Barr.
— *Sara Borschow Bormaster*

— **Meyer Perlstein**

August Lorch moved to Texas from Mainz, Germany, in the 1890s and opened stores in Wills Point, Greenville, and Bowie. He peddled and later founded a jobbing firm in Dallas in 1909. In 1920, he and his son Lester founded Lorch Manufacturing Company to make women's apparel.
— *Dorothy M. and Henry S. Jacobus Temple Emanu-El Archives, print by Andy Reisberg*

The apparel industry

Jews were at the center of the apparel industry from its beginning in Texas in 1897. Abraham Finesilver founded Texas' first apparel manufacturing company in San Antonio, and by the 1930s he was selling men's shirts to 700 J.C. Penney stores. Other family-owned businesses were founded in Houston, El Paso, and Fort Worth.

By 1930, Dallas was the center for apparel manufacturing in the Southwest. In spite of the Depression, the garment industry boomed. Companies like Nardis, Marcy Lee, and Sidran combined hard work, wise management, and good luck with low labor costs, adequate capital, and weak unions to compete successfully with New York and California clothing centers.

The most exceptional of the companies was Lorch Manufacturing, the nation's oldest privately owned women's apparel company. Established in

1920 by August Lorch and his son Lester, Lorch Manufacturing prospered during the Depression while others failed. The Lorches manufactured lower-priced house dresses, developed new lines of sportswear geared to the warmer Southwest climate, adapted an early form of polyester, and decentralized production to smaller towns. In the 1930s, Lester Lorch was president of the Apparel Division of the Manufacturers Association and promoted Dallas as a fashion center with the establishment of the "Dallas Alice" Award.

During World War II, Lester Lorch represented the apparel industry before the Office of Price Administration (OPA) in Washington, D.C., and requested lower minimum wages. The OPA granted the request. While New York garment workers earned ninety cents per hour and other Texas workers $1 per hour, Texas garment makers, predominantly women, began to earn fifty-four cents.

Lorch found his nemesis in another Jew, Meyer Perlstein. Perlstein was vice-president of the Southwest Division of the International Ladies Garment Workers Union from the 1930s to 1956 and organized workers in Dallas, Houston, and San Antonio. During the 1935 strike of 150 Dallas garment workers, the stage was set for a ten-month confrontation between Lorch and Perlstein. One social histo-

rian, Dr. Dorothy DeMoss, wrote that "the two leaders employed methods legitimate and illicit in the lengthy and disorderly dispute."

The union worked for better wages, benefits, and recognition as a collective bargaining agent, all of which the owners refused. Fights between police, pickets, and scabs broke out, and Lester Lorch began carrying a gun. On August 7, 1935, twelve female scabs were disrobed by strikers and police during Market Week in Dallas. Public sentiment swung toward management and by the end of the year, the strike ended with no union gains.

In 1936, union activity shifted to a San Antonio company, where most of the garment workers were Mexican women earning an average of $5.60 per week.[16] Other strikes occurred in 1937 in Dallas, and the ILGWU won status as a collective bargaining agent. But Dallas remained almost completely unorganized, and "open shop" sentiments prevailed. The passage of the federal Fair Labor Standards Act in 1938 established a twenty-five-cent-an-hour minimum wage, and gradually, working conditions improved.

Meyer Perlstein, front row, center, the Southwest regional vice-president of the International Ladies Garment Workers Union, poses with delegates at the 25th ILGWU Convention, c. 1935.
— *People's History in Texas*

Bernard Gold modernized the Dallas apparel industry by using power machines at Nardis Company. He also encouraged his employees to belong to the union.
— *From the Collections of the Dallas Jewish Historical Society*

Olivia Rawlston of Dallas was president of the segregated local of the International Ladies Garment Workers Union (ILGWU). She remembered Bernard Gold as a wonderful man who was sympathetic to the union.
— *People's History in Texas*

Olivia Rawlston, Dallas ILGWU president

Although the ILGWU was segregated into black and white locals, the women worked well together. Olivia Rawlston was president of the Dallas "B," or segregated, local in 1936 and remembered Bernard Gold:

"Bernard Gold . . . was a Jew, he was a wonderful man, and I had a lot of respect for him . . . he took the Negro woman out of the kitchen and put her on power machines in the city and it paid off for him . . . he made beautiful operators out of them . . . [we made] money for him and yet it helped us too . . . He was experimenting and it really worked. We made lovely money . . . Mr. Gold himself was sympathetic towards unions . . . I think Mr. Gold must have been a pretty smart man because he could see what the union could do for him, too . . ." [19]

Bernard Gold

Bernard Gold said that he believed in using the best talent he could find. Operating under that premise, he bought a controlling interest in the Nardis Company in Dallas in 1939, moved it to a modern building with 200 machines, and made it an outstanding example of the application of mass production techniques to apparel manufacturing. By hiring nationally known designers and production managers, his company developed into an $8 million annual business in women's fashions.

Gold came to the U.S. from Russia in 1914 and for seventeen years owned a cab company in New York City. Nardis had been started by Joe Sidran in 1937 with the backing of Bernard's brother, Irving Gold. Bernard Gold, who was a political liberal, believed he should not delay union organization by the ILGWU, and by 1943, Nardis had almost 500 union members. Bernard never attempted to sabotage union affiliation by his factory workers and, in turn, the ILGWU extended him a good contract agreement. [18]

The Frankfurt sisters of Dallas, led by Elsie, founded the Page Boy Company in 1939 to sell fashionable maternity wear. Left to right: Edna, Louise, and Elsie Frankfurt.
— *Dallas Public Library*

"I never wanted to be the biggest, just the best."
— Elsie Frankfurt

Elsie Frankfurt of Dallas thought her pregnant sister looked like an unmade bed in her maternity clothes, so she cut an oval hole in the front of her sister's normally sized skirts so they fit neatly and slimly. She added a boxy jacket to cover the cutout area and created a new look for expectant mothers. It was 1939, and Elsie had graduated only the year before from Southern Methodist University. She and her sisters, Edna and Louise, borrowed $500 to open a small shop in the Medical Arts Building in downtown Dallas. Their Page Boy Company was so successful that others clamored for the fashion. By 1940, their retail store in Hollywood attracted movie stars. The firm's first style show was held in 1947 at New York's Stork Club. In 1951, Elsie Frankfurt became the first woman inducted into the Young Presidents Organization, of which all executives of million-dollar corporations were under the age of forty. In 1952, she won *Mademoiselle's* Merit Award.

In 1939, the Wonder Bar was a ten-cents-a-dance night spot in downtown Dallas over the old gas company building owned by Sam Goldberg and Joe Utay.
— *From the Collections of the Dallas Jewish Historical Society*

Jewish communities

South Dallas was the focus of social, cultural, and religious activities for Dallas Jews from about 1915 until after World War II. Fram's Butcher Shop, Blatt's Bakery, and Jewish congregations dotted the area. Jewish youth attended Colonial and Brown elementary schools, and Forest High School had many absences on Jewish holidays. Many of the city's most prominent families lived in the district, the best known being those of the Marcus, Linz, and Kahn families. Two of the streets, South Boulevard and Park Row, have been designated as an Historic District.

In Houston, the majority of Jews during the 1930s and 1940s lived east of Main Street and Almeda Road in Washington Terrace and Riverside Terrace, and most Jewish students attended San Jacinto High. Jews shopped at Lang's Kosher Meat Market and ate at Schwartzberg's Restaurant and Delicatessen. The more Reform and/or wealthier Jews lived farther south, around Glen Haven and Underwood streets, and a few in the Post Oak area.[20] A documentary film about the Riverside area has been made by Houston filmmaker Jon Schwartz, "This is Our Home — It Is Not For Sale."

Friedman's Drugs in South Dallas was a popular neighborhood hangout in the 1930s and 1940s.
— *From the Collections of the Dallas Jewish Historical Society*

Rebecca "Mama" Leva served Hungarian-Jewish food in the Hungarian Cafe she owned and operated with her husband, David, in Lubbock in the 1930s and '40s.
— *Southwest Collection, Texas Tech University*

Mrs. Moskovitz' Cafe at 2216 Elm (Deep Ellum) in Dallas featured "Kosher and American Cooking" around 1930.
— *From the Collections of the Dallas Jewish Historical Society*

"I've got those Deep Ellum blues."
— Song by Leadbelly

Mrs. Moskovitz' Cafe on Deep Ellum in downtown Dallas was one of many Jewish businesses in the area made famous by blues singer Leadbelly (Huddie Ledbetter). Deep Ellum, where ethnic groups came together, was bounded by Main, Commerce, and Elm streets between Harwood and the railroad tracks (now Central Expressway). Settled after the Civil War by ex-slaves, it developed into a trading center in the 1870s. Farmers came with their horses and wagons to trade and spend the day; working men and women came to buy tools, clothes, groceries, and supplies. Jews were among the earliest merchants who not only lived behind their stores but supplied the needs of a growing urban community.

The area reached its zenith in the 1920s and 1930s with Jewish and black residents and businesses co-existing. One of the most famous landmarks was Jake's (Goldstein's) Pawn Shop. The area declined with the construction of Central Expressway in the 1950s.

Sam Schwartz (1885–1969), owner of the Aztec Theater in Eagle Pass, poses with the MGM lion, c. 1935, as he celebrated his twenty-fifth anniversary in the theater business.
— *William J. (Billy) Munter, grandson*

Sam Schwartz

Sam Schwartz was brought to America from Hungary in 1900 by his uncle, Adolph Schwartz of El Paso. Sam worked for ten years in his uncle's store, The Popular. When Sam decided to strike out on his own in 1910, he chose Eagle Pass on the Texas border.

Silent movies and vaudeville were sweeping the nation, and Sam decided that motion pictures presented a good opportunity. He purchased an old pool hall, installed benches and projection equipment, and rented films from traveling salesmen. Admission at his Majestic Theater was ten cents for adults and five cents for children, and live piano music accompanied the films. Schwartz sold tickets, swept the floors, and slept in the theater. With 16,000 soldiers garrisoned nearby during the Mexican Revolution, the Majestic was a success.

By 1915, Sam built the Aztec Theater and in 1929 was one of the first in South Texas to feature a sound movie, *The Jazz Singer* (with Al Jolson). After twenty-five years in the theater business, Schwartz received an award from Adolph Zukor of Para-

mount. When he died in 1969, he was the owner of the oldest theater in Texas.

Sam Schwartz was mayor of Eagle Pass (1920–1924) and school board member (1925–1952). He owned two farms, and was co-founder of the Maverick County Water Control and Improvement District.[21]

She wore her hair short and never married.

Gussie Oscar's career as a pianist and entertainer began in Calvert, entertaining her parents' guests in their 300-seat Casimir's Opera House and four-story Grand Hotel. In 1913, Gussie toured the U.S. and Canada as the accompanist of the singer May Irwin. In 1916, Gussie was one of only six female members of the International Alliance of Theatrical Employees.

Gussie moved to Waco in 1905 to conduct the orchestra for vaudeville acts at the Majestic Theater. She shocked Waco society by living alone in the honeymoon suite of a downtown hotel. She wore her hair short, slept until noon, and never married.

As manager of the Waco Auditorium from 1915 to 1928, she brought in many controversial programs such as *Birth of a Nation*, a film favorable to the Ku Klux Klan, which she showed on Sunday (in violation of the Blue Laws) to a sold-out house. The court offered to drop the charges if she

Gussie Oscar (1875–1950) was a musician and entertainment impresario who brought lively and controversial programs to Waco.
— *The Texas Collection, Baylor University, Waco, Texas*

would promise not to violate the law again. She refused. The judge sent her a box of candy and dropped the charges.

In 1917, Gussie scheduled a lecture on birth control together with a workshop performance of *Her Unborn Child*. Matinees were for ladies and evenings for gentlemen. She allowed only men to attend wrestling matches; they could bring their dogs, but not their women. Gussie also booked the Russian ballerina Pavlova, the Ziegfeld Follies, and William Jennings Bryan, who lectured against evolution.

During the Jazz Age, Gussie Oscar sponsored plays with half-dressed women and racy, off-color humor. When members of the city's censorship board came to review the performance, she tricked them by showing an innocuous production, which they approved. In presenting Irving Berlin's "The Music Box Revue," she defied the censorship board, and twenty actresses were arrested. The Waco *Times Herald* supported her, but the censorship board finally won. Shows were canceled, and the building was torn down. In the ensuing years, she booked events in other auditoriums.[22]

— **Rosella Werlin**

Perry Kallison (1904–   ) broadcast a farm and ranch radio show for forty years in San Antonio. Originally, the show was a commercial broadcast to promote his business, Kallison Farm and Ranch Store. It became a public service broadcast in which he helped locate missing persons, announced benefits, and promoted soil and water conservation. Kallison is the recipient of the Joe Freeman Award for Outstanding Service to Agriculture. He has also been active in Jewish affairs, serving as president of both the San Antonio Federation and Temple Beth-El. When the Israeli Ministry of Agriculture decided the country needed a mohair industry, Kallison raised a herd of Angora goats for Kibbutz Yadfat in Galilee, Israel.

— Perry Kallison

Rosella Horowitz Werlin (1904–1985) was a journalist for fifty years and wrote for a number of publications. She interviewed such luminaries as Golda Meir, Al Capone, and Eleanor Roosevelt. As a public relations professional for the City of Galveston, she promoted the island as a tourist center with a variety of clever schemes: a cotton turkey was sent to President Hoover to remind him of Galveston's role in the economy, a reunion of three sets of quadruplets was convened, and Jack Dempsey was posed dressed in a suit, holding a fishing pole upside down. As a reporter, she covered the red light district in Galveston and worked as a travel editor. In describing women in journalism in the 1920s, she said, "Jobs for women in the newspaper business were nonexistent in those days. In fact, 'nice girls' didn't do that kind of work — it was like being in the theater . . . We started work at 7:00 A.M. and often worked into the night . . . Nothing was handed to us on a silver platter. We learned work was what we had to do."[24]

— Rosenberg Library, Galveston, Texas

Anita Brenner (1900–1974) was an author who grew up in San Antonio but spent much of her life in Mexico. In 1925, she won $50 for her short story, "A Jewish Girl in Mexico," sponsored by *The Forward*, a Yiddish newspaper. She wrote *Idols Behind Altars, The Wind that Swept Mexico* (a narrative of the Mexican Revolution), and many children's books. During the Spanish Civil War, Brenner wrote dispatches from Spain for the *New York Times* and *The Nation*, and later edited *Mexico this Month*. As a member of the literati, she was able to bring Leon Trotsky to Mexico. She also helped her friends, Diego Rivera and his wife, Frida Kahlo, find recognition in New York.[23]

— The San Antonio Light *Collection, UT Institute of Texan Cultures*

David H. White (1903–1972) was the editor and publisher of Houston's *Jewish Herald Voice* from 1936 to 1972. He was an early advocate of civil rights and a leader in many Jewish and civic causes. He married Ida Schwartzberg in 1929, and together they traveled the world while he was a Far East correspondent for the International News Service. Ida worked at the *Jewish Herald Voice* alongside her husband until the paper was sold in 1972.

— Jewish National Fund

Wrestler Abe Coleman, the "Jewish Adonis," poses in wrestling stance with clenched fists as he prepares to challenge John Kilonis at the Exposition Arena in San Antonio, February 1931.
— *The* San Antonio Light *Collection, UT Institute of Texan Cultures*

Some East Texans enjoy splash day in the spring of 1910 on a Galveston pier. Third from left is Goldie Pandres; seventh from left is Goldie's father, Simon Hart.
— *Kay Goldman*

The Ehrlichs of Texarkana

Harry Ehrlich (1875–1933) of Texarkana was secretary-treasurer and business manager of the Shreveport baseball club when it won a league pennant in 1919. Well-known to players and fans alike, he attended every home game, stationed in his box on the third-base line, cigar in mouth, hat tilted, following every play. He and his brothers were entertainment entrepreneurs who owned theaters in Texarkana, as well as many towns in Louisiana and Mississippi. Harry even purchased an interest in a traveling carnival known as the Castle-Ehrlich-Hirsch Shows. He was a generous but modest philanthropist who donated huge sums to orphanages and homes for the aged. The Ehrlich Educational Building was donated by the family to Texarkana's Mount Sinai Congregation.

The Lion Auto Store Baseball Team of Dallas, 1939. Back row, l. to r.: Morris Wolfe, Ben Okon, Frank Singer, Sidney Smith, Carl Weill, and Aaron Gordon. Middle row, l. to r.: Joe Hafter, Sol Barzune, Erwin Waldman, F. Leslie, and Iuda Levy. Front row, l. to r.: Simon Smith, Reuben Levy, Donnie Love (mascot), Simon Okon, Frank Rose, and Charlie Lewin, manager.
— *From the Collections of the Dallas Jewish Historical Society*

Marie Levi (Mrs. Bernard) Bitterman of Dallas defended her title as Dallas Women's Golf Association champion in 1939. She was also champion in 1941 and 1942. More than a sports champion, Mrs. Bitterman has been president of the Dallas Section, National Council of Jewish Women, 1956 to 1958, and active in Dallas civic affairs, including the Dallas Jewish Historical Society.

— *Marie Bitterman*

Yetta Wexler (Schmidt) (1912–), born in Texarkana, is shown here at age five with a Knabe grand piano given to her by the company as a gift. When she was about three, it was discovered by her sisters' piano teacher that she had absolute pitch and could play by ear any of the pieces her sisters played. During World War I, she played for a concert to raise funds for the Red Cross. When she was seven, the visiting world-famous pianist Fannie Bloomfield Zeisler heard her play and offered to give her lessons. Yetta and her mother, and later the whole family, moved to Chicago, where Yetta studied with Zeisler. Yetta made such progress that at age twelve, she appeared with the Chicago Symphony. She graduated from Juilliard in New York and launched a career as a soloist, teacher, accompanist, and lecturer. During World War II, she joined the Women's Army Corps and served in Europe. She said, "I speak proudly of my Jewish heritage and my Texas birthplace."

— *Yetta Wexler Schmidt*

How much *gefilte* fish can be made from a 365-pound deep-sea bass? Oscar Sommer of Brownsville, shown here, and his wife, Laura, found out in 1929.

— *Ray S. Leonard*

"I never told a story that didn't have a point."

— Dr. Hyman J. Ettlinger

Celia's roping her man at the Delta Phi Epsilon Round Up, UT Austin, 1953.
— *Photo by Jack's Party Pictures*

One of the earliest Jewish fraternities at UT Austin was Phi Sigma Delta, 1929–1930.
— *Hirsh Nathan Schwartz, copy from UT Institute of Texan Cultures*

Aubrey L. Goodman played football at Baylor University in Waco, c. 1920.
— *The Texas Collection, Baylor University, Waco, Texas*

On the college campuses

In the 1920s and 1930s, increasing numbers of Jewish men and women attended college and headed for professional life. The campuses at UT Austin and Texas A&M each established Hillel Foundations in the late 1920s, and the first Jewish fraternity at the University of Texas, Phi Sigma Delta, formed in 1929. Other Jewish fraternities and sororities at UT opened, including Tau Delta Phi, Zeta Beta Tau, Alpha Epsilon Pi, Sigma Alpha Mu, Delta Phi Epsilon, Alpha Epsilon Phi, and Sigma Delta Tau. They provided a Jewish network for youngsters and an open door to a "Greek" system otherwise closed to Jews.

Jewish faculty members reached out to Jewish students. Particularly remembered are Drs. Hyman J. Ettlinger, UT Austin, and Jacob J. Taubenhaus, Texas A&M. They were both long-time faculty members, outstanding scholars, teachers, and Hillel supporters.

Dr. Ettlinger began at UT in 1913 after earning degrees at Washington University (where he lettered in three sports) and Harvard. He chaired the UT Mathematics Department for twenty-five years and co-authored a groundbreaking calculus textbook. He promoted science and math careers to high school students and re-

fereed 15,000 high school and collegiate football games. He organized the Menorah Society for Jewish students with Temple Beth Israel's Rabbi David Rosenbaum in 1913. (It was succeeded by Hillel in 1929.)

Dr. Taubenhaus was born in Safed, Palestine, where he attended an educational institute before completing his education at Cornell and the University of Pennsylvania. He went to Texas A&M in 1916, becoming chief of the Division of Plant Pathology and Physiology. He founded College Station's Hillel Foundation.

Dr. Hyman J. Ettlinger (1889–1986) taught in the Mathematics Department at UT Austin for many years. As a teacher, he integrated sports with math. "You have to count to play football and you have to count in mathematics," he said. "I always start them on their fingers."
— *Jewish National Fund*

— **Pirket Avot** *(The Sayings of the Fathers)*

Dr. Harry Joshua Leon (1896–1967) was an author, scholar, and chair of the Department of Classics at UT Austin for twenty years. He was also a trustee of Temple Beth Israel.
— *Barker Texas History Center, UT Austin*

Ernestine Phelps Leon (1896–1968), the wife of Harry Leon, taught classics at UT Austin and was the author of numerous articles.
— *Isabel Leon Samfield*

Dr. Max Sylvius Handman (1885–1939), a native of Rumania, was a rabbi and later a professor of economics at UT Austin and the University of Michigan. He was knighted by King Carol of Rumania in 1932 for his study of race and culture.
— *Ruth Ruben*

Dr. Harry and Ernestine Leon

Two scholars of classical literature and languages, Dr. Harry Leon and Ernestine Leon, joined the faculty of UT Austin in 1932.

Harry Leon was born in Worcester, Massachusetts, and received his Ph.D. from Harvard in 1927. His enjoyment of his subject and his clear and witty speaking style made him one of the most popular lecturers ever to teach at UT Austin, filling a large auditorium with his Classical Civilization course every semester. He chaired the Classics Department from 1947 to 1967 and was the first to teach Hebrew for credit there. He was also involved with the Hillel Foundation.

Ernestine Phelps was born in the Bronx, New York. She received her degrees from Hunter College and Columbia University but was denied her doctorate because her dissertation advisor died. She and her husband met while studying in Italy. After they arrived in Texas, Mrs. Leon taught Latin and Greek in the Classics Department. When anti-nepotism laws prevented husband and wife from working in the same department, Mrs. Leon taught in the Correspondence School.

Dr. and Mrs. Leon shared many intellectual interests. Together they researched the Hebrew, Latin, and Greek inscriptions in the catacombs of ancient Rome, proving that a large community of 50,000 Jews lived along the Via Appia more than 2,000 years ago. These Jewish catacombs, vast underground tombs, were later copied by the Christians. Dr. Leon's book on this subject is *The Jews of Ancient Rome*.

The Leons were well-known for the clever papers they gave at conferences, and both wrote prolifically on many subjects. Dr. Leon's last paper was on Hrotswitha, the tenth-century nun who was the first Christian playwright. Mrs. Leon enjoyed cultural detective work like diagnosing the diseases of the ancients by interpreting descriptions of their symptoms in light of modern medical knowledge.

With his command of Hebrew and Jewish subjects, Dr. Leon was a lay participant in the Kallah of Texas Rabbis and was sometimes called upon to conduct High Holy Day religious services in Hallettsville. The day after Dr. Leon's death, Mrs. Leon went to the classroom to teach his graduate seminar. A month later, she also died.[25]

Dr. Max Sylvius Handman

Dr. Max Handman came to the U.S. from Rumania in 1903. He was rabbi for Marshall's Temple Moses Montefiore in 1910 and married Della Dopplemayer, a local woman. Handman publicly opposed the reading of the Bible in the Marshall public schools. In 1917, he received a Ph.D. at the University of Chicago and became a professor of sociology and economics at UT-Austin, where he stayed until 1931.

Dr. Handman was a special investigator for the Library of Congress in 1918. He was also on the staff of the U.S. Inquiry on the Terms of Peace after World War I. He directed the Red Cross Social Service Institute for Texas in 1919, and was president of the Texas Conference on Social Welfare in 1924.

In 1932, Dr. Handman returned to his home country of Rumania to study race and culture. The results were published and led to his decoration by King Carol as Knight First Class of the Order of Cultural Merit. From 1931 to 1939, he was professor of economics at the University of Michigan.[26] He is buried in the Marshall Hebrew Cemetery.

The National Council of Jewish Women has long supported schools, libraries, and educational institutions. On June 1, 1936, the San Antonio Section, NCJW, donated 2,000 books to the public library. Left to right, Mrs. L. Lauterstein, president of the San Antonio Council of Jewish Women; Mrs. J. M. Frost, delegate, and Mrs. C. J. Matthews, president, City Federation of Women's Clubs.
— *The* San Antonio Light *Collection, UT Institute of Texan Cultures*

Henrietta Blum (Mrs. I. H.) Kempner (1882–1970) was the first president of the Parent Teacher Association of Galveston and served on the Galveston School Board from 1921 to 1926. She was also president of the Galveston Little Theater, a member of the State Committee on Child Welfare, and was active in the Girl Scouts, the Galveston Art League, and several literary clubs.[27]
— *Rosenberg Library, Galveston, Texas*

Nathan Moses (Nat) Washer of Fort Worth and San Antonio had a long history of civic involvement that culminated in his 1929 appointment as first chairman of the Texas State Board of Education, on which he served until 1935. Born in Tennessee, Nat Washer and his brother Jacob established Washer Bros. Clothing Store in Fort Worth in 1887, which supplied clothing to many famous cowboys and luminaries like Teddy Roosevelt. They advertised themselves as "The Western outpost of Texas." A past Grand Master of Masonry, Nat Washer was instrumental in the founding of a Masonic home and school for widows and orphans in Fort Worth.

After moving to San Antonio in 1899, Nat Washer served as president of Temple Beth El from 1902 to 1907. Under his presidency, a new temple building was dedicated in 1903 and was in use for twenty-eight years. Washer also served on the San Antonio Public Library Board (1913–1934) and was an orator, poet, and singer who promoted cultural institutions.[28]
— *Temple Beth-El, San Antonio, copy from UT Institute of Texan Cultures*

— **Ruth Cohen Frisch**[29]

Marguerite (Mrs. Mose) Marks (1897–
) was president of the Texas Committee
on the Cause and Cure of War from 1938
to 1945. She and her husband established
three libraries: two in Dallas at the Girls
Foundation Club and Golden Acres
Home for the Aged, and one at the Hospice Resource Center, Carmel, California.
— *Dorothy M. and Henry S. Jacobus Temple
Emanu-El Archives, Dallas,
print by Andy Reisberg*

Temple Emanu-El Sisterhood, Dallas,
1930s or 1940s. The Sisterhood organized
a Peace and World Relations Committee
around 1921.
— *Dorothy M. and Henry S. Jacobus Temple
Emanu-El Archives, Dallas,
print by Andy Reisberg*

Jewish women worked for peace

As the ominous signs of war became visible in Europe, Jewish and
non-Jewish women worked together
to avoid a worldwide conflagration.
Marguerite Marks of Dallas represented the National Council of Jewish
Women at the founding meeting of
the Texas State Cause and Cure of
War Committee and was elected president in 1938.

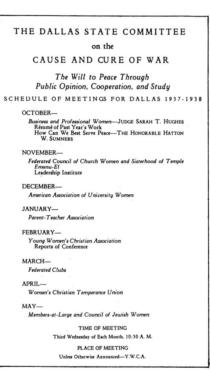

THE DALLAS STATE COMMITTEE
on the
CAUSE AND CURE OF WAR

*The Will to Peace Through
Public Opinion, Cooperation, and Study*
SCHEDULE OF MEETINGS FOR DALLAS 1937-1938

OCTOBER—
Business and Professional Women—JUDGE SARAH T. HUGHES
Résumé of Past Year's Work
How Can We Best Serve Peace—THE HONORABLE HATTON
W. SUMNERS

NOVEMBER—
Federated Council of Church Women and Sisterhood of Temple
Emanu-El
Leadership Institute

DECEMBER—
American Association of University Women

JANUARY—
Parent-Teacher Association

FEBRUARY—
Young Women's Christian Association
Reports of Conference

MARCH—
Federated Clubs

APRIL—
Woman's Christian Temperance Union

MAY—
Members-at-Large and Council of Jewish Women

TIME OF MEETING
Third Wednesday of Each Month, 10:30 A. M.

PLACE OF MEETING
Unless Otherwise Announced—Y.W.C.A.

A program of the Dallas State Committee
on the Cause and Cure of War, announcing a schedule of meetings in Dallas in
1937–1938.
— *Dorothy M. and Henry S. Jacobus Temple
Emanu-El Archives, Dallas*

Mrs. Marks was born in Galveston,
where she was inspired by the good
works of her grandmother, Elizabeth
Gaertner Levy, and her mother, Estelle Meyer. After settling in Dallas,
Mrs. Marks became president of the
National Council of Jewish Women,
1941–1943, and the Temple Emanu-
El Sisterhood, 1947–1948. She was
an early peace worker. In 1936, she
addressed Dallasites on Radio Station
WFAA: "Peace will come . . . but
only after each nation has stopped its
own economic misery and inequality;
only after blind nationalism has given
way to international good will."

Under her leadership, the Texas
State Committee on the Cause and
Cure of War formed a coalition of organizations, which included the Business and Professional Women, the
Federated Council of Church
Women, Temple Emanu-El Sisterhood, NCJW, American Association
of University Women, PTA, YWCA,
and the Woman's Christian Temperance Union. She reached out to
Negro women of the Dallas YWCA:
"They were very interested and came
to our meetings. The color made no
difference whatsoever." Mrs. Marks
recalled, "We invited history professors from SMU who were interested
in the peace movement. We continued to study . . . so that when the war
was over, we would be ready to talk
to the women's organizations about
the new United Nations."

In 1941, Marguerite was invited to
join the National Committee on International Relations and Peace. During World War II, she organized civil
defense activities, war bond sales, and
kindergartens serving the children of
mothers who worked in defense factories.[30] Since World War II, she has
continued her work. In 1988, she sent
greetings to the International Wom-
en's Conference, "Global Peace,"
which met in Dallas: "Work with intelligence, pray for the peace that
shall bring well-being to the children
of the world and all mankind."

Purim services were held for servicemen stationed in Amarillo during World War II by Temple B'nai Israel.

The Sisterhood of Congregation Adath Yeshurun in Houston entertained at the Soldiers' Service Bureau.
— *Copy from* The Golden Book of Congregation Adath Yeshurun, 1891–1941

Answering the call to fight

As World War II broke out in Europe, sons and daughters of Jewish Texans heeded the call to action and joined the armed forces. The war effort had a special meaning for Jews because of Adolph Hitler's extreme anti-Semitism. Hundreds of Jewish men went to fight on both fronts. Sgt. Marcel Sommer of Brownsville was awarded the Distinguished Flying Cross for numerous high-altitude attacks on targets within Nazi Germany. Capt. Harry A. Badt of Tyler, a graduate of the Naval Academy in 1908, had an unusual adventure story. As commander of the *Tuscaloosa,* he rescued almost 600 Nazis whose ship was burning and on the verge of being scuttled. Many Jewish servicemen were killed in action.

Many servicemen and -women from other states trained at Texas installations. Clarice Fortgang Pollard from Brooklyn, New York, recalled her experiences as a WAC in Nacogdoches, Texas. During Passover, she and the other Jewish WACS were invited to a *seder* at the home of Lena and Leon Aron. They were greatly amused to hear the Hebrew passages recited in a Texas drawl, and finally broke into laughter: "It was the unaccustomed accents. Our frankness and his [Leon's] responsive wit surrounded us with a feeling of closeness and comradery [*sic*] for the rest of the evening."[31]

Alice Taub of Waco in uniform. Women joined the WACS, WAVES, and WASPS to help defend their country.
— *The Texas Collection, Baylor University, Waco, Texas*

Louis Stein of Brownsville was killed in action near Strasbourg, France, in 1945. His mother, Mae Rose Weil Stein (1896–1983), donated $500,000 to build a Sunday school for Temple Beth El in Brownsville in memory of Louis, who had been a religious school teacher. — *Ruben Edelstein*

Haskell and Motley Harelik sold war
bonds at their Hamilton store, while their
sons served in the armed forces.
— *From the family album of the Harelik family,
compiled by Harry Harelik, Waco, Texas*

Victory gardens and scrap campaigns

On the home front, Texas Jews supported the war effort by working in defense industries, buying war bonds, volunteering for the ambulance corps, and working with other organizations like the Red Cross and USO. They planted victory gardens and saved their scrap for the war effort. Joseph Applebaum, the owner of a junk yard in Marshall, traded defense bonds to local citizens in exchange for scrap metals they brought to his yard. Born in Cuvalk, Poland, then in the possession of the Nazis, Applebaum said, "It belongs to the Germans today, but I'm trying to do my part to take it away from them again."

Brownsville Jews did their part and more. Isadore Dorfman was commanding officer of the Texas State Defense Guard, Ely Holtzman was the driving force behind a scrap campaign, insuring that thousands of tons of metal and rubber were shipped for the war effort, and Ben Freudenstein worked for the U.S. Rent Control Agency in San Antonio. In Houston, Rebecca Nathan was Texas State Conservation chair, and Rosella Werlin was the Galveston County chair of the American Women Volunteer Service and a member of Bundles for Britain.

Harry Schneider of Dallas was a World War I veteran and junior vice-commander of the Jewish War Veterans, 1943, which donated an ambulance to the Red Cross.
— *Sylvia Greenspan, official photograph of
U.S. Army Air Forces, Love Field, Dallas*

Elva Godshaw Levy and Isidora "Dodo" Levy Naman were Red Cross Gray Ladies during World War II in Waco.
— *The Texas Collection, Baylor University, Waco, Texas*

How Rosenberg became the only city on the Mainland to be attacked by the Japanese

During the war years, everyone did their part, even children. In Rosenberg, Joe and Robert Schechter volunteered through their Boy Scout troop to man an air-control tower about a mile from town after school. The tower, located in Mrs. Henry Strempel's backyard close to Needville, was sixty feet high, and together the two boys would climb to the top. One boy held the binoculars, and the other staffed the telephone. Their task was to report planes that flew overhead.

One afternoon, Joe saw three planes flying overhead in formation. He was sure they were Japanese Zeros! Robert called Ellington Air Force Base in Houston immediately to report that the Japanese were attacking Rosenberg!

Interceptor planes were sent right away, only to find that the fighter planes were actually AT6 Texans (similar in silhouette to the Japanese Zeros), trainers which were flown by the Women's Airforce Service Pilots (WASPS), stationed at Avenger Field in Sweetwater. The boys were reprimanded for the alarm, but as Robert recalled, "We bravely stood our posts even though we were under attack."[32]

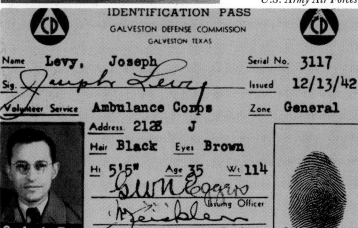

Joseph Levy was a member of the Ambulance Corps in Galveston.
— *Helene Levy, print by Steve Nussenblatt*

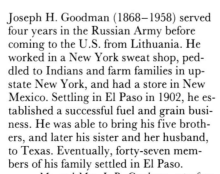

Recha Sara Levy obtained "Quota Immigration Visa No. 8317," dated May 21, 1941, from the American Consul in Berlin and left Hanover, Germany, on the last ship. She was one of the few German Jews who managed to get out in 1941. Her German passport indicates she traveled through Lisbon, Portugal; she settled in Waco.

— *Rae Levin, Waco*

German Jews seek safety

On November 9, 1938, the infamous *Kristallnacht* (Night of Broken Glass), the violent pogrom against German Jews, signaled the intensification of Nazi suppression. Many Jews believed that the wave of anti-Semitism would pass; others gathered what they could and fled. Entry to the U.S. was difficult because of immigration quotas. However, some, like Recha Sara Levy, were able to flee Nazi Germany. She settled in Waco.

Hundreds of families like Maurice and his brother Nandor Schwartz of El Paso frantically struggled to rescue relatives from annihilation. With the help of both U.S. senators from Texas, the Schwartzes brought four nephews from Hungary before the war, and after the war, they rescued four nieces who had been in concentration camps.

Joseph H. Goodman (1868–1958) served four years in the Russian Army before coming to the U.S. from Lithuania. He worked in a New York sweat shop, peddled to Indians and farm families in upstate New York, and had a store in New Mexico. Settling in El Paso in 1902, he established a successful fuel and grain business. He was able to bring his five brothers, and later his sister and her husband, to Texas. Eventually, forty-seven members of his family settled in El Paso.

— *Mr. and Mrs. I. B. Goodman, copy from UT Institute of Texan Cultures*

— **Chaya Rochel Andres**

Auschwitz, an oil painting on canvas,
30″ x 24″, 1967, by Houston artist Frank
Freed (1906–1975), in the collection of
Mr. and Mrs. Jack Lapin, Houston.
                         — *Eleanor Freed*

"The Numbers on Your Arm" [34]
— Chaya Rochel Andres
I ponder over arms with numerals
        tattooed . . .
You've felt the sear of lash,
Upon skin, upon your flesh . . .
And in your blood . . .

I feel your forehead is heating . . .
You no longer feel
the searing electrical numbering needle —
While less human you've become . . .

Now you're merely a number upon your
        arm . . .
And engraved upon my mind
are the lives of so many beings —
annihilated!

And amongst them — my nearest . . .
My dearest . . .
My mother . . .
My three sisters . . .
My one and only brother . . .

G-d Almighty.
Why? Where did they err?
For what iniquity? . . .
And I, in dark despair,
cry out:
"Come to my aid,
G-d of the universe!"

You have dug your own deep grave —
The order comes — to leap!
A forceful push —
And down you go . . .
You are buried deep . . .
A gun's discharged —

And there you lay
Motionless,
In a pool of blood . . .
Earth covered, your body lies . . .
No longer one of the human race . . .
You are now only a number . . .
And I wonder —
Shall I not ask of you now,
When you yourself are puzzled
As to how???

Do not ask of me now
How safety I found . . .
How I was able to remain alive —
To relate all that horror!

In reality, I'm no longer human . . .
only gore . . .
I'm only the numerals on my arm . . .
Ask of me no more . . .
For I do not understand . . .
I no longer remember . . .
And talk of it, I can't.

Too deep is the bloody incision . . .
In my great desolation
Do not ask . . .
Do not question . . .

JEWISH
HERALD-VOICE
Since 1906 The Voice Of Southwestern Jewry

VOLUME 43.   HOUSTON, TEXAS   MAY 20, 1948   NUMBER 7

REPUBLIC OF ISRAEL PROCLAIMED MAY 14

TEL AVIV, (JTA)—The state of Israel was born this week. The Provisional Jewish Government, meeting in Tel Aviv on the eve of the Sabbath, on the fifth day of Iyar, 5708—May 14, 1948—announced to the world:

"We, members of the National Council representing the Jewish people in Palestine and the Zionist movement of the world, met together in solemn assembly on the day of the termination of the British Mandate for Palestine, and by virtue of natural and historic right of the Jewish people, and by resolution of the General Assembly of the United Nations, hereby proclaim the establishment of a Jewish state in Palestine to be called 'Israel.'

"As from the termination of the mandate at midnight and until the setting up of duly-elected bodies in accordance with the Constitution to be drawn up by the Constituent Assembly not later than the first of October, 1948, the present National Council shall act as the Provisional Government of the state of Israel.

"The state will be open to all Jewish immigrants, will promote the development of the country for all its inhabitants, will be based on the precepts of liberty, justice and peace taught by the Hebrew prophets, will uphold full social and political equality for all its citizens without distinction of race, creed or sex, and will guarantee full freedom of education and culture."

The proclamation of the state of Israel also promised to safeguard all religious shrines and Holy Places and pledged the new state to dedicate itself "to the principles of the Charter of the United Nations." The state of Israel also appealed to the United Nations to aid the Jewish people in building the state and asked for admission to

(Continued on Page 3)

EMANU EL ELECTS H. KRAKOWER AT ANNUAL MEETING; WM. NATHAN AND MARTIN NADELMAN VICE-PRESIDENTS

Congregation Emanu El at its annual meeting on Monday, May 17, held at the Central Presbyterian Church elected Herman W. Krakower, prominent business man and communal leader, to the presidency of the Congregation. Mr. Krakower had served as vice-president of the Congregation for four years. A charter member, Mr. Krakower has been in the forefront of congregational activities and has manifest a great interest in the progress of Emanu El.

M. M. Feld, outgoing president, was elected honorary president of the Congregation.

Elected to serve with Mr. Krakower were: William M. Nathan, 1st vice-president; Martin Nadelman, 2nd vice-president; D. H. White, secretary. Mitchell Horwitz was re-elected treasurer.

Dan Hirsh and N. J. Klein were re-elected to serve a two year term on the Board of Directors. Newly elected Board members for a two year term include: E. N. Bender, Mrs. Harry Caplovitz, A. I. Lack, Al Natkin, Adolph Salsburg, Julian Shapiro, M. M. Slotnick.

Ben Epstein was elected to the Board for a one year term. Rabbi Robt. I. Kahn was elected for a tenure of three years.

Reports of the Synagogue Committees were given and the

HERMAN KRAKOWER
. . . reward for services, ability

progress of the Congregation noted by the members. A report of the progress of the Synagogue building was given by committee chairman, Julius Fohs. Indications point to the completion of the structure early in '49.

A resolution in appreciation of the exceptional service rendered the Congregation by outgoing president M. M. Feld was presented. In the resolution, Mr. Fohs pointed out that Mr. Feld

(Continued on page 12)

CHAIM WEIZMANN
. . . an idel realized, an age-old dream come true

Weizman Elected

TEL AVIV, Israel, (JTA) — Dr. Chaim Weizmann, veteran Zionist statesman who has worked for the establishment of a Jewish state in Palestine since the turn of the century, was elected this week President of the Provisional Government of Is-

(Continued on Page 12)

Houston Lodge To Celebrate Fifty Years of Service Sunday, May 23

Milton J. Mehl, prominent attorney of Ft. Worth, and newly elected 2nd vice-president of District Grand Lodge No. 7 B'nai B'rith, will be the principal speaker at the Golden Jubilee Celebration of Houston Lodge No. 434, Sunday evening, May 23 at the Crystal Ballroom of the Rice Hotel.

Mr. Mehl is well known throughout the District as an able speaker and communal leader. He served with distinction in World War II and was one of the prosecutors of the war crimes trials at Nuremberg, Germany. He has been prominent in youth activities and is himself a graduate from AZA ranks.

There will be an informal reception at 6:30 in the evening according to the announcement by Lodge resident Irving Passman. The Dinner will begin promptly at 7:00.

District recognition will be given to the members of Houston Lodge who have been members of the Order for the past 50 or 25 years. Golden Certificates will be presented to those members with fifty years of affiliation and Silver Certificates

(Continued on page 3)

NEW YORK, MAY 17 (Palcor)—Arms for the embattled new state of Israel, Marshall Plan aid for the settlement of DPs in the infant Jewish republic and swift sanctions against the Arab states now attacking the world's youngest democracy, were demanded with a single voice last night by scores of thousands of Americans, Christian and Jew, in an unprecedented series of mass demonstrations, blanketing the United States and Canada, in a salute to Israel and its fighting Army, Haganah.

Major demonstrations occurred in New York, in neighboring Jersey City, in Washington, D. C., Cincinnati, Chicago, and across the border, in Montreal.

The largest demonstration, sponsored by The American Zionist Emergency Council, took place in New York, with nearly 100,000 persons inside and outside Madison Square Garden. It was addressed by Senator Robert A. Taft, of Ohio, former Governor Herbert H. Lehman, former Secretary of the Treasury Henry Morgenthau, Jr., Mayor William O'Dwyer, Dr. Abba Hillel Silver, Chairman, and Dr. Emanuel Neumann, Mrs. Rose Halprin and Haim Greenberg, members of the American Section of the Jewish Agency Executive, Dr. Jorge Garcia Granados, Guatemalan delegate to the U. N., Dr. Stephen S. Wise, veteran American Zionist leader, Frank Goldman, President of B'nai B'rith, and Brigadier General Julius Klein, National Commander of the Jewish War Veterans of the U. S.

Senator Robert A. Taft, addressing the rally, congratulated President Truman on being the first chief of state to recognize Israel, but scored the vacillation which has marked American policy during the recent weeks of debate in the United Nations Charging that American vacillation had contributed to the present war in Palestine, the Ohio Senator proposed the following policy for U.S.A.

(Continued on Page 12)

DANNENBAUM ELECTED PRESIDENT OF CONG. BETH ISRAEL; SHLENKER AND SUSMAN NAMED VICE-PRESIDENTS

M. N. DANNENBAUM
. . . a well deserved honor

M. N. Dannenbaum, communal and civic leader, was elected president of Congregation Beth Israel at the annual meeting of the Congregation held Wednesday, May 19 at the Abe M. Levy Memorial Hall. Mr. Dannenbaum has been active in Temple affairs for many years and has served as vice-president, chairman of the Religious School Committee. He is a past president of District Grand Lodge

No. 7 B'nai B'rith, past president of the Jewish Community Center, National ADL Commissioner and has held numerous other committee assignments in various civic, communal and religious organizations. He succeeds Simon Sakowitz who served the Congregation as President for three years.

Elected to serve with Mr. Dannenbaum are: Irvin M. Shlenker, 1st vice-president; Harry Susman, 2nd vice-president; Sam Suravitz, treasurer. A. A. Kaufman was reelected secretary.

Trustees elected at the annual meeting include: I. S. Brochstein, Matthew Karn and Sam W. Levy for a three year term; Eli Marks and J. O. Berlowitz for a 1 year term.

Plans were discussed for the enlargement of the Religious School quarters; the improvement of the Abe M. Levy Memorial Hall facilities; the air conditioning and improvement of the Sanctuary. The Congregation has acquired the property adjacent to the present building and will work out plans to beautify the entire square block. A preliminary plan was discussed and a committee will develop the detail of this project.

FRONT PAGE OF HOUSTON
JEWISH HERALD VOICE

Houston Jewish Herald Voice, May 20, 1948, announced the birth of the State of Israel on May 14, 1948.
    — *Houston* Jewish Herald Voice

1945 to 1990

"As long as there are Jewish hearts."[1]
THE TEXAS JEWISH COMMUNITY SINCE 1945

In 150 years, Texas Jewish communal life has evolved from burial societies and religious institutions to secular organizations supporting a variety of social welfare programs, political causes, and the State of Israel. As the immigrant generations passed and the Jewish populace became urbanized and better educated, involvement in secular Jewish causes became a morally and ethically justifiable way to retain Jewish identity without necessarily participating in religious rites. The loss of spirituality for some led to assimilation; for others, it precipitated a mini-renaissance of questioning and seeking meaningful ways to enhance their Jewish identity.

Immediately following World War II, the Texas Jewish community focused on rescuing victims of the Holocaust; many survivors settled in the Lone Star State. Political action in favor of a Jewish homeland in Palestine was also at the top of the agenda. Although some influential Texas Jews still did not support a Jewish homeland, the creation of the State of Israel in 1948 reflected the feelings of the majority, who responded with a generous outpouring of funds, time, and energy.

On the home front, postwar prosperity, particularly in defense, high technology, and petroleum-related industries, attracted thousands of Jewish residents from other parts of the U.S. and the world. Second- and third-generation Jewish sons and daughters from small Texas towns attended universities, and as they entered the professions, they moved to urban areas. As the Jewish populations in smaller towns decreased, temples and synagogues were left behind that today either hang by a thread or are all but extinct. The Jewish population doubled from 50,000 in 1945 to almost 100,000 in 1989, with more than eighty percent living in the metropolitan areas of Houston and Dallas.

The increased Jewish population in urban areas prompted the creation and expansion of religious and social infrastructures to meet burgeoning needs. Community planning became vital, as welfare federations developed Jewish family services, homes for the aged, and vocational guidance programs. The construction of Jewish community centers in the larger cities represented the collaborative efforts of Reform, Conservative, Orthodox, and secular Jews as old tensions slowly evolved into respect and cooperation.

Support for Israel and the apparatus for communal organizations has been augmented by a broad array of volunteer groups, from Sisterhoods and Brotherhoods to Zionist and social clubs. Jewish volunteerism runs the gamut from veterans groups to women's organizations working for reproductive rights. Local, state, and national news items are highlighted, and controversial issues are aired in the Anglo-Jewish press; of note are the *Jewish Herald Voice* of Houston, the *Texas Jewish Post* of Fort Worth/Dallas, and the *Jewish Journal of San Antonio*.

Congregations in suburban areas have also grown, along with the population. Temples and synagogues have been remodeled and new ones built; some are modest structures and others are elaborate religious-educational complexes. Lines between Conservative and Reform synagogues have blurred somewhat as Reform has added more traditional elements to its liturgy and ritual. The women's movement of the 1970s prompted increased participation by women in congregational and institutional life. Women in the Reform and Conservative movements now receive *aliyas* and read from the Torah. The high incidence of intermarriage has led to outreach by Reform congregations, and conversion classes are widely attended not only by converts, but by Jews seeking to renew their faith.

Still, almost half of the Texas population calling themselves Jews in 1989 remain unaffiliated with a religious institution. Whatever their reasons, many remain "cultural Jews" who send their children to Jewish day-care centers, play handball at the Jewish community center, and participate in Jewish social or political causes. Others form *chavurot,* groups of like-minded friends similar to an extended family.

With the destruction of European institutions, books, records, and cemeteries, historical preservation has become a vital concern. The Dallas Memorial Center for Holocaust Studies and the Texas Jewish Historical Society are two organizations founded in the 1980s to preserve the records of Jewish life for future generations.

Since World War II, anti-Semitism has declined, yet in spite of general acceptance by the larger community, pockets of anti-Semitism still exist. The Ku Klux Klan, the American Nazi Party, and more recently the

Skinheads have used time-worn stereotypes to slander Jews and other minority groups. Many of their canards have fallen on sympathetic ears and have resulted in acts of vandalism and destruction aimed at Jewish institutional buildings. Local Jewish Community Relations Councils, along with the Anti-Defamation League and the American Jewish Committee, continue to monitor and counteract the activities of the hate groups.

For Texas Jews who have for years been pained by more subtle and perhaps even unintentional forms of anti-Semitism, a well-honed sensitivity to church-state issues has unified Jews into activism. In 1956, the Houston Jewish Community Council opposed the distribution of Gideon Bibles in public schools, the use of evangelists in public school assemblies, and the formation of religious clubs in high schools.

Most Jews rejoiced at the 1963 Supreme Court ruling in *Murray et al v. Curlett et al* that Bible readings and recitation of the Lord's Prayer in public schools were unconstitutional. In 1983, Jewish state legislators led a successful fight for legislation requiring excused absences to students observing religious holy days. In 1985, the law was extended to include college students. As late as 1989, Rabbi Sam Stahl (Temple Beth-El) organized a chapter of Americans United for Separation of Church and State in San Antonio to combat efforts to "christianize" public schools.

The single most unifying factor in the Texas Jewish community, however, has been support for the survival of the State of Israel. As author and historian Irving Howe noted, "[support for Israel] has become the 'civil religion' of American Jews . . . Israel brought new meaning to Jewish life; new perceptions of a collective self . . ." [Howe and Libo, *We Lived There Too*]

For the first thirty-five years of its existence, support for the social programs and foreign policy of Israel was almost universal among American Jews. Because of the external threat of war and war itself (the 1956 war with Egypt, the Six-Day War of 1967, and the Yom Kippur War of 1973), American Jews were stalwart in their support. They contributed generously, traveled to Israel as tourists and on study missions, and sent their teenagers on Teen Tours; some even made *aliyah*. A 1989 study of the Dallas Jewish community revealed that support for Israel remains the unifying force, with ninety-five percent continuing to favor economic aid.

Since 1982, however, American Jews have been reevaluating their relationship with Israel. The 1982 Israeli invasion of Lebanon and the Palestinian *intifada* (uprising), which broke out on the West Bank and Gaza Strip in 1987, have called in question previous attitudes of "Israel Right or Wrong." The 1988 controversy over "Who Is a Jew," which would deny automatic Israeli citizenship to converts to Judaism converted by any

but Orthodox rabbis, created an uproar. The Israeli Supreme Court ruled that those converted to Judaism by non-Orthodox rabbis have the right to immigrate to Israel as Jews. Opinions about these issues have divided Israelis, as well as American Jews.

Jewish sentiments critical of Israeli military actions have increased, along with activities of both Israeli and U.S. peace organizations. In 1988, Texans were among those who signed an advertisement in the *New York Times* urging the U.S. government to press for negotiations between Israel and the Palestinians to work for a peaceful solution and an end to the occupation. Almost fifty Austin Jews signed the same statement in an ad in their local *Jewish Outlook*. These issues are widely argued in the Jewish community with no easy solutions in sight.

There is an old saying that if you put two Jews together, you will get three opinions. That is certainly no less true now than ever. The Texas Jewish community today continues to be energetic and diverse, though sometimes diffuse and fragmented in its effort to provide "something for everyone." On the following pages, we present a very small sample of the many faces of Jewish leaders, activities, and institutions. As the twenty-first century lies just over the horizon, a vibrant Texas Jewish community is growing and preparing for yet another century.

Mike Jacobs

World War II was over. While Texas Jewish veterans returned home to the joy of their families, some Holocaust survivors traveled to the Lone Star State to find a new home and build a new family.

Mike Jacobs was one Holocaust survivor who went to Texas with a number still tattooed on his forearm — B-4990. Born in Konin, Poland, Jacobs lost his entire family — three brothers, two sisters, both parents, and eighty other relatives — at Treblinka. Another brother, who fought in the Polish underground, was killed by the Nazis. Jacobs was imprisoned as a teenager in the Auschwitz/Birkenau death camp and survived years of forced marches, starvation, severe winters, and the brutalities of Nazi guards. He remembered, "I never could understand how the SS troops who were fathers and husbands could go with blood on their hands from killing young children to their own homes and play with their own children."[2]

After the war, Jacobs lived in Germany for six years, earning a teaching certificate and playing soccer. He helped other Jews work their way through Germany to illegal entry into Palestine. In 1951, Jacobs decided to emigrate to the U.S. and settled in Dallas. He worked as a part-time recreational director for the Jewish Community Center, where he met his future wife, native Dallasite Ginger Chesnick. Mike and Ginger went into business, Jacobs Iron and Metal, and became heavily involved in Jewish communal affairs. He was the area chairman for Israel Bonds and has served on numerous boards, including Congregation Shearith Israel and the Jewish Federation of Greater Dallas. He is the recipient of the Prime Minister's Award from Israel Bonds, the Torch of Conscience Award from the American Jewish Congress, and Man of the Year Award from the Zionist Organization of America.

Mike Jacobs served as the first president of the Memorial Center for Holocaust Studies in Dallas, and was one of its founders along with Holocaust survivors Ann Stein, Henry Goldberg, Leon Zetley, Frank Bell, Sam Szor, and Martin N. Donald. He lectures extensively on the Holocaust and leads study missions to Poland to visit the concentration camps.

Mike Jacobs, a survivor of the Auschwitz concentration camp, led a group of Holocaust survivors who founded the Dallas Center for Holocaust Studies. The Center, located in the Jewish Community Center at 7900 Northaven, opened in 1984.
— *Courtesy* The Dallas Morning News, *photo by David Woo*

Jewish War Veterans of Texas and their wives and sweethearts held their state convention in Waco, May 3–4, 1947.
— *Sylvia Schneider Greenspan*

— **Mike Jacobs**

Fannie Schaenen, national United Jewish Appeal leader, greeted Golda Meir in Dallas during the 46th General Assembly of the Council of Jewish Federations and Welfare Funds, November 12, 1977. Schaenen was the campaign chairman for the Dallas Federation in 1949 and chair of the National Women's Division, United Jewish Appeal, 1969–1971.
— *Jewish Federation of Greater Dallas*

Golda Meir visited Houston in 1949 and was greeted by Jewish leaders. Pictured left to right are Meyer Gordon, Hyman Finger, Tom Needham (mayor pro-tem of Houston), A. I. Lack, Irvin Shlenker, and Joe Weingarten.
— *Copy from* Golden Jubilee, The Jewish Federation of Greater Houston 1936–1986

Texas Jews support Israel

When World War II ended, many of Europe's ten million refugees found their way home, but displaced Jews had no homes left. With the horrors of the Holocaust revealed, political conditions were ripe for international recognition of the Jewish people's right to an independent state. Jews headed toward Mediterranean ports, hoping to book illegal passage to Palestine. British ships intercepted vessels like the *Exodus*, carrying illegal immigrants. When seized, the ships were towed to Haifa, and the illegals were detained in camps on Cyprus. World Jewry demanded the establishment of a Jewish state.

In August 1947, the United Nations Special Committee on Palestine (UNSCOP) recommended the termination of the British Mandate and the partition of Palestine into a Jewish state and an Arab state with international status for Jerusalem. But Palestinian Arabs and the governments of all the Arab countries declared they would forcibly oppose these recommendations. The General Assembly of the U.N. voted on November 29,

Jacob (Jake) Feldman, Fannie Schaenen's brother, has been a major benefactor of Jewish causes for fifty years. In November 1948, shortly after the establishment of Israel, Jake and Fannie attended the Council of Jewish Federations and Welfare Funds meeting in Chicago. Upon hearing Golda Meir's heart-rending appeal for funds, Jake Feldman borrowed a half million dollars, which constituted the first large gift ever made to the new State of Israel. — *From the Archives of Congregation Shearith Israel, Dallas*

1947, to adopt UNSCOP's recommendation to partition Palestine. A majority of thirty-three favored the recommendation, including the U.S. and the Soviet Union; thirteen opposed, ten abstained, and two were absent. The next day, the Arab High Committee of Palestine declared a general strike, and an Israeli bus was attacked on its way to Jerusalem. The Israeli War of Independence had begun.

A few Texas Jews, like Walter Cohen of Austin, went to Israel and fought for the Haganah. Sending money was a more typical response. Relief work in Texas for international Jewry now took on great urgency. The United Jewish Appeal (UJA), formed in 1939, began allocating the bulk of its donations to support refugee resettlement and to strengthen Israeli institutions.

Israel Bond drives were held to sponsor investment in Israel, and millions were sold to financial institutions and individuals. Houston's Jewish community brought stars like Jack Benny and Eddie Cantor to promote support for Israel. On one memorable occasion in 1959, Eleanor Roosevelt spoke to an Israel Bond dinner at Shearith Israel in Dallas, held to commemorate the synagogue's seventy-fifth anniversary. Coincidentally, it was Eleanor's seventy-fifth birthday, as well.

Support for Israel reached a pinnacle in 1967, during the Six-Day War between Egypt and Israel, when the Jewish Federation of Greater Dallas raised $3.5 million for Israel in twenty-four hours.

Charles Bender of Breckenridge was
known as the Texas Zionist Cowboy. He
is pictured in 1960 with Bedouin Sheik
Audeh Abu Muamer at the Azazme tribal
encampment near Beersheba, Israel.
Bender was visiting as a member of the
Southern Region Israel Bond Delegation.
— *Houston* Jewish Herald Voice, *July 7,
1960*

Charles (1880–1970) and Bertha Bender
(1888–1990) are shown here on one of
their five visits with David Ben-Gurion at
his kibbutz in Sde Boker, Israel. Ben-Gurion declared the establishment of the State
of Israel on May 14, 1948, and later
served as prime minister.
— *Bertha Bender*

Charles Bender, the Texas Zionist Cowboy, and his wife, Bertha

Bertha Segalin (Bender) was born
in Lithuania and learned French,
Russian, and German from a govern-
ess and Yiddish from a *yeshiva bocher*.
She wrote letters for gypsies and
helped her father, an advocate (attorney), copy legal documents. In 1903,
the Jews of Kishinev experienced a
terrible pogrom, and as revolutionary
conditions swept through the country,
Bertha's father took his family to the
U.S. They settled first in New York,
where Bertha learned English from
reading the children's books of her
cousins. Like many other immigrant
girls, she got a job in a neckwear factory. She joined her family in Norfolk,
Virginia, in 1908, where she became
the secretary of the local Zionist organization and met Charles Bender.
They married later that year.

The couple settled in Dallas, and
Charles established the Star Bottling
Company in 1912. Around 1915, he
organized the Texas Young Zionists.
When the oil boom hit Breckenridge
in West Texas, they opened the two-
story Bender Department Store
(1919–1953), and a store and hotel in
nearby McCamey. Bertha remembered, "It [his Zionist activities] kept
Charles on the go while I was in the
business all those years."

Charles was president of the Southwest Zionist Region and the first
president of B'nai B'rith in West
Texas. Because there were no synagogues in the area, he raised funds
and contributed generously to build
Temple Beth Israel in Breckenridge,
which was dedicated in 1929. A rabbi
was hired for the High Holidays, and
Jews from Abilene and other small
towns came to worship. The Benders
were also leaders in the non-Jewish
community: Charles raised funds for
the YMCA, and Bertha was a poet
and active in the Wednesday Study
Club. Following Charles' death in
1970, she moved to Houston.

The Legendary Charles Bender

Charles Bender, the legendary Texas
Zionist Cowboy, traveled around the
world to Zionist meetings in western boots
with Stars of David imprinted on them
and took every opportunity he could to
promote his favorite cause — Israel.

Fay Brachman recalls the story of
Charles taking a bus home to Breckenridge. The bus stopped in a small West
Texas town, and Charles got off to have a
look around. He visited stores with Jewish
names on them, and as he walked back to
the bus station, he noticed a crowd entering a building. He went in and found a funeral in process. The young pastor began
the eulogy by stating that he didn't know
the deceased and asked if anyone had a
few words to say. No one stood to speak.

So Charles Bender arose and said, "I
didn't know the deceased either, but if
you have a moment, I'd like to say a few
words about the Zionist Organization of
America."

The Houston Jewish Federation sponsored the Israel Philharmonic with Leonard Bernstein conducting in 1951. The profits went to the building fund for a new Jewish Community Center on Hermann Drive. The same year, the Federation funded the Kashruth Association for the first time, marking a commitment to the growing number of Houston Jews who adhered to dietary laws. Pictured from left to right: (standing) Lewis Pulaski, Irvin Shlenker (president), and Morris Rauch; (seated) Joe Weingarten, Irving Alexander, and I. S. Brochstein.
— *Copy from* Golden Jubilee: The Jewish Federation of Greater Houston 1936–1986

The Federations train leaders, and every community has a Super Sunday — a fundraising event to finance Jewish projects. Super Sunday participants in Houston, c. 1981, include: (front row) Elise Wolf, Bruce Holzband, Don Aron, Lynne Aronoff, Al Aron, Gary Kornblith; (middle row) Scott Davis, Jack Goldfield, Sylvia Berner, Eta Paransky, Joe Williams, Sonia Raizes; (top row) Sheryl Falik, Harold Raizes, Willy Goldberg, Miriam Mendell, Honey Donsky, and Lynn Goldberg.
— *Copy from* Golden Jubilee: The Jewish Federation of Greater Houston 1936–1986

Sandra Weiner was elected president of the Jewish Federation of Greater Houston, 1988–1989. In 1980 and 1981, she chaired the Federation's United Jewish Campaign, raising a record-breaking $6 million for activities such as the resettlement of Soviet Jews, the Jewish Community Center, and the Jewish Home for the Aged. She has been president of Congregation Brith Shalom, national vice-chair of the United Jewish Appeal, and has served on the board of the Jewish Museum of New York. She has also been a major contributor to the I. Weiner Secondary School of Houston, a private Jewish high school.
— *Sandra Weiner*

Jacob (Jack) Kravitz (1909–) went to Dallas in 1943 as the executive director of the Jewish Welfare Federation (now the Jewish Federation of Greater Dallas), a position he held until 1973. Under his guidance, all of the local agencies expanded their programs and facilities. He constructed a highly successful fundraising campaign organization recognized nationally as a leader for cities of its size. He was a consultant to the Dallas business community and the Committee of 100, which worked for peaceful racial integration of Dallas' public facilities and schools in the late 1950s and early 1960s. Following the Camp David Peace Treaty, he was a consultant to an international committee for enhanced cooperation between Egyptian and Israeli social and health agencies.
— *Courtesy Jack Kravitz, photograph by D'Aquino*

The Jewish Community Center of Houston sent a group of its Chalutzim travel campers to Washington, D.C. in the summer of 1988. They are shown visiting with Harris County Congressman Mike Andrews.

— *Houston* Jewish Herald Voice

Dr. Herbert Shore has been director and later executive vice-president of Golden Acres Dallas Home for the Jewish Aged since 1953. Under his guidance, Golden Acres has expanded from one building with seven residents to a thirty-acre campus consisting of a nursing home and intermediate care facility, the Byer and Kahn Apartments, the ECHAD elderly low income HUD housing, and the Byer Activity Center. He has been president of both the American Association and the Texas Association of Homes for the Aged, and the National Association of Jewish Homes for the Aged. He was appointed to a task force on nursing homes by President Lyndon B. Johnson and has been a consultant to numerous professional, religious, and governmental bodies. He is the recipient of awards from the American Association of Retired Persons, the National Association of Social Work, Dallas Chapter, and the American College of Nursing Home Administrators, among others.

— *Herbert Shore, Ed.D.*

In support of the community

After World War II, Jewish organizations and institutions expanded to serve a growing population. They developed new programs, hired additional staff, and in many cases constructed new buildings. Jewish family services assist families through counseling services; the elderly are served by homes for the aged. Pre-schools and summer camping for young people are growing, and in larger cities, Jewish Community Centers have facilities for sports, exhibitions, historical archives, camps, and recreational and educational activities for all age groups. Homes and apartments for the aged include Seven Acres in Houston, Golden Manor in San Antonio, Chai Manor in El Paso, and the Mollie and Max Barnett B'nai B'rith Apartments in Fort Worth.

In 1988, at the age of ninety-eight, Frieda Weiner continued to lead her weekly Oneg Shabbat for senior citizens at the B'nai B'rith Goldberg Towers in Houston. For many years, she taught Yiddish at the Houston Jewish Community Center and conducted the Yiddish Winkle for young people.

— *Photo by Ruthe Winegarten*

Ruth Fred was the director of Houston's Jewish Family Service during the critical years 1940–1977. She wrote a column for the *Jewish Herald Voice* and had a radio program for ten years, "Ask Ruth." She has served on the boards of the Texas Mental Health Association, the Red Cross, and Planned Parenthood. In 1985, she received the Medallion of Achievement from the Houston American Jewish Committee.

— *Jewish Family Service of Houston*

Growth brings new temples, synagogues

In post-World War II boom times, Jewish populations in Texas urban centers grew as Jews left the mercantile establishments of their parents in small towns and moved to the cities to attend college and enter the professions.

Temple Emanu El's building at 1500 Sunset Boulevard opposite Rice University was dedicated in 1949. With 65,000 square feet of floor space and a sanctuary seating 855, it was, at that time, one of the largest spaces in the world under a cantilever roof. Since 1978, Rabbi Roy A. Walter has been senior rabbi.
— *Temple Emanu El, Houston, photo by David Lee Bayliss*

Congregation Beth Yeshurun in Houston has been at 4525 Beechnut Blvd. since 1962. It is the largest conservative congregation in the Southwest and the third largest in the U.S. Rabbi Jack Segal has been senior rabbi since 1973.
— *Copy from* Shalom, Welcome to Congregation Beth Yeshurun, *Houston*

Congregation Beth Israel of Houston grew rapidly after World War II, and a demographic shift from the inner city to the suburbs of southwest Houston occurred. In 1969, the congregation moved to a stunning new temple at 5600 North Braeswood.
— *UT Institute of Texan Cultures*

Dr. Robert I. Kahn went to Houston in 1935 as assistant rabbi for Congregation Beth Israel. He served overseas as a chaplain during World War II. When Beth Israel split over the adoption of "Basic Principles," Rabbi Kahn became the first spiritual leader of the newly formed Temple Emanu El, a position he held from 1944 to 1978, when he became rabbi emeritus. He was president of the Houston Rabbinical Association and the Central Conference of American Rabbis, and on the boards of the World Union for Progressive Judaism, the Boy Scouts, and Houston Metropolitan Ministries. He has lectured widely and is the author of *Lessons for Today, Ten Commandments for Today,* and *The Letter and the Spirit.*
— *Temple Emanu El, Houston*

Rabbi William Malev (1889–1973) joined Congregation Beth Yeshurun in 1946 following the merger of Adath Yeshurun and Congregation Beth El, and remained until his death. He was a graduate of City College of New York, Columbia University, and the Teachers Institute, Jewish Theological Seminary. In 1972, he celebrated fifty years in the rabbinate.
— *Congregation Beth Yeshurun, Houston*

Dr. Hyman Judah Schachtel (1907–1990) was born in London, England, and served as chief rabbi of Congregation Beth Israel from 1943 to 1975, when he became rabbi emeritus. He participated in a weekly radio broadcast and was a popular book reviewer. The author of many books, including *The Real Enjoyment of Living* and *How to Meet the Challenges of Life and Death,* he also composed liturgical music. He delivered the invocation at the inauguration of President Lyndon B. Johnson in 1965. Dr. Schachtel was president of the Central Conference of American Rabbis and a member of the Governor's Committee for Texas on Human Relations. In 1987, he received the Ima Hogg Award for distinguished service in the cause of mental health.
— *Temple Beth Israel Archives, Houston*

Rabbi Gerald Klein joined Temple Emanu-El in Dallas in 1952 as associate rabbi, was elected chief rabbi in 1961, and rabbi emeritus in 1988. Rabbi Klein has served as adjunct professor of religion at Southern Methodist University and on the board of the Hebrew Union College-Jewish Institute of Religion. He has been involved in numerous community activities, including the Dallas Pastor's Association, Child Guidance Clinic, and the Mental Health Society.
— *Dorothy M. and Henry S. Jacobus Temple Emanu-El Archives*

Rabbi Levi Olan (1903–1984) was spiritual leader and rabbi emeritus of Temple Emanu-El in Dallas from 1949 to 1970. Born in Cherkassy, Russia, he was ordained at Hebrew Union College in 1929. He served as president of the Dallas United Nations Association and the Central Conference of American Rabbis. A noted intellectual, scholar, writer, book reviewer, and community activist, he was on the faculty of several universities and a regent of UT Austin. He was a democratic socialist and an outspoken opponent of poverty and racism. His legendary radio broadcasts in the 1950s and 1960s were followed by Jew and Christian alike. In the period of introspection following the assassination of President John F. Kennedy in Dallas in 1963, Rabbi Olan pointed out the disparities between the Dallas affluent and the "shacks without indoor plumbing." He asked Dallasites "to accept responsibility for its behavior" and to nurture the less fortunate.
— *Dorothy M. and Henry S. Jacobus Temple Emanu-El Archives*

Temple Shalom, a Reform congregation at 6930 Alpha Road, was dedicated in March 1973. It was organized in 1965 by members of Temple Emanu-El who left amicably to form a smaller, more intimate temple. Its first president was Henry Jacobus, Jr. Dr. Kenneth Roseman is the senior rabbi.
— *Temple Shalom Archives, Dallas*

Temple Emanu-El at 8500 Hillcrest in Dallas was dedicated in 1957. It won an architectural award and was featured in *Life* magazine.
— *Dorothy M. and Henry S. Jacobus Temple Emanu-El Archives, print by Andy Reisberg*

In 1956, Tiferet Israel, originally Orthodox, moved from its South Dallas location on Grand Avenue and Edgewood Street to a new building at 10909 Hillcrest Road in North Dallas. Tiferet Israel, led by Rabbi Stewart Weiss, describes itself as "totally modern, yet strongly traditional," but retains its Orthodox charter.
— *UT Institute of Texan Cultures*

Cantor Max Wider sereved as *chazan* and *schochet* for Agudas Achim, an Orthodox congregation in Dallas, from 1951 to 1954. He then served Corpus Christi's B'nai Israel, 1954–1965, returning to Dallas' Tiferet Israel from 1965 to 1969.
— *Dallas Public Library*

President Lyndon Baines Johnson, in his first non-official presidential address, dedicated Congregation Agudas Achim in Austin on December 30, 1963. He is shown talking with Dr. Marion Stahl. Lady Bird Johnson is to the president's right. In 1989, Agudas Achim dedicated a new sanctuary adjacent to its old building at 4300 Bull Creek Road. Rabbi Marc Sack is the spiritual leader.
— *Elaine Novy Shapiro*

A synagogue in the shape of a Star of David was consecrated by Congregation Shearith Israel in Wharton in 1956. In 1988, the congregation, which also serves El Campo and Bay City, celebrated its seventy-fifth birthday.
— *Photo by Kaye Marvins Studio*

Jim Novy (c. 1900–1971) of Austin was a charter member of Congregation Agudas Achim in 1924 and president from 1938 to 1940. Novy was active in the Zionist movement and in the Democratic Party. He arranged for his friend, President Lyndon Baines Johnson, to dedicate Agudas Achim's new building at 4300 Bull Creek in 1963. Novy represented Texas at the 10th celebration of Israeli Independence in 1958, and in 1964, President Johnson appointed him to deliver a message to the 26th World Zionist Congress in Jerusalem.
— *Jewish National Fund*

In 1972, members of Agudath Jacob in Waco carried the Torahs from their old synagogue to their current location at 4925 Hillcrest. Today, they are led by Rabbi Max Zucker.
— *Ima Joy Chodorow (Mrs. J. E.) Gandler*

— **Rabbi Samuel Karff**

Kallah of Texas Rabbis

In 1927, Congregation Adath Yeshurun in Houston hired Rabbi Abraham I. Schechter as its rabbi. One of his first achievements was to found the Kallah of Texas Rabbis, formed to bring together rabbis of all branches of Judaism with a forum to hold discussions, give papers, and share the task of serving Jews in out-of-the-way places as their circuit-riding predecessors did in the nineteenth century. The Kallah's first meeting was held at Adath Yeshurun's Hebrew Institute, and Rabbi Schechter was chosen as president. Since then, the Kallah has remained the only organization of its kind in the U.S.

Rabbi Samuel Karff of Temple Beth Israel in Houston was elected president of the Central Conference of American Rabbis (CCAR) for the 1989–1990 term. The CCAR is the umbrella organization of Reform rabbis in the U.S. with a current membership of 1,500, serving 800 congregations. Karff is one of the youngest rabbis ever to be elected. Upon his election, he discussed the pioneering role of Reform rabbis in the movement to ban child labor and to recognize trade unions. He added, "participation in the civil rights movement within the Jewish community came in a substantial way from the Reform rabbinate . . ." [5]

Rabbi Karff moved to Houston in 1975 after serving congregations in Hartford, Connecticut; Flint, Michigan; and Chicago. He was the first rabbi to teach at the University of Notre Dame.
— Houston Chronicle, *photo by Paul Howell*

Distinguished Rabbis of the Past

For over 100 years, Texas Jews have been served by distinguished rabbis, cantors, educators, *mohalim,* and *schochetim* devoted to preserving Judaism in the Lone Star State. Some achieved state and national prominence, and others served more than fifty years in the same pulpit. The community is richer for their presence, and their impact continues to be felt in dozens of cities and towns. Among the deceased rabbis who have served with longevity were:

Jonathan Abramowitz — Agudas Achim, Dallas (1925–1950)

Pierce Annes — Tiferet Israel, Dallas (1943–1959)

Henry Barnston — Beth Israel, Houston (1900–1943)

Abraham Blum — B'nai Israel, Galveston (1871–1885)

Charles Blumenthal — B'nai Zion, El Paso (1921–1923) and Agudath Jacob, Waco (1928–1944)

Henry Cohen — B'nai Israel, Galveston (1888–1952)

Maurice Faber — Beth El, Tyler (1900–1934)

Floyd Fierman — Mt. Sinai, El Paso (1949–1979)

H. Raphael Gold — Shearith Israel, Dallas (1928–1941)

Isadore Garsek — Ahavath Sholom, Fort Worth (1946–1979)

Jacob Geller — Hebrew Benevolent Society (Bikur Cholim), Galveston (1892–1910), Adath Israel, Houston (1910–1930)

Max Geller — B'rith Abraham, Houston (1914–1917), Adath Israel, Houston (1917–1937), Beth Jacob (1937–1958)

David Lefkowitz — Emanu-El, Dallas (1920–1948)

Joseph Levine — Mount Sinai, Texarkana (1956–1981)

Wolfe Macht — Rodef Sholom, Waco (1919–1952)

Charles Mantinband — Emanu-El, Longview (1963–1971)

Samuel Marks — Beth-El, San Antonio (1897–1934)

William Malev — Beth Yeshurun, Houston (1946–1973)

Aaron Moskowitz — Ahavath Achim, Tyler (1924–1943)

Levi Olan — Emanu-El, Dallas (1949–1985)

David Rosenbaum — Beth Israel, Austin (1911–1922)

Joseph M. Roth — B'nai Zion, El Paso (1923–1953)

David Shnayerson — Beth Israel, San Angelo (1951–1971)

Kalmon Taxon — Ahavath Achim, Tyler (1966–1988)

Harvey Wessel — Beth El, Tyler (1939–1970)

Wolf Willner — Beth Israel, Houston (1890–1892); Adath Yeshurun, Houston (1907–1924)

David H. Wittenberg — Moses Montefiore, Marshall (1928–1938, 1941)

Martin Zielonka — Mt. Sinai, El Paso (1900–1940)

Rabbi Shimon Lazaroff, left, and Rabbi Moshe Traxler, right, lead prayers at Chabad Lubavitz in Houston. The boxes strapped on the rabbis' foreheads *(tefillin)* contain verses from the Torah.
— Houston Chronicle, *September 17, 1988, photo by Larry Reese*

In May 1972, 350 Dallas youths marched under the leadership of Cathy Bouton of the B'nai B'rith Youth Organization from the Julius Schepps Community Center (now the Jewish Community Center) to McFarlin Auditorium at SMU for a rally in support of Soviet Jews. Social consciousness is a staple of most Jewish youth groups.
— *Copy from* Federation News, *Jewish Federation of Greater Dallas*

Three Camp Bonim campers enjoy the summer 1946 session at Lewisville. (Bottom) Mildred Lahasky, (top) Renee (Pee Wee) Mendlovitz and Hannah Webberman (Rubin).
— *Photo by Ruthe Winegarten*

Four-year-old Ryan Soroka explores the world of dinosaurs on his classroom's computer at the United Orthodox Synagogue's Montessori School in Houston.
— *United Orthodox Synagogues Houston Montessori School*

Educational programs

In earlier times, Jewish education outside of *bar mitzvah* and confirmation was left to the realm of the home. But today, educational programs for Jewish youth begin as early as infancy with Jewish day-care and pre-school programs, and in larger cities can extend through high school. Youth organizations such as B'nai B'rith Youth, Young Judaea, United Synagogue Youth, and the Texas Oklahoma Federation of Temple Youth (TOFTY) provide a social and educational outlet to reinforce Jewish identity through club work and camping.

Since World War II, a number of Jewish pre-schools, day schools, and high schools have been established in larger Texas cities. In 1950–1951, Austin's Temple Beth Israel established the Joe Koen Nursery School in honor of a man who had served as their president for forty-five years (1899–1944).

In 1954, Congregation Beth Yeshurun in Houston founded the first con-

gregational school in the U.S. to offer both secular and religious education in a combined curriculum. Other Houston schools include the Shlenker School (Beth Israel), the Hebrew Academy, the Torah Day School, and the I. Weiner Jewish Secondary School. Dallas has Akiba Academy and the Solomon Schechter School, and in San Antonio there is the Jonathan Netanyahu Academy and the San Antonio Community High School for Jewish Studies.

As the number of working mothers in the Jewish community has increased, day-care and pre-school programs have taken on greater importance. Infants and children as young as one year old can be found throughout Texas celebrating Shabbat on Fridays with teachers and rabbis.

Camping programs have been an important part of the educational life of Texas youth since the 1940s. Young Jews have enjoyed camping as a way to reinforce Jewish identity and meet others from different cities. Camping has been particularly important for Jewish youth from small

towns, where Jewish education was unavailable. The Labor Zionist youth movement in Texas was organized in 1929 by Jacob Levin of Dallas, and by the summer of 1939, Habonim groups were functioning in Dallas, Houston, and San Antonio. The camp ran from 1941 to 1951 (the 1943 season was canceled due to the polio epidemic).

Young Judaea is a national peer-led Zionist youth organization sponsored by Hadassah. Camp Young Judaea was founded in 1952 and serves Jewish children from Texas, Oklahoma, and Louisiana at the Ben G. Barnett Camp in Wimberley.

The Greene Family Camp in Bruceville was built in the 1970s to serve the Texas and Oklahoma affiliates of the National Federation of Temple Youth. The Edward Greene family of Dallas were major benefactors. Camp Echo Hill in Kerrville, owned by Dr. Thomas Friedman, is a camp which, though unaffiliated with any Jewish movement, has introduced Jewish children for many years to the joys of "roughing it."

"For some rabbis, their love is scholarship. For me, what people **171**

needed was first." — **Rabbi Isadore Garsek**

Rabbi Isadore Garsek (1913–1985) was born in Liserka, Ukraine, Russia, and served as the spiritual leader of Ahavath Sholom in Fort Worth from 1946 to 1979. He had previously served Congregation Shaarith Israel in Lubbock, 1939–1944. He is shown, right, with his adult Bible class. Rabbi Garsek was a leader in the field of adult education and a popular lecturer. An outspoken opponent of racism and bigotry, he spoke out in the 1960s for busing and marched for racial equality — actions that drew threats from local hate groups. He was a leader in ecumenical affairs and chair of the Human Relations Commission. He was president of the Tarrant County General Ministers Association, the Kallah of Texas Rabbis, and the Southwest Region of the Zionist Organization of America. He was honored as Jewish Man of the Year by B'nai B'rith, which named a Fort Worth lodge for him.
— *Congregation Ahavath Sholom*

Education spans the ages

Jewish education doesn't end with childhood; in Jewish congregations across Texas, adults attend classes covering everything from Midrash to medical ethics. Men and women celebrate *bar* and *bat mitzvot* and study Torah and Talmud. Book clubs and Bible classes are established facts of congregational life. Conversion classes for those wishing to convert to Judaism (primarily those who are planning marriage to a Jewish mate or who are already intermarried) are also offered in many synagogues and temples.

Jewish community centers sponsor adult education classes including book reviews, speakers, and courses ranging from Jewish cooking to Yiddish, literature and history to parenting and stress management. Book fairs, art, film, and dance festivals, theatrical and music performances, and exhibitions of history, archaeology, and Israeli life are staples of Jewish communal and cultural life. Activities for all ages provide a hub for Jews to study as well as socialize.

The importance of *bat mitzvah* as a religious innovation is shown by the hundreds of adult women who have undertaken religious training and gone through the initiation ceremony that was not available to them as thirteen-year-old girls. Here, a group of women at Congregation Agudas Achim in Austin celebrate their *bat mitzvah* together on January 16, 1986. Front row, l. to r.: Pam Reznick and Bea Joseph; second row: Donna Schmidt, Rabbi Marc Sack, Joan Postles, June Cohen, Joan Dattner, Hatte Blejer, and Harriet Kirsh Pozen; third row: Dorothy Miller, Patrice Baksht, Rowena Chodorow, Bobbi Saulmon, and Janet Marz; fourth row: Margo Sack (instructor), Diane Radin, Roberta Long, Blinzia Oldak, Phil Schmidt (instructor), and Sharon Wishnew.
— Austin American Statesman, *photo by David Kennedy*

Milton Smith, a native of Detroit, Michigan, has been a leader in the Austin community for over fifty years. He is shown here in his capacity as president of the Texas Jewish Historical Society in the summer of 1989, preserving artifacts and photographs from the Delta Phi Epsilon sorority house, which was closed.

Milton founded Economy Furniture Industries in 1930, which is currently run by his wife Helen and himself. In the late 1940s, Smith was instrumental in the building of the B'nai B'rith Hillel House in Austin. In 1953, he was president of Temple Beth Israel and building chairman for its new facility, president of the District Grand Lodge #7, B'nai B'rith in 1965, and chair of the Austin Jewish Federation and the UJA Drive. He has served two terms on Austin's Urban Renewal and Human Relations committees. He was president of the Southwest Furniture Manufacturing Association and chairman of the Dallas Furniture Mart.

— *Photo by Ruthe Winegarten*

Billy Goldberg of Houston has held many positions in B'nai B'rith International (BBI), including the presidency of District #7 B'nai B'rith and honorary member of the BBI's board. He was international vice-president of the B'nai B'rith Foundation. In addition to his B'nai B'rith activities, Goldberg was national vice-chairman of the United Jewish Appeal, a member of the board of the State of Israel Bonds (receiving their Gold Medal in 1988), and an advisor to the American Israel Public Affairs Committee.

Goldberg has been active in the state and national Democratic Party, attaining prominence when he served as assistant attorney general for Texas, chair of the Texas State Democratic Executive Committee, and a member of the Democratic National Committee. He has been a major fundraiser for the Democratic Party, working for Senators Hubert Humphrey and Ed Muskie in their presidential campaigns.

The Houston housing project, Goldberg Towers, is named for Goldberg's father, J. B. Goldberg. In 1988, Billy Goldberg led a delegation of Israel Bond leaders to Israel for its fortieth anniversary celebration. A neonatal clinic outside Jerusalem was funded by Goldberg in honor of his wife, Rosalie Ackerman Goldberg. In 1988, Goldberg conceived the idea of forming a B'nai B'rith unit in the Soviet Union. Soon thereafter, it was organized by thirty-eight Moscow Jews working with a visiting U.S. delegation.

— *B'nai B'rith International Archives*

Helen (Mrs. Milton) Smith of Austin, a native of Brooklyn, New York, is the only Texan elected as international president of B'nai B'rith Women (BBW), an office she held from 1974 to 1976. She is shown with President Gerald Ford at the White House during BBW's International Convention in 1976. Happy Rockefeller and Susan Ford are to President Ford's left and right.

BBW has a membership of 150,000 with educational, civic, and philanthropic programs serving communities in the U.S., Canada, and twenty-two other countries. Helen chaired the building campaign for the BBW Children's Home in Israel for emotionally disturbed boys. Her many other positions include national commissioner for the Anti-Defamation League; advisory board of B'nai B'rith Hillel Foundation, UT-Austin; and chair of the fundraising committee for the construction of a sanctuary for Austin's Temple Beth Israel. The auditorium was named for Helen and her husband, Milton Smith. In 1969, the couple received the Gold Medal B'nai B'rith Humanitarian Award.   — *B'nai B'rith Women*

From "gentlemen's agreements" to violence

Covert, overt, and sometimes violent anti-Semitism has persisted in parts of Texas since the end of World War II. In 1951, a tenured professor at Southern Methodist University, Dr. John Beaty, published his eighth edition of *Iron Curtain Over America*, which alleged leftist infiltration of SMU and the English Department. It was widely viewed as a vicious piece of anti-Semitic literature, and the controversy eventually involved the entire SMU faculty, which condemned Beaty. In 1954, the new president of SMU, Dr. Willis Tate, took a strong stand against Beaty's views.

In Houston, the Jewish Welfare Federation and the American Jewish Committee grappled with discrimination in housing and anti-Semitism in the 1950s. They attempted to combat "gentlemen's agreements" restricting the sale of homes to Jews, and they opposed restrictions on the hiring of Jews by certain industries and corporations. They protested a performance by Wagnerian opera star Kirsten Flagstad (alleged to be a Nazi sympathizer), the distribution of Gideon Bibles in public schools, and the presentation of a Passion Play.[6] In 1940, Irving Lang, a Jewish student at Rice Institute, took a German course under a professor who belonged to the Deutscher Americanischer Bund — a Nazi-sympathizing group. When the professor tested the students on the lyrics to the "Horst Wessel," Lang wrote out the lyrics to the "Star Spangled Banner" in German. He got an "A." Lang was later killed in World War II.

Another Houston issue has been the refusal of certain oil companies who do business in the Middle East to hire Jews for work abroad, even though such refusal is a violation of federal law. Dr. Max Samfield, Rice, Class of 1940, recalls that Jews were the only Rice engineering graduates who did not get jobs with oil companies. An interviewer at a major oil company told him, "Jews don't make good engineers." Dr. Samfield now works for the Environmental Protection Agency.

In 1963, there was a fire bomb at Temple Emanu-El in Dallas, and a bullet was fired through a stained glass window at Dallas' Shearith Israel. The Dallas American Nazi Party organized in 1965. Their stickers with swastikas on them, reading "Communism is Jewish" and "We are Back," were pasted into books in Dallas libraries and on Jewish-owned stores. American Nazi Party troopers picketed an Israel Bonds banquet in Dallas in 1965, and from 1973 to 1975 they marched regularly at Dealey Plaza.

The American Nazi Party marched regularly in downtown Dallas at Dealey Plaza from 1973 to 1975. They carried banners reading "Communism is Jewish." The B'nai B'rith Anti-Defamation League and the American Jewish Committee monitor anti-Semitic incidents in Texas and across the nation.
— *Ruthe Winegarten*

The problem of anti-Semitism continues to manifest itself in various ways. In 1987 and 1988, the Jonathan Netanyahu Academy in San Antonio was vandalized three times, and in 1989 vandals set fire to the building.

On October 8, 1988, three Dallas religious sites were vandalized — Temple Shalom, the Jewish Community Center, and the Islamic Mosque of Richardson. Vandals shot out windows and spray-painted Nazi, anti-Semitic, and anti-Islamic racial slurs. The Interfaith Commission of Dallas, representing the Jewish Federation and the Greater Dallas Council of 300 Christian Churches, condemned the vandalism. On January 12, 1989, Daniel Alvis Wood, allied with the Ku Klux Klan and Skinheads, was tried for the October 8 incidents. During the trial he pled repentance and assured the court he had rethought his allegiance to Nazi and racist ideology. After he was judged guilty and sentenced to ten years in prison and a $5,000 fine, he shocked those in the courtroom by raising his arm twice in the Nazi salute. On June 16, 1989, Governor Bill Clements signed into law a bill sponsored by State Rep. Steve Wolens, D-Dallas, which makes desecration of a place of worship, a cemetery, or a community center a felony.

In January 1989, the Anti-Defamation League issued a survey indicating that the number of anti-Semitic incidents in 1988 rose to a five-year high. In Texas, twenty-three anti-Semitic incidents were reported, with more than a dozen in Dallas, according to Dallas ADL Director Mark Briskman. The Houston ADL Director, Sheldon Filger, reported that "The skinheads are emerging as a problem across the country."

Abram Geller (1898–1989) of Houston was active in Jewish communal affairs for seventy years. He was secretary of the Jewish Literary Society in 1917 and president of the Menorah Society at Rice University from 1917 until he graduated in 1920. A leader in the Orthodox and Zionist movements, he served as president of almost fifty organizations, including the United Orthodox Synagogue, Brith Abraham, and the Hebrew Academy. An insurance agent for many years, he was president of the Houston Association of Life Underwriters.

— *Jewish National Fund*

Fort Worth's Bernard S. Appel, a native of Boston, is president of Radio Shack, a division of the Tandy Corporation. Appel has been president of the Jewish Federation of Fort Worth and Congregation Ahavath Sholom, and a member of the National United Jewish Appeal Cabinet. He has been active in other agencies such as the Dancinger Jewish Community Center and Jewish Family Services. In 1985, he was selected as Fort Worth B'nai B'rith's Jewish Man of the Year.

— *Bernard S. Appel*

Reuben Askanase (1908–) of Houston, a long-time business and community leader, was chairman of the board of Dunhill International. He was a trustee of Congregation Beth Israel, president of the Jewish Community Center from 1954 to 1956 and again in 1959, and chair of the United Jewish Campaign. In 1965, he received the American Jewish Committee's Max H. Nathan Award. He has been active in the Houston Symphony, Houston Council on Human Relations, and the Alley Theatre.

— *Copy from* The Jewish Community Center of Houston: A History, 1936–1986

Dr. Vincent Ravel was one of the founders of El Paso's Jewish Federation and Jewish Community Center. In the 1950s, he and his mother, Mrs. Joe Ravel, brought the Israeli Symphony, conducted by Leonard Bernstein, to El Paso.

— *Copy from El Paso Jewish Federation,* 50th Anniversary Booklet 1937–1987

Henry Jacobus, Jr., was the first president of Temple Shalom in Dallas when it was founded in 1965. Temple Shalom, Dallas' first new Reform congregation in almost 100 years, met in many houses of worship before building its own facility in 1971: Perkins Chapel at SMU, St. Mark's School, Northaven Methodist Church, and St. Luke's Episcopal Church.

— *Temple Shalom Archives, Dallas*

Harry A. Wood, Jr., of Waco has been president of the United Way as well as regional president and national campaign chairman of the Union of American Hebrew Congregations. He is also past president of Congregation Rodef Sholom.

— *Harry A. Wood, Jr.*

Dallas board members of Pioneer Women (now Na'Amat-USA), a Labor Zionist organization, in 1953. Na'Amat-USA helps provide social, educational, and legal services for Israeli women, teenagers, and children. It also advocates legislation for women's rights and child welfare in the

U.S. L. to r., back row: Rose Davis, Sarah Munves, Freda Green, ?, Myrtle Steinberg, Freda Elphant, Dora Goodman, and Sonie Green. Center: Ray Werner, Mollie Oxman, Sarah Goodman, Pearl Eberstein (president), Lena Minsky, Tama Bloom, and Lil Mendelsohn. Seated on the floor: Dorothy Steinberg, Martha Stoller, Ruth Brodsky, and Adrienne Steinberg.
— *From the Collections of the Dallas Jewish Historical Society*

Dolores Wilkenfeld of Houston's Temple Emanu El was president of the National Federation of Temple Sisterhoods (NFTS) from 1985 to 1989. NFTS represents over 100,000 women of Reform Judaism. She was president of Temple Emanu El, 1983–1985, and on the board of the Union of American Hebrew Congregations and the Association of Reform Zionists of America. She was also a founding member of the Texas-Israel Agricultural Exchange Program organized by the Texas Commissioner of Agriculture, and active with St. Joseph Hospital and the Houston Day Care Association. She has written and directed musicals, radio, and television programs.
— *National Federation of Temple Sisterhoods*

Ann Sikora was the first woman ever elected president of the Jewish Federation of Greater Dallas, 1981–83. Sikora, a descendant of pioneer Texans, was a member of the United Daughters of the Confederacy, based upon her great-grandfather's position as a Confederate officer. She has held dozens of leadership positions in the non-Jewish and Jewish communities: United Way, Women's Council of Dallas, National Jewish Community Relations Advisory Council (vice-chair for women's issues), Council of Jewish Federations, and all the local agencies.
— *Jewish Federation of Greater Dallas*

Davna Blum Brook of Houston was the first woman to be regional president of the Union of American Hebrew Congregations when she served two terms, from 1984 to 1988. Her jurisdiction included the states of Texas, Oklahoma, Arkansas, Louisiana, Mississippi, and western Tennessee. She is a member of Temple Emanu El.   — *Work of Art Studio, Houston*

Joan Johnson was president of the Jewish Federation of El Paso, 1988–1990. She was chair of the Federation's Personnel Committee and a member of the Budget and Allocations Committee. She was formerly vice-president of B'nai B'rith District #1 in New York and for twenty-five years, active in the Anti-Defamation League.   — *Jewish Federation of El Paso*

Rabbi Jimmy Kessler, left, is shown presenting a miniature of Phineas de Cordova along with an autographed copy of *Minding the Store* by Stanley Marcus to Dr. Don Carleton, director of the University of Texas at Austin Barker Texas History Center. Rabbi Kessler was founding president of the Texas Jewish Historical Society in 1980. The Society's collection of archival materials is housed at the Barker Center.
— *Barker Texas History Center, UT Austin*

Though born in Cleveland, Rabbi Floyd Fierman (1916–1989), spiritual leader of Temple Mt. Sinai in El Paso from 1949 to 1979, conscientiously documented the history of the Jews in the Southwest through numerous articles and books. From 1979 to 1989, he was resident scholar and rabbi emeritus at Temple Mt. Sinai and a visiting lecturer in philosophy at UT El Paso. In 1986, Fierman was honored by the National Conference of Christians and Jews for building bridges between different religious organizations and eliminating prejudice and bigotry.
— *Temple Mount Sinai, El Paso*

Cynthia Salzman Mondell (second from left) and Allen Mondell (third from left) are shown on the set of the award-winning film, "West of Hester Street," a production of Media Projects, Inc., Dallas. The Mondells produced and directed the film, which portrays the Galveston Movement and documents the immigration of Jews through the port city from 1907 to 1914. The Texas Jewish Historical Society was one of the film's sponsors.
— *Allen and Cynthia Salzman Mondell*

Darin Grodin, left, a student at the Solomon Schechter Academy in Dallas, and her great-grandmother, "Great Bobi" (Anita) Grodin, of El Paso. Darin won the Texas Jewish Historical Society Essay Contest in 1987 for her work, "How my Great-Grandparents Came to Texas."
— *Mrs. Jake Grodin*

How my great-grandparents came to Texas

Darin Grodin, Fifth Grade, Dallas

I have chosen to write about my Great Bobi Kaplan who was born in Savalke, Poland and worked as a butcher there. Her husband my great Zaydee Kaplan was drafted into the Polish army. He wanted to live a free life so he deserted the army and crossed the Polish border. He took a ship to Vera Cruz, Mexico and worked as a street vendor. When he made enough money he sent two tickets to Great Bobi Kaplan and her son. Soon they too, crossed the border and took a ship to Vera Cruz. There they met Zaydee and opened up a restaurant together. Soon they decided to move on, so they moved to El Paso, Texas . . . crossing the Rio Grande bridge with a pushwagon. They lived in a little house in South El Paso. Great Bobi Kaplan owned a second hand clothing store in downtown called Anita's Dry Goods. She was elected woman of the year for taking care of the Jewish soldiers in World War II. I think my Great Bobi Kaplan is a very strong and supportive woman to her children and grandchildren, and great-grandchildren.

History of Jews lives in TeJHaS

In 1980, Rabbi Jimmy Kessler of Galveston published a letter in the *Jewish Herald Voice* of Houston and the *Texas Jewish Post* of Dallas/Fort Worth, calling for the creation of a historical society to preserve the history of the Texas Jewish experience. The first gathering took place in San Antonio in March 1980. The Texas Jewish Historical Society (TeJHaS) was organized with Rabbi Kessler as its first president. Subsequent presidents have been Frances Kallison of San Antonio, Lionel Schooler of Houston, the late Ed Lax of Dallas, Ginger Jacobs of Dallas, and Milton Smith of Austin.

The Texas Jewish Historical Society is devoted to the preservation and dissemination of the history of the Jews in Texas. A permanent TeJHaS collection of source materials, documents, and family, community, and organizational histories has been established at the Barker Texas History Center of the University of Texas at Austin. TeJHaS sponsors annual essay contests for youth, has been instrumental in erecting historical markers, and has supported films such as "West of Hester Street" (about the Galveston Movement) and "This is Our Home, It's Not for Sale" (about Houston's Riverside neighborhood). The Society has 400 members and a growing endowment fund.

L. to r., Harold Rubin, Ruth Kahn, Ginger Jacobs, and Stanley Kaufman, Dallas. Rubin and Kaufman are shown donating historic 1890s Dallas B'nai B'rith records to Kahn and Jacobs, founders of the Dallas Jewish Archives (now part of the Dallas Jewish Historical Society) in 1971. Jacobs was president of the Dallas Jewish Archives, 1971–1987, and president of the Texas Jewish Historical Society, 1987–1989. The Dallas Jewish Archives, located in the Jewish Community Center, contain photographs, business and financial records, family histories, and congregational and organizational materials.
— *From the Collections of the Dallas Jewish Historical Society*

Lonnie Schooler, a Houston attorney and former president of the Texas Jewish Historical Society, has made videotapes of older Texas Jews telling their stories, as well as recording the various activities of TeJHaS.
— *Lonnie Schooler*

Ima Joy Chodorow (Mrs. J. E.) Gandler, chair of the Waco Jewish Federation Texas Sesquicentennial Committee, and Archie Hoppenstein, master of ceremonies, are shown on August 24, 1986, at the dedication of the Jacob de Cordova Texas Historical Marker. De Cordova was honored as one of Waco's founders. The ceremony was attended by many of de Cordova's descendants, none of whom are now Jewish. Gandler was the 1986 recipient of the McLennan County Pathfinders Award for Religion, and Hoppenstein was the nominee for the Liberty Bell Award by the Waco-McLennan County and the Texas State Junior Bar Associations in 1973.
— *The Texas Collection, Baylor University, Waco, Texas*

Beginning with the ordination of Sally Preisand in 1972, women rabbis and cantors have become more numerous and widely accepted. Rabbi Ellen J. Lewis (left) became the first woman to serve as rabbi in Texas when she was hired by Dallas' Temple Emanu-El in 1980. Cantor Sharon Kohn (above) has served Congregation Emanu El in Houston since 1985. Invested at the Hebrew Union College-Jewish Institute of Religion, Kohn has been assistant cantor at HUC-JIR's campus in Jerusalem and cantor at Old York Road Temple Beth Am in Abington, Pennsylvania. She has been a featured soloist in operas and oratorios.
— *Dorothy M. and Henry S. Jacobus Temple Emanu-El Archives*
— *Photo by Barbara Loeser*

Answering the call for change

The late twentieth century has seen a reversal of ritual roles in Jewish homes and institutions. No longer is the woman's domain the kitchen and the man's realm the higher calling of prayer. Today, the kitchen and the *bimah* are shared among the genders as men cook and nurture their children, and women study and pray as equals in the Reform temples and Conservative synagogues.

The evolution of Judaism to answer the call for change attests to its vitality as a religion and to the abiding love of its people for using its tenets as a guideline to living in modern times.

Women in the Rabbinate

In 1978, Rabbi Jack Segal preached a sermon at Houston's Congregation Beth Yeshurun, "Should We Have Women in the Conservative Rabbinate?" His answer: a resounding yes. His own congregation had a female president, one of the first in the U.S., Houston pediatrician Dr. Helen Schaffer. And the Reform movement had ordained its first woman rabbi, Sally Preisand, in 1972. In 1985, Amy Eilberg became the first woman ordained by the Conservative movement.

In 1988, Rabbi Marcia Plumb of Houston became the first Texas-born woman to be ordained, and today, the number of women serving Texas congregations has increased. However, many female rabbinical graduates still face difficulty in finding posts, and others, once hired, sometimes meet with resistance from congregants.

As early as 1943, a woman served as a cantor in a small Texas town. When Dr. Harry Leon, classics professor at the University of Texas, led Yom Kippur services in Hallettsville during World War II, no cantor was available. The Kol Nidre was sung by his sixteen-year-old daughter, Isabel Leon (Samfield). One of the members of the congregation mentioned after the service that women had sung Kol Nidre at his Reform congregation in Germany.

Although female cantors are relatively common in the Reform movement, they have yet to receive membership into the Cantors' Assembly, an arm of the Conservative movement.

The *bat mitzvah* of Jacqueline Silberman in Brownsville's Temple Beth El, June 4, 1977. Jacqueline is shown here wearing a *yarmulke,* traditionally a man's head covering. Holding the Torah is Rabbi Jonothan Gerard. The ritual role of women was hotly debated among Jews in Brownsville, and Orthodox members of the congregation walked out when women began receiving *aliyahs,* or blessings recited prior to reading the Torah portion.
— *Sam and Eva Silberman Private Photo Collection*

Dr. Bernard Roth, a physicist at UT Austin, prepares chicken soup for a Passover *seder,* a task traditionally performed by women. The *seder* was held at Temple Beth Israel in 1988. Roth is a member of the Austin chapter of the New Jewish Agenda, a national progressive Jewish organization founded in 1980, which works for peace and social justice by applying Jewish history and values to domestic and international concerns.
— *Photo by Ruthe Winegarten*

Jewish Synagogue, Marshall, Texas

Congregation B'nai Zion in El Paso dedi-
cated its newest building in 1983.
— *Hymer E. Rosen, historian, Congregation
B'nai Zion*

El Paso: "Our oasis in the desert."
— Rabbi Joseph Roth

Congregation B'nai Zion in El Paso
organized in 1900, the same year that
Marshall's Moses Montefiore built its
temple. Yet Marshall's Jewish community waned during the twentieth
century, while El Paso's grew.

The Orthodox congregation, B'nai
Zion, met for ten years in the Masonic Hall, the Old Christian Science
Church, the Gem Saloon, and the
Old Opera House until its first synagogue was dedicated in 1912. In
1920, another Orthodox congregation, Achim Neemonim, consolidated
with B'nai Zion.

In 1921, the congregation hired
their first rabbi, Charles Blumenthal,
who served until 1923. Their second
rabbi, Dr. Joseph Roth of Hungary,
served for thirty years (1923–1953).
Under his leadership, membership increased and a new building was dedicated in 1926. Haymon Krupp, the
famed wildcatter, donated the synagogue wing, and in 1959 an educational wing was constructed. The congregation continued to grow, and in
1983 a new building was dedicated. A
memorial in Memory of the Six Million, designed by congregational historian Hymer Rosen, stands in the
congregation's cemetery. The congregation is now Conservative.

Dr. Roth exhorted his congregants
to concentrate on achievements in the
sciences, medicine, education, and literature and less on material accomplishments. He established a non-sectarian day-care center for working
mothers and was a chaplain at Fort
Bliss. Roth taught philosophy at the
College of Mines for twenty-two
years.

Temple Moses Montefiore in Marshall
was dedicated in 1900, but by 1972, the
handful of Jews left could not sustain the
building. They voted to sell the deterio-
rating building to the city, and the land-
mark was razed in 1973 to provide a site
for the city's new fire and police station.
Audrey Kariel, former congregational
leader and chair of the Harrison County
Historical Commission, said, "It is still
difficult to drive by the corner of Fulton
and Burleson . . . When it came time to
dismantle the synagogue, so many memories crowded our minds. We approached
the temple's front doors, and crossed the
same hexagonal steps worn by so many
footsteps of our ancestors. We looked at
the temple where so many hearts had
worshipped through the years." The ark
and many of the temple's artifacts are on
display at the Harrison County Historical
Museum.

— *Bee Goldberg*

El Santo de la Sinagoga

As the demands of the busy lives of
Texas Jews took much of their time, the
task of being the *shamas,* or guardian of
the synagogue, fell upon others who were
paid to perform the duties. Throughout
the state, caretakers, many of whom were
black or Mexican-American, became synagogue stalwarts beloved by the members
of the congregations they served.

For forty-one years, José Cruz Burciaga
(1905–1985) took care of El Paso's Congregation B'nai Zion. He and his wife
lived in the basement of the *shul,* where
they raised their six children. He cleaned
and maintained the building, saw the congregation through *bar mitzvahs,* weddings,
brisses, and funerals, and was beloved by
the children of the congregation. When he
retired in the 1970s, the congregation's
700 members turned out to honor him.

Cruz knew more about Jewish lore than
many young rabbis. Rabbi Stanley Herman recalled trying to compute the proper
amount of ice for the women's *mikvah* to
conform to Hebraic law. At wit's end, he
finally consulted Cruz. Said Rabbi Herman, "He knew immediately."

Hymer Rosen, the synagogue's historian, recalled that "back in the '50s, we
had received a bomb threat. That didn't
scare Cruz. He stayed up all night guard-
ing our treasure, our silver plates of the
Torah." Another time when thieves broke
in, Cruz Burciaga drove them out and received a severe stab wound in the process.

Burciaga said, "I never learned much
English, but it didn't matter. So many
Jews here speak perfect Spanish. But what
I did learn and come to admire was the
old Jewish way of life — the strength of
their faith, their principles, their love of
family."

When A. R. "Babe" Schwartz, a Galveston attorney, was first elected to the Texas House of Representatives in 1955, the McCarthy era was coming to an end. Babe recalled, "During the segregation battles, we all got cards in the mail making us honorary members of the Ku Klux Klan. I got up in the House and renounced the membership because one couldn't be an honorary member of a dishonorable organization . . . the threats came by the score, but the best news came in the next mail advising me that I couldn't be a member anyhow because I was ineligible as a Jew. Thank God for little favors."[1]

Babe Schwartz served in the Texas legislature for twenty-six years, from 1955 to 1981. He served three terms in the House of Representatives (1955–1961) and six terms in the Senate (1961–1981). During his tenure, he fought segregation, was an environmentalist, and sponsored numerous bills to regulate nuclear disposal. In one session alone, he carried ninety-nine bills and major resolutions, of which fifty-three passed and went to the governor's desk. *Texas Monthly* consistently named Schwartz to its list of "Ten Best Legislators."

His friend and fellow House member, Maury Maverick, said, "For more than 25 years, Babe fought for the Bill of Rights in the Legislature. The simple truth is he has more hash marks on his arm in the defense of liberty than any other legislator, dead or alive, in the history of Texas."[2] Since 1980, the affable and popular Schwartz has been a lobbyist and has won accolades for his keen political sense.

— *Rosenberg Library, Galveston, Texas*

"All of my values come from being Jewish."[3]
THE JEWISH PRESENCE IN TEXAS

When the Morton H. Meyerson Symphony Center opened in Dallas in 1989, Meyerson, a Fort Worth native, reflected, "Only in America and Texas could the grandson of an immigrant tailor wind up with his name on a symphony hall." Meyerson's story is a familiar American tale — from marginality in Europe to mainstream in America, living and flourishing in an atmosphere of religious tolerance and returning the blessings of bounty to the community. It is an environment that has allowed many of the Texas institutions which we today take for granted, from Ben Taub Hospital to NorthPark Mall, the Marshall Public Library to the magazine *Texas Monthly,* to be created by Jews. Civic activism, creativity, and community building among Texas Jews have become a 150-year tradition: from Adolphus Sterne to Babe Schwartz, Michael Seeligson to Annette Strauss, Dr. Moses Albert Levy to Dr. William Levin, Olga Kohlberg to Gerry Beer, and Fania Feldman Kruger to Sara Borschow Burmaster, Texas Jews have been pioneers, politicians, physicians, philanthropists, and poets.

Today, as in the past, Jews have translated their traditional values of respect for learning, justice, charity, and love of family to the community at large as they have worked for education, human rights, social justice, and peace. The United States, with its democratic ideals, cultural pluralism, and open society, has proved to be a fertile ground for these values and as a result, a disproportionate percentage of Jews has moved to the forefront in business and the profes-

sions, communications and the arts, government, and social welfare.

With a well-honed sensitivity to oppression and discrimination, born of a 5,000-year history of persecution, Texas Jews have often been in the forefront in defense of the "underdogs" of our society. Rabbis and Reform congregations, in particular, have worked to help the disadvantaged and have courageously spoken out in defense of the civil rights of other minorities. Temple Beth-El in San Antonio, for example, through its Permanent Charities Foundation, launched a scholarship project in 1989, providing child-care tuition for low-income families striving to achieve economic self-sufficiency. Similarly, AIDS victims, child or spouse abuse victims, the low-income elderly, and single-parent families find concerned support from Jewish individuals and institutions today.

Defense of civil liberties and protection of ethnic diversity without fragmentation and polarization in the community is also an urgent question as the ethnic mix of our communities has undergone a radical transformation in the past twenty-five years. The American Jewish Committee's Institute for American Pluralism and Southern Methodist University, with a grant from the Meadows Foundation in Dallas, have mounted a "Consultation on American Pluralism — A Southwest Perspective" to set an agenda for the future.

The issues of black-Jewish relations have been of ongoing concern, as many Jews relate to the discrimination experienced by blacks. The Dallas American Jewish Committee was

the first in the city (1955) to hire black women as secretaries. In recent years, the Houston Anti-Defamation League has held a black-Jewish Seder. Rabbi Jack Segal of Congregation Beth Yeshurun and Pastor Kirbyjon Caldwell of Windsor Village United Methodist Church have developed a special liturgy relating black liberation from slavery to the Jewish *Haggadah.* The late Congressman Mickey Leland organized black youths for summers in Israel to enhance interracial understanding.

In the past twenty-five years, fields of endeavor previously closed to Jews — in banking, insurance, and corporate board rooms — have opened. A study conducted by the Dallas Chapter of the American Jewish Committee in 1966 revealed evidence of local discrimination against Jews in certain country clubs, service clubs, and the executive suites of some banks, insurance, and utility companies. By 1988, a national AJC study found no evidence of patterned discrimination against Jews in the last bastion of institutional anti-Semitism — the executive suites of major corporations.

While acceptance of Jews by the community at large is more the rule than the exception, anti-Semitism remains a small, though alarming, fact of life. From incidents of vandalism against Jewish institutional buildings and vituperative slander by hate groups to seemingly benign incidents of common ignorance, misunderstanding and hatred of Jews still exist.

Today's young Jews are largely immune to the discriminatory patterns of the past, in which Jews were barred from certain clubs, neighborhoods, medical schools, and corporate positions. Even so, it has only been in the late 1980s that Panhellenic, the umbrella group of campus sororities at the University of Texas at Austin, dropped the division between Jewish and non-Jewish Rush Week. Jewish youth are inspired to nurture their Jewish identity by something much different: the trend in ethnic pride. Even as the lines between groups blur, pride in ethnic Judaism helps Jewish youth retain their identity. At the same time, it becomes increasingly difficult for Jewish youth to understand the obstacles their parents, grandparents, and great-grandparents faced and overcame on the road to success.

The following pages present a representative sample of some Jewish Texans who have made major contributions to their communities, their state, and their nation. This chapter

in no way constitutes a "Who's Who of Texas Jews." For every individual featured, there could have been dozens more. While a "Who's Who" would be a voluminous and worthy undertaking, the scope of this chapter is limited to a sample of Jews, who as professionals, politicians, volunteers, philanthropists, and thinkers, have gone forth to achieve good works and make an impact on the public. Those pictured are not necessarily of equal significance; some have made ripples while others have made waves.

The connection between the accomplishments of these individuals and their Judaism, whether religious or secular, is marked; a further connection between their Judaism and their sense of responsibility to the broader community is also evident. A Brandeis University study in 1988 revealed that Jews who give to Jewish causes are also the most likely to give

to non-sectarian causes.

As Pearl Buck eloquently wrote of the Jews in her novel *Peony* (1948):

". . . where a voice sings most clearly there is one; where a line is drawn most cleverly to make a picture clear, a carving strong, there is one; where a statesman stands most honorable, a judge most just, there is one; where a scholar is most learned . . . where a woman is both beautiful and wise, there is one. Their blood is lively in whatever frame it flows, and when the frame is gone, its very dust enriches the still kindly soil. Their spirit is born anew in every generation."

The soil of Texas has indeed been kind, and indeed, the Lone Star State is enriched by the presence of Jews who have made a difference.

— Bernard Rapoport

Bernard Rapoport of Waco was once listed among the twenty most powerful men in Texas by *Texas Business*. He is a philanthropist whose interests include education and health, support for liberal causes, and the Democratic Party.
— *Bernard Rapoport*

Robert Strauss, pictured at the White House with President Lyndon B. Johnson in 1968, was chairman of the Democratic National Committee in 1974. Known as the "Disraeli with a Rolodex," he is now a lobbyist in Washington, D.C. A Dallas attorney with interests in real estate and radio stations, Strauss broke into politics as a fundraiser for John Connally's successful 1962 race for governor of Texas. For twenty years, he has raised money for many Democratic presidential candidates. *Newsweek* called him the major power broker during the 1988 Democratic Convention; that year he co-chaired the National Economic Commission to study the federal deficit. The *New York Times* called Strauss "a senior statesman who bridges partisan rivalry," and "the Capital's leading wise man."
— *Lyndon Baines Johnson Library*

Elsie and Stanley Pearle of Dallas exemplify a couple whose interests range from grassroots politics to support of the arts to involvement in many Jewish causes. They have been involved in the American Israel Public Affairs Committee and are founding members of TxPAC and supporters of many political candidates. Elsie has been active in the League of Women Voters, the Democratic Forum, the Women's Center of Dallas, the Texas Abortion Rights Action League, and the National Organization for Women. She was an associate producer for "West of Hester Street," a docu-drama film. Stanley is the founder of Pearle Vision Centers and has been president of United Way, the Jewish Federation of Greater Dallas, and a member of the Dallas Citizens Council. The couple were honored by the American Jewish Congress in 1988.
— *Elsie and Stanley Pearle*

"I have a sense of outrage and injustice."
— Bernard Rapoport

Bernard Rapoport of Waco had his beginnings in a Marxist household in San Antonio. The son of David Rappoport, a Russian revolutionary who fled Latvia in 1905, Bernard became a capitalist after his exposure to various economic theories as a student at UT Austin. He is founder and chief executive officer of the American Income Life Insurance Company, which has grown to $500 million in assets by selling insurance policies to two million union members.

Bernard Rapoport's first foray into politics was as the Central Texas manager for Homer P. Rainey's unsuccessful 1946 Texas gubernatorial race. Rapoport has been a leader in the Democratic Party and a financial supporter of many liberal political candidates ever since.

Ronnie Dugger, publisher of the *Texas Observer*, says of Rapoport, "His passion for social justice underlies everything he does." As a major benefactor of the *Texas Observer*, Rapoport established an endowment for the paper in 1989 with a gift of $50,000. He sponsors a regular column in the *Observer*, sometimes reflecting his own views or those of others. He and his wife Audre have established six professorships in government, economics, and public policy at UT Austin, founded the Bernard Rapoport Post Graduate Institute in New York, and a Chair in the History of the American Labor Movement at Tel Aviv University. He has been on the boards of many educational and religious institutions, including the Hebrew Union College and the Union of American Hebrew Congregations.

Of his great philanthropy, Rapoport says, "I don't have a choice of whether I give or not. I am forced to give; the way in which I was raised leaves me no other avenue. This is the tradition that I have to follow."

Norman W. Black, a Houston attorney, was appointed to the U.S. District Court, Southern District of Texas, in 1979 by President Jimmy Carter. Judge Black was a former assistant U.S. attorney and adjunct professor of law at the University of Houston School of Law and the South Texas College of Law.

— Norman W. Black

Judge Irving Goldberg (1906–) of Dallas was the first Jew in the South to hold a federal judgeship when he was named to the Fifth Circuit Court of Appeals in 1966 by President Lyndon B. Johnson. Born in Port Arthur, Goldberg attended UT Austin and Harvard Law School. He was president of the Dallas Jewish Welfare Federation and Temple Emanu-El, national vice-president of the American Jewish Committee, and on the boards of the Dallas United Nations Association and Golden Acres Jewish Home for the Aged. He was former vice-chair of the Texas Advisory Committee, U.S. Commission on Civil Rights. Goldberg was one of three justices on the Fifth Circuit who ruled in the *Roe v. Wade* case, which established the legal right of a woman to an abortion in 1970. Their decision was upheld by the U.S. Supreme Court in 1973.

— UT Institute of Texan Cultures

I. Allan "Babe" Lerner was elected as judge of the 56th Judicial District (Galveston County) in 1980, and reelected in 1984 and 1988. He was city attorney for the City of LaMarque from 1953 to 1981. Lerner, the son of Polish immigrants, served as president of Congregation Beth Jacob in Galveston from 1984 to 1986.

— Photo by Jim Cruz

Ruby Kless Sondock of Houston became the first woman and Jew ever to serve as a full-time justice on the Texas Supreme Court when she was appointed by Governor Bill Clements in 1982 to fill an unexpired term. Upon completing her term, she returned as presiding judge of the 234th Judicial District Court in Harris County. She was the first woman in Harris County appointed as a district judge (1973), and the first woman elected to the Court of Domestic Relations (1975). She was the first judge appointed to the newly created 234th Judicial District Court in 1977, and subsequently was reelected without opposition. A 1988 *Houston Post* survey ranked her first among Civil Court judges. In 1989, she stepped down from the bench to join a Houston law firm.

— Photo by Work of Art Studio

Houston attorney Debra Danburg was elected as a Texas state representative for District 79 (Harris County) in 1980 and was named best legislator by *Houston City Magazine.* Formerly the assistant director of Texans for an Equal Rights Amendment, she is active in dozens of community groups, supporting the rights of minorities, women, and tenants, as well as AIDS research and environmental protection. She is regional vice-president of the National Association of Jewish Legislators, and was listed in the 1986 Who's Who of Emerging Leaders in America and Outstanding Young Women of America.

— *Debra Danburg*

State Rep. Steven D. Wolens from Dallas County was elected in 1982, and is presently serving his fourth term in the Texas legislature. He is chairman of the House Business and Commerce Committee and a member of the Ways and Means Committee. *Texas Monthly* selected him as one of the "Ten Best Legislators" for 1983 and described him as an "unbeatable debator whose mind stores facts like a camel stores water." In 1985, *D Magazine* said he was considered one of the "smartest, most honest, and most effective members of the Dallas delegation." — *Steven D. Wolens*

State Rep. Alvin Granoff, representing the 108th District of Dallas County, was first elected to the Texas House of Representatives in 1982 and reelected to his fourth term in 1988. He was chairman of the Committee on State, Federal, International Relations in the 71st legislature and a member of the National Conference of State Legislators' State Federal Assembly on International Trade. He is a practicing attorney in the areas of worker's compensation and personal injury. *Texas Monthly* named him one of the most valuable members in the 71st session.

— *Alvin Granoff*

Congressman Martin Frost, a Dallas attorney, was elected to the U.S. House of Representatives from the 24th Congressional District in 1978 and was reelected to a sixth term in 1988. He has been named one of the top five representatives in the Texas delegation by the *Fort Worth Star Telegram* and the *Dallas Times Herald.* He was appointed to the House Rules Committee in 1979 and chairs the Health Task Force of the Budget Committee. Frost is descended from two pioneer Jewish families, the Frosts, founders of Frost Bros. in San Antonio, and the Marwills of Henderson. His uncle, Charles Brachfield, was Rusk County judge and a state senator. Before he was elected to Congress, Frost was a staff writer for the *Congressional Quarterly Weekly Report,* a law clerk for Federal Judge Sarah T. Hughes, and a legal commentator for KERA-TV in Dallas.

— *Martin Frost*

State Rep. Paul Colbert was first elected to the Texas legislature in 1980 from District 132, Harris County. He is chairman for Budget and Oversight of the Public Education Committee. He co-authored HB 72, the Educational Reform Act of 1984, and established the Texas Literacy Council. He supported legislation creating a center for superconductivity at the University of Houston and to establish a Child Nutrition Research Center, and sponsored a bill making it illegal for people to falsely advertise non-kosher food as kosher. He has been recognized as one of the "Ten Best" legislators by *Texas Monthly* and the *Dallas Morning News.*

— *Paul Colbert*

"I love you, too, granddaddy, but Annie's the mayor."

— Annette Strauss' granddaughter

Annette Strauss was elected mayor of Dallas in 1987 and reelected in 1989 in a landslide with a seventy-three percent majority. She had previously served on the city council (1983–1987) and as mayor pro-tem. As a volunteer, she has raised over $10 million for civic and charitable causes, and has presided over sixteen boards and served on fourteen others, including the Friends of the Kennedy Center, the Children's Medical Center Foundation, and UT (Austin and Dallas) development boards. She headed the United Jewish Appeal and has been on the boards of the American Jewish Committee, the Junior Black Academy, and the National Museum for Women in the Arts. Strauss grew up in Houston, where she played Ginger Rogers on her front porch to raise money for ice cream. Her mother was from Brenham; her father, J. B. Greenfield, was the son of a Palestinian rabbi. Strauss has a master's degree in sociology and psychology from Columbia University and worked as a John Robert Powers model before her marriage to Ted Strauss.

— Annette Strauss

When Adlene Harrison became interim mayor of Dallas in 1976, she was the first Jewish woman to be mayor of a metropolitan city in the U.S. She was on the City Planning Commission and the Dallas City Council for many years. She was appointed regional director of the Environmental Protection Agency by President Jimmy Carter (1977–1981) and was chair of the Dallas Area Rapid Transit Board (DART) from 1983 to 1986.

Harrison has been active in the Dallas Chapter, Brandeis University National Women's Committee, Girl Scouts, YWCA, Golden Acres, and the Dallas Council on Aging. With an avowed dedication to equality, she has been named Outstanding Woman Leader by the Women's Center of Dallas, Outstanding Citizen of the Year by the Black Chamber of Commerce, and received the Community Relations Award by the American Jewish Committee, and the Award for Excellence by the Dallas Historical Society.

— Adlene Harrison

When Jeff Friedman was elected as the mayor of Austin at the age of thirty in 1975, he became the youngest to hold that position. Known as the "hippie mayor," Friedman advocated environmental protection. He was successful in getting a Code of Ethics ordinance passed, as well as Equal Employment Opportunity ordinances that outlawed discrimination. In 1988, he ran an unsuccessful race for mayor. He is past president of the Jewish Community Council of Austin.

— Barker Texas History Center, UT Austin

"The answers are there. It's just a matter of digging them out." [5]   **187**

— **A. Albert Lichtenstein, mayor of Corpus Christi**

Ruben H. Edelstein served as mayor of Brownsville from 1975 to 1979. During his tenure, he established clinics for indigent health care, a training program for midwives to reduce high infant mortality, and the first emergency medical service in the Lower Rio Grande Valley. He has been involved in a number of charitable activities, including the United Way, and is active in the Jewish community as past president of Temple Beth El and custodian and historian of the Brownsville Hebrew Cemetery.

— Ruben Edelstein

Minnie Solomonson, an Amarillo native, was a Dallas attorney before moving to South Padre Island on the Texas Gulf coast to retire. Instead, she was elected as a municipal judge, serving from 1980 to 1982, and then to two terms as mayor (1982–1984 and 1984–1986). Under her leadership, the city raised the tax limit to obtain better municipal services, hired top quality staff, and developed its tourist industry.

— Minnie Solomonson

Abraham Albert Lichtenstein (1910–1978), pictured with his wife, Annie, served a tumultuous term as Corpus Christi mayor from 1953 to 1954. A prominent businessman, he was elected under the banner of the Better Government League, a group of disaffected citizens tired of the previous administration. He reluctantly agreed to head the ticket, but refused to campaign or even vote. He won, nonetheless, by over 4,000 votes, but resigned after an argument with the city council over the construction of a tunnel. He was an active member of the Jewish Community Council and Temple Beth El, and was named Outstanding Jewish Citizen by B'nai B'rith in 1947.

— Print by Applied Photographics, Inc.

Bayard Friedman (left), with architect John Street, was mayor of Fort Worth from 1963 to 1965. He joined the Fort Worth National Bank as senior vice-president in 1965, becoming president in 1972. He helped negotiate the development of the Dallas/Fort Worth Regional Airport and serves on its board of directors.

— Fort Worth Star Telegram *Photograph Collection, Special Collections Division, The University of Texas at Arlington Libraries*

"I'm a fighter. I'm also honest and tactless."[6]

— **Ruth Levy Kempner**

Ruth Levy (Mrs. Harris) Kempner, third from left, has described herself as a fighter. She was the first woman elected to the Galveston City Council, serving 1961–1963. Also shown are l. to r., (seated) T. D. Armstrong, Robert Albright, Edward Schreiber, Theodore Stubbs, T. A. Waterman, and Ed J. Harris; (standing) City Attorney James Phipps and Director of Public Works Owen Holzheuser.

A trailblazer who doesn't look back, Ruth Kempner is the daughter of City Attorney Marion J. Levy and the niece of former mayor Adrian Levy, Sr. Before her marriage in 1939 to Harris Kempner, the president of H. Kempner Cotton Co. and a director of the Imperial Sugar Company, she received a degree in history and government from UT Austin in 1937, along with a teacher's certificate. She joined the League of Women Voters in 1947, and as their leader, campaigned for the adoption of a city manager form of government. Her campaign was successful in 1961, and she was then chosen to serve on the first council elected under the new system. On her passport, she describes her occupation as "troublemaker."

— *Rosenberg Library, Galveston, Texas*

Florence Donald Shapiro, mayor pro-tem of Plano in 1989, was elected president of the Texas Municipal League in 1987. She is the third woman to head the organization, which represents 11,000 members and 900 cities. She was elected to the board of the National League of Cities in 1987. Shapiro has been on the Plano City Council since 1979, serving two previous terms as mayor pro-tem, 1980–1983. In 1983, she was elected president of the North Central Texas Council of Governments and is past president of the Texas Association of Mayors and Council Members.

— *Florence Shapiro, Mayor Pro-Tem, Plano, Texas*

Barbara Krantz Crews, mayor pro-tem of Galveston in 1989, was elected to the Galveston City Council in 1985. She is director of Women's Programs at the College of the Mainland in Texas City, on the advisory board of the Galveston Women's Resource and Crisis Center, and active in the beautification and revitalization of Galveston. She was formerly a city planning commissioner, a member of the Historical Review Board, a commissioner for the Galveston Housing Authority, and on the board of Temple B'nai Israel.

— *Barbara Krantz Crews*

James Goldman, an El Paso businessman, was elected to the El Paso City Council in 1988. In addition to being a national commissioner of the Anti-Defamation League of B'nai B'rith, he serves on the boards of the Boy Scouts, the El Paso Cancer Treatment Center, and is vice-president of the West Texas Council of Governments. He is a former board member of Temple Mount Sinai.

— *James Goldman*

J. Livingston Kosberg of Houston was appointed in 1983 by Governor Mark White to the Texas Board of Human Services and was subsequently elected chairman, serving until 1988. He founded the National Living Center, one of the nation's largest nursing home chains. He is a past president of the Jewish Federation of Greater Houston and a former chair of the United Jewish Campaign. His wife, Saranne, is a civic leader and vice-chairman of the Hebrew Union College-Jewish Institute of Religion Board and vice-president of the local Jewish Federation.
— *Texas Department of Human Services*

Susan Marks Hopkins of Corpus Christi is state director of Communities in Schools, a drop-out prevention program of the Texas Employment Commission. She was appointed by Governor Mark White in 1983 to serve on the Texas Select Committee on Public Education, was a fundraiser and lobbyist for the Texas Association of School Boards and promoter of the arts in Corpus Christi, where she has served as a board member of the Chamber of Commerce and a funding consultant to the city government. She has been involved in literacy campaigns and was special projects director for KEDT-TV Public Broadcasting Station, 1977–1980.
— *Susan Marks Hopkins*

Her interests range from garbage to government, Girl Scouts to fine art. Veta Winick of Dickinson was president of the Texas League of Women Voters from 1970 to 1975 and a national director of the League from 1976 to 1978. She is director of the O'Kane Gallery at the downtown campus, University of Houston. In 1987, she was selected as chairman of the Governor's Task Force on Waste Management Policy Committee. She has also served as president of the Gulf Coast Waste Disposal Authority, Industrial Development Authority, and Financing Authority. In 1988, she was elected to the Dickinson City Council.
— *Photo by P.L.G. Ltd.*

Jerry Kane of Corpus Christi was appointed as chairman of the Texas Rehabilitation Commission Board in 1984, having served since 1982. He is the president of Sam Kane Beef Processors, Inc., and has been on the board of the American Meat Institute. His parents were Holocaust survivors, and Kane has been on the steering committee of the U.S. Holocaust Memorial Council. He is on the national cabinet of the United Jewish Appeal and president of Temple B'nai Israel. He was dinner vice-chairman in 1984 for the Reagan-Bush victory celebration, following the election of Ronald Reagan and George Bush as president and vice-president.
— *Texas Rehabilitation Commission*

Harry Shapiro (1921–1982) of San Saba was first appointed to the Lower Colorado River Authority (LCRA) board in 1967, serving until 1973. He was reappointed in 1977 and elected chairman in 1981. The LCRA's building in Austin is named after him. Shapiro was mayor of San Saba and president of the local Chamber of Commerce. He was commander of his American Legion Post and the Veterans of Foreign Wars. In 1978, he received the Israel Bonds Leadership Award and was a member of Austin's Congregation Agudas Achim. Upon his death, the Texas legislature adjourned for a day.
— *Beatrice Shapiro*

Dr. Abe Greines (1898–1978) was a leading Fort Worth physician for sixty years who served on the local school board from 1953 to 1962. He lettered in football at Texas Christian University and graduated from Baylor Medical School. Before being elected to the school board, he was on the Park Board. He was active in the Kiwanis Club, the Fort Worth Boys Club, and the Masonic Order. He was a director of the Union Bank (now Texas Commerce Bank). In 1963, he was B'nai B'rith Man of the Year and was named Fort Worth Senior Citizen of the Year by the Women's Civic Club Council. The Wilkerson-Greines Activity Center of the Fort Worth Independent School District is named for him. His father opened the Greines Furniture Company in 1905, which was operated by the family until 1989. Abe's brothers were also prominent; David and Sol were attorneys, and Jake owned the Greines Dry Goods store.
— *Fort Worth Jewish Community Sesquicentennial Archives*

Houston artist Gertrude Barnstone served on the Houston School Board from 1964 to 1969. A leader in facilitating desegregation, she was responsible for the initial acceptance of federal breakfast and lunch programs. She worked for bilingual education and equal opportunity for minority students, teachers, and staff. Her activities have been far-ranging, from being director of community relations for KPRC-TV in Houston to being on the board of the Texas Film Commission. In 1987, she began working with anti-nuclear activists to insure that the Port of Houston is nuclear free. "Every gun," she said, "is a theft from someone who is hungry."[7] Her unusual sculpture, created over a twenty-year period, is a blend of nature and technology. Using plexiglas, metal, string, wire mesh, and sometimes tree branches, she sculpts environments, as well as functional art pieces, which have been widely exhibited.
— *Photo by Bill Stone*

Chris N. Adler was elected to an at-large position on the Corpus Christi Independent School District Board in 1988. She is former president of the Texas Region of Hadassah and serves on its national board. She has served on the boards of the South Texas Speech, Hearing and Language Center, the Palmer Drug Abuse Council, PTA, and the Corpus Christi Human Relations Commission. She is on the board of B'nai Israel and the Jewish Community Council. In 1988, she was the recipient of the Golda Meir Award from the State of Israel Bonds.   — *Chris Adler*

Cathy Mincberg was elected to the Houston School Board in November 1981. Reelected in 1985, she has served as president since 1987. She is the owner and publisher of the "Quorum Report," a bimonthly non-partisan newsletter. Mincberg has been a Houston Community College trustee, a member of the Advisory Committee to the State Board of Education on Long Range Planning, and served on the Houston Police Advisory Committee and the Executive Committee of the Gulf Coast Association of School Boards. She has been active in the YWCA, American Jewish Committee, Jewish Federation, ORT, and the Jewish Community Center.
— *Houston Independent School District*

Janey Lack of Victoria was appointed by several governors to statewide educational positions, including chair of the Texas Task Force on Literacy (1986–1987) and member of the Advisory Council for Technical-Vocational Education (1985–1986). She served on the Victoria City Council from 1979 to 1986. A graduate of the Harvard Graduate School of Business Administration, Lack was appointed to the State Treasury Assets Management Committee (1983–1987). She was treasurer and then regional director of the Texas Recreation and Parks Society from 1976 to 1979. She is active in the Victoria Arts Council and chaired the city's Parks and Recreation Commission from 1974 to 1978.
— *Janey Lack*

— *Marshall News Messenger,* **April 18, 1979**

No job is too big for Audrey D. Kariel. Audrey Daniels (Mrs. Louis, Jr.) Kariel of Marshall has been involved in education and historical preservation for many years. She coordinated the campaign to bring public library service and post-vocational/technical training to Marshall and Harrison County. As chairman of the Civic Center Advisory Board (1976–1984), she led a campaign for the con-

struction of a 1,600-seat auditorium in 1984. As the first acting chairman of the Marshall Public Library Board of Trustees from 1969 to 1975, she coordinated a successful drive to build the library. The library's Gold Auditorium was named in memory of Etta and Moses Gold, Jewish residents, whose heirs gave a seed grant of $150,000 to establish the library.

When the decision was reached to close Temple Moses Montefiore, Audrey saw that its history was preserved through publication and historical markers. When the temple was demolished, she made sure that the records and artifacts were presented to the Harrison County Historical Museum, where they are on display. She was a consultant on community services for the Marshall Memorial Hospital and an administrative assistant to State Rep. Ben Z. Grant (1978–1981).

Kariel has received numerous awards, including Most Outstanding Citizen by the Marshall Chamber of Commerce, Churchwoman of the Year by Religious Heritage of America, and the Myrtle Wreath Achievement Award by Hadassah. In 1988, she became chair of the Harrison County Historical Commission, leading a fight to save the local train depot. A leader in the Texas Jewish Historical Society, she and her husband chaired the 1989 annual meeting in Jefferson, the largest and most successful in the organization's history.

— Marshall News Messenger, *April 18, 1979*

The interior of the Hannah Landa Memorial Library, donated to the San Antonio Public Library system by Harry Landa (1863–1951) in memory of his wife. Rabbi David and Mrs. Helen Jacobson were instrumental in securing the gift for the city. Landa donated Landa Park to the City of New Braunfels. He was the son of Joseph and Helena Landa, pioneer Central Texans. He and his mother ran the Landa family businesses for many years, and a year after her death, in 1913, he married Hannah Mansfield of Tucson, Arizona. He owned the Landa Milling Company and the San Antonio Southern Railway, and was a director of the International and Great Northern Railroad.

— *Photo by Harvey Patteson, copy from San Antonio Public Library*

David Kaplan Westheimer of Houston
and Los Angeles is a member of the pioneer Westheimer family who settled in
Houston in 1859. David decided to become a writer in junior high when he won
a seventy-five-cent prize for a book report.
He later wrote fifteen novels, including
the best-seller *Von Ryan's Express* and *My
Sweet Charley*, which became a TV show.
During World War II, he was a B-24 Lib-
erator bomber/navigator stationed in Palestine and Egypt. He has held a variety of
editorial posts for magazines and has
worked as a Hollywood screenwriter and
columnist for the *Houston Post*.
— *David Westheimer*

Dr. William Breit is an E. M. Stevens
Distinguished Professor of Economics at
Trinity University in San Antonio. Breit
and co-author Kenneth G. Elzinga write
murder mysteries using economic theories
to solve "whodunits." Using the pseudonym Marshall Jevons, their mysteries
are on the reading lists of more than 400
college economics courses. Breit and Elzinga have written two books on economics dealing with the need to revise the federal antitrust laws; their recommendations were enacted into law.
— *Photo by Gittings*

San Antonio-born Marie Brenner, an author and journalist, has been called "the
best magazine writer in America" by columnist Liz Smith. Brenner's book *House
of Dreams: The Bingham Family of Louisville*
was a national bestseller praised by *Newsweek, Time,* and the *New York Times.* As
special correspondent for *Vanity Fair,*
Marie did an interview with Michelle Du-
valier of Haiti which won the Front Page
Award for the most distinguished magazine story of 1986. Now a Manhattan resident, Marie has been an editor for *New
York* magazine and a film critic for *Texas
Monthly.*   — *Photo by Elena Seiberg*

Rosellen Brown is the author of six books,
including three novels (*Tender Mercies,
Civil Wars,* and *The Autobiography of My
Mother*), two poetry collections, and a
book of short stories. She received a Gug-
genheim Fellowship, grants from the National Endowment for the Arts, and was
selected by *Ms* magazine in 1984 as one of
their twelve "Women of the Year." She is
on the creative writing faculty at the University of Houston.
— *Photo by Marv Hoffman*

Evelyn Oppenheimer is a Dallas author,
book reviewer, and literary agent. She
holds the record for the longest-running
book review radio broadcast (forty years).
She has been an instructor at Southern
Methodist University and UT Austin and
is the recipient of the Book Publishers of
Texas Media Award. She was the first
young woman ever to win a national high
school debate tournament in 1924. When
the salutatorian of her graduating class
was asked by his father why he lost valedictorian to a "mere girl," the boy answered: "Evelyn is not mere." [8]
— *Photo by Hodges, Photographers*

Frances Sanger Mossiker (1906–1985) of
Dallas, the only granddaughter of Alex
Sanger, was an award-winning novelist
with an international literary reputation.
Her books appeared in foreign language
editions, and her history of Marie An-
toinette's disappearing jewels, *The Queen's
Necklace,* won the Carr P. Collins Award
for best non-fiction book written by a
Texan in 1961. Her second book, *Napoleon
and Josephine: The Biography of a Marriage,*
was published in 1964 and also received
the Collins Award.
— *UT Institute of Texan Cultures*

John Rosenfield (1900–1966) was a nationally recognized critic whose knowledge of opera and music was legendary. He headed the amusement department of the *Dallas Morning News* from 1925 to 1957. *Time* said that culture blossomed in Dallas "like a rose on the dry plains of the Southwest, thanks largely to Rosenfield." His widely acclaimed column, "The Passing Show," became an institution. He helped revive the Dallas Symphony Orchestra in the 1920s, encouraged pioneer theater-in-the-round innovator Margo Jones, and was a key factor in the development of the Frank Lloyd Wright-designed Dallas Theatre Center. A scholarship in playwriting was established at Southern Methodist University in Rosenfield's honor. — *Dallas Public Library*

Arnold Rosenfeld began his newspaper career at the *Houston Post* in 1953. His career has included positions at the *Detroit Free Press* and the Dayton (Ohio) *Daily News and Journal Herald*. He was editor of the *Austin American Statesman* from 1984 to 1988, editor of the *Atlanta Constitution* (1988–1989), then was appointed senior vice-president and editor-in-chief of the Cox Newspaper Chain. He has been a director of the American Society of Newspaper Editors and chair of its minority affairs committee.

Rosenfeld and his family moved to Houston in 1940. He contributed to the book, *Growing Up in Texas*, which was honored by Women in Communication. In "An Outsider's Christmas" [*A Texas Christmas*, 1986], he recalled, "It was not always easy to be Jewish and to have grown up on the north side of Houston . . . I was the only Jewish kid around . . . There were occasional fist fights, and the double-wounding slur, 'Jew baby,' was sometimes flung in my direction." — *Arnold Rosenfeld*

Evelyn Hoffman, third from left, is a Waco television producer and host of the program "Better with Age." She is shown in 1987 receiving the Owl Award for the best non-fiction TV program by the Retirement Research Foundation. Also, l. to r., advice columnist Ann Landers, director Michael Thompson, and movie critic Gene Siskel. Hoffman is a consultant for the Baylor University Gerontology Institute, an advisor to the Waco Center for Battered Women, and fundraising coordinator for the Waco Community Hospice Program. She received the governor's Pathfinder Award for being the first Texas woman to develop a weekly senior citizens' talk show. — *Evelyn Hoffman*

Howard D. Gutin of San Antonio was elected chairman of the board of directors of the Corporation for Public Broadcasting in 1987. He was formerly associated with Texas public television stations KLRN-TV (San Antonio) and KLRU-TV (Austin) from 1979 to 1986. His philosophy is reflected in the following comments: "Public broadcasting is intended to be a mirror of the American people, and we aggressively reach out to women and minorities to ensure that their perspective is reflected in our programming." [9] — *Howard Gutin*

Michael Levy, pictured with his wife Becky, started the magazine *Texas Monthly* in 1973 in Austin. *Texas Monthly* is a popular magazine which highlights Texas people, politics, cuisine, and culture. It was the first magazine to win the National Magazine Award after its first year of publication. Becky founded the R. S. Levy Gallery in 1983. — *Photo by Lee Kelly,* Austin American Statesman, *February 27, 1988*

— Maurice Schmidt

Eleanor Freed stands beside the c. 1986 painting by her husband, Frank Freed, "Opening Night at the Contemporary Arts Museum," Houston. She was art critic for the *Houston Post* from 1965 to 1973. Her art criticism has appeared in many magazines, including *Art in America* and the *Texas Humanist*. She grew up in Memphis, Tennessee. During World War II, she was a staff member of the American Red Cross Military Welfare Service, and after the war, worked for Friends of Democracy and Estes Kefauver's senatorial campaign. She was a founder of the Harris County Democrats, helped establish the Houston Council on Human Relations, and was chairman of the YWCA's public affairs committee. Her husband was Frank Freed, a well-known Houston artist. They were both active in the Houston Contemporary Arts Museum.

— Eleanor Freed

Houston artist Frank Freed (1906–1975) began to paint toward the end of World War II and gained recognition with his depiction of the human comedy in art. His self-taught style was often described as "sophisticated primitivism," but found wide respect by artists and critics alike. His paintings have been exhibited nationwide, in Japan, Mexico City, and Israel, and are in many collections. He is shown with his painting "Antique Garden," c. 1960. His philosophy: "I'm mostly involved with conveying ideas . . . I have particularly felt a sense of kinship with Breughel, Hogarth, Daumier, Shahn, and Hopper." [11]

He was born in San Antonio to active Zionists Louis and Fannie Freed. He moved to Houston in 1913 and attended Rice Institute. He was one of the founding members of Congregation Emanu El, a founder of Houston's American Jewish Committee, and president of the Houston United Nations Association.

— Eleanor Freed

Maurice Schmidt is a painter, sculptor, printmaker, muralist, and art critic in Kingsville. His art is in private collections throughout the U.S. and abroad and has been exhibited in museums and universities throughout Texas and at the Museo De Belles Artes in Mexico City. Much of his art contains Jewish themes. He is shown painting a portrait of his wife, Becky. Maurice is the grandson of a pioneer New Braunfels Jew, Jacob Schmidt, one of the founders of Congregation Agudas Achim in San Antonio. Maurice grew up in New Braunfels, where ten Jewish families from both his hometown and Seguin worshiped at the Schmidt home.

— Maurice Schmidt

"This work is my accusation of those who keep silent when human   **195**

beings are reduced to the level of 'non-persons.' "
— **Maryanne Meltzer on her "Alienation Series"**

Dallas artist Maryanne Meltzer is shown with her painting entitled "And Who Speaks?" ("Alienation Series," 1985, acrylic — 50″ x 60″). In addition to her many exhibitions throughout Texas and the nation, she taught art in the Dallas public schools and in the Dallas Community College District. She is a national board member of the Women's Caucus for Art and vice-president and a founder of the Dallas Women's Caucus for Art.

— Maryanne Meltzer

"Oracle of the Mother Goddess" is a 12′ x 8′ multidimensional polyethylene painting by Jan Statman of Longview. The painting was displayed at Kilgore College in 1977. Statman asks, "Why the Mother Goddess? Every culture, every language . . . whispers legends of the mother goddess . . . the beautiful . . . embodiment of the vastness of life . . . with all the female virtues; loyalty, steadfastness, honor, courage, wisdom, strength, benevolence, beauty, dignity." [12] Statman is a writer and art critic whose paintings hang in permanent collections of museums in Spain and Italy. She is currently writing a history of Jewish participation in the East Texas oil boom of the 1930s.

— Photo by Max Statman

Architect Howard Barnstone (1923–1987) was best known for his design of the Rothko Chapel in Houston. He also developed condominium projects and assisted John and Dominique de Menil, international art collectors, with their home. He was co-author of *The Galveston That Was.*

— Houston Metropolitan Research Center, Houston Public Library

Raymond Nasher of Boston, a Dallas real
estate developer, who created one of the
first post-World War II shopping centers
(NorthPark), and his wife Patsy amassed
a stunning collection of modern art —
paintings, sculpture, and ephemera —
over a twenty-year period.
— *Copy from Dallas Museum of Art*

Patsy Nasher of Dallas (1929–1988), educated at Hockaday in Dallas and Smith
College, was an internationally recognized
connoisseur of art whose collections are
recognized worldwide.
— *Copy from Dallas Museum of Art*

A Century of Modern Sculpture

One of the world's finest private
collections of modern sculpture, as-
sembled by Dallas residents Patsy
and Raymond Nasher, was featured
in the exhibition *A Century of Modern
Sculpture: The Patsy and Raymond Nasher
Collection*. The exhibition was organized by the Dallas Museum of Art,
where it opened in April 1987. It then
traveled to the National Gallery of
Art and made its international debut
in Madrid, Spain, at the Centro de
Arte Reina Sofia in April 1988.

It was on display at the sixteenth-
century Forte di Belvedere in Florence, Italy, from July 8 through October 29, 1988. Its final stop was at the
Tel Aviv Museum of Art in Israel in
1989. Mrs. Nasher died after a long
illness just days before the Florence
opening.

Large Seated Nude by Henri Matisse (1869–
1954), c. 1923–1925, bronze,
$30^1/_2$ x $31^5/_8$ x $13^5/_8$ inches.
— *The Patsy and Raymond Nasher Collection
of Modern Sculpture, photo by Lee
Clockman, copy from Dallas Museum of Art*

Jocelyn L. Straus has been active in the Republican Party since 1960. She was appointed by President Ronald Reagan in 1988 to serve on the National Council of the Arts, the first Texan on the Council in twenty years. Straus was founding chairman of the Foundation for Cultural Arts in San Antonio, a project to revitalize the downtown area and create a city arts district. She is also involved with the boards of the United Way, the University of Texas Health Science Center, San Antonio Youth Literacy, the Bexar County Hospital District, and the San Antonio Zoo.

— *Jocelyn Straus*

Iris Siff, Alley Theatre director

Iris Siff of Tyler, managing director of Houston's Alley Theatre, was a guiding force in the arts for thirty-five years. She founded the Alley Academy for young people, and was influential in the establishment of the National Endowment for the Arts. The Iris Siff Oral History Library honoring Jewish women is sponsored by Houston's American Jewish Committee.

Houston actress Pauline Hecht is pictured in 1978, playing the role of Berthe in the musical *Pippin* at Theater Under the Stars. Also pictured are actors Dennis Bourgeois, Kerry Durdin, Sterling Tinsley, and Rob Bobbi. Hecht, a versatile actress with forty years of experience, has appeared in theatrical productions at the Alley Theatre and Stages Repertory Theatre, among many others; her performances include "Gigi," "A Majority of One," "West Side Story," and "My Fair Lady."

— *Houston Metropolitan Research Center, Houston Public Library*

The lives of Haskell and Motley Paley Harelik, pictured on their wedding day, are portrayed in a play by their grandson, Mark Harelik, pictured in costume to the right. "The Immigrant, a Hamilton County Album," which debuted in Denver and toured nationally, dramatizes the life story of the Hareliks in the small Texas town of Hamilton. Haskell became a successful merchant, and his grandson has become a successful actor and playwright, who wrote "The Immigrant" as a tribute to his grandfather.

— *The Texas Collection, Baylor University, Waco, Texas*

— *Photo by Jay Thompson*

Dallas-born Aaron Spelling is the most successful independent producer in television history. The youngest of five children born to David Spelling, a Russian-Jewish immigrant tailor, and Pearl Wall, Aaron was raised on Browder Street in a poor South Dallas working-class neighborhood. His father was a tailor who made suits for Eddie Cantor and Al Jolson as they passed through on vaudeville tours.

Aaron recalls the Cotton Mill Gang who lived in their neighborhood and beat up Jewish boys: "We used to get our butts whipped every day on the way home from school." During World War II, he entertained on a troop ship and wrote comedy routines for GIs during the Nazi blitz of London. After the war, he attended Southern Methodist University on the GI bill. At SMU he was part of a comedy team and won the national Eugene O'Neill Award for best original one-act play in 1947 and 1948.

He lived briefly in New York and then moved to California in 1951, where he broke into show business as a band boy and talent scout. After writing, acting, and directing, he became a producer in 1959 with the CBS series *Johnny Ringo*. Among the successful television shows produced by his company, Aaron Spelling Productions Inc., are *Charlie's Angels, The Mod Squad, Dynasty*, and *The Love Boat*. He has often been criticized for his formulaic bent toward television violence, but responds, "we often have to make the choice between 150 critics and 150 million Americans . . . I have always felt that my job was to please [the viewers]. To entertain them."

In 1989, Spelling, his wife, Candy, and their children, Victoria and Randall, moved into a 65,000-square foot home in Beverly Hills, costing about $45 million.[13]
— *From the Collections of the Dallas Jewish Historical Society*

"The only Jews in the Hill Country are Jesus and Kinky Friedman," says Kinky Friedman, a self-described Jewish Will Rogers living in Kerrville. He is a singer/songwriter and mystery novelist whose country-western musical group, Kinky Friedman and the Texas Jewboys, was popular during the 1970s. Two of his showier titles were, "They Ain't Makin' Jews Like Jesus Anymore" and "Get Your Biscuits in the Oven and Your Buns in the Bed." He wrote the first song on the Holocaust, "Ride 'em, Jewboy."

The "twisted and folksy" Friedman is currently carving a successful career as a mystery author with three novels, one of which, *Greenwich Killing Time*, is being made into a movie. He ran as a Republican for justice of the peace in Kerr County, but lost, attributing his defeat to the prevalence of "Kerrverts."
— *Poster by Micael Priest, copy from Barker Texas History Center, UT Austin*

Dr. Daniel Sternberg was dean of the Baylor School of Music in Waco from 1949 to 1981, and has been music director and conductor of the Baylor Symphony Orchestra since 1962. Born in Poland, he was raised and educated in Vienna, beginning his music studies at age five. He experienced anti-Semitism at the University of Vienna, where he studied law. He studied conducting at the Vienna National Academy of Music. After graduation in the 1930s, he moved to the USSR, where he was assistant conductor of the Leningrad Philharmonic and the Leningrad Grand Opera. When offered a more attractive position in Kiev if he became a Soviet citizen, he declined and returned to Vienna, where he was arrested by the Gestapo in 1938 and given forty-eight hours to leave the country. He arrived in the U.S. in 1939. Since his retirement from Baylor, he has been a guest conductor with the Dallas Symphony Orchestra.
— *The Texas Collection, Baylor University, Waco, Texas*

Fredell Lack (Eichhorn) of Houston is a world-famous concert violinist who began music studies at the age of five, gave her first concert at age eight, and at seventeen, entered the Juilliard School of Music from which she graduated. The winner of many competitions, she has made numerous tours of Europe, Central America, Canada, and Hawaii. She starred on her own network radio program and recorded with the New York Philharmonic. She is artist-in-residence and professor of violin and chamber music at the University of Houston. She received the Mayor's Award as Houston's outstanding performer, the Teacher of the Year Award for 1987 by the Houston Music Teachers Association, and was the first recipient of the Young Audiences Fredell Lack Award. In 1989, she was honored by the Houston Symphony and Youth Symphony for her work as a teacher of outstanding students.
— *Photo by Kay Marvins*

Gisele Ben-Dor, a new Texan, was appointed resident conductor of the Houston Symphony Orchestra in 1989, having served one year as assistant conductor. The Uruguayan-Israeli has conducted orchestras on three continents, including the Israel Philharmonic and the Berlin Symphony. She has been tutored in master classes by Maestros Leonard Bernstein and Zubin Mehta and was the winner of the 1986 Bartok Prize of the Hungarian Radio and Television International Conductor's Competition.
— *Houston Symphony Orchestra*

From floor sweeper to the president of the South's largest bank — that is the life story of Dallasite Fred Florence (1891–1960). The son of Lithuanian parents, he began his career as a bank janitor in Rusk, Texas. He became president of the State Bank in nearby Alto, served in the Army Air Corps in World War I, and upon his return, was named Alto's mayor. In 1920, he moved to Dallas and helped found the Guaranty Bank and Trust Company. By 1929, he was president of its successor, the Republic National Bank, the South's largest financial institution. His lifetime civic involvement included the Community Chest, the Jewish Welfare Federation, and scouting. In 1936, Florence was president of the Texas Centennial Exposition. He and business leader Robert L. Thornton worked together on many civic endeavors, including the creation of the Dallas Citizens Council, later known as the "oligarchy." In 1959, Florence received the Benemerenti Medal from Pope John XXIII, the only Jew to be so honored.
— *Dallas Public Library*

Healthy competition in civic leadership

Stanley Marcus said that Dallas had a unique quality. "In the absence of any one or two civic benefactors, the business interests of the city have long recognized the necessity of plowing back a good share of their corporate profits into the cultural and charitable institutions of the community . . . there is a healthy competition in civic leadership . . ."[15]

Although Marcus was referring primarily to leaders in the non-Jewish community, Jewish men like Julius Schepps and Fred Florence personified that blend of civic and business interests typical of Dallas and other Texas cities.

Julius Schepps (1895–1971) helped dedicate the Julius Schepps Community Center in Dallas in 1962. The Center was named after Schepps in a compromise reached after a heated controversy over the need for a Jewish facility.[16] In 1975, it was renamed the Jewish Community Center.

Schepps became prosperous in businesses from banking to insurance to liquor distribution. During World War II, he contributed $120,000 for the relief of European Jews. A Dallas Home for the Jewish Aged was one of his projects. He headed Dallas' first bi-racial commission, won the Linz Award in 1953, and in 1954 was named Dallas' most outstanding citizen. After his death the Texas Legislature named him "Mr. Dallas."
— *Copy from* Jewish Community Center of Dallas Dedication Book

Neiman-Marcus is a name synonymous with exquisite merchandise and innovative marketing. Stanley joined the family business upon graduating from the Harvard School of Business in 1926 and became president in 1950. He developed sales promotion events like the Fortnights, the Zodiac Room fashion shows, and the *Christmas Book*. Despite the store's reputation for catering to the wealthy, Stanley contended that "the lady who spends $250 a year is our darling." Style-conscious women, from Paris, Texas, to Paris, France, have shopped at Neimans, including royalty and wives of U.S. presidents. His books include *Minding the Store* and *Quest for the Best*.

In an interview in *Texas Monthly* [February 1988], Marcus said that leaving behind his religion was not leaving behind his identity. "I'm a Jew," he said. He believes in the separation of church and state and resents grace being given at business lunches. Dallas' best-known citizen, Marcus is equally comfortable in the worlds of business and the arts.
— *Neiman-Marcus Archives*

— **Isadore Roosth**

"Rise to the top" is the favorite expression of Isadore Roosth, a Tyler philanthropist and oil producer. Roosth is well-loved and respected for his civic interests and generosity. He serves on thirty boards, including the Texas Board of Health, the East Texas Hospital Foundation, the Tyler Junior College Foundation, and the Mental Health and Mental Retardation Regional Center of East Texas. He was the 1988 recipient of the Dallas-Fort Worth Hospital Council's Distinguished Health Service Award. He is also past president of Congregation Ahavath Achim in Tyler.
— *Photo by McWhirter*

William Zale (1903–1983) of Dallas visits with children from the Avance Project, one of numerous programs funded by the Zale Foundation, created in 1951, to provide money for educational and health programs. Other programs funded by the Zale Foundation have included the Greater Dallas Communications Committee to seek harmonious solutions to community conflicts; an inner-city high school in Brooklyn, New York; and a program for El Paso health workers. The latest benefactor of the Zale family's generosity is the Zale-Lipshy University Hospital, scheduled to open in 1990, as a part of UT Southwestern Medical School in Dallas.

William and his brother, Morris Zale, emigrated from Russia and founded the Zales Jewelry Store in Wichita Falls in 1924. Their stores quickly grew into a large national retail chain. Their success was due to many factors, including the wise management of assets, an innovative credit policy that made jewelry affordable to the masses, the promotion of jewelry as gifts for special occasions, a mail-order service, and extensive newspaper advertising. Today, Zales is one of the largest retail jewelry chains in the world.
— *Zale Foundation, copy from UT Institute of Texan Cultures*

Harold M. Freeman (1889–1983), pictured here, and his brother, Joe Freeman (1885–1971), were South Texas philanthropists whose San Antonio beneficiaries have included the Boysville Foundation, Aganier Home for Homeless Girls, the Mission Road Foundation for Handicapped Children, and the Santa Rosa Hospital. Joe and Harold both worked to create the San Antonio Livestock Exposition, whose coliseum is named for them. Harold bequeathed his 3,500-acre ranch in Hays County to Southwest Texas State University. In 1983, SWT named its aquatic biology building for him. He was also the chairman of the first fundraising drive to build Golden Manor Jewish Home for the Aged in San Antonio. Joe was president of the San Antonio Chamber of Commerce and established the Freeman Forest in Israel in 1973.
— *Southwest Texas State University News Service Photo*

Edwin Gale of Beaumont is pictured with his wife, Becky. He and his parents endowed the Gale Professorship of Judaic Studies, and the Gale Chair in the College of Business Administration at UT Austin. They also established the Gale Professorship in Psychiatry at UT Medical Branch in Galveston. Edwin has served as president of the Beaumont Jewish Federation.
— *The University of Texas Medical Branch, Galveston*

202   *"Human dignity. That's what's left to work on."*

— **Ben Rogers**

Julie and Ben Rogers of Beaumont.   — *Ben Rogers*

Regina Rogers of Beaumont and Houston
is the daughter of Ben and Julie Rogers.
— *Regina Rogers*

Julie and Ben Rogers

If one were to combine the *vitaes* of Julie and Ben Rogers and their daughter, Regina, the boards of over 100 charitable organizations would be represented. Millions of Texans, whether indigent, ill, involved in the arts, or interested in Jewish causes, interfaith relations, or the perpetuation of scholarship, have benefited from their acts of charity and kindness.

At the height of the Depression, Ben Rogers and his brother, Sol, arrived in Texas practically penniless. They chose to settle in Beaumont, and Ben recalled that they spent their first night in the car. They awoke in the morning to a cow licking Sol's nose. Undaunted, the Rogers brothers remained, and even named their business — Texas State Optical — after their adopted state. The business prospered, and the Rogers family have shared their prosperity with thousands of others.

Ben married Julie, a graduate at age nineteen from the De Paul University School of Law, Chicago. Together, they have served organizations ranging from the Mental Health Association to the Salvation Army, M.D. Anderson Hospital to the National Conference of Christians and Jews, the Beaumont Civic Opera to

Houston's Theater Under the Stars, and ethnic groups from the United Negro College Fund to the Institute of Hispanic Culture.

Julie has received awards from the Texas Safety Association, the Salvation Army, the Texas Association for Mental Health, and the National Association of Social Workers. In 1982, the City of Beaumont named a theater in her honor for her four-decade commitment to the arts. In 1987, she was named the American Jewish Committee's Woman of Achievement. And in 1988, she was named National Volunteer of the Year by the National Mental Health Association.

Ben Rogers was the first Jew to receive the National Medal of Honor from the Daughters of the American Revolution. He also won the Good Samaritan Award from the Mormon Church, the F. D. Patterson Award from United Negro Colleges, Man of the Year from the American Cancer Society, and the Diamond Jubilee Award from the National Jewish Hospital in Denver. He has been president of the Babe Didrikson Zaharias Foundation and the Joe Louis International Sports Foundation. Among his civic interests have been St. Elizabeth Hospital, the YMCA, and the International Seamen's Center. In honor of Ben's seventy-fifth birthday, his wife and children committed

$150,000 to establish the "Ben Rogers/Lamar University [Beaumont], I Have a Dream" program to establish seventy-five scholarships for economically disadvantaged youth.

Together, Ben and Julie Rogers have been honored by Business and Professional Women, the NAACP for supporting and working with Negro colleges, the Southeast Texas Council of the Arts, the National Conference of Christians and Jews, and the American Heart Association.

Their daughter, Regina, has established several awards in honor of her parents, including the Julie and Ben Rogers Ecumenism Award of the Anti-Defamation League and the Julie and Ben Rogers Award for Excellence at M.D. Anderson Cancer Center.

Regina has a long list of "firsts": first girl in Beaumont to have a *bat mitzvah*, first woman regent of Lamar University, and first woman law clerk for a judge in Beaumont. An attorney, Regina is also involved in numerous social and civic causes in both Houston and Beaumont, including the chairmanship of the Texas Higher Education State Coordinating Board's Equal Education Opportunity Committee, the University of Houston Law School Foundation, the Houston Symphony, and the American Jewish Committee.

— **Leopold Meyer**

Ben Taub (1889–1982) is a Houston name synonymous with health care for the indigent. Ben Taub Hospital, which opened in 1964, is named for him. The son of a Hungarian immigrant, Taub was a financier who worked for more than fifty years to provide quality health care for everyone. He worked first in his father's tobacco wholesaling business, then became a real estate developer and a member of twenty-three corporate boards.

In 1936, Ben Taub donated land for the University of Houston campus. He was board chairman for Jefferson Davis Hospital from 1935 to 1964 and continued as honorary chairman of the Harris County Hospital District. Dr. Michael E. DeBakey credits Taub with shaping the destiny of the nation's fourth largest public hospital system, which operates the Lyndon B. Johnson and Ben Taub hospitals and many neighborhood clinics. Taub's Sunday hospital visits were legendary, as he moved about quietly distributing coins and candy to sick children. He was also credited with persuading the Baylor College of Medicine to move to Houston in 1943. (The Jewish Institute for Medical Research, a division of the Baylor College of Medicine, was built with contributions from Houston Jews.) Through a family foundation, Taub gave millions of dollars for medical research, scholarships, and a home for indigent children.[17]

— *Photo by Gittings*

J. J. Abercrombe (left) and Leopold Meyer (right) at the dedication of the Texas Children's Hospital in Houston, 1951. Leopold Meyer (1892–1982), a Houston businessman and philanthropist, was a major supporter of Texas Children's Hospital. A 1912 graduate of Tulane University, Meyer and his brothers purchased department stores and ultimately developed Meyerland, one of Houston's first suburban retail shopping centers. He was associated with Foley Brothers from 1918 to 1945.

Leopold enjoyed rubbing elbows with Hollywood stars who appeared at the legendary Pin Oak Charity Horse Show, which benefited Texas Children's Hospital. He supported other institutions, such as the Houston Livestock Show and Rodeo and the Houston Symphony Orchestra. He was named Cultural Leader of the Year by the Houston Youth Symphony and Ballet in 1981. He said, "I don't read detective stories and I don't waste my leisure in playing cards. There is only so much time in a man's life and I think we ought to take advantage of what time we can get."[18] His wife, Adelena (1897–1967), was on the board of the Florence Crittendon Home for Unwed Mothers. Her hobby was making exquisite clothing for dolls, often auctioned off for charity.

— *Houston Metropolitan Research Center, Houston Public Library*

Dr. Michael Brown, left, and Dr. Joseph Goldstein, right, professors at the University of Texas Southwestern Medical School in Dallas, received the Nobel Prize in Medicine in 1985. It was the first medical Nobel ever awarded to Texans. Their mutual interest in the prevalence of heart disease among families led to the remarkable discovery of a complex tiny molecule which acts as a receptor of cholesterol into cells and designates it for metabolism. The two scientists isolated the human gene for low density lipoprotein (LDL) receptors. They noted that some families have defective genes, placing them at higher risk for heart disease and possible premature death. They also received the Albert D. Lasker Award in Basic Medical Research (1985) and in 1988, the National Medal of Science from President Ronald Reagan.
— *Photo by Gittings*

Dr. Ralph D. Feigin, shown with a young patient, is executive vice-president and physician-in-chief of the Texas Children's Hospital in Houston. He is also professor of pediatrics and chairman of the Department of Pediatrics at the Baylor College of Medicine. Dr. Feigin has lectured throughout the country and is a widely published expert in the field of pediatrics; his publications number over 300. His numerous honors include the McGovern Outstanding Faculty Member, Baylor College of Medicine, in 1986. He has been president of the Midwest Society for Pediatric Research and the Harris County Medical Society.

— Photo by Jim de Leon

Dr. William Cohn Levin was president of the University of Texas Medical Branch in Galveston (1974–1987) and is their Ashbel Smith Professor in the Department of Internal Medicine. He is also executive director of the Center for Health Manpower and Allied Health Sciences with the World Health Organization. Born in Waco, Dr. Levin has been active in many civic and social causes involving public health issues and has had numerous articles published in medical journals. His awards include the Nicholas and Katherine Leone Award for Administrative Excellence in 1977 and the Commandeur des Palmes Academiques in 1981 — the highest honor that can be conferred upon an academician by the French government. He was the president of Temple B'nai Israel in Galveston. His wife, Edna Seinsheimer Levin, is a member of a pioneer Galveston family. Her parents, Joe and Blanche Fellman Seinsheimer, were married in 1879. Her father, Joseph Fellman Seinsheimer, Jr., established the American Indemnity Insurance Company in 1913, the first of its kind in Texas.

— Photo by Korsh, Ottawa

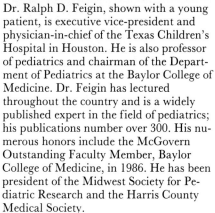

Dr. Ludwig Anigstein (1891–1975) traveled throughout the world as a surgeon and epidemiologist and for fifteen years was a member of the Malaria Commission of the League of Nations. From 1946 to 1975, Anigstein chaired the Preventive Medicine and Public Health departments at the University of Texas Medical Branch in Galveston.

— Rosenberg Library, Galveston, Texas

Harvey J. Graff is a professor of history at the University of Texas at Dallas. A social historian, Dr. Graff is internationally known for his books and articles on the history of literacy and the importance of that history to today's issues. Best known are his books *The Legacies of Literacy, The Labyrinths of Literacy: Literacy and Social Development in the West,* and *The Literacy Myth.* His works have appeared in foreign language editions and have brought him numerous awards and honors. Graff is currently writing a history of growing up in Anglo-America.

In 1988, Dr. Robert Abzug, professor of history at UT Austin, won the Friar Society's $15,000 award for excellence in teaching. The annual award, presented by the university's most prestigious honor society, is based on the evaluations of undergraduate students. Abzug, shown during his class on the Holocaust, said, "I just do what I like to do. It's very rewarding . . . like all awards given by students, you have a sense that that's your original audience. It's their response, it isn't filtered through academic politics."
— Austin American Statesman, *April 6, 1988, photo by Lynne Dobson-Keeble*

Robert S. Schechter is a professor of chemical and petroleum engineering at UT Austin who has done pioneer research in the study of the surface recovery of oil. Formerly the chairman of the Department of Petroleum Engineering, he is an internationally noted scientist, lecturer, and teacher. He has received many awards for teaching excellence and research, including the Chavalier dans l'Ordre Palmes Academiques from the French government (1980), the Billy and Claude Hocott Distinguished Centennial Engineering Research Award (1984), and the General Dynamics Award for excellence in teaching engineering (1987). He is a member of the National Academy of Engineering and the author of numerous books and articles.

— *Mary Ethel Schechter*

Dr. Ilene Busch-Vishniac is an award-winning acoustician and engineer who has developed micro robots designed to improve the manufacture of computer chips with potential medical applications. She was promoted to the rank of associate professor of mechanical engineering at UT Austin after only four years — six years is the norm. She was formerly with AT&T's Bell Labs in New Jersey.
— Austin American Statesman, *February 21, 1988*

Mark Yudof, pictured with his wife Judy, is the dean of the UT Austin Law School and a nationally recognized legal scholar. His book, *When Government Speaks: Politics, Law and Government Expression in America,* has won several awards. Judy Yudof is the president of New Milestones Foundation, Inc., a non-profit corporation which raises money for mental health. She is vice-chair of the Mental Health Advisory Committee to the Commission of the Texas Department of Mental Health-Mental Retardation, a past president of Congregation Agudas Achim in Austin, and a vice-president of the Southwest Region, United Synagogues of America.
— Austin American Statesman

Norma (Mrs. Mordecai) Podet, a native of Chicago, is a Waco social worker who served as chair of the McLennan Community College Board of Trustees from 1984 to 1986. She was first elected to the Board in 1977 and reelected for a second six-year term, ending in 1990. From 1974 to 1985, she was administrator of the Waco Family Home Care Agency. Her previous positions included director of in-service training at the Methodist Home (1965–1974) and adjunct associate professor at Baylor University, teaching courses in social work (1966–1971).

— *Norma Podet*

Aaron Farfel (1906–1988) was chairman of the Board of Regents of the University of Houston from 1971 to 1988. He was first appointed to its board in 1963. Farfel was a director of the Houston Chamber of Commerce and on the boards of the Houston Symphony and Alley Theatre. He was a leader in the American Jewish Committee, Jewish Family Service, Congregation Beth Yeshurun, and the Pauline Sterne Wolff Memorial Foundation.

— *The University of Houston*

Sam Barshop of San Antonio was appointed to the University of Texas Board of Regents in 1987. He is the owner of La Quinta Motor Inns, Inc. He has served as a trustee for a number of university and medical foundations and was chairman of the 1988 United Way of San Antonio and Bexar County. His wife, Ann, has been a leader of O.R.T., the Community Guidance Clinic, and the Longhorn Association for Excellence in Women's Athletics, UT Austin.

— *Sam Barshop*

Dr. Shirley Strum Kenny, the president of Queens College in New York, grew up in Tyler, the granddaughter of pioneer Tyler Jews. She has combined teaching and research with administrative leadership, and is the author of five books and numerous articles on Restoration and eighteenth-century British drama.

— *Shirley Strum Kenny*

Dr. Seth L. Wolitz has been Gale Professor of Jewish Studies at UT Austin since 1983. He organized the Jewish Studies Program and created the largest Yiddish-Hebrew literature collection in the Southwest. He is on the editorial board of *Tikkun*.

"Together we shall overcome bigotry, oppression, and lack of opportunity." — Rabbi David Jacobson

David Jacobson of San Antonio was the first rabbi to be elected president of the National Conference of Social Welfare in 1976. He served Temple Beth-El in San Antonio for fifty years (1938–1988); in 1942, he was elected senior rabbi, and in 1976 rabbi emeritus. In the 1980s, Rabbi Jacobson served Temple Mitzpah in Abilene one weekend each month. A leader in many ecumenical activities, he was president of United Community Services of Texas and the Worden School of Social Service at Our Lady of the Lake University. He received the Aristotle-Aquinas Award from the Catholic College Foundation.

Over the years, Jacobson and his wife, Helen, have been involved in the NAACP and the United Negro College Fund. In the early days of the civil rights movement, he helped desegregate public facilities which barred blacks and Hispanics. In 1989, he led the city's first freedom march on Martin Luther King Day and received the Martin Luther King Award for his "contributions towards keeping the dream alive." Mrs. Jacobson was on the national board of UNICEF and the National Council on Crime and Delinquency, and was president of the San Antonio Library Board.
— *Temple Beth El, San Antonio, copy from UT Institute of Texan Cultures*

Rabbi and Mrs. Charles Mantinband of Longview are pictured in 1970 at Camp Blue Star. Rabbi Mantinband went to Temple Emanuel in Longview at age sixty-eight in 1963, after an illustrious career in Alabama and Mississippi. One of the most courageous exponents of civil rights in the South, his activities in Hattiesburg, Mississippi, were documented in Harry Golden's *Our Southern Landman*. Mantinband was state president of the Mississippi Council on Human Relations and in 1962, received an award by the Stephen Wise Free Synagogue in New

York "for exceptional devotion to the causes of individual freedom and social justice." In 1963, John F. Kennedy invited him to participate in a conference on religion and race at the White House.[19] Mantinband was a member of the Southern Regional Council for twenty years. His wife was a talented book reviewer and active in community theater. Longview's Temple Emanuel also draws congregants from the nearby communities of Kilgore, Marshall, and Gladewater.
— *Mrs. Abram Ginsburg*

In 1968, the National Council of Jewish Women, Greater Dallas Section, began providing volunteers to help the staff at the Frederick Douglass School. The program became a model for all Dallas public school volunteer programs that followed.
— *National Council of Jewish Women, Greater Dallas Section*

There is little in the field of social services that has not felt the special touch of Austin resident Bert Kruger (Mrs. Sidney S.) Smith of Austin. She is a special consultant to the Hogg Foundation for Mental Health, having been associated with them since 1952. A widely recognized gerontologist, she is the author of seven books. Smith is president of the Austin Groups for the Elderly (AGE). Under her leadership, the group purchased the old Confederate Woman's Home and turned it into a multi-purpose facility providing low-cost space and enhancing cooperation among member agencies. She was chair of the Governor's Older Workers Task Force and has participated in several White House Conferences on Aging. The UT Austin School of Social Work established a Bert Kruger Smith Professorship in 1983, and in 1988 she was inducted into the Texas Women's Hall of Fame.

— Personal Collection of Bert Kruger Smith

Rabbi Robert Schur began to serve Temple Beth El in Fort Worth in 1956 and became rabbi emeritus in 1987. In the 1960s, he was involved in the civil rights movement, courageously marching in Fort Worth beside blacks and whites of all faiths to show sympathy after the shooting of Rev. James Reeb in Selma, Alabama. It was the first such local demonstration. He was active in other social causes, particularly counseling drug-addicted youths. Said Schur, "If young people are rebellious, it is based on their disappointment that adult society is not what it professes to be. They see the gap between principle and practice." He was the recipient of the National Conference of Christians and Jews Brotherhood Award in 1966.

Rabbi Mordecai Podet of Waco has long been an advocate for social services and civil rights. Before beginning to serve Temple Rodef Sholom in Waco in 1964, he was a chaplain during the Korean War. During his previous tenure as rabbi at Temple B'nai Israel in Salt Lake City, he testified before the Utah legislature on behalf of civil rights and mental health legislation. He has been chairman of the Waco Human Relations Commission and co-chaired the United Negro College Fund Drive. He is winner of the Humanitarian Award of the Waco Conference of Christians and Jews. He is the author of *Pioneer Jews of Waco* and was president of the Southwest Association of Reform Rabbis, and the Waco Ministerial Alliance. He retired in 1988.

— Mordecai Podet

Mrs. Yetta W. Edelstein received an award for over 3,000 hours of volunteer service as a member of the Brownsville Medical Center Auxiliary.

— Ruben Edelstein

Milton Brenner of San Antonio was one of the first retailers in town to hire black workers, including many in management positions, with the assistance of the NAACP, who helped him recruit qualified persons. He said, "I started hiring blacks for all jobs years before the Civil Rights Law . . . Our only standard was ability."

In 1919, Brenner's father, Isidore, started Solo Serve, one of the first department store chains which discounted fine clothing and dry goods. Milton later joined the business. During World War II, he was chief of finance for the Air Transport Command and received the Legion of Merit. In 1973, he successfully prevented San Antonio's power structure from ousting a large number of elderly widows from their homes. His fight was conducted in hearings before the Texas Senate.

— Marie Brenner

Leaders of the movement

Many Texas Jewish women have been leaders in the women's movement. Dr. Carolyn Galerstein was the first chair of the Dallas Commission on the Status of Women in 1975. The director of the state's first battered women's shelter was Lois Ahrens of Austin, c. 1975. Carolyn Farb of Houston has been a major fundraiser for the Ms. Foundation.

The Women's Haggadah was written and compiled by Frieda Werden and Dina Samfield in Austin around 1979, adapted from an earlier Lesbian *Haggadah* by Austinites Nina Wouk and Norma Funderberg.

Julia Wolf Mazow is the editor of *The Woman Who Lost Her Names: Selected Writings of American Jewish Women,* and is fiction editor of the Jewish women's magazine *Lilith.* She is co-chair of a Texas Jewish Feminist Conference scheduled in 1990, sponsored by the Houston chapter, American Jewish Committee.

Sherry Merfish is a Houston attorney whose campaign against the so-called "Jewish American Princess (JAP)" jokes has resulted in national media coverage and the organization of a special task force. Her position is that "JAP" jokes contribute to the negative stereotyping of Jewish women, the lowering of Jewish women's self-esteem, and an increase in anti-Semitism on college campuses.
— *Photo by Phyllis Segal and Roeanne Stern*

Gerry Beer of Dallas was founder and first president of the Family Place, a shelter for battered women and their children, which opened in 1979. A longtime civic leader, she chaired the Rhoads Terrace Project for pre-schoolers in an inner-city neighborhood sponsored by Temple Emanu-El and was a counselor at the Dallas Women's Center. In 1989, she received the Hannah G. Solomon Award of the NCJW, Greater Dallas Section.
— *Gerry Beer*

Hermine Tobolowsky, a Dallas attorney, is known as the Mother of the Texas Equal Legal Rights Amendment for leading a fifteen-year successful fight for its adoption. Texas voters, by a 4–1 majority, approved a state amendment to the Texas Constitution in 1972. Her victory resulted in the removal of forty discriminatory laws from the statutes.[20] She was inducted into the Texas Women's Hall of Fame in 1986.
— *Photo by Zavell's, Inc.*

Houstonites Adelyn Bernstein and Doris Nathan Lasher were founders and board members of the Houston Area Women's Center and organizers of the Women's Information Referral and Exchange Service (WIRES) in 1977. Bernstein chaired the United Women for an Effective Housing Code, an interfaith coalition of the Temple Emanu El Sisterhood, Church Women United, and the Diocesan Council of Catholic Women, which secured passage of a municipal minimum housing code. She also organized the

Temple's Committee for the Homeless and Women for Justice, a multi-purpose program for female inmates in the county jail.

Lasher has been active in the Family Service Center, the Florence Crittendon Home for Unwed Mothers, Lighthouse for the Blind, the Task Force Committee for the Homeless, and the Houston Public Library's Community Information Service.
— *Adelyn Bernstein*
— *Doris Nathan Lasher*

— Florence Frosch Blum

A nationally recognized expert, Billie Frauman of Dallas has worked in the field of human relations for thirty years. From 1956 to 1976, she was human relations specialist and Southwest regional director of the American Jewish Committee. The Dallas office was the first in the city to hire a black secretary in a job usually filled by a white.

— American Jewish Committee

Florence Frosch (Mrs. Ben) Blum of Houston began her volunteer career in the first grade when, "I was put in charge of a rag box for those who needed a hanky." Blum has been chair of the Interfaith Workshop and a volunteer at St. Joseph's Hospital, the Jewish Community Center, the YWCA, and Jewish Family Service, among many others.

— Florence Blum

Virginia (Mrs. Ben) Battelstein was the first woman president of the Jewish Home for the Aged (now Seven Acres), president of the Houston Section, NCJW, and chair of the UJA's President's Council. An author, artist, and actress, she was also secretary of the Houston Interfaith Housing Corporation.

— Photo by Gulf Photo, Houston

Miriam Mendell was president of the Houston League of Women Voters and a member of the state board. She served on the Board of the Institute of International Education. In 1985 she won an AJC Medallion of Achievement.

— Jewish Federation of Greater Houston

On July 3, 1989, members of the Greater Houston Section, National Council of Jewish Women, participated in a citywide pro-choice demonstration in front of the local federal building, along with 150 other advocates. L. to r., Cookie Portnoy, president, Deedee Ostfeld, Anita Cohen, Rosine Chappell, Ferne Winograd, Mady Amsterdam, and Jeanne Saletan. Other Jewish organizations with a pro-choice position include Hadassah, B'nai B'rith Women, the American Jewish Committee, the New Jewish Agenda, and National Federation of Temple Sisterhoods.

— National Council of Jewish Women, Greater Houston Section

Mark L. Briskman, regional director of the Anti-Defamation League of B'nai B'rith in Dallas (left) is pictured with the late Egyptian president Anwar Sadat (center), and Larry Schoenbrun (right), ADL Board chair, during an ADL Congressional mission to Israel and Egypt in 1980. — *Anti-Defamation League, Dallas*

This ad was placed by Joe Weingarten (1884–1967) in the *Houston Chronicle* on New Year's Day, 1966, during the early years of protest against the Vietnam War. Weingarten was the president and founder of the World Institute for World Peace to develop alternatives to war. Impressed during a 1950 visit to Israel with the traditional greeting, "Shalom Aleichem" (Peace be unto you), Weingarten began a personal crusade to promote world peace. In 1959, he visited European heads of state and Pope John XXIII to discuss his ideas. In 1965, Dr. Raga S. Elim of Egypt was hired as director.

Born in Poland, Joe came to the U.S. with his parents as a child. His father opened the first Weingarten's Grocery Store in downtown Houston in 1901. His mother's $300 nest egg helped buy the first store at Congress and Crawford. In 1920, Joe incorporated and opened a second store. He pioneered the concept of "cash and carry" self-service, and his chain of stores grew to a total of seventy by 1967. He was the first president of the Supermarket Institute of America and served on the boards of the Texas Medical Center and the Baylor Medical Foundation. Weingarten was a generous supporter of many Jewish institutions, including Congregation Beth Yeshurun and the Jewish Theological Seminary. Following World War II, he provided 1,000 blank affidavits guaranteeing that refugees would not be dependent on the government. He was the UJA chairman in 1949.
— *Jewish National Fund*

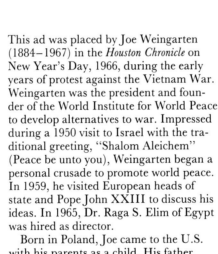

The late Thelma Vogel and Dr. Joan Weston hosted a meeting of Dallas Jewish leaders in August 1988 to foster a dialogue with Israeli women attending an International Peace Conference. The Israelis, both Jewish and Palestinian, live with their families in an experimental Arab-Jewish village, Neva Shalom, designed to build friendship between the two peoples.

Vogel was a founding member of the Southwest Region, American Jewish Congress, and a national officer. She was a leading activist for the homeless, helping organize in 1986 the Dallas Jewish Coalition for the Homeless and later a shelter for children of the homeless. She coordinated services to the Stew Pot, a downtown food program for the homeless. Thelma and her husband Phil Vogel were killed in a crash at Dallas-Fort Worth Airport on August 31, 1988. On June 4, 1989, the Thelma and Philip Vogel Child Care Center for the Homeless was dedicated. Their friends shared many personal memories of the Vogels' warmth. Gerry Beer remembered, "Who else would talk Yiddish in front of their dog when they had to leave him at home?"

Dr. Joan Weston has been an instructor of sociology and anthropology for the Dallas County Community College District since 1972. In 1989, she won their award for best instructor in the entire district. Weston has traveled extensively throughout the world, participating in conferences on conflict resolution and the development of school peace curricula programs. She was a founder of the Family Place, a Dallas shelter for battered women and their children. — *Photo by Ruthe Winegarten*

— **Sara Borschow Bormaster**

Dr. Joseph S. Werlin (1900–1964), a Houston sociologist, worked tirelessly to make Mexico better understood and appreciated by American students. He was honored in 1951 by Mexico with a medal of Distinguished Visitor. He helped found the People's Junior College at the Jewish Peoples Institute in Chicago. In 1934, he joined the faculty of the University of Houston, then known as the Houston Night School, and helped create the Department of Sociology. Werlin conducted field trips with his sociology classes to penal institutions. After World War II, he developed summer study centers for American students under the auspices of the University of Houston in Mexico, Cuba, Guatemala, and the Sorbonne in Paris.

— Rosella H. Werlin, copy from UT Institute of Texan Cultures

Sara Borschow Burmaster, an award-winning poet and author, won a Golden Poet Award in 1988 from the World of Poetry. Her pen name is Rita Barr. Formerly of San Antonio, she now lives in Joplin, Missouri.

— Sara Borschow Burmaster

Idelle Rabin of Dallas is pictured here with Njeri Mungai, Kenya's largest string bean farmer, at the International Women's Conference at Nairobi in 1985. She represented the American Jewish Committee as a national vice-president. Idelle and her husband Leon, also a national AJC leader, are owners of Delanns, a women's high-fashion store. They have made significant contributions to the world of art and intergroup relations. She was a founder of the Dallas Historical Society's Fashion Collection, an associate of the Dallas Museum of Fine Arts, and active in the Dallas Theatre Center and Dallas Civic Opera. She is a director of the National Association of Women Business Owners, Dallas/Fort Worth Chapter.

— Idelle Rabin

The Prayer: That Joyful Tomorrow
Rita Barr (Sara Borschow Bormaster)

(Dedicated in 1988 to USSR Secretary General Mikhail Gorbachev and U.S. President Ronald Reagan for their efforts to bring about international peace and understanding.)

Let the taproots of justice and truth
    sink far deeper
Than stones that are dropped in a
    bottomless pool;
And let each son of man be his
    brother's keeper
In a world whose *law* is the Golden
    Rule.

Let the children grow old without
    knowledge of hating,
For hate is the offspring of envy and
    fear;
Then the sweet wine of peace which
    the world is awaiting
Will flow from those hopes that our
    hearts have held dear.

There will be no more boundaries, no
    nations, no races . . .
But all men, as brothers, will walk in
    the light
With uplifted hearts and glad, radiant
    faces
Extolling the ultimate triumph of
    right.

And never again will there be want or
    sorrow,
And never again will a child be
    afraid —
Then, come, let us welcome that
    joyful tomorrow —
The day we have longed for . . . and
    hoped for . . . and prayed!

Julius and Helen Schwartz pose with their
son, Hirsh Nathan Schwartz (1909–1981),
in 1913. Hirsh grew up to become a business and civic leader, serving as mayor of
Schulenburg, a small town about sixty
miles west of Houston, from 1963 to 1981.
— *UT Institute of Texan Cultures*

11

FROM BIRTH TO OLD AGE TO REBIRTH

The synagogues and temples, organizations, societies, businesses, and schools are but skeletons of Jewish Texana. The flesh and blood and strength of any community lies with its people.

The heart of Jewish life has always been the family and the shared milestones and celebrations: births and deaths, weddings and *bar mitzvahs*, the holidays from Rosh Hashanah to Passover. Collective memory is full of the sound of broken glass under the *chupah*, shouts of *"Dayenu!"* at the *seder* table, and the voices of siblings and cousins playing after a family dinner into the twilight of a hot Texas summer night.

On these pages, we share our favorite photographs of holidays and life cycle events, from birth to old age to rebirth, from deep in the heart of Texas.

Annie (Mrs. Sam) Finger with her children, Rozella and Sammie, in Shepherd in 1916.

— *Mrs. Joe Kost*

Laura Hirshfeld of Austin.
— *Hirshfeld Papers (AR/H.24), Austin History Center, Austin Public Library*

Albert D. Lasker of Galveston.
— *Mrs. Albert Lasker, copied from John Gunther,* Taken at the Flood, *print from Barker Center, UT Austin*

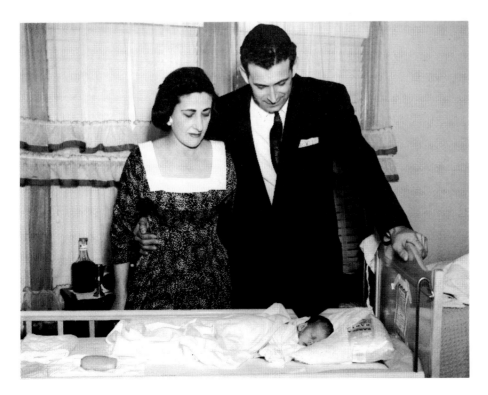

Sarah and Bill Winston admire their youngest son, Jaron Lerner Winston, on the day of his *bris,* March 1956, in Galveston.
— *Sarah and Bill Winston*

Jeanette and Moselle Littman of Austin win a doll in a children's cakewalk dance contest around 1910.
— *Queenie Littman Collection*

Members of Waco's Pansy Aid Society, pictured here, are (l. to r.), Juliette Cohn, Rosalie Hirshberg, and Carrie Sanger (Godshaw), c. 1895. The Pansy Aid Society, organized by Emma Beer in 1896 for Jewish children, raised money for charity through benefit shows. Ninety members paid monthly dues of ten cents.
— *The Texas Collection, Baylor University, Waco, Texas*

The Lewin cousins in South Dallas around 1908. (L. to r.), Ernestine Lewin (Feagans), her brother Leo Lewin, their first cousin Charles Lewin, and Morris Lewin (brother of Ernestine and Leo). Ernestine, Leo, and Morris Lewin have lived in Los Angeles since the late 1920s.
— *Mildred Lewin Baltar*

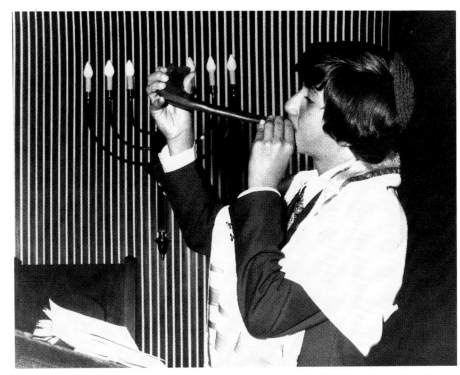

Aubrey Rubinsky blows the *shofar* at Temple Beth El to announce Rosh Chodesh (the new month) during his *bar mitzvah* in Brownsville, October 23, 1976.
   — *Sam and Eva Silberman private photo collection*

An unidentified young Dallas man seems to be dressed for his *bar mitzvah*. He is holding a book entitled *A Ritual of Jewish Soldiers*.
   — *From the Collections of the Dallas Jewish Historical Society, print by Andy Reisberg*

Temple Beth El confirmation class in Corsicana, 1927. (L. to r.), Natalie Dreeben (Rosenblum), Helen Goldman (Mrs. Milton) Kay, Rabbi Wolfe Macht (Waco), James H. Cerf, Gabe Goldberg, Sidney Marks and Sam Brooks, teachers, Elise Miller (Mrs. Leo) Davis, and Thelma Miller (Mrs. Jerry) Nasits.
   — *Natalie Rosenblum*

Dallas AZA members hold a Hobo Dance
in 1933.
— *From the Collections of the Dallas Jewish
Historical Society*

Before their marriage, Joe Meyer and
Edna Oppenheimer take a ride in 1904
around San Antonio's beautiful Brackenridge Park.
— *Mrs. Harry Halff, copy from UT Institute
of Texan Cultures*

In 1924, Bessie Antweil married Labe H. Golden in an elaborate Fort Worth wedding. Present were (l. to r.), first row: Estelle Shanblum, Marie Cohn, Ruth Gilbert, Ida Antweil, the bride Bessie Antweil, the groom Labe H. Golden, Lizzie Goldman, Fanny Antweil, Henrietta Wolf, and Bess Lipschitz. Second row: Melville Goldman, Mace Golden, Hannah Antweil, Dr. A. Antweil, Dr. Maurice Cohn, Sol Weinstein. Third row: Dr. M. Silverman and Eddie Gilbert. Flower girls in front are Jessonda Gilbert and Sylvia Silberman.

     — *Mr. and Mrs. L. H. Golden, copy from UT Institute of Texan Cultures*

"I will give you the dowry gift of your virginity."

Jewish religious marriages are solemnized by the signing in advance of a *ketubah* (marriage contract). Following is the text of the marriage contract of Ruben Gandler and Feigel Beerman, who were married in Waco.

The Ketubah of Ruben Gandler and Feigel Beerman, Sunday, September 1, 1916

On the fourth day of the week, the first day of the month of Elul of the year 5676 [i.e., Sunday, September 1, 1916] after the creation of the world according to the reckoning that we use, here at Waco, Texas . . . the bridegroom Reuveyn son of Reb (an honorific) Yakov Efrayim said to the virgin Feigel daughter of the Reb Menachem Mendel:

Be my wife according to the law of Moses and Israel, and I will work for, and honor, and nourish, and maintain you according to the practice ("halacha") of Jewish men, who work for and honor and nourish and maintain their wives on truth. I will give you the dowry gift of your virginity, 200 silver zuzim, that is due you according to the Torah, and your food, sufficiency [general needs], clothing, companionship [conjugal obligation] according to the way of all the earth.

And Miss Feigel daughter of Reb Menachem Mendel, the virgin, consented to be his wife. And the dowry which she brings with her from her father's house, whether in silver, gold, ornaments, clothing, household utensils or bedding, all this has received Reb Reuveyn son of Reb Yakov Efrayim, the groom, in the sum of 100 pure silver pieces.

And Reb Reuveyn son of Reb Yakov Efrayim, the groom, consented to add to this from his own another 100 pure silver pieces, the total amount being 200 pure silver pieces.

Newlyweds Anna Breier and Morris Gruber celebrate with family and friends on January 24, 1915, at the home of Mr. and Mrs. Bernard Gruber, 2913 Swiss Avenue, Dallas.

     — *From the Collections of the Dallas Jewish Historical Society, print by Andy Reisberg*

Alex and Alma Halff of San Antonio are
shown on their honeymoon trip to Bal-
anced Rock near Fredericksburg, January
1899. Behind them are their friends, Dave
and Ida Straus.

— *Mrs. Harry Halff, copy from UT Institute
of Texan Cultures*

The Garonziks enjoy a family *seder* in 1903 at 1400 Corinth in South Dallas. (L. to r.) Mary Garonzik Michaelson, Max Michaelson, Bertha Tobias Garonzik, Herbert Garonzik, Philip Garonzik, Uncle Harry Garonzik, Grandparents Matthias and Fannie Garonzik, Uncle Morris Garonzik, Israel Garonzik, Uncle Charlie Garonzik, and Will Garonzik.
— *From the Collections of the Dallas Jewish Historical Society*

A 1943 Purim celebration at Temple Emanu-El in Dallas. Because the holiday was celebrated during World War II, a number of the children dressed up as soldiers and nurses, and others as Adolph Hitler, who is likened to the traditional villain, Haman.
— *Dorothy M. and Henry S. Jacobus Temple Emanu-El Archives, print by Andy Reisberg*

Mrs. Rose Brilling of Houston lights the Hanukah candles in November 1959.
— *Copy from* Beth Israel Bulletin, *November 30, 1959*

Laredo Sunday school children celebrated Succoth in the backyard of Mr. and Mrs. Harry Granoff, c. 1938, before a congregation was formed in the city.
— *Blanche Sheiness*

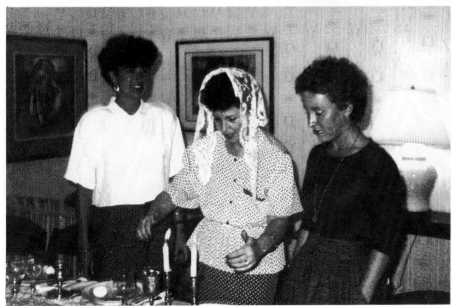

Eva Silberman, center, and her daughters, l. to r., Jackie Silberman and Marsha Silberman, bless the candles for the first night of Passover, April 1, 1988 in Brownsville.
— *Sam and Eva Silberman private photo collection*

Isaac Lazerowitz of Galveston was one of
the patriarchs pictured in *The Forward*, a
New York Yiddish newspaper, symboliz-
ing the patriarchs of old, around 1919.
— *The Texas Collection, Baylor University,
Waco, Texas*

Pauline Steiner Goldberg (1861–1942)
was born in Columbus, Texas, and lived
in many small Texas towns, including
Colesmaniel, Corrigan, Brenham, and
later Houston. She was widowed young
with five small children, and supported
the family in part by selling her handwork. Her granddaughter, Bettie
Schlamme, remembered that the greatest
treat of her childhood was to spend a day
with her "Nannie."
— *Bettie Westheimer Schlamme*

Rabbi Sheldon Zimmerman of Temple Emanu-El in Dallas blesses David Gerhardt on Shavuot, 1988. David is the son of Paula Schlinger and James Gerhardt.
— *Paula Schlinger and James Gerhardt*

Molly Suzanne (Ivria Miriam) Winston, born in Austin on July 30, 1988, embodies the Jewish experience in Texas as a descendant of both pioneer German Jews and Eastern Europeans, who came via the Galveston Movement. Molly, the daughter of Cathy Schechter and Jaron Winston, attends the Child Development Center at Temple Beth Israel in Austin.
— *Cathy Schechter*

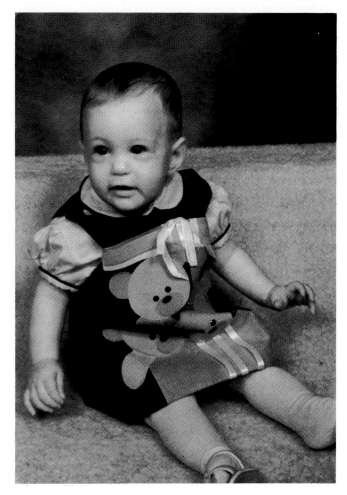

Note: unless otherwise indicated, foreign words are in Hebrew and translations are found in the parentheses.

aliyah (going up): refers either to immigration to Israel, or to one who is called to the *Torah* to recite one of the blessings before and/or after reading of the text.

auto de fé: the ceremony accompanying the pronouncement of judgment by the Inquisition and followed by the execution of sentence by the secular authorities. (Spanish)

bar mitzvah [male], *bat mitzvah* [female]: lit. (son/daughter of the commandment) refers both to the person who has attained religious maturity (thirteen for boys, twelve or thirteen for girls) as well as the occasion at which this status is assumed.

bimah: the raised platform from which the worship service is read and/or upon which the reading table for the *Torah* rests.

bris/brit milah (covenant of circumcision): the ceremony at which male children are circumcised on the 8th day after birth and enter into the covenant of Abraham.

brit: covenant between God and the children of Israel.

challah: egg bread, usually braided, served on Sabbaths.

Chanukah: (Hanukah) commemorates the rededication of the Temple of Jerusalem after its defilement by Antiochus of Syria, probably the first struggle for religious freedom in world history. Candles are lit for eight days.

chasid (pious one): originally referred to Jewish mystics; now refers to offshoot groups that formed the movement started by the *Baal Shem Tov* in Poland, c. 1700.

chavurah (company, group, fellowship): a recent movement among American Jews to organize small, informal, family-like groups for prayer, study, and/or celebration of Jewish festivals.

chazan: one who chants at a ritual event or prayer service.

cheder (room): general term for afternoon Hebrew school.

converso: one who converted to Christianity from Judaism during the time of the Spanish Inquisition. (Spanish)

crypto-Jew: a modern term for *converso* used by some historians.

frum: one who is observant of Jewish ritual (Yiddish).

Galitzianer: a person from Galicia.

Gemorah: ninth/tenth century compiled commentary on the *Mishnah;* called the *Talmud* when in combination with the *Mishnah.*

goldena medina (golden state): a Yiddish term used in Europe to refer to the United States with its "streets of gold."

Haganah (defense): The underground military organization of the settlers in Palestine during the British rule from 1920 to 1948. With the establishment of the State of Israel, the *Haganah* became the official army of the state.

Haggadah: prayerbook used for the Passover *seder.*

halacha (path/way): Jewish law encompassing both the written *Torah* and the oral tradition.

hamentashen: fruit-filled pastry eaten on Purim, in the shape of Haman's three-cornered hat.

hanukiyah: nine-branched candelabrum used in the observance of Chanukah.

Haskalah (enlightenment): a movement to promote modern European culture among Jews during 1700s and 1800s.

kashrut (fit): refers to Jewish dietary laws.

ketubah: a Jewish marriage contract.

Kol Nidre: the major prayer of *Yom Kippur* (the Day of Atonement).

Litvak: a Jew from Lithuania.

Marrano: a term for converts to Christianity from Judaism during the Spanish Inquisition. (Spanish)

m'chitzah: the partition which separates a men's seating section from a women's section in a synagogue, usually found in Orthodox congregations.

menorah: the seven-branched candelabrum used in the tabernacle and temple.

mikveh (pool, hope): a ritual pool of water used for purification.

minhag: custom or practice in Jewish tradition.

minyan: a quorum of ten men required for certain communal activities including some prayer services.

Mishnah: traditional doctrines originally transmitted and committed to writing in the third century.

mitzvah (commandment): deeds performed by Jews in the observance of Judaism.

mohel: ritual circumciser.

New Christian: see *Marrano.*

Passover (Pesach): An eight-day holiday in the spring commemorating the deliverance of the Jews from bondage in Egypt.

Pentateuch: five books of Moses; first five books of the Hebrew scriptures; Torah.

Pesach: Passover.

Purim: Festival of Lots, marking the deliverance of the Jews from Haman's plot to exterminate them (Book of Esther).

Rosh Hashanah: religious New Year celebrated in the fall.

schochet: ritual slaughterer who insures observance of dietary laws.

schule: school (Yiddish).

seder: ritual service for a Passover dinner in tradition of Haggadah.

Sepher Torah: a parchment scroll containing the first five books of the Torah.

Shabbat (sabbath): the seventh day of the week which extends from sundown Friday to sundown Saturday, in Yiddish, *shabbas.*

shamas: guard; sexton of a synagogue.

shaygetz: non-Jewish male (Yiddish).

shofar: the ram's horn used in ritual services.

shtetl: village (Yiddish).

shul: synagogue (Yiddish).

Simchat Torah (rejoicing in the Torah): an observance at the end of *Sukkot* celebrating the conclusion of the reading of the Torah reading cycle and the beginning again of that cycle.

Sukkot (booths): the fall pilgrimage festival commemorating the Jewish wandering in the desert following the Exodus.

talith: prayer shawl.

Talmud: rabbinic literature containing the *Mishnah* and the *Gemorah* compiled in the ninth/tenth centuries; two compilations, Babylonian and Jerusalem.

Talmud Torah: religious school.

Torah (teaching): refers to the first five books of Moses, as well as the entire body of all Jewish literature.

tzedakah: charity; good deeds.

Yeshivah: Jewish academy.

Yom Kippur: Day of Atonement.

SELECTED EVENTS RELATING TO TEXAS JEWISH HISTORY

1579 Don Luis de Carvajal, a Portuguese *converso*, is appointed governor by Spanish king of the New Kingdom of Leon (what is now South Texas and northern Mexico). He and family members, most of whom secretly practice Judaism, are victims of the Inquisition.

1826 Adolphus Sterne, a German Jew, settles in Nacogdoches, becomes *alcalde* (mayor), treasurer, postmaster, and keeps a diary.

1835–1836 A handful of Jews fight in various battles for Texas independence (Goliad, the Alamo, San Jacinto), including Dr. Moses A. Levy, surgeon-in-chief of Texas Army.

1836 Eugene Chimene, a veteran of Battle of San Jacinto, settles in Houston.

1839 Jacob de Cordova settles in Houston; Isadore Dyer, Joseph and Rosanna Osterman settle in Galveston.

1842 Henri Castro founds Castroville.

1845 Jacob de Cordova founds De Cordova Land Agency in Houston.

1847 Adolphus Sterne and Jacob de Cordova become first Jews elected to Texas legislature.

1848 Simon Mussina founds Brownsville.

1849 Jacob de Cordova is a founder of Waco.

1850s Schutze brothers open a store in El Paso.

1852 Galveston Jews establish city's first Jewish cemetery, consecrated by Rev. M. N. Nathan from New Orleans; possibly first time a rabbi officiates in Texas.

1853 Michael Seeligson is elected mayor of Galveston.

1854 Houston Jewish cemetery is established.

1855 Lewis Levy forms Texas' first Jewish organization in Houston, the Hebrew Benevolent Society.

1856 San Antonio Jewish cemetery is founded.

1857 Sanger Bros. is founded in McKinney by Isaac Sanger.

1858 Jewish section of city cemetery is set aside in Victoria.

Alexander and Julia Simon are first Jews to settle in Dallas.

1859 Hebrew Congregation Beth Israel, Houston, is chartered.

1860 Rev. Zachariah Emmich, Houston's Congregation Beth Israel, is Texas' first resident rabbi.

1862 Jefferson Mt. Sinai Cemetery is founded.

1864 Religious school is organized by Houston women.

1861–65 Texas Jews fight in both Union and Confederate armies.

1866 Rosanna Osterman bequeaths large sums to build synagogues in Houston and Galveston, as well as many Jewish and non-sectarian institutions.

1867 Julius Joske opens a store in San Antonio.

1868 Congregation B'nai Israel, Galveston, oldest Texas temple established from beginning as Reform, is chartered.

Hebrew Benevolent Society is organized in Marshall.

1870 Temple B'nai Israel in Galveston and Temple Beth Israel in Houston dedicate buildings.

Texas' first Ladies Hebrew Benevolent Society is organized in San Antonio.

1872 Victoria's Temple Beth Israel is organized.

1873 Jefferson Hebrew Sinai Congregation buys building from Catholic Sisters for synagogue.

Texas' first B'nai B'rith lodge is founded in Waco.

1874 First Jewish Community Center program begins in Houston.

1875 First synagogue in South Texas, Temple Beth-El in San Antonio, dedicated.

1876 Temple Beth Israel, Austin, is founded.

Temple Emanu-El in Dallas is chartered and sponsors non-

sectarian school.

Moritz Kopperl represents Galveston in state legislature.

1879 John Peter Smith donates land for Hebrew cemetery in Fort Worth.

YMHA is formed in Dallas.

1880 Texas rabbis organize system of "circuit preaching."

1880s and 1890s A number of Orthodox synagogues are founded, including Shearith Israel (Dallas), B'nai Abraham (Brenham), Agudas Jacob (Waco), Agudas Achim (San Antonio), Adath Yeshurun (Houston), Ahavath Shalom (Fort Worth).

1881 Solomon Schutz is elected mayor of El Paso.

Sid Samuels and Belle Doppelmayer are in UT-Austin's first graduating class.

Hebrew Immigrant Aid Society sends colonists to Texas to farm.

Temple Rodef Sholom, Waco, is dedicated.

1887 Temple Beth El is chartered in Tyler.

1888 Rabbi Henry Cohen comes to B'nai Israel in Galveston.

1892 Olga Kohlberg, El Paso, organizes state's first private kindergarten.

1895 Morris Lasker, Galveston, is elected to Texas Senate.

1897 Dr. Sigmund Burg organizes Zionist group in San Antonio.

1898 Temple Mt. Sinai is founded in El Paso.

1899 Leo N. Levi is the first Jew to deliver commencement address at UT.

1900s First interfaith activity in Dallas is Silver Tea to benefit a non-sectarian ladies' home for the elderly.

1900 There are 15,000–17,500 Jews and about twenty B'nai B'rith lodges in Texas.

Congregation B'nai Zion, El Paso, is organized, and Moses Montefiore, Marshall, dedicates temple.

Great Storm devastates Galveston.

1901 Texas' first chapter, National Council of Jewish Women, founded in Beaumont.

1903 Leo N. Levi, Galveston, frames Kishinev Petition protesting massacre of Russian Jews.

Congregation Ahavath Achim, Orthodox, is chartered in Tyler.

1904 Charles Brachfield, Henderson, is elected state senator.

1905 Texas Zionist Association is organized by Dr. Sigmund Burg, president.

1906 Houston *Jewish Herald Voice* is founded and Jewish Literary Society is organized.

1907–1914 Galveston Movement: 10,000 European Jews come through Galveston for resettlement.

1907 Neiman-Marcus is founded in Dallas.

Victor Hexter is president of Dallas School Board.

1909 Anna Hertzberg becomes one of the first women elected to public office in Texas upon winning seat on San Antonio school board. In 1911, she is president, Texas Federation of Women's Clubs.

1910 Simon and Tobias Sakowitz open Houston store.

B'nai B'rith, under Henry J. Dannenbaum of Houston, campaigns against prostitution.

1911 Godcheaux A. Levi is president of state's first United Jewish Charities in Dallas.

Alex Sanger, Dallas, becomes first Jew appointed to UT

Board of Regents.

1913 Jewish Welfare Association founded in Houston by merging a number of organizations.

1914 Hadassah founder Henrietta Szold establishes one of the first Texas chapters in Wharton.

1916 UT regent Rabbi Maurice Faber of Tyler defies Governor Jim Ferguson's efforts to control UT.

1917 Isaac Kempner is elected mayor of Galveston.

Rabbi Martin Zielonka, El Paso, promotes concept of Jewish chaplains in U.S. Army.

1917–1918 Texas Jews serve in armed forces and on home front during World War I.

1920s San Antonio has two Jewish newspapers, *Jewish Journal* and *Jewish Record*.

Resurgence of Ku Klux Klan in Texas.

1920 Texas Jewish population is about 30,000.

1922 Rabbi Henry Cohen chairs CCAR committee which favors ordination of women as rabbis.

1923 El Paso oilman Haymon Krupp brings in Santa Rita Oil Well #1, producing millions of dollars in royalties for UT System's Permanent Fund. West Texas oil boom results in growing Jewish population and construction of new temples.

1924 Zionist leader Chaim Weitzman visits Dallas.

1925 Dallas attorney Hattie Henenberg is appointed to special state All-Woman Supreme Court.

1926 Charles Brachfield, Henderson, is the first Jew to run for statewide office — attorney general — but loses.

1927 Kallah of Texas Rabbis is founded in Houston.

1929 Hillel Foundation and first Jewish fraternity, Phi Sigma Delta, are founded at UT Austin.

1930s Anti-Zionist American Council for Judaism opens Dallas office.

There is a Jewish Art Theatre in Dallas, and Arbeiter Rings (Workmen's Circles) in several cities.

1934 Meyer Perlstein, Southwest ILGWU organizer, begins organizing Texas garment workers.

1936 Jewish Community Council of Houston is founded.

Fred Florence, Dallas, is president of Texas Centennial Exposition.

Ben and Jacob Taub donate land for University of Houston.

1937 Women win right to vote in congregational matters of Houston's Temple Beth Israel.

1941–45 Texas Jews serve in armed forces and on home front during World War II.

1942 Home for Aged Sons and Daughters of Israel is organized in Houston.

1943 Conflict over Zionism erupts in Houston's Congregation Beth Israel, resulting in split and formation of Temple Emanu El.

1944 Forerunner of Dallas Jewish Home for Aged is founded.

1945 Texas Jewish population about 50,000.

1947 *Texas Jewish Post* is founded in Fort Worth.

1948 Texas Jews support establishment of State of Israel by UN.

1950s–1960s Many Jews, including Reform rabbis, work for peaceful desegregation and in civil rights movement.

1951 Dallas Jews protest anti-Semitic book, *Iron Curtain Over Amer-*

ica, by SMU professor Dr. John Beaty.

Houston JCC building is dedicated.

1952 Dr. Ray Daily is defeated by McCarthyite opponent after serving on Houston School Board for twenty-four years.

1953 Golden Acres Dallas Jewish Home for Aged dedicates building.

1954 Congregation Beth Yeshurun, Houston, founds first congregational day school in U.S. offering secular and religious education.

1960 A. R. "Babe" Schwartz, Galveston, is elected to Texas Senate.

1962 Julius Schepps Community Center, Dallas, is dedicated.

1963 President Lyndon B. Johnson dedicates Congregation Agudas Achim's new building in Austin.

1964 Houston's charity hospital is named for Ben Taub.

1966 Irving L. Goldberg of Dallas becomes first Jew in the South appointed to a federal judgeship; is named to 5th Circuit Court of Appeals by President Lyndon B. Johnson.

1967 Dallas Federation raises $3.5 million in twenty-four hours on heels of Six-Day War in Israel.

1970s Texas Jews organize in support of Soviet Jews' right to emigrate.

Women's movement results in increased leadership and ritual roles for Texas Jewish women.

1971 Founding of Dallas Jewish Archives.

1972 Ratification of Texas Equal Legal Rights Amendment to Texas Constitution by Texas voters, in a 4–1 majority, spearheaded by Dallas attorney Hermine Tobolowsky.

1973 Texas Jews organize political support for Israel at time of Yom Kippur War.

1974 Robert Strauss is chairman, Democratic National Committee.

Helen Smith, Austin, is international president, B'nai B'rith Women.

1977 Texas has 71,000 Jews.

Gerry Beer founds Dallas' first shelter for battered women.

1978 Dallas attorney Martin Frost is elected to U.S. House of Representatives.

1980 Texas Jewish Historical Society is founded by Rabbi Jimmy Kessler.

Texas has its first female rabbi — Temple Emanu-El in Dallas hires Rabbi Ellen Lewis.

1981 Debra Danburg, Houston, becomes first Jewish woman elected to state legislature.

1982 Ruby Sondock is appointed to fill an unexpired term on Texas Supreme Court; first woman and Jew to serve.

1984 Dallas Memorial Center for Holocaust Studies opens.

1987 Annette Strauss is elected mayor of Dallas.

1988 Texas has 92,000 Jews (.6 percent of state's population). U.S. has 5.9 million Jews (2.5 percent of nation's population).

Texas' first chapter, New Jewish Agenda, is founded in Austin.

1989 Rabbi Samuel Karff, Temple Beth Israel, Houston, is elected president, Central Conference of American Rabbis.

Austin History Center = archival collection of Austin at Austin Public Library
Barker = Barker Texas History Center, University of Texas at Austin
TJHS = Texas Jewish Historical Society; collection at Barker Texas History Center, UT Austin

CHAPTER 1

1. Jacob Beller, *Jews in Latin America* (New York: Jonathan David, 1969), 2.
2. Carlos Montalvo Larralde, "Chicano Jews in South Texas," Ph.D. dissertation, Univ. of Calif. at Los Angeles, 1978.
3. Richard G. Santos, "Chicanos of Jewish Descent in Texas," *Western States Jewish Historical Quarterly* 15, no. 4 (July 1983); "Crypto-Jews in New Mexico," *All Things Considered*, National Public Radio, April 3, 1988.
4. Harriet and Fred Rochlin, *Pioneer Jews — A New Life in the Far West* (Boston: Houghton Mifflin, 1984), 1–3.
5. Nathan Ausubel, *Pictorial History of the Jewish People* (New York: Crown, 1954), 211.
6. Cleofas Calleros, El Paso, letter to Frances Kallison, December 14, 1966; Calleros, El Paso, letter to Seymour B. Liebman, September 20, 1966; Liebman, Miami, FL, letter to Frances Kallison, September 27, 1966 (TJHS Coll., Inquisition file).
7. Carlos E. Castañeda, *Our Catholic Heritage in Texas*, Vol. I. (Austin: 1936), 181–184; Dorothy Hull, "Castaño de Sosa's Expedition to New Mexico in 1590," *Old Santa Fe* 3, no. 12 (October 1916): 307–332.
8. Susan A. Roberts and Calvin A. Roberts, *New Mexico* (Albuquerque: 1988), 1–2.
9. Martin A. Cohen, *The Martyr* (Philadelphia: Jewish Pub. Society, 1973), 249.
10. *Ibid.*
11. *Ibid.*, 256.

CHAPTER 2

1. *Galveston Daily News*, December 18, 1921, 16.
2. Harold Sharfman, *Jews on the Frontier* (Chicago: Regency, 1977), 132–154.
3. B. Korn, "American Jewish Life in 1849," in *Eventful Years and Experiences; Studies in 19th Century American Jewish History* (Cincinnati: American Jewish Archives, 1954), 29; Lester G. Bugbee, "The Old Three Hundred," *Quarterly of Texas State Historical Association* I (1897–1898); Rabbi Henry Cohen et al., *100 Years of Jewry in Texas* (Chicago: 1936), 6; Maud Isaacs and Judge Samuel Isaacks, "Isaacks Family" (El Paso, 1955), 4–5; Texas State Archives, Genealogy Dept.
4. *Occident* IV (1846): 270–271.
5. According to Halacha (Jewish law), being born of a non-Jewish mother, Sterne would not be recognized as Jewish. He apparently identified himself as Jewish, as witness references in his diary.
6. Archie McDonald, ed., *Hurrah For Texas! The Diary of Adolphus Sterne, 1838–1851* (Austin: Eakin, 1986), xii.
7. Henry Cohen, "Settlement of the Jews in Texas," *Pubs. of the American Jewish Hist. Society*, no. 2 (1894): 141.
8. McDonald, *passim*.
9. Saul Vierner, "Surgeon Moses Albert Levy: Letters of a Texas Patriot," *Pub. of the American Jewish Hist. Soc.* 46, nos. 1–4 (September 1956–June 1957): 105.
10. Bernard Postal and Lionel Koppman, *American Jewish Landmarks*, 2nd ed., vol. 2, *The South and Southwest* (New York: 1979), 257; Julie Hilton Danan, "The Jews of Texas — A Sesquicentennial Retrospective," *Jewish Journal of San Antonio*, August, p. 10, col. 2.
11. Henry Cohen, et al., *100 Years of Jewry*, 9–10.
12. Daniel N. Leeson, "In Search of the History of the Texas

Patriot Moses A. Levy — Part I," *Western States Jewish History* 21, no. 4 (1989): 292.
13. Vierner, *passim;* Leeson, 291–306; Entry no. 48, Episcopal Parish of Christ Church register, Matagorda, Texas, May 23, 1848; letter received from Jessie Foss, August 1, 1989.
14. Vierner, 105–109.
15. David L. Kokernot, "Reminiscences," *Gonzales Inquirer*, August 17, 1878, rpt. *Gonzales Inquirer*, July 19, 1923.
16. *Ibid.*
17. Steven G. Kellman, "The Yellow Rose of Texas," *Journal of American Culture* (Summer 1982): 45–48.
18. Jacob de Cordova, *Texas, Her Resources and Her Public Men*, 1st ed. (Philadelphia: Lippincott, 1858), 21.
19. Henry Cohen, "The Jews in Texas," in *Pubs. of the American Jewish Historical Society*, no. 4 (1895): 1–7.
20. Henry Samuel Morais, *The Jews of Philadelphia* (Philadelphia: Levytype Co., 1894), 45, 445-A.
21. Cohen, "The Jews in Texas," 5.
22. Frances Kallison, "Phineas de Cordova," *Texas Jewish Historical Society Newsletter* (Spring 1987): 3.
23. de Cordova, *Texas, Her Resources*, 22.
24. *Ibid.*, 64.
25. *Ibid.*, 28.
26. *Ibid.*, 22.
27. *Ibid.*, 21.
28. *Ibid.*, 24.
29. *Asmonean* [New York], May 24, 1850.
30. Cohen, et al., *100 Years of Jewry*, 13–15.
31. Bobby D. Weaver, *[Henri] Castro's Colony: Empresario Development in Texas, 1842–1865* (College Station: Texas A&M Press, 1985); Henry Cohen, "Henry Castro, Pioneer and Colonist," *Pubs. of the American Jewish Historical Society*, no. 5 (1897): 40–43; Texas Historical Commission (Austin), unpublished paper, "The Henry Castro Homestead," December 8, 1975.
32. Walter P. Webb, et al., eds., *Handbook of Texas*, vol. 2 (Austin: Texas State Hist. Assn., 1952), 253; Cohen, et al., *100 Years of Jewry*, 8–9.
33. Corinne A. Krause, "The Jews in Mexico, 1857–1930," Ph.D. dissertation, Univ. of Pittsburgh, 1970. (Microfilm #4562 at Benson Latin American Collection, UT Austin.)
34. Ysleta Edition, *El Paso Times*, April 1, 1881.
35. Carol Tefteller, "Diaspora to Texas, or, The Jewish Community in Frontier Jefferson" (Jefferson: c. 1974), unpublished paper, 2. (TJHS Coll., Jefferson file.)
36. *Tri-Weekly Telegraph* [Houston], December 20, 1860.
37. Frances Kallison, "100 Years of Jewry in San Antonio," thesis, Trinity Univ., San Antonio, 1977, *passim*.
38. *Occident* V (1852): 58–59.
39. Rebecca H. Mayer, typescript (Chicago: April 23, 1917). (American Jewish Archives.)
40. Information about early-day San Antonio from Frances Kallison, "100 Years of Jewry in San Antonio."
41. Rev. M. N. Nathan's remarks at the dedication of the Hebrew Cemetery No. 1 on August 29, 1852, were published in the *Occident* X and reprinted in A. Stanley Dreyfus, "Hebrew Cemetery No. 1 of Galveston" (Galveston, March 22, 1965). (Rosenberg Library, Galveston.)
42. Dreyfus, "Hebrew Cemetery No. 1."
43. Henry Cohen Papers (Barker Center, Box 3Y16).
44. Henry Samuel Morais, *The Jews of Philadelphia*, 406; Henry Cohen Papers, Draft of Henry Cohen's article for *Pubs of American*

Jewish Hist. Soc. (Box 3M325, Barker Center); David Kaufman vertical file (Texas State Archives, Genealogy Dept.)

45. *Occident* 19 (June 1853).

46. Henry Cohen, et al., *100 Years of Jewry,* 29; Morais, 406; Letter to Jimmy Kessler from Kevin R. Young, Goliad County Hist. Com., February 16, 1987 (TJHS Coll., Michael Seeligson File).

47. Cohen, et al., *100 Years,* 11–12; James E. and Jennie Noland Johnson, "The George Seeligson House at 1208 Ball, Galveston, Texas," unpublished paper, Texas Hist. Com., Austin, n.d.

48. Letter to Rosanna Osterman from three Confederate soldiers, reprinted in Charles W. Hayes, *History of the Island and the City of Galveston* (Cincinnati: N.p., 1879; rpt. Austin: Jenkins Garrett Press, 1974), 2: 891–892.

49. Henry Cohen Papers (Barker Center, Box 3Y16, caption under photo of Isadore Dyer home).

50. Cohen, et al., *100 Years,* 10–11, 19; *Galveston News,* December 18, 1921 (Dyer Scrapbook, Rosenberg Library); Hayes, 891–894; Elizabeth Turner, "Rosanna Dyer Osterman," unpublished article, Houston, 1989.

51. Rosanne Leeson, "Brief Description of the Life of Mary A. Levy," typescript (Los Altos, Calif., 1989); Deed, Jacob de Cordova to Mary L. Levy, March 2, 1844; Deed, Sam Houston to Lewis A. Levy, November 11, 1843. (Copies in private collection of Rosanne Leeson.)

52. Information about the early history of Houston comes from Helena Schlam, "The Early Jews of Houston," thesis, Ohio State Univ., 1971; Annie Nathan Cohen, *The Centenary History, Congregation Beth Israel of Houston, Texas, 1854–1954* (Houston: privately published, 1954).

53. Morris Lasker, "Letter from a Texas Pioneer," *Menorah Journal* 24 (April 1936): 193–203; Leon Rosenberg, *Sangers: Pioneer Texas Merchants* (Austin: Texas State Hist. Assn., 1978), 9–11.

54. Adah Isaacs Menken, "To the Sons of Israel," *American Israelite* 5, no. 30 (June 28, 1859): 236.

55. Leo Shpall, "Adah Isaacks Menken," *Louisiana Hist. Quarterly* 26 (January–October 1943), 162–168.

56. Adah Isaacs Menken, *Infelicia* (New York, London, Paris: n.p., 1868), 86–91.

57. Shpall, 162–168; Menken, *Infelicia;* Jacob R. Marcus, *The American Jewish Woman: A Documentary History* (New York and Cincinnati: 1981), 273–285; Edward T. James, et al., eds., *Notable American Women 1607–1950,* vol 2, "Adah Isaacs Menken," 526–529.

58. *San Antonio Daily Herald,* December 17, 1859.

59. Harry Landa, *As I Remember* (San Antonio: Carleton, 1945), 26–27; Landa Estate, *The Oasis of Texas,* 2nd ed. (San Antonio: 1904), *passim.*

60. "Auntie" Clara Anderson, "Slave Narratives of Travis County," 13–14, typescript. (Austin History Center, Austin Public Library.)

61. Gen. T. L. Waul's testimonial was written in a letter to Leo N. Levi, May 17, 1894, and reprinted in *Galveston Daily News,* June 10, 1894.

62. Cohen, et al., *100 Years of Jewry,* 9; Phil Hewitt, *The Jewish Texans* (San Antonio: UT Institute of Texan Cultures, 1984), 7.

63. Letter to Ruthe Winegarten from Frances Kallison, December 15, 1988.

64. Myer Levy, "A History of Navasota Citizens of the Jewish Faith," typescript (Box 2C 493, TJHS Coll.).

65. Quoted in Schlam, 57.

66. Waul, letter to Leo N. Levi, May 17, 1894.

67. August Bondi, *The Autobiography of August Bondi, 1833–1907* (Galesburg, IL: His [Bondi's] Sons and Daughters, 1910), 30.

68. Telephone interview with Pauline Schlinger Frankl, February 1989. (TJHS Coll., Leopold Schlinger file.)

69. Robert Shosteck, "Leopold Karpeles: Civil War Hero," *American Jewish Hist. Quarterly* 52 (September 1962–June 1963): 220–233.

70. Bondi, 30–31; Morris U. Schappes, *The Jews in the United States 1654–1875* (New York: Citadel, 1950), 352ff, 666ff.

CHAPTER 3

1. Louis Schmier, ed., *Reflections of Southern Jewry: The Letters of Charles Wessolowsky* (Macon, GA: Mercer Univ., 1982), 86–87.

2. Isaac Metzger, *A Bintel Brief* (New York: Behrman House, 1971), 1: 97.

3. William Toll, "Judaism as a Civic Religion in the American West," in *Religion and Society in the American West,* ed. by Carl Guerneri and David Alvarez (Lanham, MD and London, England: Univ. Press of America, 1987), 197–219.

4. Judy Cohen, biographical sketch of Samuels family, Fort Worth Jewish Community Sesquicentennial Archives, 1986.

5. Documents and biographical information about the Kuttner family (Texas Collection, Baylor University).

6. David Carb, *Sunrise in the West* (N.p.: 1931); Ted E. Frank, "The Image of the German-American Immigrant in Historical Fiction: An Analysis of David Carb's *Sunrise in the West,*" typescript (UT Arlington, n.d.). (Tarrant County Historical Commission; Fort Worth Jewish Community Sesquicentennial Archives.)

7. All information from Hirshfeld Family Papers (Austin History Center, Austin Pub. Lib.)

8. Mrs. Arch McKay and Mrs. H. A. Spellings, *A History of Jefferson,* 20th printing (Jefferson: n.p., n.d.), 42–43.

9. Jacob Sterne, Civil War letters. Jefferson Museum, comp. J. A. R. Mosley.

10. Carol Tefteller, "The Jewish Community in Frontier Jefferson," *Texas Historian* 35, no. 1 (Austin: September 1974), 2–7.

11. Eva Sterne, *The Little Immigrant, A True Story* (New York: privately printed, 1921).

12. *Ibid.,* 84–85.

13: *Ibid.,* 40–42.

14. Mrs. Richard G. Mayer, "Memoir and Genealogy of the Ferdinand and Jette Steiner Mayer Family 1832–1971," typescript (San Angelo: 1972). (American Jewish Archives; TJHS Coll., Ferdinand Mayer file.)

15. Kallison, 88–90.

16. The stable is shown on a lithograph of a January 1, 1869, map of Houston.

17. Interview with Hettie Westheimer Ray, Houston paper, July 8, 1951. (TJHS Coll., Box 2C 495, Westheimer file.)

18. "Westheimer—If You Don't Know the Name, You Don't Live in Houston," *Jewish Herald Voice,* April 24, 1986, 104–106; "Hurwitz-Wagner, An Early Wedding of Note," *Jewish Herald Voice,* 107–108. (TJHS Coll., Westheimer and Hurwitz Files.)

19. Personal interviews with Helene Levy, Galveston, May 1988. (TJHS Coll., Levy Funeral Home File.)

20. John Gunther, *Taken at the Flood* (New York: Harpers, 1960), 22.

21. Phil Hewitt, *The Jewish Texans,* 8; Morris Lasker, "Letter from a Texas Pioneer — 1909," *Western States Jewish Historical Quarterly* 15, no. 4 (July 1983): 305–316; Morais, 184–186; Elizabeth Turner, Houston, unpublished research about Mrs. Morris Lasker; Nettie Lasker obituary, *Galveston Tribune,* 19 and 20 June 1930; Gunther, *Taken at the Flood, passim.*

22. Paul Burka, "Galveston, Grand Dame of the Gulf," *Texas Monthly* (December 1983).

23. Phil Hewitt, *The Jewish Texans,* 9–10.

24. Sam B. Graham and Ellen Newman, *A Historical and Biographical Record of Galveston and Galveston County* (Galveston: A. W. Cawston, 1945), 238–239; "Mrs. H. Kempner . . . Succumbs," *Galveston Daily News,* September 27, 1947; Elizabeth Turner, Houston, unpublished research about Elizabeth Kempner.

25. Phil Hewitt, *The Jewish Texans,* 7–8; Kallison, "100 Years of Jewry in San Antonio," 33.

26. Fay Brachman, "The Story of Rachel and Abraham Ros-

enthal," typescript, c. 1985 (TJHS Coll., Abe Rosenthal File.)

27. In 1987, a headstone was erected in honor of Simon Suhler in San Antonio's National Military Cemetery.

28. Kallison, *passim.*

29. Hewitt, 9; Kallison, 36–37.

30. San Antonio *Express News*, August 30, 1988, 1-C.

31. Larry Meyer, "D. & A. Oppenheimer, Bankers (Uninc.), Transcribed Interviews with Mr. Dan Oppenheimer," Oral Business History Project (Austin: UT Austin, 1971); Jesse Oppenheimer, "Letter to customers," San Antonio, September 14, 1988.

32. Letter from Godcheaux Levi to Rabbi Henry Cohen, March 25, 1895 (Henry Cohen Papers, Box 3M 219, Barker Center).

33. Levi to Henry Cohen; "Address of Godcheaux Levi to the Victoria Historical Society, Sept. 1973" (TJHS Coll., Levi Family file); personal interview with Marie Bitterman, Dallas, May 16, 1988; Lawrence S. Johnson, *A Century of Service, The Concise History of Victoria Bank & Trust Co.* (Victoria: n.p., 1979); Mrs. Robert Earl Cliburn, "The Abraham Levi Home" (Austin: Texas Hist. Com., January 1965); organizational records of the Ladies Hebrew Benevolent Society, Victoria, 1876–1901 and cash book, 1877–1923 (Barker Center); letter from Mrs. M. L. Potash to Henry Cohen (Cohen Papers, Box 3M 219, Barker Center).

34. Ad reproduced in Lt. W. H. Chatfield, *The Twin Cities, Brownsville, Texas, Matamoras* [sic], *Mexico of the Border and the Country of the Lower Rio Grande* (New Orleans: Brandao, 1893), n. pag.

35. "Exhibit narrative," Raphael showcase, Charles Stillman House Museum, Brownsville.

36. Alice Raphael Coll., Barker Center.

37. Claire R. Reis, *Composers in America*, rev. ed. (New York: DeCapo Press, 1977).

38. Alice Raphael, trans., *Faust, Wolfgang Von Goethe* (New York: Jonathan Cape, 1930); *Los Angeles Herald Express*, August 22, 1938; *The Nation*, April 29, 1931. (Alice Raphael Coll., Barker Center.)

39. Ernst Kohlberg, *Letters of Ernst Kohlberg 1875–1877*, trans. Walter L. Kohlberg (El Paso: UT El Paso Press, 1973).

40. *Ibid.*, 4.

41. Series on the Kohlberg family in *El Paso Times*, September 20 and 27, 1964; Floyd S. Fierman, *El Paso Jewish Historical Review* 1, no. 2 (Spring 1983): 152–155; Hewitt, 10–11.

42. Temple Beth El, *History of the Jewish Community* (Corpus Christi: Temple Beth El, 1957), 8–9, 12.

43. Eleanor Weinbaum, *Shalom America* (Burnet, TX: Nortex, 1981).

44. *Ibid., passim.*

45. B. G. Rudolph, *From a Minyan to a Community, A History of the Jews of Syracuse* (Syracuse, NY: Syracuse Univ., 1970), 13–15, 75–77.

46. Audrey Daniels Kariel, "The Jewish Story and Memories of Marshall, Texas," *Western States Jewish Historical Quarterly* 14, no. 3 (April 1982): 195–206.

47. *Ibid., passim;* Juliet George, "Zahor!" *Marshall News Messenger*, April 12, 1979; Benjamin Joseph Cramer, "Marshall Hebrew Cemetery: Memorial of People and Their History," *Texas Historian* 44, no. 4 (March 1985): 9–13.

48. Eliza Bishop, *Mini-History Houston County, Texas* (Crockett: Houston County Hist. Comm., 1980).

49. "Plum Creek Almanac," *Texas State Gazette and Business Directory, Caldwell County Listing 1882–1883*, 3, no. 1 (Spring 1985): 47; Gravestones in Luling Jewish Cemetery recorded by Ruthe Winegarten and Kay Goldman, October 31, 1988.

50. Letter received from Frances Kallison, November 6, 1988, with information from Dr. Milton Jacobs, San Antonio, descendant of Luling pioneers.

51. Anne C. Huff Bridges with corrections and additions by Mary Louise Bridges Watt, *Early Days in Luling* (Luling: n.p., 1967), 29.

52. *Ibid.*, 16.

53. Letter to Ruthe Winegarten from Charles Schultz, April 26, 1988.

54. Visit to Luling Jewish Cemetery, October 31, 1988, by Ruthe Winegarten and Kay Goldman, with notations made of tombstone inscriptions of Louis Goodman and family members.

55. Telephone interviews with Mrs. Jules (Mickey) Breitenbach and Mrs. Philip (Martha) Hirsch, Houston, June 20, 1988; personal interview with Eleanor Freed, Houston, June 20, 1988; letter received from Helen Jacobson, San Antonio, December 6, 1988; letter received from B. J. Mayer, San Angelo, May 16, 1988.

56. Leon Rosenberg, *Sangers* (Austin: TSHA, 1978), 1–2; Leon Harris, *Merchant Princes: An Intimate History of Jewish Families Who Built Great Department Stores* (New York: Harper, 1979), 158.

57. Mordecai Podet, *Pioneer Jews of Waco — Part II*, *Western States Jewish History* 4 (1989): 338.

58. Sanger Bros. Collection (Texas Collection, Box 3B61, Baylor Univ.)

59. Richard Denny Parker, *Historical Recollection of Robertson County* (Salado: Anson Jones Press, 1950), 195.

60. Rosenberg, *Sangers, passim;* Harris, 156–169.

61. Rosenberg, *Sangers*, 22.

62. Harris, 161–162.

63. Rosenberg, *Sangers*, 21.

64. Susan Porter Benson, *Counter Culture: Saleswomen, Managers, and Customers in American Department Stores, 1890–1940* (Urbana: Univ. of Ill. Press, 1986).

65. Rosenberg, *Sangers*, 30.

66. Harris, 165.

67. "Death of Mrs. Alexander Sanger," *Beau Monde* (Dallas, November 1898).

68. Rosenberg, *Sangers, passim.*

69. D. D. Garber, "Sanger Home Built in '85 Stands as Monument to Fabulous Era," *Dallas Morning News*, September 19, 1951.

Chapter 4

1. Letter received from Frank Wagner, Corpus Christi, June 2, 1988.

2. Temple Beth El, *Corpus Christi, History of the Jewish Community* (Corpus Christi: Temple Beth El, 1957), 9; Letter received from Frank Wagner, June 2, 1988.

3. Letter to Henry Cohen from Grace Rice, October 11, 1896 (Henry Cohen Papers, Box 3M 219, Barker Center).

4. Temple Beth El, *Corpus Christi, History of the Jewish Community* (Corpus Christi, 1957), 9–10.

5. Cemetery records of the Hebrew Cemetery of Brownsville (Collection of Ruben Edelstein, Brownsville).

6. Schmier, 93.

7. *75th Anniversary Diamond Jubilee Shearith Israel Congregation* (Wharton: Shearith Israel, 1988), 34.

8. Shmier, 89.

9. *Ibid.*

10. *Ibid.*, 90–91.

11. As reprinted in Anne Nathan Cohen, *Centenary History*, 30–31.

12. Schmier, 90–91.

13. Letter to Henry Cohen from Jonas Dannenbaum, October 3, 1985 (Cohen Papers, Box 3M 219, Barker Center).

14. Corsicana local paper, September 28, 1900.

15. *Ibid.*

16. Rabbi Ernest Joseph, "The Jewish Community of Corsicana, Texas," typescript, October 17, 1988, 1–2; "Corsicana, Texas: A Most Unlikely Canaan," typescript (Austin: Texas Hist. Com., c. 1977), *passim.*

17. Patty George, "Rope Walker, Rope Walker, What Was Your Name" (song), words reprinted in *Corsicana Daily Sun*, October 30, 1988.

18. Rabbi Ernest Joseph, "Rope Walker's Tombstone," paper given at Kallah of Texas Rabbis, Galveston, February 23, 1976.

19. Anne Nathan and Harry I. Cohen, *The Man Who Stayed in Texas: The Life of Rabbi Henry Cohen* (New York: Whittlesey House, 1941), *passim;* A. Stanley Dreyfus, ed., *Henry Cohen, Messenger of the Lord* (New York: Bloch, 1963), *passim;* Kessler, "B.O.I.," *passim.*

20. Rabbi Samuel M. Stahl, "A Brief History of Congregation B'nai Israel" (Galveston: December 1972); Rabbi James Lee Kessler, "B.O.I., A History of Congregation B'nai Israel, Galveston Texas," diss., Hebrew Union College, Jewish Inst. of Religion, Calif. School, 1988, *passim.*

21. Congregation B'nai Israel, *The First Hundred Years* (Galveston: 1968); "Congregation B'nai Israel Synagogue," typescript [Austin: Texas Hist. Com. narrative, taken from Howard Barnstone, *The Galveston That Was* (New York: Macmillan, 1966].

22. *San Francisco Jewish Progress,* June 10, 1878, reprinted in Kenneth Libo and Irving Howe, *We Lived There Too* (New York: St. Martin's, 1984), 157–158.

23. *Dedication Volume of Congregation Beth Jacob* (Galveston: December 1, 1963).

24. *Archives Israelites,* April 1, 1865.

25. *The American Israelite,* November 12, 1875, reprinted in *Western States Hist. Quarterly* (April 1976).

26. Information about the early history of Temple Emanu-El in Dallas comes from their archives.

27. Information about Shearith Israel comes from Jennie Zesmer, ed., *Golden Book of Shearith Israel, Commemorating the Congregation's Fiftieth Anniversary, 1884–1934* (Dallas: 1935); and *Centennial Journal: Congregation Shearith Israel, Dallas, Texas, 1884–1984* (Dallas: 1984).

28. Ann Ackerman, "Snatches of Life in Goosevalley," paper presented at American Jewish Hist. Soc. Natl. Conv., Denver, CO, May 17–20, 1986, *passim.*

29. *Ibid.;* Congregation of Tiferet Israel, *Congregation Tiferet Israel, 1890–1965* (Dallas: 1965); *Congregation Tiferet Israel, 1890–1980* (Dallas: March 15, 1980); *Congregation Tiferet Israel, 75th Anniversary* (Dallas: April 17, 1966).

30. Rose-Mary Rumbley, *A Century of Class: Public Education in Dallas, 1884–1984* (Austin: Eakin, 1984), 29.

31. Letter to a Mr. Mayer from Johnnie B. Terrell, Littleton, CO, November 16, 1963 (TJHS Coll., Ferdinand Mayer File).

32. Information about early San Antonio from Kallison, "100 Years of Jewry," *passim,* and from Temple Beth-El, *Diamond Jubilee 1874–1949* (San Antonio: 1949), *passim.*

33. Schmier, 100–102.

34. Jay Lawrence Silberberg, "The First One Hundred Years: A History of the Austin Jewish Community, 1850–1950," senior thesis, Bachelor of Arts, Plan II, UT Austin, August 1974, 36.

35. *Ibid., passim;* Mary Starr Barkley, *History of Travis County and Austin, 1839–1899* (Waco: Texian Press, 1963), 285–286.

36. Schmier, 103–109.

37. Congregation Agudath Jacob, *Golden Jubilee Year Book, 1884–1934* (Waco: 1934), *passim.*

38. Mordecai Podet, *Pioneer Jews of Waco* (Waco: privately published, 1986); "Waco, Texas and its Jewish Community," *The Owl,* 14, no. 5 (October 1902), 14–21; Rabbi Harry Weiss and I. A. Goldstein, *Synagogue Fair and Bazaar Souvenir Fair Book* (Waco: Knight Prtg. Co., 1899); I. A. Goldstein, "The Waco Jewish Community," *Waco Heritage & History* 13, no. 4 (Winter 1982) (Texas Coll., Baylor Univ.)

39. Mrs. Sam Tobin, "History of B'nai Abraham Synagogue [Brenham]." (Austin: Texas Hist. Com., n.d.)

40. Obituary, *American Israelite,* November 1, 1900, rpt. in *Western States Jewish Hist. Quarterly* (January 1987), 132–133; Podet, 63; H. Schwarz, "Talmudic Alphabet" (in German and Hebrew), Hempstead, typescript, tr. Alix Magnus, Fort Worth,

1988 (Henry Cohen Papers, Barker Center).

41. Alex Simon Family Papers (TJHS Coll., Box 2C 495, Barker Center).

42. Schmier, 84–86.

43. Houston *Jewish Herald Voice,* April 24, 1986.

44. Telephone interview with Edis (Mrs. H. D.) Schwarz, Hempstead, December 16, 1988; Letter received from Edis Schwarz, January 4, 1989.

45. *Jewish Herald,* December 23, 1909, vol. 2, no. 14; Schwarz Family Bible owned by Cathy Schechter, Austin; Letter received from Edwin Gale, Beaumont, December 2, 1988; Other family records (private collection of Edwin Gale, Beaumont); Letter received from Edwin Gale, November 7, 1985.

46. Typescript of Gussie Schwarz Galewsky's remarks at dedication of Schwarz Training School in 1928 (TJHS Coll., Schwarz Family File).

47. Schmier, 99–100.

48. "The Mystery and Murder of Diamond Bessie," *Dallas Morning News,* January 8, 1933, Sec. IV, p. 1; "East Texas First and Most Famous Big Name Trial," *Marshall News Messenger,* August 23, 1936, 1; Fred Tarpley, *Jefferson: Riverport to the Southwest* (Austin: Eakin, 1983), 136–150.

49. Deolece Parmelee, *The Deadly Jewels of Diamond Bessie, Historical Tragedy* (N.p.: D. M. Parmelee, 1968); James W. Byrd, "A Texas Folk Drama: 'The Diamond Bessie Murder Trial'," in Ed Wilson and M. Hudson, eds., *Diamond Bessie and the Shepherds* (Austin: Encino, 1972), 3–13; Tarpley, 318–323.

50. "Bessie's death in 1877 still causes debate," in Kent Biffle's "Texana," *Dallas Morning News,* April 30, 1989.

51. "Texas Articles of Inc. for Hebrew Sinai Congregation"; "Constitution and By-Laws of Hebrew Sinai Congregation, Jefferson, Texas" (TJHS Coll., Jefferson File).

52. Typescript, Jefferson's Hebrew Sinai Synagogue (Austin: Texas Hist. Com., c. 1965).

53. Carol Tefteller, "The Jewish Community in Frontier Jefferson," *Texas Historian* 35, no. 1 (September 1974), 8.

54. Marguerite Marks, "Philip Eldridge," *News from the Residents of Golden Acres* (Dallas: December 1976); Obituary of Philip Eldridge, *Jefferson Journal,* October 21, 1924, rpt. in *Jewish Record,* date unknown.

55. Personal interview with Elizabeth Eldridge Bettelheim in Jefferson, March 10, 1989.

56. Libo and Howe, *We Lived There Too,* 158.

57. A. D. Kariel and Gail K. Beil, ed. by Jennifer Larned, "Temple Moses Montefiore, Marshall," typescript (Austin: Texas Hist. Com., n.d.); Audrey Kariel, "Application for Texas Historical Marker, Marshall Hebrew Cemetery," typescript (Austin: Texas Hist. Com., 1988).

58. Max S. Lale, "The Hochwald House, Marshall," typescript (Austin: Texas Hist. Com., May 9, 1978).

59. Schmier, 119.

60. *Ibid.*

61. Lisa Mack, "Emanuel Hebrew Rest Cemetery" (Austin: Texas Hist. Com., c. 1981).

62. Dan Danciger Jewish Community Center, Fort Worth Jewish Community Sesquicentennial Committee, "Celebration and Tour Brochure," June 29, 1986; Ellen Mack, "History of Beth-El Congregation, Fort Worth" (Austin: Texas Hist. Com., January 9, 1986); *Beth El Congregation Fort Worth, Texas, 70th Anniversary, 1902–1972* (Fort Worth: 1972).

63. Judith Cohen, biographical sketch of Shanblum family, Fort Worth Jewish Community Sesquicentennial Archives, 1986; *Seventy-Fifth Anniversary Congregation Ahavath Sholom* (Fort Worth: 1967).

64. Harvey Wessel, "A History of the Jews of Tyler and Smith County, Texas," in Robert W. Glover, ed., *Tyler and Smith County: An Historical Survey, Bi-Centennial Edition* (Tyler: Walsworth Pub., 1976), 201–212; Bridget C. (Mrs. Harvey) Mann, *100 Year Anni-*

versary 1887–1987, Temple Beth El (Tyler: 1987).

65. Wessel, *passim;* Rabbi Abraham Herson, ed. and pub., *Golden Jubilee and Dedication Book, Ahavath Achim Congregation, 1899–1949* (Tyler: 1949).

66. Schmier, 123–124.

67. Barbara Glick, ed., *Centennial Journal of Mount Sinai Congregation 1885–1985* (Texarkana: 1985); *Mount Sinai Jubilee Texarkana, 1885–1935* (Texarkana: Charles Grossman, 1935).

68. Schmier, 120–122.

69. *Ibid.*, 105–106.

70. Mary S. Cunningham, *The Woman's Club of El Paso, Its First Thirty Years* (El Paso: Texas Western Press, 1978); "Builders of El Paso . . . Mrs. [Ernst] Kohlberg," prod. Peyton Packing Co., Inc., KTSM Radio, El Paso, July 2, 1939; Hewitt, 10–11.

71. Temple Emanu-El Archives, Dallas.

72. Amelia Barr, *All the Days of My Life* (New York and London: Appleton, 1913), 207.

73. *Houston City Directory, 1886–87.*

74. Silberberg, 39.

75. Jan Hart, "Annie the Immigrant," typescript, c. 1988 (TJHS Coll., Harelik File).

76. Josephine J. Goldman, "Women of Galveston," *Galveston Tribune*, August 1, 1924; *12th Annual Historic Homes Tour Booklet* (Galveston: Galv. Hist. Found., 1986), 22–24.

77. Catalogue is in Kidd-Key College Collection, SMU Archives, Dallas.

78. Waco Community File (TJHS Coll.).

79. Frances E. Willard and Mary A. Livermore, *American Women*, vol. 1 (Detroit: Gale, 1973), 357–358, rev. ed.; Willard and Livermore, *Woman of the Century* (New York: Mast, Crowell, 1896).

80. Lee Cohen Harby, *Messenger*, January 12, 1883, January 18, 1883, rpt. in Jacob Marcus, *The American Jewish Woman: A Documentary History* (New York and Cincinnati: KTAV and Amer. Jewish Archives, 1981), 343–350.

81. Waco Community File (TJHS Coll.).

82. Rochlin and Rochlin, *Pioneer Jews*, 144, 159.

83. Floyd S. Fierman, *Insights and Hindsights of Some El Paso Jewish Families, El Paso Jewish Historical Review* 1, no. 11 (Spring 1983): 225–228.

84. Samuel Freudenthal, "El Paso Merchant and Civic Leader," *Southwestern Studies*, Monograph 11 (El Paso: Texas Western College, 1965).

85. Cited in *American Israelite*, November 23, 1888.

86. *Sabbath Visitor* (Cincinnati, September 1, 1890, September 15, 1890), rpt. *Western States Jewish Hist. Quarterly* (July 1976).

87. "Prominent Galveston Man Dies Suddenly," *Galveston Daily News*, October 8, 1917, 2 (Rosenberg Library).

CHAPTER 5

1. Unpublished oral history of Celia Cohen Lewin, interviewed by her daughter, Ruthe Winegarten, 1983.

2. Certificate in private collection of Bernard Rapoport, Waco.

3. "Her Search Continuing," *Austin American*, September 22, 1961.

4. "Books," *Austin American Statesman*, May 23, 1971; Obituary, *Austin American Statesman*, July 17, 1977; Biographical materials at Institute of Texan Cultures, San Antonio; Institute of Texan Cultures, "The Kruger Family: Texas Immigrants," videotape, c. 1986; Fania Feldman Kruger Collection (Humanities Research Center, UT Austin).

5. Freida Esther Mirochnik Weiner, untitled biography, typescript, June 2, 1968.

6. Freida Weiner, "My Shtetl Korostishev" ("My Little Town Korostishev"), tr. Sam Miron, typescript, n.d.; Freida Wei-

ner, "Jewish Folk Remedies," in *I Remember When* (Houston: National Council of Jewish Women, 1983); Personal interviews with Freida Weiner, May 2, 1988 and June 15, 1988; Letter received from Phyllis Weiner, Temple, Texas, April 26, 1988 (TJHS Coll., Freida Weiner File).

7. Jan Hart, *passim.*

8. Henry Cohen, et al., *100 Years*, 24–25; International Order of B'nai B'rith, *To the Memory of Leo N. Levi* (Chicago: Hamburger Prtg., 1905); Hewitt, 11.

9. Sigmund Burg, "As I Remember and See It," in H. R. Gold, ed., *Book of Redemption* (Houston: White Pub., for Jewish Natl. Fund, 1939).

10. Louis A. Freed, "Zionism in Texas Thirty-five Years Ago," in H. R. Gold, *Book of Redemption*, 70–71.

11. Minutes in Texas Collection, Baylor University.

12. David Geffen, "A Sentimental Journey — Early Zionist Activities in the South — The Diary of Jacob de Haas' Trip in 1904," in *Forum*, rept. of "Diary" in *Maccabaean*, VIII–I, 22–31.

13. Cynthia and Allen Mondell, "West of Hester Street, A documentary about the Galveston Movement"; *The Texas Humanist* 3, no. 8 (May 1981): 3–6; "The Galveston Movement," *The Jewish Herald* [Houston], November 12, 1908, 1; Bernard Marinbach, *Galveston, Ellis Island of the West* (Albany, NY: State Univ. of New York Press, 1983).

14. Nathan and Cohen, *The Man Who Stayed in Texas*, 195.

15. Abram Geller, Houston, handwritten note with attached sketch for a play about Geller family in Galveston, March 10, 1983.

16. Henry Cohen Papers (Barker Center, prison records, Boxes 3M 296-3M 305, Picurd letter in personal correspondence, Box 3M 223, Schwartz letter in personal correspondence, Box 3M 224).

17. Rosella H. Werlin, typescript about Werlin family, January 3, 1974 (TJHS Coll., Joseph Werlin File).

18. "Hey! Zhan Koye," a Crimean Yiddish folk song about an area of Soviet Jewish collective farms; English words by Pete Seeger.

19. Uri D. Herscher, *Jewish Agricultural Utopias in America, 1880–1910* (Detroit: Wayne St. Univ., 1981), 37–38.

20. Mordecai Podet, "Pioneer Jews of Waco, Texas," *Western States Jewish History* 21, no. 4 (1989): 330.

21. Martin A. Davidson, Dallas, "A Texas Jewish Historical Lead," typescript, undated; telephone interview with Mary Peoples, Genealogy Section, Conroe Pub. Lib., July 21, 1988; records in private collection of Susan Abramson, Dallas (TJHS Coll., Farmers File).

22. Personal interview with Frank Wagner, Corpus Christi, March 3, 1988.

23. Biographical sketch of Sam Rosen (Fort Worth Jewish Community Sesquicentennial Archives); Obituary, Fort Worth paper, December 21, 1932.

24. Information from Dallas Jewish Historical Society Archives.

25. Hewitt, 23; Biographical sketch sent by Sandra Hodges, county judge, Rusk County; Letter received from Sandra Hodges, October 1988 (TJHS Coll., Brachfield File).

26. Bishop, "The Bromberg Family," *passim.*

27. Lewis L. Gould, *Progressives & Prohibitionists* (Austin: UT Press, 1973), 185–221.

28. Marilyn McAdams Sibley, *George W. Brackenridge* (Austin: UT Press, 1973), 230.

29. Correspondence relating to controversy between Rabbi Faber and Governor Ferguson, as well as other documents, are in private collection of Faber's grandson, Eugene J. Lipstate, Lafayette, LA (TJHS Coll., Faber File).

30. "Sakowitz: A Houston Tradition," typescript from Sakowitz, Houston, c. 1985; Alison Cook, "The Fraying Empire of Bobby Sakowitz," *Texas Monthly* (December 1985): 132–136, 232–258.

31. Lois Burkhalter, *San Antonio Light*, April 15, 1973; Marianne Odom and Gaylon Finklea Young, *The Businesses That Built San Antonio* (San Antonio: Living Legacies, 1985); "Joske's Dates Back to 1873," *San Antonio Light*, November 14, 1976, 2J.

32. Harold M. Hyman, "I. H. Kempner and the Galveston Commission Government," *Houston Review* 10 no. 2 (1988): 57, based on forthcoming book *Oleander Odyssey: The Kempners of Galveston, 1870–1980* (College Station: Texas A&M Press, 1990).

33. *History of the Jewish Literary Society of Houston, Texas, June 27, 1906, to June 30, 1916* (Houston, June 1916), 13.

34. *History of the Jewish Literary Society*, 44.

35. Samuel Rosinger, *My Life and My Message* (Beaumont: privately published, 1958), 20.

36. *Ibid.*

37. Shmuel Geller, *Mazkers Ahavah, Remembrance of Love, Rabbi Yaakov Geller: From Galicia to Texas 1863–1930* (Zichron Yaakov, Israel: Institute for Pub. of Books and Study of Manuscripts, Torah Ed. Center, January 1988), 28.

38. Kallison, "100 Years," 113A–115.

39. Letters received from Morris Riskind, Eagle Pass, August 21, September 30, and October 10, 1988 (TJHS Coll., Riskind File).

40. Floyd S. Fierman, *The Schwartz Family of El Paso*, Southwestern Studies, monograph No. 61 (El Paso: Texas Western Press, 1980), *passim*.

41. Obituary, *Brownsville Herald*, August 19, 1971; Personal interviews with Dr. Philip Leonard, Austin, grandson, and Mrs. Ray Leonard, Harlingen, daughter, May 1988; *H. Matamoras*, Tamaulipas, Mexico, Domingo 29 de Agosto de 1971.

42. Hymer Rosen, "Sam Dreben, Half-Pint Warrior," typescript, El Paso, 7 (TJHS Coll., Dreben File).

43. Hewitt, 18; *El Paso Herald-Post*, May 30, 1961.

CHAPTER 6

1. "Jewish Woman Lawyer Talks to Literary Society," *Houston Chronicle*, January 12, 1916, 5.

2. *Galveston Tribune*, June 14, 1913.

3. Ackerman, 9.

4. Nancy Goebel, "Small Inns of Texas," *Dallas Morning News*, January 23, 1983, 4J.

5. Frank Tolbert, *Neiman-Marcus, Texas* (New York: Holt, 1953), 35.

6. Tom Peeler, "Story of the Store," *D Magazine* (August 1984): 166–171; Stanley Marcus, *Minding the Store* (Boston: Little Brown, 1974), *passim*.

7. Ackerman, 6, 18; Telephone interview with Ann Ackerman, June 11, 1988.

8. Letter received from Mary Hirsch Stern, Ontario, CA, October 2, 1988.

9. Letter to Gov. Coke Stevenson from Rev. Robert E. Lucey, San Antonio, December 15, 1944; Letter to Gov. Coke Stevenson from Rabbi David Jacobson, January 5, 1945; Betty Brown Cohen, "Carrie Pfeiffer Brown," typescript, August 1988; Letter from Philip Pfeiffer Brown, December 17, 1988 (TJHS Coll., Carrie Brown File).

10. Miriam Hirshfeld Frees, *An Autobiography* (n.p.: n.d.), n. pag. (Hirschfeld Papers, Austin History Center).

11. *Ibid.*; Obituary, "In Memoriam — Miriam Hirshfield [sic] Frees," Austin, paper not known, May 1918.

12. Don E. Carleton, *Red Scare!* (Austin: Texas Monthly Press, 1985), 38–39, 169–170, 172, 175, 277.

13. Tom Mulvany, "Dr. Ray K. Daily Reflects on a Full Life," *Houston Chronicle*, May 31, 1970 (Ray Daily Coll., HMRC, Houston Pub. Lib.).

14. Personal interview with Fannie Pravorne Wienir, December 1985 (TJHS Coll., Fannie Wienir File).

15. Letter received from Tillie Harris Harmel, Dallas, c. June 1988; letter received from Eunice H. Reiter, Houston, 18 May 1988 (TJHS Coll., Harmel File).

16. Bishop, "Bromberg Family."

17. Personal collection of Brilling papers owned by Cathy Schechter, Austin.

18. Fay Lucas Oringel, "The National Council of Jewish Women," *Jewish Herald Voice*, Houston, April 24, 1986.

19. *Waco Section, National Council of Jewish Women, 50th Anniversary, 1913–1963* (Waco: NCJW, 1963). (Texas Collection, Baylor Univ.)

20. Estelle Goodman Levy Collection at Western Jewish Hist. Center, Judah L. Magnes Museum, Berkeley, CA.

21. Marguerite Marks, "Elizabeth Gaertner Levy," in Evelyn Carrington, ed., *Women in Early Texas* (Austin: Jenkins for Amer. Assn. of Univ. Women, 1975), 157–161.

22. *Dallas Section, National Council of Jewish Women, 1913–1963* (Dallas: NCJW, 1963); *Greater Dallas NCJW Section 1913–1988, A History* (Dallas: 1988).

23. "Ten Commandments." (Henry Cohen Papers, scrapbook Box 3Y-16, Barker Center.)

24. Copy of letter from Henrietta Szold, December 11, 1939 (TJHS Coll., Hadassah File).

25. Littman Family Collection (Austin History Center).

26. Jeanette Littman Hammer, "The Littmans," Fort Lauderdale, FL, July 9, 1971, typescript (Littman Family Coll., Austin History Center).

27. Information on Minnie Bertha Hirsch (TJHS Coll., Ferdinand and Jette Mayer File).

28. Letter to Mrs. Percy V. Pennybacker, July 29, 1902 (Texas Fed. of Womens Clubs Papers, Texas Woman's Univ.).

29. Letter from Frances Kallison, San Antonio, February 27, 1986.

30. Kallison, "Early History," 106–109.

31. Ruthe Winegarten, *Texas Women, A Pictorial History* (Austin: Eakin Press, 1986), 103.

32. Jewish Literary Society, 51.

33. Janet G. Humphrey, *A Texas Suffragist* (Austin: Ellen C. Temple, 1988), 127, 140.

34. Edward J. Bristow, *Prostitution-Prejudice: The Jewish Fight Against White Slavery, 1870–1939* (New York: Schocken, 1983), 180.

35. George Fox, "The End of an Era," in Stanley F. Chyet, ed., *Lives and Voices* (Philadelphia: Jewish Pub. Society, 1972), 280.

36. Charlotte Baum et al., *The Jewish Woman in America* (New York: New Amer. Lib., 1975), 170–175.

37. Bristow, *passim*.

38. Fox, 279–281; Speech by Ellen Mack, Texas Jewish Historical Society Annual Meeting, Fort Worth, March 1986.

39. Bristow, 160–161, 178–180, 271–272.

40. *New York Times*, January 30, 1913, 1.

41. "Credits Ballot With Influence," Houston newspaper clipping, no date (Ray Daily Scrapbook, MSS 9, Box 3, Daily Collection, Houston Metropolitan Research Center, Houston Pub. Lib.).

42. *Galveston Tribune*, June 14, 1913; Larry J. Wygant, " 'A Municipal Broom': The Woman Suffrage Campaign in Galveston, Texas," *Houston Review* 6, no. 3 (1984): 117–134.

43. Elizabeth Enstam, "The Forgotten Frontier, Dallas Women and Social Caring, 1895–1920," *Legacies, A History Journal for Dallas and North Central Texas* 1, no. 1 (Spring 1989): 20–28; *Who's Who in American Jewry*, 388.

44. Ruthe Winegarten and Judith N. McArthur, eds., *Citizens At Last: The Woman Suffrage Movement in Texas* (Austin: Ellen C. Temple, 1987).

45. Research notes, private collection of Elizabeth Turner, Houston; Betty Ewing, "First bride at Cohen House returns special gift to school," *Houston Chronicle*, May 1, 1988, sec. 9, p. 4.

46. Research notes, private collection of Elizabeth Turner,

Houston; Obituary of Etta Lasker (Mrs. Samuel) Rosensohn, *New York Times*, September 21, 1966; Biographical data, November 1959 (Hadassah, NYC); *Encyclopedia Judaica*, 14: 289; Gunther, 25–26.

CHAPTER 7

1. Cohen, *Centenary History*, v.
2. *Ibid.*, 53–58.
3. Marion Bernstein and Jeanne Samuels, *A Half Century of the Houston Jewish Federation, 1936–1986* (Houston: printed by M. Lefkowitz, December 11, 1986), 1.
4. *Jewish Herald Voice*, Houston, April 24, 1986.
5. Bernstein and Samuels, 4.
6. *Houston Post*, August 30, 1974.
7. Max Blumer, *Diamond Jubilee 1874–1949* (San Antonio: Temple Beth-El, 1949).
8. Jennie Zesmer, ed., *Golden Book of Shearith Israel, 1884–1934* (Dallas: 1959), n. pag.
9. Gold, *Book of Redemption*, 140.
10. Ginger Jacobs, "The Jewish Community Center of Dallas," unpublished paper, December 1982; Lyssa Bossay, *JCC of Dallas Dedication Book* (Dallas: Taylor Pub., 1980).
11. Telephone interviews with Ginger Jacobs and Rose Biderman, Dallas, August 7, 1989; letter received from Dr. Herbert Shore, August 4, 1989.
12. Gold, 119.
13. Barbara Rosenberg, "Jewish History of San Angelo," typescript (Sugar Land, May 1988); Avril Suckow, "Amarillo Jews in Service to the Panhandle, Ethnic Geography of the Panhandle," typescript, November 23, 1982; Herbert and Carolyn Timmons, "Temple B'nai Israel," *Amarillo Sunday News*, no date (Amarillo Pub. Lib.); Lee Inselberg, "Changing Worlds: Jewish Women in Lubbock, Texas," thesis, Texas Tech Univ., 1982.
14. Barbara Rosenberg, 5.
15. Obituary of Joe Hirsch, *Marshall News Messenger*, May 25, 1966; Joe W. Hirsch, biographical sketch of Valrie Weisman Hirsch, typescript, n.d.
16. Personal interview with Barbara and Mel Kusin, Texarkana, May 1989.
17. Barbara Glick, ed., *Centennial Journal of Mount Sinai Congregation, 1885–1985* (Texarkana: 1985).
18. Gaylon Finklea Young, "Self-Made Itinerant Rabbi 'Perl' of the Rio Grande," *San Antonio Express News*, no date (probably March of 1979 or 1980).
19. Harriett Denise Joseph, "A Tribute to Sam Perl, 1898–1980," in *Studies in Brownsville History* 2 (1988).
20. *Gonzales Inquirer*, no date (TJHS Coll., Zellen File).
21. *Ibid.*
22. Rochlin, 213.
23. Louis Freed, lecture to the Texas-Louisiana Zionist Association, Beaumont, November 12, 1933 (TJHS Coll., Freed File).
24. *Who Was Who in America* 7 (1977–81): 491.
25. Louis A. Freed, "Zionism in Texas Thirty-Five Years Ago," in Gold, 70–71.
26. Freed, lecture, 1933.
27. Bernstein, 12.
28. Chaya Rochel Andres, *Zahnen Yorn Gelofn: Mayn Lebns Eschikhte [Years Have Sped By]*, ed. Jeanette Cohen (Dallas: H. R. Andres, 1981), 32.
29. *Ibid.*
30. "Minutes, YMHA" (Dallas: 1925). (TJHS Coll., Dallas JCC File.)
31. Jacobs, "The JCC of Dallas."
32. Ginger Jacobs, *The Levin Years* (Dallas: Dallas Jewish Hist. Soc., 1989).
33. San Jacinto County Historical Commission, *Dim Trails and Blurred Footprints: A History of San Jacinto County, Texas* (Cold-spring, TX: Taylor Pub. for San Jacinto County Hist. Com., 1982).
34. *Jewish Herald Voice*, Houston, March 4, 1954.

CHAPTER 8

1. Tommy Stringer, *The Zale Corporation . . . From the Beginning* (Dallas: Zale Found., c. 1985), 11.
2. Jacquelyn Dowd Hall, *Revolt Against Chivalry, Jessie Daniel Ames and the Women's Campaign Against Lynching* (New York: Columbia Univ. Press, 1979), 178, 242.
3. Gunther (quoting Albert Lasker), 11.
4. Hymer E. Rosen, "Sam Dreben, Half-Pint Warrior," El Paso, typescript, no date, 10.
5. Ouida Nalle, *The Fergusons of Texas* (San Antonio: Naylor, 1946), 163.
6. Hall, 114, 134–135.
7. David Ritz, "Inside the Jewish Establishment," *D, the Magazine of Dallas*, 2 (November 1975): 52–54; Stringer, 11.
8. *Houston Jewish Herald*, April 3, 1924.
9. Norman D. Brown, *Hood, Bonnet, and Little Brown Jug, Texas Politics, 1921–1928* (College Station: Texas A&M Press, 1984), 211–252.
10. John William Stayton, "The First All-Woman Supreme Court in the World," *Holland's Magazine* (March 1925), 5–6.
11. Gunther, 11.
12. *Ibid., passim.*
13. Floyd Fierman, *Roots and Boots, From Crypto-Jew in New Spain to Community Leader in the American Southwest* (Hoboken, NJ: KTAV, 1987), 114.
14. Edward C. Rowland, "A Rose Blooms in the Desert — The Saga of the Santa Rita #1," in *Hoein' the Short Rows* (Dallas: SMU Press for Texas Folklore Soc., 1987), 92–99.
15. Meyer Perlstein, telegram to Charlotte Duncan, ILGWU leader, November 19, 1936 (UT Arlington Labor Coll.).
16. Dorothy DeMoss, "Looking Better Every Year," in Donald Whisenhunt, ed., *Texas: A Sesquicentennial Celebration* (Austin: Eakin, 1984), 281–291; Dorothy Dell DeMoss, "The History of Apparel Manufacturing in Texas, 1897–1981," diss., Texas Christian Univ., 1981.
17. Rawlston quotation in Richard Croxdale and Melissa Hield, eds., *Women in the Texas Workforce: Yesterday and Today* (Austin: People's History in Texas, 1979).
18. Croxdale and Hield, *passim.*
19. *Ibid.*
20. Elaine H. Maas, "The Jews of Houston: An Ethnographic Study," diss., Rice Univ., 1973, 58.
21. Lupe Ramos, "Sam Schwartz: A Pioneer of the Theatre Industry," *Texas Historian* (January 1974): 8–9; "Narrative for Historical Marker Aztec Theatre and Sam Schwartz Eagle Pass," typescript, Texas (Austin: Texas Hist. Com.).
22. Patricia Ward Wallace, *A Spirit So Rare* (Austin: Nortex, 1984), 156–168.
23. *Contemporary Authors*, 49–52 (Detroit: Gale, 1975) 78; Hayden Herrera, *Frida, A Biography of Frida Kahlo* (New York: Harper, 1983), 131, 186, 204, 234, 287, 301, 357, 384.
24. Eve Lynn Sawyer, "Covering the Beat for 50 Years," *San Antonio Express News Scene*, June 24, 1978, 1-E; Joel Kirkpatrick, "Library Given 2-Era Material," *Galveston Daily News*, 1-E. (Werlin Collections at Rosenberg Library, Galveston, and Barker Center.)
25. "In Memoriam, Harry Leon" (vertical file, Barker Center); biographical sketch by Frieda Werden, granddaughter, San Francisco, 1989 (TJHS Coll., Leon File).
26. *National Cyclopedia of American Biography*, 38: 319.
27. Graham and Newman, 241–242; "Henrietta Blum Kempner Has Received Many Honors," *Galveston News*, October 6, 1968.

28. "HemisFair Exhibit to Tell History of Firm," *Daily Star-Telegram,* Fort Worth, August 4, 1967; Telephone interview with Mrs. Harris K. Oppenheimer, September 19, 1988; Kallison, "100 Years," 102–104.

29. Lecture to Texas Federation of Temple Sisterhoods Convention, San Antonio, 1924.

30. Information from the Marguerite Marks Collection (Temple Emanu-El Archives, Dallas).

31. Clarice Fortgang Pollard, "WAACS in Texas during the Second World War" XCIII, no. 1, *Southwestern Historical Quarterly* (July 1989): 64.

32. Telephone interviews with Joe and Robert Schechter, May 1989.

33. Chaya Andres, *Zahnen Yorn Gelofn,* "To You My Songs I Dedicate," 59.

34. *Ibid.,* 67–68.

CHAPTER 9

1. Audrey Daniels Kariel, "The Jewish Story and Memories of Marshall, Texas" in *Western States Jewish Hist. Quarterly* 14, no. 3 (1982): 206.

2. *Dallas Morning News,* April 18, 1988.

3. *Ibid.*

4. *Jewish Herald Voice,* Houston, June 8, 1989.

5. *Ibid.*

6. Bernstein and Samuels, 15.

7. Kariel, "The Jewish Story," 206.

CHAPTER 10

1. *Houston Chronicle,* June 22, 1986, sec. 3, p. 6.

2. *Ibid.*

3. Personal interview with Bernard Rapoport, June 14, 1988, Waco.

4. *Ibid.*

5. *Corpus Christi Times,* December 11, 1976.

6. *Galveston Daily News,* February 28, 1982.

7. Speech sponsored by the Houston Area Women's Center, 1987.

8. Rumbley, 342–343.

9. "Vita," Howard D. Gutin (TJHS Coll., Howard Gutin File).

10. "Jewish Tradition Through South Texas Culture," program brochure, Hillel Jewish Student Center Gallery, Cincinnati, Ohio, February 1, 1988.

11. Frank Freed, "Artist on Art," magazine article, name and date not known.

12. "Legends of the Mother Goddess," Art Exhibit Program, Kilgore College, November 1977.

13. Ed Bark, "Aaron Spelling," *Dallas Morning News,* March 12, 1989, sec. E, 1–3; *Current Biography Yearbook* (1986), 539–543; *People Weekly,* April 4, 1988, 40–41.

14. Interview by Houston chapter, American Jewish Committee, for their AJC Iris Siff Medallion of Achievement Award, 1985.

15. Tolbert, 35.

16. Ritz, 113.

17. "City philanthropist Ben Taub, 93, dies," *Houston Post,* September 10, 1982.

18. Obituary, *Houston Post,* November 2, 1982, 10A.

19. Sandra Galoob Sachnowitz, *The Roots of Temple Emanu-El* (Longview: n.p., n.d.), 44–45.

20. Carolyn Lesh, "Hermine Tobolowsky," *Dallas Morning News,* October 19, 1986, sec. E-1.

Major archival collections of materials about Texas Jews include:

American Jewish Archives, Cincinnati, Ohio
Austin History Center, Austin Public Library (Hirshfeld Papers)
Barker Texas History Center, University of Texas, Austin (Henry Cohen Papers, Henri Castro Collection, Texas Jewish Historical Society Collection, Alice Raphael Collection)
Dallas Jewish Historical Society Archives, Jewish Community Center
Texas/Dallas History and Archives Division, Dallas Public Library
Fort Worth Jewish Community Sesquicentennial Archives
Houston Public Library, Houston Metropolitan Research Center (Papers of Dr. Ray Daily, Leopold Meyer, Beth Israel)
Institute of Texan Cultures, University of Texas, San Antonio
Rosenberg Library, Galveston (Papers of Joseph O. Dyer, Ruth Levy Kempner, Rosella Werlin)
Temple Emanu-El, Dorothy M. and Henry S. Jacobus Archives, Dallas
Temple Beth Israel Archives, Houston
Texas Collection, Baylor University, Waco
Texas Historical Commission, Austin (Historical Marker Files)
Texas State Archives, Texas State Library, Austin
Texas Woman's University (Texas Women's History Project Files; Hermine Tobolowsky Papers)

Other valuable sources include county historical societies and county histories, public libraries, city directories, temples and synagogues, Jewish organizational and institutional records, the *Jewish Herald Voice* (Houston) and the *Texas Jewish Post* (Fort Worth).

Copies of almost all the articles and many of the items in the "Manuscripts" section, as well as many congregational histories, are in the Texas Jewish Historical Society Collection at the Barker Texas History Center, University of Texas at Austin. This collection also includes extensive biographical, institutional, organizational, and topical files, and about 200 responses to a survey questionnaire sent in 1987 by the TJHS.

Locations of some items are listed in parentheses at the end of the entry.

Abbreviations:

AJA	American Jewish Archives
AJHQ	*American Jewish Historical Quarterly*
BC	Barker Texas History Center, UT Austin
ITC	Institute of Texan Cultures, UT San Antonio
PAJHS	*Publications of the American Jewish Historical Society*
THC	Texas Historical Commission
TWU	Texas Woman's University, Denton
WSJH	*Western States Jewish History*
WSJHQ	*Western States Jewish Historical Quarterly*

BOOKS

American Jewish Year Book. Baltimore: Jewish Publication Society of America, 1899/1900– . Annual.

Andres, Chaya Rochel. *Zahnen Yorn Gelofn: Mayn Lebns Geschikhte [Years Have Sped By]*. Edited by Jeanette Cohen. Dallas: H. R. Andres, 1981. (BC)

Ausubel, Nathan. *Pictorial History of the Jewish People*. New York: Crown, 1954.

Barkley, Mary Starr. *History of Travis County and Austin, 1839–1899*. Waco: Texian Press, 1963.

Barnston, Dr. Henry. *History of the Jews of Houston*. Houston, n.d.

Barr, Amelia. *All the Days of My Life, An Autobiography*. New York: D. Appleton, 1913.

Baum, Charlotte, et al. *The Jewish Woman in America*. New York: New American Library, 1975.

Beaty, John. *Iron Curtain Over America*. 8th prtg. Dallas: Wilkinson, 1951.

Bemporad, Jack, ed. *A Rational Faith: Essays in Honor of Rabbi Levi A. Olan*. New York: KTAV Pub., 1977.

Benson, Susan Porter. *Counter Cultures: Saleswomen, Managers, and Customers in American Department Stores, 1890–1940*. Urbana, IL: University of Illinois Press, 1986.

Berman, Henry. *The Galveston Movement for Distributing Jewish Immigrants*. (Reprinted from *The American Hebrew*. A speech before District B'nai B'rith's Grand Lodge). N.p., n.d. (BC)

Bernstein, Marion, and Jeanne Samuels. *The Jewish Federation of Greater Houston Golden Jubilee 1936–1986*. Houston: printed by Michael Lefkowitz, December 11, 1986.

Beth El Congregation Fort Worth, Texas. 70th Anniversary, 1902–1972. Fort Worth, 1972.

Bishop, Eliza. "The Bromberg Family [of Crockett]." In *Houston County History*, 277–278. Tulsa: Heritage Publishers, 1908.

Blue Book for Visitors, Tourists and Those Seeking a Good Time While in San Antonio, Texas, 1911–1912. Distributed by San Antonio Chamber of Commerce and cab drivers. (TWU)

Blumer, Dr. Max. *Diamond Jubilee, 1874–1949, Temple Beth-El*. San Antonio: Temple Beth-El, 1949.

Bondi, August. *The Autobiography of August Bondi, 1833–1907*. Galesburg, IL: His Sons and Daughters for its Preservation, 1910.

Bossay, Lyssa. *JCC of Dallas Dedication Book*. Dallas: printed by Taylor Pub., 1980.

Bristow, Edward J. *Prostitution-Prejudice: The Jewish Fight Against White Slavery, 1870–1939*. New York: Schocken, 1983.

Brodsky, Ruth S. "The Shamus and the Shikse." In *Her Work, Stories by Texas Women*, edited by Lou Rodenberger, 26–33. Bryan: Shearer Pub., 1982.

Brooks, Elizabeth. *Prominent Women of Texas*. Akron, OH: Werner, 1896.

Brown, Norman. *Hood, Bonnet, and Little Brown Jug, Texas Politics, 1921–1928*. College Station: Texas A&M Press, 1984.

Byrd, James W. "A Texas Folk Drama: 'The Diamond Bessie Murder Trial.'" In *Diamond Bessie and the Shepherds*, ed. by Ed Wilson and M. Hudson, 3–13. Austin: Encino, 1972.

Carb, David. *Sunrise in the West*. N.p., 1931.

Carleton, Don E. *Red Scare!* Austin: Texas Monthly Press, 1985.

Carrington, Evelyn M., ed. *Women in Early Texas*. Austin: Jenkins, 1975.

Chatfield, W. H. *The Twin Cities, Brownsville, Texas, Matamoras [sic], Mexico . . .* New Orleans: Brandao, 1893.

Christian, Stella L., ed. *The History of the Texas Federation of Women's Clubs*. Houston: Dealy-Adey-Elgin, 1919. (BC)

Chyet, Stanley F., ed. *Lives and Voices, A Collection of American Jewish Memoirs*. Philadelphia: The Jewish Pub. Soc. of America, 1972.

Clemens, Gus. *The Concho Country*. San Antonio: Mulberry Ave. Books, 1980.

Cohen, Anne Nathan. *The Centenary History — Congregation Beth Israel of Houston, Texas, 1854–1954*. Houston: Privately published, 1954.

Cohen, Henry. *National Loyalty, a Jewish Characteristic*. New York: Press of Philip Conner, 1893. (BC)

Cohen, Henry, David Lefkowitz, and Ephraim Frisch. *One Hundred Years of Jewry in Texas, the Original Researches of Dr. Henry Cohen*. Prepared for Texas Centennial Religious Program in Dallas. Chicago: Regensteiner, 1936. (BC)

Cohen, Martin A. *The Martyr: The Story of a Secret Jew and the Mexican Inquisition in the Sixteenth Century*. Philadelphia: Jewish Pub. Soc. of America, 1973.

Congregation Adath Emeth Golden Jubilee. Houston, 1968.

Congregation Agudas Achim. *Dedication.* Austin, 1963.

Congregation Agudath Jacob. *Golden Jubilee Year Book, 1884–1934.* Waco, 1934.

Congregation Beth Israel. *Policy Formulation Committee.* Houston. (Adopted in 1943). A Handbook of the Facts Concerning the Basic Principles of Congregation Beth Israel. Houston, n.d. (BC)

Congregation Beth Jacob. *We Remember.* Galveston, 1934 (?).

Congregation Beth Yeshurun Sisterhood. *Let My People Eat: A Jewish Cookbook.* Houston, 1976.

Congregation B'nai Israel. *The First Hundred Years.* Galveston, 1968.

Congregation Shearith Israel. *Centennial Journal: Congregation Shearith Israel, Dallas, Texas, 1884–1984.* Dallas, 1984.

———. *Diamond Anniversary, 1884–1959, Seventy-Fifth Year.* Dallas, 1959.

Congregation Tiferet Israel. *The Congregation of Tiferet Israel, 1890–1965.* Dallas, 1965.

Congregation Tiferet Israel, 1890–1980. Dallas, March 15, 1980.

Congregation Tiferet Israel, 75th Anniversary. Dallas, April 17, 1966.

Congregation Tiferet Israel. *Tiferet Israel Congregation: Past (Its Origin), Present (You), Future (Your Children).* Dallas, March 4, 1962.

Crook, Cornelia E. *Henry Castro and His Homestead.* Castroville, TX: Privately published, 1978.

Croxdale, Richard, and Melissa Hield. *Women in the Texas Work Force: Yesterday and Today.* Austin: People's History in Texas, 1979.

Cunningham, Mary S. *The Woman's Club of El Paso, Its First Thirty Years.* El Paso: UT El Paso, Texas Western Press, 1978.

Dallas Free Kindergarten Association. Dallas: n.p., c. 1905. (TWU)

Dallas Section, National Council of Jewish Women, 1913–1963. Dallas: NCJW, 1963.

Day, James. *Jacob de Cordova, Land Merchant of Texas.* Waco: Texian Press, 1962.

De Cordova, Jacob. *The Cultivation of Cotton in Texas. The Advantages of Free Labor.* Delivered by him before the Cotton Supply Association, Manchester, [England], September 28, 1858. London: J. King & Co., 1858.

———. *Lecture on Texas delivered by Mr. J. De Cordova at Philadelphia, New York, Mount Holly, Brooklyn and Newark.* Also read by him before the New York Geographic Society, April 15, 1858. Philadelphia: Ernest Crozet, 1858. (BC)

———. *New Map of the State of Texas* (revised and corrected by Charles W. Pressler). New York: J. H. Colton and Company, 1857. (BC)

———. *Texas, Her Resources and Her Public Men.* 1st ed. Philadelphia: J. B. Lippincott, 1858. Reprint. Waco: Texian Press, 1969.

Dedication Volume of Congregation Beth Jacob. Galveston: December 1, 1963.

De Moss, Dorothy. "Looking Better Every Year." In *Texas: A Sesquicentennial Celebration,* ed. by Donald Whisenhunt. 281–291. Austin: Eakin, 1984.

Dranov, Alexander. "From Moscow to Houston: An Uneasy Journey of the Spirit." In *Studies of the Third Wave: Recent Migration of Soviet Jews to the United States,* ed. by Dan N. Jacobs and Ellen Frankel Paul. Boulder, CO: Westview Press, 1981.

Dreyfus, A. Stanley, ed. *Henry Cohen, Messenger of the Lord.* New York: Bloch Pub., 1963. (BC)

Encyclopaedia Judaica. Jerusalem: Macmillan Company, 1971. "Texas," 15:1034–1036; "Dallas," 5:1229–32; "Houston," 1049–1052.

Falk, Bernard. *The Naked Lady or Storm Over Adah [Menken].* London: Hutchinson, 1934.

Fenwick, Marin B., ed. *Who's Who Among the Women of San Antonio and the Southwest.* San Antonio: n.p., c. 1917. (BC)

Fernea, Elizabeth E., and Marilyn P. Duncan, eds. *Texas Women in Politics.* Austin: Texas Foundation for Women's Resources, 1977.

Fierman, Floyd S. *Guts and Ruts, The Jewish Pioneer on the Trail in the American Southwest.* New York: KTAV, 1985.

———. *Peddlers and Merchants on the Southwest Frontier 1850–1880* (rpt. from *Password* of the El Paso County Hist. Soc., 8, no. 2, 1963).

———. *Roots and Boots, From Crypto-Jew in New Spain to Community Leader in the American Southwest.* Hoboken, NJ: KTAV, 1987.

———. *Samuel J. Freudenthal (1863–1939): Southwestern Merchant and Civic Leader.* El Paso: UT El Paso, Texas Western College Press, 1968.

———. *The Schwartz Family of El Paso: The Story of a Pioneer Jewish Family in the Southwest.* El Paso: UT-El Paso, Texas Western Press, 1980.

———. *75th Anniversary Temple Mt. Sinai, 1898–1973.* El Paso, 1973.

———. *Some Early Jewish Settlers on the Southwestern Frontier.* El Paso: Texas Western Press, 1960.

Freedman, Warren. "Jews of Texas." In *Jewish Press.* New York, July 25, 1980.

Frees, Miriam Hirshfeld. *An Autobiography.* N.p., n.d. (Austin History Center)

Gamoran, Emanuel. *Survey of Jewish Education in Dallas.* Cincinnati, 1945.

Geller, Shmuel. *Mazkeres Ahavah, Remembrance of Love, a Biographical Account of Rabbi Yaakov and Sara Geller and Family — The Transplanting of Jewish Life from Galicia to Texas, 1863 to the Present.* Zichron Yaakov, Israel: Institute for Publication of Books, January 1988.

Glick, Barbara, ed. *Centennial Journal of Mount Sinai Congregation 1885–1985.* Texarkana, 1985.

Gold, H. R., ed. *Book of Redemption.* Houston: Printed by D. H. White & Co. for Jewish National Fund, 1939. (BC)

Golden Book of Adath Yeshurun. Houston: D. H. White & Co, 1942.

Goldstein, Isaac A. *The Waco Jewish Community: Some Historical and Reminiscent Notes.* Waco: Historic Waco Foundaton, 1982. (BC)

Goodman, Fanny Sattinger, comp. *"In the Beginning": The Jewish Community of El Paso, Texas.* El Paso, 1970.

Goodman, Mrs. I. B. "The Jewish Community," in *El Paso, A Centennial Portrait,* edited by Harriett Howze Jones. El Paso: Superior Print, 1972.

Gould, Lewis L. *Progressives and Prohibitionists.* Austin: UT Press, 1973.

Graham, Sam B., and Ellen Newman. *A Historical and Biographical Record of Galveston and Galveston County.* Galveston: A. W. Cawston, 1945.

Greater Dallas NCJW Section 1913–1988, A History. Dallas, 1988.

Griffin, S. C. *History of Galveston, Texas.* Galveston: A. W. Cawston, 1931.

Gunther, John. *Taken at the Flood: The Story of Albert D. Lasker.* New York: Harpers, 1960.

Hall, Jacqueline Dowd. *Revolt Against Chivalry, Jessie Daniel Ames and the Women's Campaign Against Lynching.* New York: Columbia Univ. Press, 1979.

Harris, Leon A., Jr. *Merchant Princes: An Intimate History of Jewish Families Who Built Great Department Stores.* New York: Harper, 1979.

Hayes, Charles W. *Galveston: History of the Island and the City.* 2 vols. Austin: Jenkins Garrett Press, 1974, 891–893. Rpt. Cincinnati: n.p., 1879.

Herrera, Hayden. *Frida, A Biography of Frida Kahlo.* New York: Harper, 1983.

Herscher, Uri D. *Jewish Agricultural Utopias in America, 1880–1910.* Detroit: Wayne State Univ., 1981.

Herson, Abraham, ed. and pub. *Golden Jubilee and Dedication Book, Ahavath Achim Congregation, 1899–1949.* Tyler: 1949.

Hewitt, Phil. *The Jewish Texans*. San Antonio: UT-San Antonio, Institute of Texan Cultures, 1974.

Hewitt, W. Phil, and Marian L. Martinello. *A Teacher's Guide to the Jewish Texans*. San Antonio: UT-San Antonio, Institute of Texan Cultures, 1978.

Humphrey, Janet A. *A Texas Suffragist, Diaries and Writings of Jane Y. McCallum*. Austin: Ellen C. Temple, 1988.

Hyman, Harold M. *Oleander Odyssey*. College Station: Texas A&M University Press, 1990.

International Order of B'nai B'rith. *To the Memory of Leo N. Levi*. Chicago: Hamburger Prtg. Co., 1905.

Jacobs, Ginger. *The Levin Years*. Dallas: Dallas Jewish Historical Society, 1989.

Jewish Community Center of Houston: A History 1936–1986. Houston: JCC, 1987.

Jewish Community Council of Metropolitan Houston. Population Survey Committee. *Report on Part I: Survey of the Known Jewish Population of Metropolitan Houston, 1955–56*. Houston: 1956.

Jewish Community Yearbook, 1986–87. Dallas: Publication of Jewish Community Center, 1987.

Jewish Encyclopedia. Edited by Isidore Singer. 2 vols. New York: Funk & Wagnalls, 1901.

Jewish Literary Society, Houston. *History of the Jewish Literary Society of Houston, Texas, June 27, 1906 to June 30, 1916*. Houston, 1916. (BC)

Jewish National Fund of Texas. *The Book of Redemption*. See H. R. Gold, ed.

Johnson, Lawrence S. *A Century of Service, The Concise History of Victoria Bank & Trust Co.* Victoria: n.p., 1979.

Joseph, Harriett Denise. "Temple Beth-El, 1931–1981." In *Studies in Brownsville History*, edited by Milo Kearney, 230–244. Brownsville: Pan American University, 1986.

———. "A Tribute to Sam Perl, 1898–1980." In *More Studies in Brownsville History*, ed. by Milo Kearney, 2 (1989):367–373.

Kallah Yearbook: An Annual Convention of Texas Rabbis. Publisher and location vary. 1927–1936? (BC)

Kempner, I. H. *Recalled Recollections*. Dallas Egan, 1961. (BC)

Kohlberg, Ernst. *Letters of Ernst Kohlberg 1875–1877*. Trans. by Walter L. Kohlberg. El Paso: Texas Western Press, 1973.

Kruger, Fania. *Cossack Laughter*. Dallas: Kaleidograph Press, 1949.

———. *Selected Poems*. Austin: American Universal Artforms, 1973.

———. *The Tenth Jew*. Dallas: Kaleidograph, 1949.

Landa Estate. *The Oasis of Texas*. 2nd ed. San Antonio: Press of Guessey & Ferlet, 1904.

Landa, Harry. *As I Remember*. San Antonio: Carleton Prtg., 1945.

Lea, Tom. *Wonderful Country*. Boston: Little, Brown, 1952.

Levi, Leo N. *Memorial Volume*. Chicago: Privately published, 1905. (BC)

Libo, Kenneth, and Irving Howe. *We Lived There Too: In their Own Words and Pictures — Pioneer Jews and the Westward Movement of America 1630–1930*. New York City: St. Martin's, 1984.

Liebman, Seymour B. *The Enlightened: The Writings of Luis de Carvajal, el Mozo*. Coral Gables, FL: Univ. of Miami Press, 1967.

Maas, Elaine. *Jews in Houston*. Houston: Houston Center for the Humanities, 1982.

Mann, Bridget C. *100 Year Anniversary 1887–1987, Temple Beth El*. Tyler, 1987.

McCoy, Lois Rich. *Millionairess: Self Made Women of America*. New York: Harper, 1978.

McDonald, Archie, ed. *Hurrah for Texas! The Diary of Adolphus Sterne, 1838–1851*. Austin: Eakin, 1986.

McKay, Mrs. Arch, and Mrs. H. A. Spellings. *A History of Jefferson*. 20th printing. Jefferson: n.p., n.d.

Marcus, Jacob Rader. *The American Jewish Woman: A Documentary History*. New York and Cincinnati: KTAV and AJA, 1981.

———. *The American Jewish Woman: A Documentary History*. Cincinnati: KTAV — American Jewish Archives, 1986. 742–744.

Marcus, Stanley. *Minding the Store*. Boston: Little Brown, 1974.

———. *Quest for the Best*. New York: Viking Press, 1979.

Marinbach, Bernard. *Galveston, Ellis Island of the West*. Albany, NY: State Univ. of New York Press, 1983.

Maynard, Betty J. *The Dallas Jewish Community Study*. Dallas: Jewish Welfare Federation, 1974.

Mazow, Julia, comp. and ed. *The Women Who Lost Their Names: Selected Writings by American Jewish Women*. New York: Harper, 1980.

Members of the Texas Legislature, 1846–1980. Austin: Texas Legislature, 1981. (BC)

Menken, Adah Isaacs. *Infelicia*. London, Paris, and New York: Privately published, 1868.

Metzger, Isaac. *A Bintel Brief*. Vol. I. New York: Behrman House, 1971.

Meyer, Leopold L., and Newell E. Fance. *The Days of My Years, Autobiographical Reflections of Leopold L. Meyer*. Houston: Privately published, 1975.

Morais, Henry Samuel. *The Jews of Philadelphia. Their History From the Earliest Settlements to the Present Time*. Philadelphia: Levytype Co., 1894.

Moreland, Sinclair. *Texas Women's Hall of Fame*. Austin: Biographical Press, 1917.

Nalle, Ouida. *The Fergusons of Texas*. San Antonio: Naylor, 1946.

Nathan, Anne, and Harry I. Cohen. *The Man Who Stayed in Texas: The Life of Rabbi Henry Cohen*. New York: Whittlesey House, 1941.

National Council of Jewish Women. *Proceedings of the First Convention of the National Council of Jewish Women*. New York: Jewish Pub. Assn., 1896.

Odom, Marianne, and Gaylon Finklea Young. *The Businesses That Built San Antonio*. San Antonio: Living Legacies, 1985.

Oppenheimer, Jesse D. *I Remember*. San Antonio?, 196-.

Parmelee, Deolece. *The Deadly Jewels of Diamond Bessie, Historical Tragedy*. N.p.: D. M. Parmelee, 1968.

Podet, Mordecai. *Pioneer Jews of Waco*. Waco: Privately published, 1986.

Postal, Bernard, and Lionel Koppman. *American Jewish Landmarks*. 2nd ed. Vol. 2, *The South and Southwest*. New York: Fleet Press, 1979.

Potter, Fannie C. *History of the Texas Federation of Women's Clubs, 1918–1938*. Denton: Wm. H. McNitsky, 1941.

Raphael, Alice, trans. *Faust, Wolfgang Von Goethe*. New York: DeCapo Press, 1977.

Reckles, Burton et al., comp. *Shalom! Welcome to Congregation Beth Yeshurun*. Houston, n.d.

Reisberg, Gertrude Turner. *Life is . . . an autobiography in poetic form*. New York City: Vantage Press, 1975.

Roberts, Susan A., and Calvin A. Roberts. *New Mexico*. Albuquerque, NM, 1988.

Rochlin, Harriet, and Fred Rochlin. *Pioneer Jews — a New Life in the Far West*. Boston: Houghton Mifflin, 1984.

Rosen, Hymer Elias. *'Joe' (Joseph) H. Goodman, Patriarch and Pioneer*. El Paso: n.p., December 1978.

Rosenberg, Leon. *Sangers: Pioneer Texas Merchants*. Austin: Texas State Hist. Assn., 1978.

Rosinger, Samuel. *My Life and My Message*. Beaumont: Privately published, 1958.

Rowland, Edward C. "A Rose Blooms in the Desert." In *Hoein' the Short Rows*, edited by F. E. Abernethy, 92–99. Dallas: SMU Press and the Texas Folklore Society, 1987.

Rudolph, B. G. *From a Minyan to a Community, A History of the Jews of Syracuse*. Syracuse, NY: Syracuse Univ., 1970.

Rumbley, Rose-Mary. *A Century of Class: Public Education in Dallas, 1884–1984*. Austin: Eakin, 1984.

Sachnowitz, Mrs. Gary. *The Roots of Temple Emanu-El of Longview, Texas*. Longview, 1985.

San Antonio Section, National Council of Jewish Women. *Year*

240

Book, 1976–1977. San Antonio, 1976.

San Jacinto County Historical Commission. *Dim Trails and Blurred Footprints, A History of San Jacinto County, Texas.* Coldspring, TX: prt. by Taylor Pub., Dallas, 1982.

Sanger, Hortense. *90th Anniversary [of Temple Emanu-El].* Dallas: Temple Emanu-El, 1962.

Schappes, Morris U. *The Jews in the United States 1654–1875.* New York: Citadel, 1950.

Schmier, Louis, ed. *Reflections of Southern Jewry: The Letters of Charles Wessolowsky.* Macon, GA: Mercer Univ. Press, 1982.

Schulman, Sam. *A Social and Demographic Survey of the Jewish Community of Houston, Texas.* Houston: Jewish Community Council of Metropolitan Houston, 1976.

75th Anniversary Diamond Jubilee Shearith Israel Congregation. Wharton: Shearith Israel, 1988.

Sharfman, I. Harold. *Jews on the Frontier.* Chicago: Henry Regency Company, 1977.

Sibley, Marilyn. *George W. Brackenridge.* Austin: UT Press, 1973.

Smith, Bert Kruger. *A Teaspoon of Honey.* Nashville: Aurora Pub., 1970.

Soble, Mrs. Howard A., ed. *5000 Years in the Kitchen.* Dallas: Temple Emanu-El Sisterhood, 1965.

Stahl, Samuel M. *A Brief History of Congregation B'nai Israel.* Galveston: December 1972.

Sterne, Eva. *The Little Immigrant, A True Story.* New York: Privately printed, 1921.

Stringer, Tommy. *The Zale Corporation . . . From the Beginning.* Dallas: Zale Foundation, c. 1985.

Tarpley, Fred. *Jefferson: Riverport to the Southwest.* Austin: Eakin Press, 1983.

Temple Beth-El. *Diamond Jubilee, 1874–1949.* San Antonio, n.d.

———. *History of the Jewish Community, Corpus Christi.* 25th Anniversary Issue. Corpus Christi, 1957.

Temple Beth Israel, Austin, The First 100 Years. Austin, 1976.

Temple Emanu-El. *From Generation to Generation, Hallelujah.* 100th Anniversary. Dallas, December 1972.

Temple Mount Sinai, Dedication Services. El Paso, 1916. (BC)

Temple Mt. Sinai. *Yearbook, 1898–1928.* El Paso, 1928. (BC)

Texas Federation of Women's Clubs, ed. *Who's Who of the Womanhood of Texas* v. 1923–1924. Fort Worth: Stafford-London, 1924.

Tolbert, Frank X. *Neiman-Marcus, Dallas, Texas.* New York: Holt, 1953.

Toll, William. "Judaism as a Civic Religion in the American West." In *Religion and Society in the American West,* ed. by Carl Guarneri and David Alvarez. Lanham, MD and London, England: Univ. Press of America, 1987.

Universal Jewish Encyclopedia. New York, 1941.

von der Mehden, Fred R. *The Ethnic Groups of Houston.* Houston: Rice Univ., 1984.

Waco Section, National Council of Jewish Women, 50th Anniversary, 1913–1963. Waco: NCJW, 1963.

Wallace, Pat. *A Spirit So Rare.* Austin: Nortex, 1984.

Waugh, Julia Nott. *Castro-Ville and Henry Castro.* San Antonio, 1934.

Weaver, Bobby D. *[Henri] Castro's Colony: Empresario Development in Texas, 1842–1865.* College Station: Texas A&M Univ. Press, 1985.

Webb, Walter Prescott, et al., eds. *Handbook of Texas.* 2 vols. Austin: Texas State Hist. Assn., 1952.

Weinbaum, Eleanor Perlstein. *Shalom, America.* Burnet: Nortex Press, 1981.

Weiss, Rabbi Harry, and I. A. Goldstein, eds. *Souvenir Fair Book.* Waco Synagogue and Bazaar Assn., March 13–16, 1899. Waco: Knight Prtg., 1899. (BC)

Werden, Frieda, et al. *The Woman's Haggadah.* Austin: Feminist Events Committee of the First Unitarian Church, April 1979. (BC)

Wessel, Rabbi Harvey. "A History of the Jews, Tyler and Smith County, Texas." In *Tyler and Smith County: An Historical Survey,* 201–212. Tyler: Walsworth Pub. Co., 1976. (BC)

Who's Who in American Jewry. 1980 Edition. Incorporating the Directory of American Jewish Institutions. Los Angeles.

Who's Who in World Jewry: A Biographical Dictionary of Outstanding Jews. Edited by I. J. Carmin Karpman. New York: Pitman, 1972.

Wilkins, Thurman. "Adah Isaacs Menken." In *Notable American Women,* edited by Edward T. James, et al., 526–529. Cambridge, MA: Belknap Press of Harvard Univ. Press, 1971.

Willard, Frances E., and Mary A. Livermore. *American Women.* Vol. 1. Detroit: Gale, 1973. "Lee Cohen Harby," 357–358. Rev. ed., *Women of the Century.* New York: Mast, Crowell, 1896.

Winegarten, Ruthe. *Texas Women, A Pictorial History: From Indians to Astronauts.* Austin: Eakin Press, 1986.

———, ed. *Texas Women's History Project Bibliography.* Austin: Texas Foundation for Women's Resources, 1980.

Winegarten, Ruthe, and Judith N. McArthur, eds. *Citizens At Last: The Woman Suffrage Movement in Texas.* Austin: Ellen C. Temple, 1987.

Zesmer, Jennie, ed. *Golden Book of Shearith Israel, Commemorating the Congregation's Fiftieth Anniversary, 1884–1934.* Dallas, 1935. (BC)

PERIODICALS

"Alley Theatre director [Iris Siff] found dead." *Houston Post,* January 14, 1982.

Axelrod, Ronald A. "Rabbi Henry Cohen and the Galveston Immigration Movement, 1907–1914." *East Texas Historical Journal* 15 (Spring 1977): 24–37.

"Bicentennial History: First Jew, First Woman [Adlene Harrison] Becomes Mayor of Dallas." *Texas Jewish Post,* February 5, 1976, p. 1.

B'nai B'rith Hillel Scribe. Austin, University of Texas. Miscellaneous issues (BC)

Bugbee, Lester. "The Old Three Hundred." *Quarterly of Texas State Hist. Assn.* I (1897–1898).

Burka, Paul. "Galveston, Grand Dame of the Gulf." *Texas Monthly,* December 1983.

Burkholter, Lois Wood. "The Enjoyable Joske Store." San Antonio *Light,* April 15, 1973.

Cohen, Henry. "The Galveston Movement." *WSJHQ.* (January 1986).

———. "Henry Castro, Pioneer and Colonist." *AJHQ* 5 (1897): 39–43.

———. "The Jews in Texas." *PAJHS* 4 (1895): 1–7; 4 (1896): 9–19.

———. "Rabbi Cohen Traces Careers of Jewish Leaders." *Houston Post,* April 28, 1938.

———. "The Settlement of the Jews in Texas." *PAJHS* 2 (1894): 139–56.

Cook, Alison. "The Fraying Empire of Bobby Sakowitz." *Texas Monthly,* December 1985.

Dyer, J. O. "Some Foreign Born Pioneers." *Galveston Daily News,* December 18, 1921.

"Early Texas Patriot and Wife [Jacob de Cordova and Rebecca de Cordova] Who Did Much to Develop State Reburied in Official Cemetery." *Dallas News,* December 9, 1935?

Enstam, Elizabeth. "The Forgotten Frontier, Dallas Women and Social Caring, 1895–1920." *Legacies, A Historical Journal for Dallas and North Central Texas* I, no. 1 (Spring 1989): 20–28.

Fierman, Floyd S. *Insights and Hindsights of Some El Paso Jewish Families.* El Paso Jewish Historical Review I, no. 11 (Spring 1983).

———. *Insights and Hindsights of Some More El Paso Jewish Families.* El Paso Jewish Historical Review (1984).

———. "The Kohlberg Family." *El Paso Jewish Historical Review.* I, no. II (Spring 1983): 152–155.

Gardner, Sue. "When Texas Jews Dreamed of a Jewish Homeland." *Pioneer Woman*, March-April 1979, 9–10.

Geffen, David. "A Sentimental Journey — Early Zionist Activities in the South." In *Forum*, rpt. of "Diary" in *Maccabaean* 8, no. 1, 22–31.

Goldberg, Irving. "The Changing Jewish Community of Dallas." *AJA* 11 (April 1959): 82–97.

Hagen, Cecil V. "The Jewish Community in Gonzales County." Parts I and II. *Gonzales Inquirer*, Gonzales, May and July, 1987.

Hull, Dorothy. "Castaño de Sosa's Expedition to New Mexico in 1590." *Old Santa Fe* 3, no. 12 (October 1916): 307–332.

Hyman, Harold M. "I. H. Kempner and the Galveston Commission Government." *Houston Review* 10, no. 2 (1988): 57–85.

"Jacob de Cordova, Publicity Man for an Empire." *Dallas Morning News*, September 18, 1932, section IV.

"Jacob de Cordova, Who Owned It, Called Site for Waco the Most Beautiful Town Location in Texas." *Waco Tribune-Herald*, October 30, 1949, 19.

Jennings, Diane. "Gerry Beer, the Founder of the Family Place, . . ." *Dallas Morning News*, October 27, 1985, E-1.

Jewish Beacon [Houston], April 10, 1947. (BC)

Jewish Herald Voice [Houston]. Miscellaneous issues. (BC Newspaper Collection)

Kallison, Frances. "Phineas de Cordova." *Texas Jewish Historical Society Newsletter*. (Spring 1987): 3.

Kariel, Audrey D. "The Jewish Story and Memories of Marshall." *WSJHQ* 14, no. 3 (1982): 195–206.

Kellman, Steven G. "The Yellow Rose of Texas." *Journal of American Culture* (Summer 1982): 45–48.

Kramer, William M. "Pioneer Lawyer of California and Texas: Henry J. Labatt [1832–1900]." *WSJHQ*, October 1982.

Kramer, William M., and Reva Clar. "Rabbi Abraham Blum: From Alsace to New York by Way of Texas and California," Part I. *WSJHQ*, October 1979.

Lasker, Morris. "Letter from a Texas Pioneer." *Menorah Journal* 24 (April 1936): 193–203.

Leeson, Daniel N. "In Search of a History of the Texas Patriot Moses A. Levy — Part I." *WSJH* 21, no. 4 (1989): 291–306.

Lesh, Carolyn. "Hermine Tobolowsky." *Dallas Morning News*, October 19, 1986, Section E-1.

Marks, Rabbi Samuel. "History of the Jews of San Antonio." *Reform Advocate*, January 24, 1914.

Meyer, Larry. *D. & A. Oppenheimer, Bankers (Uninc.).* Transcribed interviews with Mr. Dan Oppenheimer. Oral Business History Project. Austin: UT Austin, 1971.

Mondell, Cynthia, and Allen Mondell. "West of Hester Street, A Documentary about the Galveston Movement." *Texas Humanist* 3, no. 8 (May 1981): 3–6.

Moorhead, Dean. "Texas' All-Woman Supreme Court." *Texas Star*, February 11, 1973.

Oppenheimer, Evelyn. "High Profile." *Dallas News*, August 17, 1986, 9E.

Podet, Mordecai. "Pioneer Jews of Waco, Texas." *WSJH* 21, nos. 3 and 4 (1989).

Pollard, Clarice Fortgang. "WAACS in Texas during the Second World War." *Southwestern Hist. Quarterly* XCIII, no. 1 (July 1989).

Ritz, David. "Inside the Jewish Establishment." *D Magazine*, (November 1975): 52–55, 108–116.

Robinson, Lynette M. "The First Jewish Congregation in Texas [Houston's Beth Israel]." *Jr. Historian* (Texas) 20 (November 1959): 5–8, 16.

Rosenswaike, Ira. "Levy L. Laurens (1816–1837): An Early Texan Journalist." *AJA* 27 (April 1975): 61–66.

Sanger Bros. Monthly Magazine 1, vols. 1 and 2 (BC)

Santos, Richard. "Chicanos of Jewish Descent in Texas." *WSJHQ* 15, no. 4 (1983).

———. "Mexican-Americans, A Jewish Background?" *San Antonio Express*, July 2, 1973.

Sherry, Lynn. "Remembering Judy [Resnik]." *MS* (June 1986): 56–58.

Shook, Robert W. "Abraham Levi: Father of Victoria Jewry." *WSJHQ*, January 1977.

Shosteck, Robert. "Leopold Karpeles: Civil War Hero." *AJHQ* 52 (September 1962–June 1963): 220–233.

Shpall, Leo. "Adah Isaacks Menken." *Louisiana Historical Quarterly* 26 (January–October 1943): 162–168.

Southwest Jewish Chronicle [Oklahoma City], 1934, 1942, 1943. (BC)

Stern, Norton B. "The Final Resting Place of Los Angeles Jewry's First President [Waco]." *WSJHQ*, July 1986.

Stayton, John William. "The First All-Woman Supreme Court in the World." *Holland's Magazine*, March 1925.

Tefteller, Carol. "The Jewish Community in Frontier Jefferson." *Texas Historian* 35, no. 1 (1974).

"Temple [Temple Emanu-El] in Texas, Dallas." *Time* 69 (February 11, 1957): 54.

"Texas Merchants after the Civil War, 1871." *AJA* 12 (April 1960): 71–74.

Toohey, Mark. "Out of the Mouth of Babe [Schwartz] Comes a Colorful Career." *Houston Chronicle*, June 22, 1986.

University Jewish Voice 1 (May 1970). (Hillel, UT Austin).

Vierner, Saul. "Surgeon Moses Albert Levy: Letters of a Texas Patriot." *PAJHS* 46 (September 1956–June 1957): 101–113. Supplement: 49 (March 1960): 202–207.

"Waco Jewish Community, The." *Waco Heritage & History* 13, no. 4 (1982).

Waldman, Morris D. "The Galveston Movement." *Jewish Social Service Quarterly* 4 (March 1928): 197–205.

Western States Jewish History (unsigned articles)
October 1974: "Letter from Galveston, Texas — 1878."
April 1976: "Dallas Jewry Engages Their First Rabbi: Congregation Emanu-El in 1875." (Reprinted from *The American Israelite*, November 12, 1875).
July 1976: "A Jew Views Black Education: Texas — 1890."
July 1977: "A Congregation for Beaumont, Texas — 1895." (Rpt, *The American Israelite*, October 3, 1895, 3.)
January 1978: "From the Capital of Texas [Austin] — 1873."
January 1978: "First Synagogue in Dallas, Texas — 1876." (Rpt., *Jewish Times* (NY), June 16, 1876, 245.)
July 1978: "Two Views of an International Jewish Community: Brownsville, Texas and Matamoros, Mexico. [1876]."
October 1978: "First Jewish Organization in Texas: Houston — 1855." (Rpt., *The Occident* (Philadelphia), July 1855, 199–200.)
July 1979: "Passover in a Texas Town in 1891 [Hempstead]." (Rpt., *Jewish Voice* (St. Louis), May 1, 1891, 7.)
July 1981: "Central Texas Jewry in 1875 [Hempstead, Austin and San Antonio]." (Rpt., *The American Israelite*, November 2, 1875.)
January 1982: "Calvert, Texas: Two Views — 1880."
April 1983: "Brownsville, Texas District Attorney — 1913."
July 1985: "A Texas Orphan — 1877."
January 1987: "From Kempen, Poland to Hempstead, Texas: The Career of Rabbi Heinrich Schwarz."
January 1988: "Religious Life in Dallas a Century Ago."

Winegarten, Ruthe. "Remarkable Jewish Women." Series in *Texas Jewish Post* (Dallas), February 27–May 15, 1975.

Wolff, Kurt H. "Traditionalists and Assimilations: A Sample Study of the Jewish Population in Dallas, Texas." *Studies in Sociology* 4 (nos. 1/2, 1940): 20–25.

Woods, J. M. "The Jews' Early Contribution to Texas." *Frontier Times* (Bandera) 14 (1937): 208–211.

Zuber, W. P. "Captain Adolphus Sterne." *Quarterly of the Texas*

State Hist. Assn. 2 (January 1899): 211–16.

MANUSCRIPTS

Ackerman, Ann. "Sketches of Life in Goosevalley." Paper given at American Jewish Historical Society National Convention. Denver, Colorado. May 17–20, 1986.

American Jewish Committee. Oral history transcripts. Typescript. Houston.

Axelrod, Ronald. "Rabbi Henry Cohen and the Galveston Immigration Movement 1907–1914." Thesis, UT Austin, 1974.

Ben-Zedeff, Evitar. "Coverage of the Yom Kippur War (October 1973) in the Texas Press: A Comparative Content Analysis." Thesis, UT Austin, 1981.

B'nai B'rith. District No. 7 Grand Lodge. Miscellaneous Programs Various Annual Conventions. (BC)

Cohen, Henry. "The Hygiene and Medicine of the Talmud." Lecture, University of Texas Medical Branch, Galveston. Austin, 1900? (BC)

DeMoss, Dorothy Dell. "The History of Apparel Manufacturing in Texas, 1897–1981." Ph.D. dissertation, Texas Christian University, 1981.

Dinnerstein, Leonard. "Jews in the South." Master's thesis, Louisiana State University, 1973.

Dreyfus, A. Stanley. "The Hebrew Benevolent Society: A Saga of Service." [Galveston], 1966. (Rosenberg Library)

———. "Hebrew Cemetery No. 1 of Galveston." Galveston: March 22, 1965. (Rosenberg Library, #71-0207-A)

Hammer, Jeanette Littman. "The Littmans." Typescript. July 9, 1971. (Austin History Center)

Henry, Maurice. Papers. Brazoria County Clerks Office, Angleton. (Jacob Henry)

Hill, Marilyn Wood. "A History of the Jewish Involvement in the Dallas Community." Master's thesis, Southern Methodist University, 1967.

Inselberg, Lee Bradley. "Changing Worlds: Jewish Women in Lubbock, Texas." Master's thesis, Texas Tech Univ., 1982.

Jacobs, Ginger. "A Comparison of the Dallas Jewish Population of 1953–1954 with that of 1939–40." Master's thesis, SMU, Dallas, August 1954.

———. "A History of the Dallas Jewish Community Center." Typescript. Dallas, December 1982.

Jefferson. Hebrew Sinai Synagogue Files (Jefferson Historical Museum Archives).

Joseph, Ernest. "The Jewish Community of Corsicana, Texas." Typescript. October 17, 1988.

Kallison, Frances. "100 Years of Jewry in San Antonio." Master's thesis, Trinity University, San Antonio, 1977. (BC)

Kariel, Louis. "Transcript of a Speech: The History of the Jewish People in Marshall, Texas." N.d. (AJA)

Kemp, L. W. Fannin Notes I-K [Edward Isaack Johnson] (BC Archives, B 16/32.)

Kessler, Rabbi James Lee. "B.O.I., A History of Congregation B'nai Israel, Galveston, Texas." Doctor of Hebrew Letters dissertation, Hebrew Union College, Jewish Institute of Religion, California School, 1988.

———. "The Mexican Inquisition." Rabbinic thesis, Hebrew Union College, Jewish Institute of Religion, 1972.

Krause, Corinne A. "The Jews in Mexico, 1857–1930." Ph.D. dissertation, Univ. of Pittsburgh, 1970.

Larralde, Carlos. "Chicano Jews in South Texas." Ph.D. dissertation, Univ. of Calif. at Los Angeles, 1978. (BC)

Lefkowitz, David. "Why I Am a Jew" (Speech, Fair Park, March 18, 1931). Dallas, 1931? (BC)

Levi, Leo N. "Judaism in America." Speech, Union of American Hebrew Congregations. New Orleans, December 4, 1894. New Orleans: Simmons & Loomis, Printers, 1894.

Levy, Myer. "A History of the Navasota Citizens of the Jewish Faith." Typescript. (TJHS Coll. BC)

Lewandoski, Shirley. "Neiman-Marcus." Master's thesis, Ryerson Institute of Technology, 1960.

Maas, Elaine H. "The Jews of Houston: An Ethnographic Study." Ph.D. dissssertation, Rice University, 1973.

Mack, Ellen. "History of Beth-El Congregation, Fort Worth." Narrative for THC. Austin, January 9, 1986.

Manaster, Jane. "The Ethnic Geography of Austin, Texas, 1875–1910." Master's thesis, UT Austin, 1986.

Mayer, Mrs. Richard G., San Angelo, Texas. "Ferdinand and Jette Steiner Mayer Family. Memoir and Genealogy, 1832–1971." Privately published, 1972. (AJA) (BC)

National Council of Jewish Women. "I Remember When." Typescript. Houston, 1983.

———. Items in Minnie Fisher Cunningham Papers, Box 17, folder 263, Houston Public Library.

———. Items in papers of Mrs. Sally Ward Beretta, Daughters of the Republic of Texas Library at the Alamo, San Antonio.

NJCRAC. *Papers from the June 23–26, 1974 Plenary Session.* Southfield, Michigan. "Equal Rights for Women — A Panel Discussion." (Sec. 11, MSS. 20-Jewish Women, Part C: TWU)

North Texas College, Kidd-Key Conservatory, Sherman. *Catalogue,* 1910–1911. (SMU Archives, Dallas)

Pines, Mrs. Jack (Ruth Herzstein). "A Picture of Jewish Life in Dallas from 1872 to 1955." Dallas: National Council of Jewish Women. (Bridwell Library, SMU)

Rosenberg, Barbara. "Jewish History of San Angelo." Typescript. Sugar Land, May 1988.

Rosenberg, Leon Joseph. "A Business History of Sanger Brothers, 1857–1926." Ph.D. dissertation, New York Univ., 1967.

Rosenthal, Arlene. "Fort Worth Attitude Study: The Position of the Jewish Community in the Larger Society." Master's thesis, Texas Christian Univ., 1966.

Santos, Richard G. "Sephardic Jews and the Mexican Americans of Texas." Paper read at Trinity Univ., San Antonio, May 23, 1973.

Sarvia (or Sarvis), Lois Ann Tausch. "Anna Hertzberg's Dream: A History of the Tuesday Music Club." Master's thesis, Trinity Univ., San Antonio, 1980.

Schlam, Helena. "The Early Jews of Houston." Master's thesis, Ohio State Univ., 1971.

Silberberg, Jay Lawrence. "The First One Hundred Years: A History of the Austin Jewish Community, 1850–1950." Senior thesis, Bachelor of Arts, Plan II, UT Austin, August 1974.

Sterne, Adolphus. Items at Stephen F. Austin University, Ralph Steen Library, Nacogdoches.

Sterne, Jacob. Civil War letters. Jefferson Museum, J. A. R. Mosely (comp.)

Texas Jewish Post [Dallas-Fort Worth]. Miscellaneous issues. (BC).

Texas Jewish Press [San Antonio]. Miscellaneous issues. (BC).

Texas Judaen Outlook; Young Judaea [Waco] Miscellaneous issues. (BC).

Tobin, Mrs. Sam. "History of B'nai Abraham Synagogue [Brenham]." Typescript. Austin: THC, n.d.

Torrence, L. F. "The Ku Klux Klan in Dallas, 1915–1928." Master's thesis, Southern Methodist University, 1948.

University of Texas. "The Abraham I. Schechter Collection of Hebraica and Judaica. A Check List of Judaica with other related materials in the University of Texas Library." Compiled by the UT Library Catalog Dept. Austin, 1943. (BC)

Victoria Ladies Hebrew Benevolent Society, Victoria. Organizational records and minutes, 1876–1901. Cash Book, 1877–1923. (BC)

Weston, Joan Laveson. "School-Directed and Non School-Directed Aspirations of Middle and Upper-Middle Class Jewish High School Students in a Large Urban Texas Community." Ed.D. dissertation, North Texas State Univ., 1974.

Winegarten, Ruthe. "A Leisure Time Interest Survey of Adult

Jews in Dallas County." Master's thesis, UT Arlington, 1970.

Winer, Mark L. "The History of Temple Emanu-El of Dallas, Texas, during the Nineteenth Century." Submitted to HUC-JIR, as a term paper, New York School, 1969. Typescript.

Zubatsky, David S. "A Preliminary Bibliography for the Study of Jewish Life in the Trans-Mississippi West." (Champagne, IL), February 1982 (BC)

NONPRINT AND OTHER TYPES OF MATERIALS

"Builders of El Paso . . . Mrs. [Olga] Kohlberg." Radio script of KTSM, El Paso, July 2, 1939.

"Crypto-Jews in New Mexico." *All Things Considered*. National Public Radio, April 3, 1988.

Friedman, Kinky. Record albums. *Sold American*. New York, Vanguard Records, 1973. *Kinky Friedman*. Los Angeles, ABC Records, 1974. (Sound Archives, BC)

Harelik, Mark. "The Immigrant, A Hamilton County Album." A play, c. 1986.

Mondell, Cynthia, and Allen Mondell. "West of Hester Street." A docu-drama film about the movement of Jews through the port of Galveston from 1907 to 1914.

Silberman, Sam, and Eva Silberman. "Jewish Life in Brownsville — A Salute to the State of Texas on its Sesquicentennial." Brownsville, 1986.

Index

Steven D., 185
Wolf, Elise, 164
  Isaac, 44
  Joyce Dannenbaum, 106
Wolfe, Morris, 148
Wolff, Pauline Sterne, 107
Wolhberg, B., 83
Wolitz, Seth L., 201, 207
Women's Crusade, 140
women's movement, 107, 117, 210, 211
women's suffrage, 39, 107, 117, 119
Wonder Bar, 144
Wood, Harry A., Jr., 174
Woody, Sam, 29
Workmen's Circle (*see* Arbeiter Ring)
World Union for Progressive Juda-

ism, 136
World War I, 58, 78, 103, 104, 105, 135
World War II, 121, 123, 130, 135, 141, 154
Wortham, Texas, 139
Wouk, Nina, 210
Wyll, Issie, 91

Y
Yarborough, Ralph, 103
Yiddish Culture Club, 81
Yiddish *Vinkle*, 81
YMHA Congregation (Galveston), 125
Young Hebrew Literary Society (Austin), 72
Young Judaea, 83, 116, 130, 170

Young Men's Hebrew Association (YMHA), 34, 56, 59, 60, 62, 64, 73, 74, 100, 125, 132
Young Men's Hebrew School, 101
Youth Aliyah, 116
Yudof, Judy, 206
  Mark, 206

Z
Zale, Morris, 134, 201
  William, 201
Zale Foundation, 201
Zangwill, Israel, 84
Zeidman, Beatrice, 116
Zeisler, Fannie Bloomfield, 149
Zellen, Ida Orinovsky, 129
Zesmer, David, 132
  Jennie Hesselson, 112

Zeta Beta Tau, 150
Zetley, Leon, 161
Ziegfeld Follies, 146
Zielonka, Rabbi Martin, 118, 129, 169
Zimmerman, Sheldon, 225
Zimmerman-Glatzer, Schmuel Mordecai, 132
Zionism, 69, 77, 81, 83, 84, 98, 116, 117, 122, 130, 163
Zionist Organization of America, 163
Zork, Bertha Krakauer (Mrs. Gus), 107
  Louis, 15, 17, 19
  Mrs. Louis, 62
Zuber, Abraham, 11
  William, 11
Zucker, Rabbi Max, 168